This collection of essays looks at the music of Webern from several new perspectives. The most recent Webern scholarship, based on the sketches and other primary material now owned by the Paul Sacher Stiftung in Basel, the Pierpont Morgan Library in New York and the Library of Congress in Washington, has emphasised Webern's lyricism, and this is a theme running through *Webern Studies.* Other techniques not generally associated with Webern are explored as well: two of the chapters illustrate and examine his apparent early interest in octatonic and pitch-specific motivic collections. Most of the essays are the result of work with primary material, much of which has not been published elsewhere. The volume includes, for example, previously unpublished entries from Webern's diaries, and all of the row tables for his twelve-note music. A new and comprehensive Webern bibliography covers thoroughly the period since Zoltan Roman's bibliography of 1978.

Webern studies

# Weber studies

EDITED BY KATHRYN BAILEY

CAMBRIDGE
UNIVERSITY PRESS

Published by the Press Syndicate of the University of Cambridge
The Pitt Building, Trumpington Street, Cambridge CB2 1RD
40 West 20th Street, New York, NY 10011-4211, USA
10 Stamford Road, Oakleigh, Melbourne 3166, Australia



First published 1996

Printed in Great Britain at the University Press, Cambridge

*A catalogue record for this book is available from the British Library*

*Library of Congress cataloguing in publication data*

Webern studies / edited by Kathryn Bailey.
p. cm.
Includes bibliographical references and index.
ISBN 0 521 47526 0 (hardback)
1. Webern, Anton, 1883–1945 – Criticism and interpretation.
I. Bailey, Kathryn.
ML410.W33W43 1996
780'.92–dc20 95-42777 CIP

ISBN 0 521 47526 0 hardback

TAG

# Contents

# Plates

# Preface and acknowledgments

I should like to have dedicated this volume to Arnold Whittall, on the occasion of his sixtieth birthday, but since he is one of the contributors (for which the book is richer) it seemed inappropriate to do so. The thought is there nonetheless.

Several of the contributors to this volume have benefited from the generosity and good will of the Paul Sacher Stiftung in Basel and the Pierpont Morgan Library in New York, and I am sure they join me in acknowledging the debt that Webern scholarship owes these institutions. I am particularly grateful to Felix Meyer, Curator of the Sacher Stiftung's Webern collection, for his considerable help and support during various stages of the project. I am also grateful to Penny Souster of Cambridge University Press, for her patience and good humour.

It is a pleasure as well as a duty to acknowledge permissions when they have been so graciously forthcoming. The extracts from the early Avenarius songs which appear in Chapter 1, those from the Op.7 pieces in Chapter 5 and the row tables in Chapter 6 are all the authors' transcriptions from materials in the Sacher Stiftung's Sammlung Anton Webern; the plates in Chapters 5 and 6 are reproductions of materials also in this collection and are used with the permission of the Sacher Stiftung. Excerpts from Schoenberg's *Gurrelieder* and Webern's Opp.25 and 30 in Chapters 2, 7 and 8 are used with the kind permission of Universal Edition Ltd, those from the songs of Opp. 3 and 4 in Chapters 3 and 4 with the permission of Universal Edition and European American Music. Excerpts from the Five Songs after poems by Richard Dehmel and the Four Stefan George Songs appear by permission of Carl Fischer, Inc.

*Kathryn Bailey*
*Cambridge, 1995*

# Introduction

KATHRYN BAILEY

13 September 1945 was Arnold Schoenberg's seventy-first birthday. How this occasion was celebrated is not generally known, but it is probably safe to assume that for Schoenberg the day did not pass without some memories of and a certain longing for his two most illustrious students and faithful friends: Alban Berg, who had died a premature death nearly ten years earlier, and Anton Webern, who had remained in Vienna throughout the dreadful war that had been the reason for Schoenberg's own removal twelve years earlier to what must have seemed to him a very alien land. It is certain that for Webern the day was one of nostalgia and thoughts of his friend and of better times. Fourteen months earlier he had written to Willi Reich, asking how Reich planned to celebrate Schoenberg's seventieth and confessing his own 'unspeakable longing' for their mutual friend.[1]

Two days later Webern was himself dead, a bizarre casualty of that war which Berg and Schoenberg had in different ways both escaped, and which had been over for four months. In an obituary published some four months later in *The Musical Times* Erwin Stein wrote that 'the circumstances of his death have so far not been revealed. Some tragic accident seems to have ended the life of one of our finest musicians.'[2] At the end of 1946 Humphrey Searle described the cause of Webern's death as 'a stray bullet fired by an Allied soldier'.[3] As the war had kept Webern's music from being known, so the politics of its aftermath kept even the exact circumstances of his death – which was, it might seem, even more than ordinarily in such situations senseless and absurd – concealed for some time. The result of a bullet, certainly, but a stray bullet, not exactly. In any case, we have just

[1] Letter dated 6 July 1944, given in *Anton Webern. Weg und Gestalt*, ed. Willi Reich (Zurich: Verlag der Arche, 1961), p. 67.

[2] *The Musical Times*, January 1946. Reprinted in Stein, *Orpheus in New Guises* (London: Rockliff, 1953), pp. 99–102.

[3] Searle, 'Webern's last works', *The Monthly Musical Record*, December 1946, p. 231.

passed the half-century mark of this appalling error, and the following collection of essays on Webern's music constitutes one of the celebrations of that watermark: not a celebration of the anniversary of a death, which is a grotesque idea, but a celebration of a life and an *œuvre* – and, particularly, of our present understanding of both.

Not only Webern's death, but the last years of his life and the history and reception of the music of these years, were shaped by the horrific situation in Europe at the time. As his music had been banned in his own country and he had little success in getting it published and performed elsewhere during the final years of his life, it was not widely known at the end of the war, though Webern himself was a well-known figure and his activities were the subject of great interest to young composers who had little or no experience of his music. Although it is often the case that the death of an artist elicits a sudden burst of interest in his work, in Webern's case the timing of the first blossoming of interest in his music had more to do with the end of the war than with the death of the composer.

The first decade following Webern's death saw frenetic activity amongst the young composers who frequented Darmstadt, and for whom Webern acquired the status of father-figure and mentor. They imagined that they saw in his carefully structured music signposts pointing the way to their own obsession with precompositional schemes. Boulez, who studied for a time with René Leibowitz, produced three important harbingers of integral serialism in 1948: the *Livre pour quatuor*, his Second Piano Sonata and *Le soleil des eaux*. His first essays date from this time as well. 'Propositions', in which his discussion of canonically organised rhythms makes reference to Messiaen rather than to either Schoenberg or Webern, appeared in 1948;[4] in 'Trajectoires: Ravel, Stravinsky, Schönberg', the following year,[5] we see his zeal for a new organisation focusing on the latter two composers, and we encounter perhaps for the first time the opinion that was to be expressed on so many subsequent occasions: that it was Webern, not Schoenberg, who understood the nature and potential of serial technique.

4 *Polyphonie* 2 (1948), pp. 65–72; trans. Stephen Walsh in *Stocktakings of an Apprenticeship* (Oxford: Clarendon Press, 1991), pp. 47–54.

5 *Contrepoints* 6 (1949), pp. 122–42; trans. in *Stocktakings*, pp. 188–208.

The serial madness reached its zenith in 1951–2. Boulez was particularly prolific during this time. *Polyphonie X* appeared in 1951, and in 1952 he not only produced the work that will probably stand for all time as the classic example of this genre – *Structures I* for two pianos – but two of the most important essays in the field as well. 'Schönberg is dead', in which he castigates Schoenberg roundly for not going all the way with his new discovery and once again presents Webern as a better model –

> Schoenberg's serial music was doomed to stalemate. First, the investigation of serialism was one-sided: it neglected rhythm, and even, strictly speaking, sound, in the sense of dynamics and mode of attack ... But the real reason for the stalemate lies in a profound misunderstanding of serial FUNCTIONS as such, as engendered, that is, by the actual serial principle ... a certain Webern ploughed the same furrow; admittedly ... hardly anyone has heard of him ... Perhaps we might, like this Webern, investigate the musical EVIDENCE arising from the attempt at generating structure from material. Perhaps ...[6]

– appeared in February, and its obvious sequel, 'Eventuellement ...' –

> The only one, in truth, who was conscious of a new dimension in sound ... was Webern ...
>
> ... We need ... to link rhythmic to serial structures through a common organization which will also embrace the other characteristics of sound: dynamics, mode of attack, timbre; and then to expand this morphology into an integrated rhetoric.[7]

– in May. Webern's name was never far from the surface in these essays; a short piece that appeared in the *New York Herald Tribune* on 28 December 1952[8] ended

> Webern is the threshold ... let us have the insight to regard him as such... we shall dismember his face, for there is no reason to surrender to hypnosis. Nevertheless music is not about to sink that face into oblivion.

6 Originally published in English in *The Score* 6 (Feb. 1952), pp. 18–22; repr. in *Stocktakings*, pp. 209–14. Capitalisation as in original.

7 *La Revue musicale* no. 212 (May 1952), pp. 117–48; trans. as 'Possibly ...' in *Stocktakings*, pp. 111–40 (current references pp. 114 and 115).

8 'A note to tonight's concert: Webern's work analysed', *NYHT* sect. 4, p. 4; repr. as 'Incipit' in *Stocktakings*, pp. 215–16.

Stockhausen first visited Darmstadt in 1951, and in that year composed his *Kreuzspiel*, to be followed shortly by *Kontra-Punkte* and the first of his *Klavierstücke*. The ideas of hyperserialisation were not restricted to Darmstadt: Milton Babbitt was doing similar things in the United States, but Darmstadt was the main centre of activity. *Die Reihe 2*, published in 1955,[9] was the first consolidated presentation of the Darmstadt view of Webern. Stockhausen and Boulez are there – but, significantly, the Boulez of December 1952 (his contribution is the piece from the *New York Herald Tribune* quoted above)[10] – as well as Herbert Eimert[11] and one Armin Klammer, who tells us more than anyone ever wished to know about the third movement of the Op.27 Variations.[12] But for all its appearance of dogma, *Die Reihe 2* represented a view of music that was already moribund. *Le marteau sans maître* appeared in the same year, and already in November of 1954 Boulez had written, in 'Recherches maintenant':

> Webern only organized pitch; we organize rhythm, timbre, dynamics; everything is grist to this monstrous all-purpose mill, and we had better abandon it quickly if we are not to be condemned to deafness. One soon realizes that composition and organization cannot be confused without falling into a maniacal inanity, undreamt of by Webern himself.[13]

And by 1957 Boulez, in his famous essay deploring the current 'obsession' with chance, was equally scornful of the 'schematisation' and 'number fetishism' of which he had been a pioneer only a few years earlier.[14]

Thus the initial – and probably the most colourful – response to the music of Webern lasted almost exactly a decade. The subsequent thirty years saw the publication of hundreds of analyses of music from all periods of Webern's life as well as a significant number of books about Webern. These

9 *Die Reihe 2*, ed. Herbert Eimert and Karlheinz Stockhausen (Universal Edition, Vienna), trans. Leo Black and Eric Smith (Bryn Mawr: Theodore Presser, 1958).

10 See Stockhausen, 'For the fifteenth of September, 1945', pp. 37–9, and, especially, 'Structure and experiential time', pp. 64–74; Boulez, 'The threshold', pp. 40–1.

11 'Interval proportions', pp. 93–9.

12 'Webern's piano variations, pp. 27, 3rd movement', pp. 81–92.

13 *La Nouvelle Revue française* 23 (Nov. 1954), pp. 898–903; trans. in *Stocktakings* as 'Current investigations', pp. 15–25 (current reference p. 16).

14 'Alea', *La Nouvelle Revue française* 59 (Nov. 1957), pp. 839–57; *Stocktakings*, pp. 26–38.

represented a wide spectrum of attitudes and perspectives, ranging from those whose primary concern was to define Webern's achievements in terms of the German-Viennese tradition (which was so important to him) to those who saw in his music revolutionary procedures which could be adequately explained only in terms of numbers, proportions and mathematical relationships. Great interest was shown, naturally, in Webern's symmetrical arrangements and in particular his love of the musical palindrome, as in his oft-expressed concern for a synthesis of the horizontal and the vertical, a concern he shared with Schoenberg but which originated in his engagement with the theories of Goethe. All of these perspectives have something to offer in our quest for a truer understanding of the unique music of Webern; all have helped to fill out the profile of a body of music which was initially rather enigmatic. But none can claim to tell the whole story, and even taken together the composite seems somehow lacking.

The outlines were fleshed out considerably with the publication, in 1978, of the Moldenhauers' biography.[15] Here for the first time one caught a glimpse of the wealth of primary materials – sketches, letters, diaries and so on – that would one day give a more comprehensive picture of Anton Webern and his work. The most important single event in the progress of Webern scholarship occurred in 1986, when Moldenhauer's considerable collection of Webern materials, which until that time had for the most part been locked up and inaccessible, was finally made available for inspection and study, at the Library of Congress, the Stadt- und Landesbibliothek in Vienna and the Paul Sacher Stiftung in Basel. At last it was possible to see how the man had worked, to examine his methods and to read his voluminous diaries and letters, the contents of which had been virtually unknown until the late 1970s[16] and from 1978 known only secondhand, through Moldenhauer's filtering of

15 Hans and Rosaleen Moldenhauer, *Anton von Webern: a Chronicle of his Life and Work* (London: Gollancz, 1978; New York: Knopf, 1979).

16 Moldenhauer allowed a carefully rationed supply of sketch materials and unpublished works to seep into circulation via six international Webern conferences which he helped to organise, the first in 1962, the publications of forty-seven pages of sketches published in facsimile in 1968 – *Anton von Webern: Sketches (1926–1945)* (New York: Carl Fischer) – and the occasional release for publication of early works (for example, in 1966 the world was introduced to several early songs, the 1905 String Quartet, an early slow movement for string quartet and *Im Sommerwind*).

them for publication in his biography. Since 1986 a number of people, including most of the authors whose work appears in the following pages, have become to some extent familiar with these materials from Webern's own hand. This familiarity will surely be – indeed, has been already – decisive in giving our portrait of Webern the breath of life.

One of the most important outcomes of our getting to know Webern firsthand is the realisation that he was perhaps first and foremost a lyricist. This is a theme which has already been explored by Anne Shreffler in two major works – a book examining Webern's compositional process in the writing of the Trakl songs of Opp.13 and 14, and her study of his mercurial engagement with twelve-note technique in writing the subsequent songs of Opp.15–18.[17] Webern's consuming interest in German turn-of-the-century lyric poetry is the subject of Susanne Rode-Breymann's chapter in the present volume on the early settings of texts by Ferdinand Avenarius, and lyricism is a theme that surfaces again in Christopher Wintle's essay on the first of the Op.25 Jone songs. Arnold Whittall, in his essay, quotes a letter written by Webern to Berg following a trip to the Hochschwab, in which he articulates his faith in contemplation of the mysteries of nature as the path to self-knowledge and revelation: a belief which was wholly in tune with that of the turn-of-the-century lyric poets and the painters with whom they were associated aesthetically. Whittall goes on to examine the Op.30 Variations for Orchestra as a discourse on Goethe's concepts of metamorphosis and self-knowledge.

*Die Reihe 2*, which contained so much that supported the Darmstadt view, opened with a section which, in contrast, was truly Webern's: testimonials, and letters written by him. In a famous epigraph Stravinsky refers to 'his diamonds, his dazzling diamonds' (p. vii). The poetess Hildegard Jone, whose words Webern had so often set, describes her first hearing of the Op.29 Cantata, and of 'its illuminating grace . . . this "perfection" of unearthly gentleness' (p. 7). Also present is Schoenberg's oft-quoted foreword to Webern's Op.9 Bagatelles, in which he refers to Webern's expression of 'a novel in a single gesture, a joy in a breath' (p. 8). And the 'Hochschwab' letter to Berg is given, in which Webern relates his great pleasure in the discovery of 'a tiny

[17] *Webern and the Lyric Impulse: Songs and Fragments on Poems of Georg Trakl* (Oxford: Clarendon Press, 1994); and '"Mein Weg geht jetzt vorüber": the vocal origins of Webern's twelve-tone composition', *JAMS* 47/2 (1994), pp. 275–339.

plant', the winter-green, which he describes as 'a little like a lily of the valley, homely, humble and hardly noticeable. But a scent like balsam! What a scent! For me it contains all tenderness, emotion, depth, purity.'[18]

Webern's lyricism is not something that has gone entirely unnoticed until recently. In the obituary cited above Erwin Stein described Webern as 'primarily a lyricist in the same sense as Schubert and Debussy were' and goes on to remark that 'the lyrical quality of his music distinguishes Webern from Schoenberg whose faithful disciple he was'.[19] And in 1955, the year of *Die Reihe 2*, Adorno, in his essay 'Webern der Komponist', wrote that 'Webern's idea [*Idee*] is one of absolute lyricism: the attempt to dissolve all musical principles and all objective elements of musical form in the sheer sound of the subject.'[20] Later in the same essay, in an attempt to define more clearly the quality of lyricism in Webern, Adorno draws a parallel with the work of Paul Klee. He sees an affinity between the two artists in terms of both intention and technique. Both men turned their backs on sentimentality and excess, and their work is eminently recognisable because of what Adorno describes as its 'linear restraint' and 'a strange kind of graphics [which he later likens to doodling, and to Kafka's prose style], . . . at the same time definite and mysterious', and possessing the same spirit of enchantment that results from accidents of colour in children's art:[21]

> Both Webern and Klee travel along an imaginary border between colour and outline. The constructions of both are shaded rather than coloured. Colour is never used autonomously, there is no insistence on it as an essential element of composition, nor is there an organised pattern of sounds.

Nine years earlier Erwin Stein had also used the language of visual art to describe Webern's lyricism, and, though the reference is not explicit, again the magic squares and wonderfully enchanting line drawings of Paul Klee come to mind:

[18] Letter of 1 August 1919, on p. 17. This is an important letter of which I quote only a small portion here, since it is quoted at greater length elsewhere in this volume: see Rode-Breymann, p. 18; Bailey, p. 173; and Whittall, p. 264.
[19] Stein, in *Orpheus in New Guises*, p. 100.
[20] In *Klangfiguren*. This essay was reprinted in *Merkur* 13/3 (March 1959), pp. 201–14; my page references are taken from this reprint (current reference, p. 202).
[21] Ibid., p. 213.

> Webern remains the lyricist. His phrases are fitted together like coloured patterns into a mosaic.
>
> ... Ecstasy was his natural state of mind; his compositions should be understood as musical visions. Webern imagined a music of ethereal sounds ... The avoidance of strong beats and of symmetrical groupings often imparts the feeling of hovering suspension ... The timbre changes perpetually, like colours and shapes in a kaleidoscope.[22]

But in spite of these early voices Webern analysis has until very recently tended not to be enchanted by the naïveté of his lyricism so much as bewitched by the complexity of his symmetries. As Anne Shreffler has written, the association of his music 'with a cerebral, detached aesthetic remains strangely unaffected' by voices 'raised now and then in favour of a more humanist Webern'.[23] It is to be hoped that the present volume may help to redress this imbalance. If the several essays to follow share a common thread, it is that they all look at a familiar figure from unfamiliar perspectives. Several chapters were referred to above, those that are concerned specifically with lyricism and with Goethean theories of metamorphosis. Other perspectives are represented as well. Allen Forte and Robert W. Wason offer convincing proof of Webern's use, early in his compositional life, of two musical means that have not traditionally been associated with him: octatonicism and specific pitch repetitions. Derrick Puffett speculates – seriously, in spite of his tongue-in-cheek transcription of a little-known sketch using Wagner tubas – on the course that Webern's music might have taken had he not got caught up with the person of Arnold Schoenberg and with the latter's Expressionist/abstract proclivities and teaching. Felix Meyer and Anne Shreffler examine in detail the interaction between composition and performance with particular reference to the Op.7 pieces for violin and piano. And I report on the changes in my own view of the composer as the result of time spent with the row tables from which he composed. Not one of these essays follows a 'party line'. Finally, Neil Boynton has compiled a new Webern bibliography containing specific references for the wealth of primary materials that have become accessible in the past decade, as well as a comprehensive list of secondary sources that

22 In *Orpheus in New Guises*, pp. 101, 99–100.

23 *Webern and the Lyric Impulse*, p. 3.

either were omitted from Zoltan Roman's bibliography of 1978 [24] or have been published since that time. This will be an invaluable tool for those wishing to get better acquainted with the Webern who has begun to emerge from behind his canons and mirrors in the past few years.

Sometime around 1908 Webern chose a poem by Stefan George to set to music; the resulting song is one of those examined by Robert Wason in Chapter 3. Some ninety years later the text seems a particularly appropriate plea from a composer whose lyricism has been for so long submerged in a mire of numbers and theorems:

> This is a song
> for you alone:
> of childish dreams
> and pious tears . . .
> Lightly it wings its way
> through morning gardens.
> Only for you
> it wants to be
> a song that stirs the heart.[25]

[24] This appeared first in Moldenhauer, *Anton von Webern*, pp. 757–73. It was then published separately: *Anton von Webern: an Annotated Bibliography* (Detroit: Information Coordinators Inc., 1983).

[25] 'Dies ist ein Lied', the first poem of George's *Der siebente Ring* and the first song of Webern's George Lieder, Op.3. Translation by S. S. Prawer in *The Penguin Book of Lieder* (Baltimore: Penguin Books, 1984).

# 1 '... gathering the divine from the earthly ...'

## Ferdinand Avenarius and his significance for Anton Webern's early settings of lyric poetry

SUSANNE RODE-BREYMANN
*Translated by Mary Whittall*

Writing to Hildegard Jone in August 1934, Anton Webern told her not to suppose that his choice of text was 'a matter of indifference' to him: that he had his 'whole life long ... demonstrated quite the opposite'.[1] Just as at that date Webern was steeped in the poetry of Hildegard Jone, so at various times in the past he had immersed himself in that of Richard Dehmel, Stefan George, Rainer Maria Rilke, Karl Kraus and Georg Trakl, and drawn from it the intuition for the stages of his *œuvre* as a vocal composer. At each stage he had taken the verses of the poet in question literally: 'that is, as a concrete utterance of the human soul's understanding of itself and the world'.[2] In a letter to Schoenberg dated 4 December 1919 he had summed up his view of the relationship between life and art in the following terms: 'I want to express only what fulfils me, unceasingly, all the days of my life. I do not want anything else.'[3] In the light of that confession, we must approach the texts set by Webern with appropriate seriousness. Lyric poetry was undoubtedly one of the things that fulfilled Webern, and his preoccupation with the verse of individual poets should not be treated as simplistically as it sometimes is.

1 Letter of 8 August 1934 in *Webern: Letters to Hildegard Jone and Josef Humplik*, ed. Josef Polnauer, trans. Cornelius Cardew (Bryn Mawr: Theodore Presser, 1967), p. 27.

2 Reinhard Gerlach, 'Die Dehmel-Lieder von Anton Webern. Musik und Sprache im Übergang zur Atonalität', in *Jahrbuch des Staatlichen Instituts für Musikforschung Preußischer Kulturbesitz 1970* (Berlin, 1971), pp. 45–100 (p. 45).

3 Typescript in the Stadt- und Landesbibliothek Wien, Musiksammlung.

Webern scholars were slow in turning their attention to the recurrent themes in Webern's choice of texts, although they are 'the most direct source of information about his compulsion to self-expression'.[4] Once Reinhard Gerlach and Elmar Budde had published their findings about the composer's Dehmel and George 'phases' respectively, in the early 1970s,[5] study of the other poets who were important to him began to gather momentum, yet still his earliest songs were left virtually untouched. In the early 1980s Albrecht Dümling addressed the question of the choice of themes in Webern's songs in the period 1906–12, but the earliest phase in which Webern displayed a marked affinity for the lyric poetry of one particular poet – the poet, editor and educationalist Ferdinand Avenarius – has received only the most general treatment, with the sole exception of Robert Schollum's study of the stylistic elements of Webern's early songs.[6]

Between 1899 and 1904 Webern set seven poems by Ferdinand Avenarius, all from his collection *Stimmen und Bilder: neue Gedichte*, published in 1897. It was Avenarius's second volume and apart from pieces in ballad style consists mainly of poems concerned with the changing moods of nature – and those of human life to a lesser extent – during the cycle of the year. The following settings date from Webern's days as a schoolboy at the Bundesgymnasium in Klagenfurt:

'Vorfrühling' ('Leise tritt auf . . .')
Klagenfurt, 1899; instrumental accompaniment Klagenfurt, 12 January 1900
published posthumously in *Drei Gedichte für Gesang und Klavier*

'Wolkennacht' ('Nacht, dein Zauberschleier . . .')
Klagenfurt, 1900
MS, forty-three bars: complete setting

4 Albrecht Dümling, '"Dies ist ein Lied für dich allein." Zu einigen Motiven von Weberns Textwahl', in *Musik-Konzepte, Sonderband Anton Webern I* (Munich, 1983), pp. 251–61 (p. 252).

5 Reinhard Gerlach, 'Die Dehmel-Lieder', and Elmar Budde, *Anton Weberns Lieder op. 3: Untersuchungen zur frühen Atonalität bei Webern*, Beihefte zum Archiv für Musikwissenschaft, Band 9 (Wiesbaden, 1971).

6 Robert Schollum, 'Stilistische Elemente der frühen Webern-Lieder', in *Österreichische Gesellschaft für Musik, Beiträge 1972/73: Webern-Kongress* (Kassel, 1973), pp. 127–34.

'Vorfrühling II' ('Doch schwer hinschnaubend . . .')
  [1900]
  MS, twenty-six bars: incomplete pencil draft
'Wehmut' ('Darf ich einer Blume still . . .')
  Preglhof, 15 July 1901
  MS, twenty-three bars: complete setting

and these from his early days at university:

'Gebet' ('Ertrage du's . . .')
  Preglhof, 1903
  published posthumously in *3 Lieder nach Gedichten von Ferdinand Avenarius*
'Freunde' ('Schmerzen und Freuden . . .')
  [Vienna], 6 January 1904
  published posthumously in *3 Lieder nach Gedichten von Ferdinand Avenarius*
'Gefunden' ('Nun wir uns lieben . . .')
  [Vienna or Preglhof], 5 April 1904
  published posthumously in *3 Lieder nach Gedichten von Ferdinand Avenarius.*

Webern's matriculation in 1902 must have been a major reason for the interval between the fourth song and the rest, but it did not prevent his continuing to immerse himself in the poetry of Avenarius. He received another volume, *Lebe*, on his birthday in 1901 – 'von Mitzi zum Geb. 1901', according to the inscription in his copy.[7] Avenarius's aim, in *Lebe* (*Live!*, in the imperative mood), was to achieve an overreaching, large-scale verse form by relating the individual poems to each other – that is, by creating an inner drama. On 8 December 1901 Webern commented enthusiastically to his cousin Ernst Diez that the volume was 'really very beautiful', and that now he knew 'all the poems of Avenarius'.

7 Webern's copy of this collection resides in the Paul Sacher Stiftung in Basel. I wish especially to thank the Stiftung for a research stipend in 1989 which made my work on the present subject possible, as well as for their helpfulness and generosity during my stay there.

Whether he really knew them all or not must remain an open question. But from the library in his Nachlaß, small as it was, and from entries in his notebooks, it is certain that in addition to *Stimmen und Bilder*[8] and *Lebe*[9] he owned copies of *Die Kinder von Wohldorf*[10] and *Wandern und Werden*,[11] and that he was very familiar with the work of Avenarius. Besides the settings, further evidence of this is given by the fact that he copied three poems from *Wandern und Werden* into his notebook at the end of 1899.[12]

| **'Waldsee'** | **'Woodland lake'** |
|---|---|
| Dich lieb ich, Waldsee,<br>Nachts, wenn ihr Haupt<br>Schlummernd die Weiden neigen,<br>Wenn über dich leise<br>Das Ried herflüstert,<br>Und, grüne Lichtlein,<br>Erglimmend, verlöschend,<br>Glühkäfer über dich hinzittern. | I love you, woodland lake,<br>At night, when the willows<br>Bow their heads in slumber,<br>When the rushes whisper<br>Softly across you,<br>And the little green lights —<br>Now glinting, now dark —<br>Of fireflies tremble above you. |
| Von einer Seele hört ich, die einst<br>Ihr Liebesweh<br>In deiner Tiefe begrub —<br>Im Vollmondscheine<br>Steige sie auf<br>Und lausche traurig<br>Den Stimmen im Schilf. | I have heard of one who buried<br>Her broken heart<br>In your depths.<br>At full moon, they say,<br>She rises again<br>And listens sorrowfully<br>To the voices in the reeds. |
| Doch du, ins Auge<br>Siehst du dem befreundet Himmel,<br>Und seiner Lichter<br>Schwankende Bilder<br>Wiegest du begütigend. | But you look up<br>Into the eyes of your friend, the sky,<br>And rock<br>His lights' wavering images<br>In your kindly cradle. |

– from the portion of *Erstes Wandern* with which Avenarius opened his second collection

8 From *Neue Gedichte* (Florence/Leipzig, 1897).

9 From *Eine Dichtung* (Leipzig, 1894).

10 (Dresden, 1886.)

11 From *Erste Gedichte* (Dresden, 1881).

12 Diary entries will be identified by the numbers given on the microfilm in the Paul Sacher Stiftung (in this case, PSS 210103–5).

**'Sonnenuntergang'**

Ganz still
Sinkt die Sonne dem Ozean zu.
Leise vor sich hin
Weinen Wellen und Wind,
Ganz leise, die Sterbende
Nicht zu betrüben durch ihren Schmerz.
Vom fern hin dämmernden Küstenland
Summen die Glocken.
Sie aber, die Königin,
In Thränenschönheit lächelt sie
Und täuscht in Liebe
Weg über den letzten Augenblick ...
Gedankenlos
Spielt eine Weile die Welt mit der Gütigen
Goldenem Totengeschenk.
Langsam erkennt sie, was geschah —
Der Wind klagt auf,
Der Himmel droben, der verlassene,
Weithin flammt er mit Totenleuchten,
Und der scheue Erbe Mond
Schleicht in das verödete Reich.

**'Sunset'**

Quite silently
The sun sinks towards the ocean.
Softly, to themselves,
The waves and wind weep,
Quite softly, So that their pain
Does not distress her as she dies.
From along the coast, fading
distantly in the twilight,
Comes the hum of bells.
But she, the queen,
Smiles in the beauty of tears,
And disguises
The last moment in love ...
Unthinking,
The world plays a while
with the benevolent light's
Golden bequest.
Slowly it understands what has happened —
The wind moans,
The widowed sky above
Is aflame with funeral torches,
And the moon, shy inheritor,
Creeps into the desolate kingdom.

– from the second part of the collection, entitled *Blätter Meer*

**'Auf einem Kirchhof'**

Auf den ernsten Trauerweiden
Weilt des Mondes Gruß,
Wie auf stillen Menschenleiden
Einer Mutter Kuß.

Wachend ist im weichen Lenze
Blütenduft allein —
Können Blumen denn und Kränze
Schmerzeszeichen sein?

Gleite dunkel, Selbstvergessen,
Über mein Gemüt,
Wie der Schatten der Zypressen
Über Gräber zieht!

**'In a churchyard'**

The moonlight rests
Upon the sombre weeping willows,
With a greeting like a mother's kiss
On silent human sorrow.

Nothing is awake in the soft spring
But the scent of blossoms —
Can flowers and garlands
Be signs of suffering?

Let self-forgetting glide darkly
Over my spirit,
As the shadow of the cypresses
Steals across the graves!

– from the third section of the book *Zweites Wandern*

The fact that Webern wrote out his copies of the three texts in the order in which they appear in the printed volume suggests that the act of copying was a kind of record of his experience, made at the moment of reading them, and reflecting his fascination.

Ferdinand Avenarius (1856–1923) was Richard Wagner's nephew, being the son of his younger half-sister, Cäcilie Geyer-Avenarius. Viewed as a whole, his literary work amounted to rather more than the volumes of his own verse, for he also compiled anthologies of the verse of others. The correspondence between those collections and the poetry set to music by Webern up to 1904 is striking. Apart from Friedrich Nietzsche, all the poets (Hans Böhm, Matthias Claudius, Richard Dehmel, Gustav Falke, Johann Wolfgang von Goethe, Martin Greif, Detlev von Liliencron, Theodor Storm, Ludwig Uhland, Wilhelm Weigand) are to be found in one, and in some cases both, of Avenarius's anthologies, the *Hausbuch Deutscher Lyrik*,[13] which groups atmospheric pieces by topics such as human life, times of day and seasons of the year, and the *Balladenbuch*.[14] Webern could even have taken the texts of 'Hochsommernacht' (Martin Greif) and 'Heimgang in der Frühe' (Detlev von Liliencron) directly from the *Hausbuch*,[15] and 'Siegfrieds Schwert' (Ludwig Uhland) is to be found in the *Balladenbuch*.[16] The significance of the coincidence is diminished, admittedly, by the observation that this spectrum of poets occupied the middle ground of popular poetry around 1900, and would have been found in countless other anthologies.

Lyric poetry at the turn of the century was one of the most important of the cultural movements that offered an alternative to Naturalism, and was the product of a society whose traditional values and ways of thought were beginning to disintegrate. Naturalism's interest in general and social

13 Collected by Ferdinand Avenarius with drawings by Fritz Philip Schmidt (Munich: Kunstwart, 1903).

14 (Munich: Kunstwart, 1907.)

15 These poems are found on pp. 43 and 124 respectively.

16 On p. 140. [This work is now known not to have been written by Webern, but arranged by him: see Martin Hoyer, 'Neues zu Anton Weberns frühen Liedern' (bibliography, p. 338).–Ed.]

questions was countered by an interest in details, the particular moment and the nuance, and by concern for what was subjective, inward and conditioned by emotion. For all of those things lyric verse was the most suitable literary genre, and in consequence reading poetry was probably more widespread among the middle classes than at any time before or since.

This was the world in which Webern grew up, wrote down in his notebooks the texts of songs which had made an impression on him (such as Eduard Mörike's poems 'Auf das Grab von Schillers Mutter', 'Neue Liebe', 'Gesang Weylas' and 'Verborgenheit') and copied out poems with which he identified. In October 1901 he copied three poems by Hermann Ubell,[17] who was born in Graz in 1876.

| **'Jenseits allen Harms'** | **'Beyond the reach of harm'** |
|---|---|
| Weiß durch weiße Schleier | White, the winter's day |
| Blickt der Wintertag. | Peers through a white veil. |
| Die Pappeln um den Weiher | The poplars stand around the pond, |
| Stehn in tiefem Schlaf. | Sunk in sleep. |
| | |
| Stille mich umfängt | Stillness embraces me |
| Und wiegt mich, weichen Arms | And cradles me in soft arms. |
| Meine Seele hängt | My soul rests |
| Jenseits allen Harms. | Beyond the reach of harm. |

| **'Die Fahrt der Todten'** | **'Voyage of the Dead'** |
|---|---|
| Es fuhr ein kalter Wind in meinen Garten, | A cold wind has blown across my garden, |
| Der seine Blumen fromm zur Sonne wandte: | Which had turned its flowers piously to face the sun: |
| Ein blauer Schatten fiel in meinen Garten, | A blue shadow has fallen across my garden, |
| Und früher war doch unbewegte Klarheit . . . | Yet earlier all was clear and still . . . |
| | |
| Zum hohen Erker steig ich müd' empor | Wearily I climb up to my high oriel |
| Und lausche in die dunkle, weiche Dämmerung, | And listen out into the dark, soft twilight |
| Die zögernd niedergleitet; schläfrig tickt | Stealing hesitantly down; the clock on the mantlepiece |
| Die Stutzuhr am Kaminsims; freundlich lädt | Ticks sleepily; the old chair |
| Der alte Lehnstuhl in die weiten Arme . . . | holds out its arms in welcome . . . |

17 PSS 210045–7.

| | |
|---|---|
| ... Und langsam schifft sich meine Seele ein, | ... And slowly my soul embarks |
| Und segelt – o der stillen weißen Segel – über | And sails – oh, the still, white sail – over |
| | |
| Das sonnenhelle, hohe Meer der Träume. Lieblich | The sunbright, high seas of dreams. The lovely |
| Blinken die vielen Wellen ... Mich umkreist | Wink of countless waves ... A garland of sweet voices |
| Ein Kranz von süßen Stimmen, die so zärtlich | Circles round me, |
| Wie Perlen und wie dünnes Silber klingen ... | As delicate as pearls and tinkling like thin silver ... |
| | |
| Im blauen Fernen dämmern Palmeninseln, | Palm islands down in the distance, |
| Von denen uns die Brise warme Düfte | Sending us the breath of warm aromas |
| Herüberathmet ... Schmale grüne Reiher | On the breeze ... Slender green herons |
| Ziehn uns zu Häupten ihre lichten Kreise ... | Draw their light circles above our heads ... |
| | |
| Selig, mit leisem Singen, landen wir | Blessed, and singing softly, we land |
| Im ruhevollen Port der sanften Dinge ... | In the peaceful haven of gentle things ... |

## 'Jugend'

Nimm dein Geschick auf dich und sei dein eigener Stern
Schreite den Pfad deiner Wahl durch das Dickicht der Nacht.
Halte die Brut der Gespenster gebärenden Stille dir fern
Bis aus den Wipfeln der blauende Morgen dir lacht!

O dann hülle den Leib in den strahlenden Panzer des Tags,
Sonnenumflossen, ein Sieger vom Scheitel bis zum Zeh,
Lausche der sehnenden Geige des Fauns am Raine des Hags,
Schmiege den Arm um den Elfenbeinrücken der Nymphen im See ...

## 'Youth'

Take your fate upon yourself and be your own star.
Walk the path of your choice through the thicket of night.
Banish the brood of the ghost-bearing silence
Till from out the treetops the breaking day laughs at you!

Then, oh then clothe your limbs in day's glowing armour,
Bathed in sunlight, a victor from head to foot,
List to the yearning violin of the faun at the grove's edge,
Wreathe your arms round the ivory backs of the nymphs in the lake . . .

While the poems by Mörike that Webern copied can be said to be typical of the taste of the time, as also reflected by Avenarius's anthologies, Ubell was far from popular or well known, and it is somewhat surprising to find his poems in Webern's notebooks. How did Webern come across them? The question is quite easily answered: the trail leads straight to his closest boyhood friend, his cousin Ernst Diez (1876–1961), seven years his senior.

Diez was to become a distinguished scholar in the field of Oriental art, but he was still a student of art history in Graz during Webern's last years at school in Klagenfurt. The cousins corresponded, and also saw each other during the summer holidays at the Preglhof or at the opera in Graz (where, for example, they saw Wagner's *Tristan* at Easter in 1901). Hans Moldenhauer describes their correspondence aptly as 'a constant exchange of their ideas in the cultural sphere'.[18] The picture Moldenhauer paints[19] does not include every facet of the exchange, however: in all likelihood Webern owed his acquaintance with the lyric poetry of Ubell to Diez, whose diary, begun in 1899,[20] contains poems by Ubell which are of a slightly earlier date than those copied by Webern. Just as this particular interest of Webern's appears to have been inspired by Diez, so there seem to have been many other – non-musical – instances in their exchange of ideas where the initiative was taken by Diez. In musical matters, in particular their shared enthusiasm for Wagner, Webern was his cousin's equal, in spite of the difference in their ages, but elsewhere he was the beneficiary in a variety of ways.

There can, for example, be no doubt that it was Diez who drew Nietzsche to his cousin's attention, as a result of which Webern set Nietzsche's poem 'Heiter' ('Mein Herz ist wie ein See . . .') in 1904. Diez filled a good ten pages of his diary in the summer of 1900 with quotations from Nietzsche, taken, interestingly enough, from a secondary source,

[18] Hans and Rosaleen Moldenhauer, *Anton von Webern: a Chronicle of his Life and Work* (London: Victor Gollancz, 1978), p. 47.

[19] Ibid., pp. 38ff.

[20] The diary of Ernst Diez is also owned by the Paul Sacher Stiftung in Basel.

Elisabeth Förster-Nietzsche's biography of her brother.[21] Not much later, in September 1901, quotations from *Also sprach Zarathustra* appear, with an entry in their midst recording the end of 'Toni''s visit. Diez would have told him about his interest in Nietzsche's conception of genius (which the quotations reflect), Nietzsche's attitude towards scientific attention to detail, Nietzsche's preference for a 'certain poetic recreation of spirits, events, characters'.[22] Last but not least, Nietzsche's opinions of Wagner's music and the Bayreuth Festival, to which Diez gave a lot of space, would have been one of the topics on which the cousins exchanged views.

The proof that Diez led the way and Webern followed is more concrete in the case of reading Nietzsche than in their appreciation of painting, but the pattern is likely to have been similar, and once again Hermann Ubell crops up. Ubell, custodian and director of the Ober-österreichischen Landesmuseum in Linz from 1903 until 1937, had played an important role in Graz during the years of Diez's art history study there, as founder of the Kunsthistorische Gesellschaft Graz and co-editor of the *Grazer Kunst*, which Webern indicated as the source for the three poems by Ubell that he copied into his notebook.[23]

Ubell lectured on a variety of subjects to the Kunsthistorische Gesellschaft Graz: for example, a talk on Hans Marées on 6 March 1900 and another on Benvenuto Cellini on 31 October of the same year were announced in the *Grazer Tagespost*.[24] The latter was given as part of the proceedings at the society's Annual General Meeting, and the *Grazer Tagespost* carried a report on 2 November 1900, including the following: 'Lectures on the history of art in more recent times were given by . . . Herr Dr H. Ubell on . . . Benvenuto Cellini and Böcklin (posthumous), [and] by Herr Curator E. Diez on Velasquez.'[25]

21 Elisabeth Förster-Nietzsche, *Das Leben Friedrich Nietzsches* (Leipzig, 1897). Concerning Webern's introduction to Nietzsche, see Susanne Rode, '"Wagner und die Folgen." Zur Nietzsche–Wagner–Rezeption bei Alban Berg und Anton von Webern', in *Der Fall Wagner. Ursprünge und Folgen von Nietzsches Wagner-Kritik*, Band 11 of the Thurnauer Schriften zum Musiktheater (Laaber: Thomas Steiert, 1991), pp. 265–92.

22 From Ernst Diez's diary.

23 'Jenseits allen Harms' and 'Die Fahrt der Todten' were also published in Ubell's collection *Der Stundenreigen* (Vienna, 1903), on pp. 40 and 4 respectively.

24 *Grazer Tagespost* (1900), nos. 64 and 279 respectively.

25 Ibid., no.294.

In view of the liveliness of Diez and Webern's exchange of views at that date it is inconceivable that this was not another area explored in their letters and conversations, and that in turn makes a lecture Ubell gave in Graz in the previous year especially interesting. The *Grazer Tagespost* of 12 November 1899 reported on the meeting of the Kunsthistorische Gesellschaft Graz held on 9 November, at which 'the writer Herr Hermann Ubell spoke about Segantini, the recently deceased master of landscape' and outlined 'the position of this Italian-Tyrolese painter in modern art':

> First his new, highly impressive technique was described . . . Then Herr Ubell proceeded to discuss the subjects themselves. Segantini's conception and execution of them were illuminated by a comparison with Jean François Millet and by contrast with a third painter of peasant life, Defregger . . . The atmosphere of Segantini's major landscape paintings was characterised by readings from some of the beautiful poems of Konrad Ferdinand Meyer and a few of the magnificent, impressionistic, landscape aphorisms of Nietzsche.[26]

Webern's enthusiasm for Segantini is well known and often referred to.[27] This account suggests the possibility that it grew in soil prepared by Diez and was not first planted when he saw Segantini's *Alpenlandschaft* in Munich in 1902; thus Eric Frederick Jensen's summary statement that 'it is surprising that Webern did not come into contact with [Segantini's] work until 1902'[28] is called into question. Jensen accepts the generally held belief that Webern's admiration for Segantini began with a visit to the Neue Pinakothek in Munich, on the return journey from the visit to the Bayreuth Festival which he and Diez made together in the summer of 1902. This assumption is based on an entry in Webern's notebook dated 2 August 1902, reporting on the art galleries and exhibitions that the cousins visited together in Munich.

> We visited the Neue Pinakothek, where there are some glorious pictures. I was especially impressed by Segantini's *Alpenlandschaft*, Böcklin's *Spiel der Wellen* . . . Then the Schack-Galerie, full of wonderful Böcklins (esp.

26 *Grazer Tagespost* (1899), no.314.

27 See for example Eric Frederick Jensen, 'Webern and Giovanni Segantini's "Trittico della natura"', *The Musical Times* 130/1751 (January 1989), pp. 11–15; and Joachim Noller, 'Bedeutungsstrukturen. Zu Anton Webern's "alpinen" Programmen', *Neue Zeitschrift für Musik* 151/9 (1990), pp. 12–18.

28 Jensen, 'Webern and Segantini's "Trittico"', p. 11.

> *Villa am Meer*) and a lot of Schwinds. Lastly we went to the Secession. This was the first exhibition of modern artists I've ever seen. To be honest! none of the paintings made an outstanding impression on me. Perhaps I was already past being able to appreciate them properly after the exertions of our journey.[29]

Although at first sight these comments appear to be a spontaneous record of Webern's impressions of the various galleries, they quickly lose their impromptu quality if they are read carefully and in association with the fact that the cousins had been comparing notes on art for some time, for the conjunction of the three names Segantini, Böcklin and Schwind points all too plainly to the third area of Ferdinand Avenarius's activity and the one which had the most valuable consequences: his foundation in 1887 of the periodical *Der Kunstwart*, and in 1902 of the Dürer-Bund, which Webern joined in 1903. The 'Dürer League' and the periodical, both of which Avenarius used to serve his educational purposes, were connected: 'the one disseminated the ideals of its members, the other can be regarded as the organisation of the readers of *Der Kunstwart*'.[30] In 1897 *Der Kunstwart* was given not only a new subtitle ('Fortnightly publication on poetry, theatre, music, fine and applied art') but also a new, rapidly expanding section, *Lose Blätter*, devoted to samples of the work of poets and thinkers, in which Avenarius already anticipated the line he would follow in his anthologies. From 1898 onwards *Der Kunstwart* began to publish art prints and printed music. To begin with, the prints took the form of single plates and inserts in the periodical itself, but before long Avenarius was producing separate, reasonably priced supplements (*Mappen*: albums) making works of art that had previously been little known outside a small circle more widely available. (See Plate 1, *Schweigen im Walde*, one of six woodcut reproductions from the *Böcklin Mappe*, published by *Der Kunstwart*.) According to Gerhard Kratzsch,

29 PSS 210055. Though Webern's diaries were not available until recently, this entry is alluded to by Moldenhauer, who, in his description of this visit, mentions 'a Segantini landscape [that] made a special impression on Webern' (*Anton von Webern*, p. 51).

30 Gerhard Kratzsch, *Kunstwart und Dürerbund. Ein Beitrag zur Geschichte der Gebildeten im Zeitalter des Imperialismus* (Göttingen, 1969), p. 11.

**Plate 1** Arnold Böcklin (1827–1901), *Schweigen im Walde*, reproduced in the *Kunstwart Böcklin-Mappe* that contained reproductions of six woodcuts by Böcklin: *Dichtung und Malerei, Heilger Hain, Schweigen im Walde, Der Überfall, Die Toteninsel*, and *Maria an der Leiche des Heilands*. The notes on Arnold Böcklin in the preface to *Schweigen im Walde* give the following description: 'We walk among the towering trees, and all the time it becomes lonelier, quieter. For hours now it has been just tree after tree, and silence. Does there really exist somewhere a world of men? Does there really exist somewhere a world of sounds? Hour after hour just tree upon tree again, and quiet, stillness, silence. Then it happens. From among the trees appears a unicorn, apparently ageless, with a wood nymph riding on its back. It is all quite natural, even inevitable. She looks at you without concern, rides on without a sound, and disappears silently amongst the trees. Then she appears once more; and once again; and now she is gone.'

> The promotion and developing of *Der Kunstwart* and the Dürer-Bund ... were Ferdinand Avenarius's major achievements. Not the poet, not the literary man alone, but the organiser gained the publicity that made his name known throughout all of Germany.[31]

In addition to Albrecht Dürer, the artists favoured by *Der Kunstwart* included the modern artists Arnold Böcklin, Max Klinger, Hans Thoma, Moritz von Schwind and Albert Welti. Segantini's work was also represented there.[32]

There is no concrete evidence of the role that *Kunstwart* played in forming Webern's taste in the visual arts, but equally there is no doubt that the periodical was so perfectly in tune with the temper of the time, and so skilful at satisfying 'the needs of a tide rising around 1900 in the arts and the taste of cultivated and educated people',[33] that it can perfectly well stand as representative of the visual culture that shaped him.

Such was the foundation on which Webern's opinions were based, and his study of art history will certainly not have been the least important factor in making those opinions more penetrating. As a result, the notes he made about the art he saw in Munich in 1905 are far more discriminating than what he had written three years earlier.

> The international art exhibition in the Glaspalast, I'll be as brief as possible. Artists from every country in the world have sent work ... Among this enormous number of pictures, only 3 made an impression on me – a fresco by Fritz Hodler, a portrait by Albert Welti and a picture by Fritz Erler, *Der Fremdling* ... I found exactly the same thing in the Neue Pinakothek as in the hideous Glaspalast! One painting by Böcklin, *Spiel der Wellen*, one each by Hartung, Kalckreuth, Schwind, Segantini, and that was all. Everything else mediocre or complete rubbish. The very building of the Neue Pinakothek is as bad – shabby – tasteless to an unbelievable degree ... Of the Lenbach exhibition I can report no better ... The Schack-Galerie. Here again, more disappointments ... The most marvellous works of art hanging alongside the ugliest dreck. Of the Böcklins, I was particularly taken with the *Ideale Frühlingslandschaft* [see Plate 2], the *Villa am Meer* is beautiful and *Die Seeschlange* is quite wonderful, perhaps my favourite Böcklin to date ... And now I come

31 Ibid., p. 141.

32 Segantini's *Die Pflüger* was reproduced in vol. 13 (1899/1900).

33 Kratzsch, *Kunstwart und Dürerbund*, p. 133.

**Plate 2** Arnold Böcklin, *Ideale Frühlingslandschaft*

to the master Schwind. His pictures make an impression of something unclouded and wondrous. *Des Knaben Wunderhorn* [see Plate 3]. A boy with fair curly hair lies beside a spring deep in the German forest, drinking from a horn, and this horn is the . . . fount of German poetry; all the magic of the German fairytale forest is contained in this magic horn, and . . . the boy drinks copious draughts from it, and he will then go out into the world and sing to the world what his magic horn has sung to him: . . . One could not imagine anything lovelier than this picture. Suddenly the thought struck me: ah, if only it were really so, and it seemed impossible, but immediately I thought better of it and said to myself, certainly it's possible, certainly that's how Schwind saw it. Only those who suffer poverty of the imagination, people without souls, only they do not see these beings when moonlight lies on the misty world or the forest sleeps its noontide slumbers.[34]

Avenarius had published an essay on Moritz von Schwind in *Der Kunstwart* in 1903, supplemented by a series of prints of Schwind's paintings.[35] We encounter another such parallel in the case of Webern's orchestration of some of Wolf's lieder, after the periodical had devoted a lot of space to Wolf.[36] The ideas mooted in setting up the Dürer-Bund[37] can also be linked without any strain to Webern's emotional mode of thought: Avenarius defined the role the League should play in the urgently needed fight against the demise of aesthetics, by which he meant that 'our people would have unlearnt, but for a few isolated phrases, the language for everything that cannot be spoken in words, that they would no longer be able to convey their feelings and views with natural confidence to others' eyes and ears'.[38] The purpose of the League must therefore be the 'cultivation of aesthetic life'. Avenarius's concept of aesthetic life was something very broad, embracing the artist's life as well as 'love for everything that bears leaf and blossoms, and for our brothers in the forest and the field', so that one part of the League's work must be to arouse and encourage 'an understanding of the thousandfold beauties of the landscape, and a relationship to our homeland'.[39] In the League's statutes, Avenarius formulated its aims as the 'cultivation of aesthetic life' and the 'cultivation of the love of nature'.[40]

34 PSS 210143ff.

35 Avenarius, 'Schwind', *Der Kunstwart* 17/1 (1903/4), pp. 477–82.

36 *Der Kunstwart* 16/1 (1902/1903).

37 See Ferdinand Avenarius, 'Zum Dürer-Bunde! Ein Aufruf', *Der Kunstwart* 14/2 (1901), pp. 468–74.

38 Ibid., p. 470.

39 Ibid., p. 471.

40 Ferdinand Avenarius, 'Wie richten wir den Dürerbund ein', *Der Kunstwart* 15/2 (1902), pp. 49–53 (pp. 49–50).

**Plate 3** Moritz von Schwind (1804–71), *Des Knaben Wunderhorn*

'The will to exercise positive effects in and through the arts . . . and the consciousness of moral responsibility'[41] were united in Avenarius with anti-intellectualism and a strong sense of homeland. He 'possessed the energy to create a forum for the interests of those cultivated people, those

[41] Kratzsch, *Kunstwart und Dürerbund*, p. 133.

ethical idealists who turned their backs on the parties where they found no assurance of their desires. In making the case for the validity of realism and objectivity, and right moral principles, and for placing a high value on art and culture, he was simultaneously working for the social validity of the representatives of a model attitude.'[42]

The synthesis of art and nature for which Avenarius strove also constitutes one of the most important fundamental convictions shaping Webern's appreciation of poetry. His lyric vision of poetry is perfectly expressed in the words of Karl Kraus, whom Webern greatly admired, when he defined a poem as 'a revelation of the poet absorbed in contemplation of nature'.[43]

That was the kind of poetry which sparked the creative process in Webern. He wrote in his diary in November 1904 of his longing for a composer who 'writes in solitude, far away from all turmoil of the world', in view of nature, 'in contemplation of the glaciers, of eternal ice and snow, of the sombre mountain giants'.[44] Unquestionably, for Webern, art and culture were based on the opening up of nature's secrets, leading to an ever greater revelation of its mysteriousness. His objective, as he explained it to Alban Berg in a letter dated 1 August 1919, was 'the deep, unfathomable, inexhaustible meaning in . . . these manifestations of nature'. And when he goes on to express his conviction that the 'physical reality [of nature] contains all the miracles [so that] studying, observing amidst real nature is for me the highest metaphysics, theosophy',[45] herein lies the key to his fascination with the poetry of Avenarius.

The poems by Avenarius that Webern chose to set to music are such as reveal 'the poet absorbed in contemplation of nature'. 'Transported worlds away from Earth', wrapped in the magic of the night, the poet surrenders to the phantasmagoria of the clouds racing overhead in 'Wolkennacht', sees 'dark lands' rise and 'glaciers grow' before his gaze. An intangible landscape is fashioned from the elements of movement and light.

[42] Ibid., p. 141.
[43] Karl Kraus, 'Um Heine', *Die Fackel* no. 199 (23 March 1906), p. 3.
[44] Quoted in Moldenhauer, *Anton von Webern*, p. 76.
[45] Ibid., p. 231.

| 'Wolkennacht' | 'Cloudy Night' |
|---|---|
| Nacht, dein Zauberschleier<br>Webt um meinen Sinn,<br>Daß ich weltenweit entrückt<br>Von der Erde bin. | Night, your magical veil<br>Wraps around my senses,<br>And I am transported<br>Worlds away from earth. |
| In den Wolkenfluten,<br>Wie das wogt und gärt!<br>Wie wenn dumpf sich eine Welt<br>Aus dem Nichts gebärt. | How the cloud-billows<br>Surge and seethe!<br>As if a world is soundlessly<br>Being born out of nothingness. |
| Und es will sich trennen,<br>Und vom Schlafe schwer<br>Tauchen dunkle Lande stumm<br>Traumhaft aus dem Meer. | And it will be separate,<br>And, heavy with sleep,<br>Dark lands silently rise up<br>Out of the sea, as in a dream. |
| Schneegebirge wachsen<br>Strahlend drüber auf,<br>Und die Märchensonne schwebt,<br>Und der Mond schwebt auf. | Glaciers grow<br>Radiantly above them,<br>And the fairytale sun is suspended,<br>And the moon rises, hovering. |

The poem is an example of the poetry of night, a field both popular and broad in range. Webern was not alone in succumbing to its appeal, and it was perhaps the most important subject in his early songs.[46] Night, whether moonlit and magical, eerie and mysterious or, at a later date, the expressionistic darkness of the city, was always more than merely a dark version of day. The fascination with the beauties and terrors of the night was correspondingly multifarious.

No other age, however, was so well attuned to the poetry of night as the Romantic era, in which thought and sensibility were saturated with the glorification of night. Thomas Mann writes:

> The night is the true domain and dwelling place of all Romanticism, its real discovery, which it invariably presents as the truth in contrast to the vain illusions of the day – the realm of sensibility contrasted with reason . . . and it is within the general orbit of this world that Wagner's *Tristan* is firmly located.[47]

[46] Other Webern songs that are settings of night poems are 'Nachtgebet der Braut', 'Tief von Fern', 'Aufblick', 'Ideale Landschaft', 'Am Ufer', 'Nächtliche Scheu', 'Helle Nacht', all on poems by Dehmel; 'Fromm' by Gustav Falke; 'Sommerabend' by Wilhelm Weigand; and 'Heimgang in der Frühe' by Detlev von Liliencron.

[47] Thomas Mann, 'Leiden und Größe Richard Wagners' [1933], in Band 9 of *Gesammelte Werke in 12 Bänden* (Frankfurt am Main, 1960), pp. 363–426.

As the ancestor of the 'quintessentially Romantic glorification of the night that we find in this sublimely morbid, consuming and magical work, thoroughly initiated in all the direst and noblest mysteries of Romanticism', Mann identifies Novalis, 'who in "Hymnen an die Nacht" laments: "Must the morning always come again? Shall the power of this earthly life never end? Shall love's secret sacrifice never burn for all eternity?" Tristan and Isolde call themselves "votaries of the night" – which is a verbatim echo of a phrase in Novalis.'[48]

Lovers' isolation from everything earthly is the subject of Avenarius's 'Gefunden', yet the second verse makes clear that here the lovers are no longer 'votaries of the night' but are conscious rather of the 'creator-spirit' all around them.

| **'Gefunden'** | **'Found'** |
|---|---|
| Nun wir uns lieben, rauscht mein stolzes Glück | Now that we love, my proud joy courses |
| hoch ob der Welt, | high above the world. |
| was kann uns treffen, wenn uns das Geschick | What can harm us if Fate |
| beisammen hält? | keeps us together? |
| Und wenn hinab in seine Nacht das Meer | And when the sea hauls the earth |
| die Erde reißt, | down into its night, |
| die Liebe schwebt über den Sternen her | love comes soaring over the stars |
| als Schöpfergeist. | as creator-spirit. |

Avenarius is not filled with despair by any thought of the inevitable return of daylight; on the contrary, in 'Vorfrühling' (a poetic depiction of nature in which he abandons strophic form for free verse) he very subtly draws an analogy between it and the springtime reawakening of nature. Here, the 'deep slumber' of night gives way to 'lovely morning scenes', and the very gentle transition between the times of day stands for the almost imperceptible onset of spring. Solitude and isolation are also conveyed by the image of an unpeopled landscape, filled only by the sound of an early blackbird's call.

48 Thomas Mann, 'The sorrows and grandeur of Richard Wagner', in *Pro and Contra Wagner*, trans. Allan Blunden (London: Faber and Faber, 1985), pp. 125–6; wording altered slightly.

| 'Vorfrühling' | 'Early Spring' |
|---|---|
| Leise tritt auf — | Enter gently — |
| nicht mehr in tiefem Schlaf | no longer in deep slumber, |
| in leichtem Schlummer nur | only lightly sleeping, |
| liegt das Land: | lies the land: |
| Und der Amsel Frühruf | And the blackbird's early call |
| spielt schon liebliche | spills lovely morning scenes |
| Morgenbilder ihm in den Traum. | into its dreams. |
| Leise tritt auf. . . | Enter gently . . . |

One group of poems by Avenarius that Webern set to music expresses a conviction that there is an order in nature which is willed by God. This means that there is something deeper to be discerned in every observation of nature – in Webern's words, the 'physical reality' of nature can reveal 'all the miracles'. This is the subject of 'Wehmut'.

| 'Wehmut' | 'Melancholy' |
|---|---|
| Darf ich einer Blume still | If I can silently look |
| Heut ins Auge sehen, | Into the face of a flower today, |
| Wie ein heimlich Grüßen will | Something like a secret greeting |
| Mirs entgegenwehen. | Seems to come towards me. |
| Schau ich nun ins Land hinaus, | And if I now look out across the open country, |
| Wills mich fast berücken, | It almost beguiles me |
| Daß ich säh ein Antlitz draus | Into seeing a face there, |
| Herzlich auf mich blicken. | Looking at me lovingly. |
| Wenn dann Lerchensänge weit | Then, when larksong pours |
| Durch den Himmel schwimmen, | Across the heavens, |
| Hör ich aus der Ewigkeit | I hear beloved voices |
| Jubeln liebe Stimmen. | Rejoicing from eternity. |

Another poem, 'Freunde', strophic in form but unrhymed, has the line 'und zwischen den Ähren lächelt auf aus Blumen die Schönheit' (between the ears of corn, beauty smiles up from flowers): this is another expression of the view of the world that Webern represented in *Tot: Sechs Bilder für die Bühne* (1913), in the words: 'Ich kam durch die Blüte zur Anschauung Gottes' (I came through the blossoms to behold the face of God).[49]

[49] Webern, quoted in *Opus Anton Webern*, ed. Dieter Rexroth (Berlin: Quadriga, 1983), p. 74.

Avenarius ends 'Freunde' with an appeal to his friends to join in gathering the divine from the earthly ('aus dem Irdischen sammelnd das Göttliche'); this reached to the very core of Webern's being, and left an indelible impression on his conception of what it meant to be absorbed in the contemplation of nature.

The Avenarius songs show Webern working out the first principles of his word-setting and discovering where he could allow himself the first, small liberties with the given text. To begin with, setting poems written in rhymed and metrically regular forms, he followed their formal structures exactly.

In 'Wolkennacht' (see text above) he separated the four stanzas with piano interludes, the first and third of which are of the same length, while the middle one, between the second and third verses, is somewhat shorter. This brings the two middle stanzas slightly closer together, which can be seen to reflect the way the third one begins, following on directly in sense from the end of the second ('. . . a world is soundlessly being born out of nothingness. / And it will be separate . . .'), and thus as an indication of Webern's sensitivity to the words. The individual lines of verse remain formally inviolate, and each is clearly separated from the following one (sometimes by rests). Metrically Webern follows in the most faithful way the metre of the poem. That is to say, he reflects directly the sequence of poetic feet in a regular sequence of musical beats: each verse is made up of two lines with three accents, one line with four, and a concluding one with

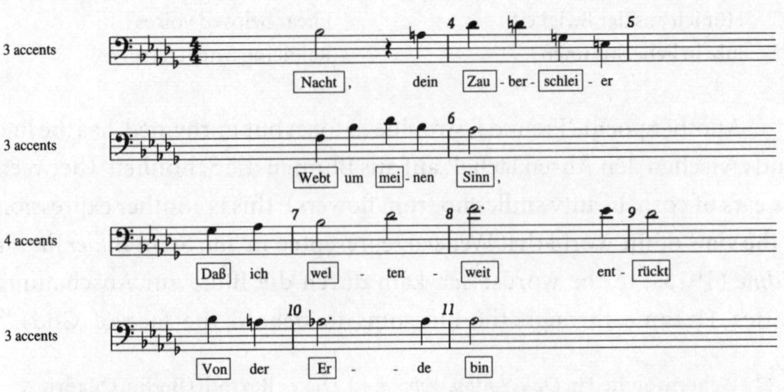


Example 1

three, and as a rule Webern allows the accented syllables of the text to follow each other at the interval of a minim (see Example 1). It is not hard to see that the departures from the norm in the succession of strong beats at minim intervals arise from conscious decisions taken by Webern in the light of his interpretation of the text. Similar extensions of the distance between accents are found in the third verse on the words 'Schlafe' (sleep) in line 2 and 'dunkle Lande' (dark lands) in line 3, as well as in the closing lines of the second and fourth verses. 'Wehmut' (see text above), composed a year later, is based on a similar relationship between musical beats and metrical feet. Here, however, Webern's manipulation of the distance between accents is not a matter of extension but of contraction, as he seeks to draw pairs of lines (3 and 4, 6 and 7) closer together (see Example 2).

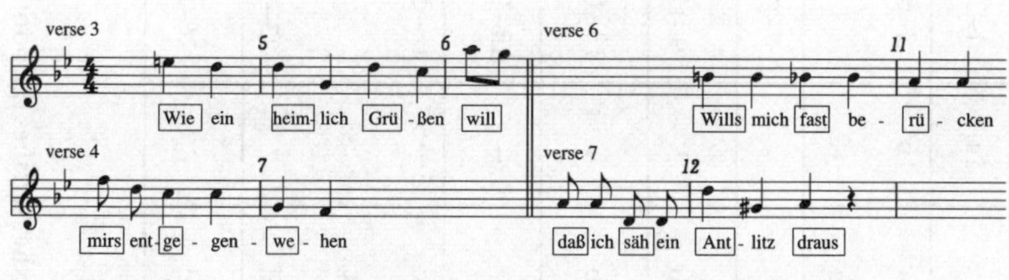


**Example 2**

Webern also employs this somewhat more variable structuring of the relationship between beat and foot in his later settings of poems by Avenarius that are in regular metres. Though here, too, he develops the rhythmic declamation of the text from the background of the poetic feet, he has in the meantime acquired a repertory of ways to enhance nuance – extension and contraction of the distance between accents, *enjambement* and the insertion of piano interludes within stanzas – whereby his growing independence and self-confidence vis-à-vis the text begin to announce themselves.

The two stanzas of 'Gebet' are regular in metrical structure, with five strong beats in each line. Webern interprets them flexibly, in the musical structure shown in Table 1. In 'Gefunden' (see text above), another poem in two verses, Webern turns again to exactly the same model, subdividing the text by means of two piano interludes. The individual elements of 'Gefunden' are unequal in length, but its layout is symmetrical: Webern seems here to adumbrate the experimentation with symmetrical structures

Table 1

| verse | text | rhyme | lines | bars | rhythm of accents |
|---|---|---|---|---|---|
| 1 | Ertrage du's, | | 1a | 1–2 | 𝅗𝅥 \|[2] 𝅗𝅥. 𝄾 |
| | lass schneiden dir den Schmerz<br>scharf durchs Gehirn und wülen Hart durchs Herz | a<br>a | 1b<br>→2 | 3–6 | 𝅗𝅥 𝅗𝅥 \|[4] 𝅗𝅥 𝅗𝅥 \|[5] 𝅗𝅥 𝅗𝅥 \|[6] 𝅗𝅥 𝅗𝅥 |
| | | | – | 7–8 | piano interlude |
| | Das ist der Pflug, nach dem der Sämann sät, | b | 3 | 9–12 | 𝅝 \|[10] 𝅝 \|[11] 𝅗𝅥 𝅗𝅥 \|[12] 𝅗𝅥 𝄽 𝄾 |
| | dass aus der Erde Wunden Korn ersteht. | b | 4 | 13–15 | 𝅗𝅥 𝅗𝅥 \|[14] 𝅗𝅥 𝅗𝅥 \|[15] 𝅗𝅥 |
| | | | – | 15–17 | piano interlude |
| 2 | Korn, das der armen Seele Hunger stillt -<br>Mitt Korn, o Vater, segne mein Gefild: | c<br>c | 5→6 | 18–23 | 𝅝 \|[19] 𝅗𝅥 𝅗𝅥 \|[20] 𝅗𝅥 𝅗𝅥 \|[21] 𝅗𝅥 𝅗𝅥 \|[22] 𝅗𝅥 𝅗𝅥 \|[23] 𝅗𝅥 |
| | doch wirf auch ein in seine Furchen Saat! | d | 7 | 23–5 | 𝅗𝅥 \|[24] 𝅗𝅥 𝅗𝅥 \|[25] 𝅗𝅥 𝄽 |
| | reiss deinem Pflug erbarmungslos den Pfad, | d | 8 | 26–8 | 𝅗𝅥 ♩ ♩ \|[27] 𝅝 \|[28] 𝅝 |

**Prayer**

Bear it,
let the pain cut sharply through your head
and thrust cruelly through your heart:
it is the plough that the sower follows sowing,
so that corn may grow from the earth's wounds.

Corn that satisfies the poor soul's hunger —
Father, bless my field with corn:
force your plough's path mercilessly,
but also drop seed into its furrows!

that is a feature of his later song-writing. This is all the more remarkable in view of the irregular construction of 'Gefunden', with *umschließendem Reim* in the first verse and *Kreuzreim* in the second,[50] and the irregular lines, each verse consisting of lines of five, two, four and two accented syllables. Thus Webern can not have arrived at the formal structure of his setting through a reflection of the poetic structure: rather, his form is the result of an autonomous arrangement (see Table 2).

This way of using musical materials is seen also in Webern's settings of poems by Avenarius in free verse. In 'Freunde' he restructures the lines, making of the five and seven lines of the two verses three four-line sections, in one case interrupting a line and combining the end of it with the line that follows: 'und zwischen den Ähren lächelt auf / aus Blumen die Schönheit' becomes 'und zwischen den Ähren / lächelt auf aus Blumen die Schönheit' in Webern's setting (see Example 3).

**Example 3**

While in Webern's settings of poems in regular metres the metrical and declamatory stresses of the text determine the musical emphases, in setting those in free forms, where the pattern of metrical and declamatory stresses is less well defined, he found himself obliged to create clarity by positioning the words within the bar according to the degrees of accentuation. At this stage in his progress as a setter of words the bar, as a self-governing construction, was unquestionably one of his most important rhetorical means.

Webern appears to have been remarkably confident about the conversion of the text into a vocal part. At all events, comparison of the sketches and final drafts of 'Gebet', 'Freunde' and 'Gefunden' reveals that he made only minimal alterations to the vocal part between the first and last stages, apart from marks of expression and articulation.

50 The rhyme is not exact between first and third lines of the first verse (aba′b), whereas alternating lines rhyme in the second (abab).

Table 2

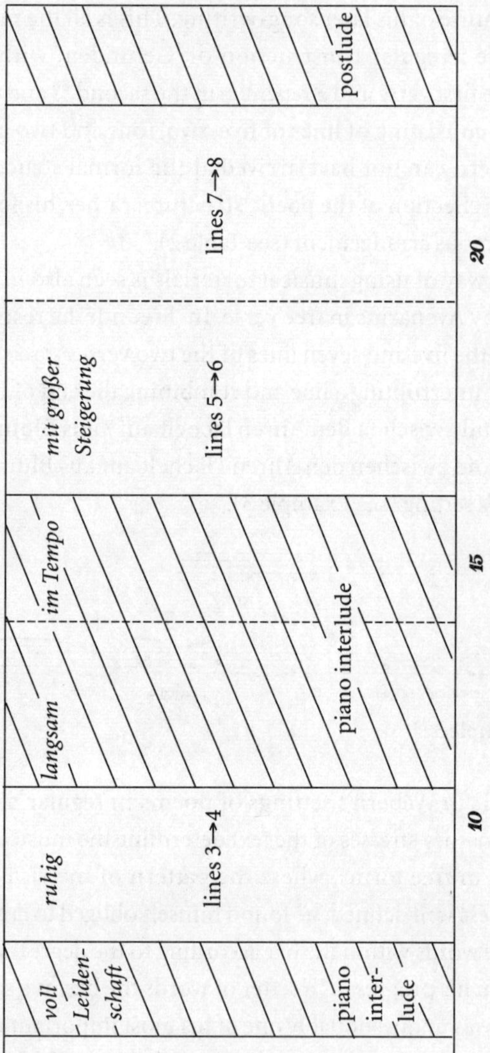

| | | | | | | | | |
|---|---|---|---|---|---|---|---|---|
| | | | *voll Leiden-schaft* | *ruhig* | *langsam* — *im Tempo* | *mit großer Steigerung* | | |
| prelude | line 1 | line 2 | piano inter-lude | lines 3→4 | piano interlude | lines 5→6 | lines 7→8 | postlude |
| 1 | | 5 | | 10 | 15 | | 20 | |

**Example 4**

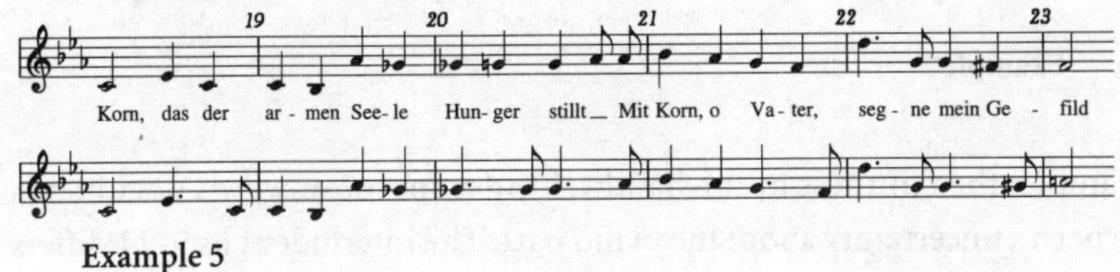


**Example 5**

sketch

Ge - fild: reiß dei

final draft

Ge - fild: reiß dei - nem Pflug er - barm- ungs los den Pfad

**Example 6**

In 'Gefunden' the alterations amount to minor retouching affecting rhythm and pitch (see Example 4). In 'Gebet' the changes are somewhat more substantial. The final version makes greater use of dotted rhythm at the start of the second verse (see Example 5). There were already two variants of the last two lines of the second stanza in the sketches, showing that Webern changed his mind about starting line 7 on a full crotchet beat, and he did not make up his mind about the pitches until the final draft (see Example 6). The sketches of the eighth line show variants in pitch, rhythm and metre as well, and again it was only in writing down the final version that Webern took the definitive decisions (see Example 7).

The piano accompaniments of these songs go through more changes between sketches and final draft than do the voice parts. Much of the accompaniment was literally only sketched in the sketches, in a hand which is visibly paler in some places than in others. In the sketch of 'Freunde', for

Example 7

example, the faintness of the handwriting from b.7 onwards documents Webern's uncertainty about the piano part. The interlude at bs 9–11 differs from the final version at several points; and although the accompaniment is close to the final version already in bs 11–14, it becomes only a schematic outline in the last part of the movement.

In 'Gebet', too, it is in the piano interlude that the greatest variation between sketch and definitive version occurs (see Example 8). As a general rule, a similar process of refinement took place between the sketch and the final draft in the composition of all of these songs, as Webern worked out the articulation, tempo markings, precise agogic details, and sometimes subtle dynamic nuances.

Example 8

Comparing the sketches of the Avenarius songs with their final versions makes it clear that in general certain formal elements – the interludes and the conclusions – gave Webern more trouble than others. It is perfectly understandable that the young composer (scarcely twenty) had less trouble with *inventio* – that is to say, the idea of setting texts melodically – than with *dispositio*, the construction of forms to contain those ideas, not to mention *elaboratio*, a test of his musical technique. After all, the structure of the poem offered an outline for that of the song, and at first (as shown above) Webern kept to it strictly, only later beginning to experiment with more independent ways of structuring the musical material.

Hans Moldenhauer writes that

> *Vorfrühling* could well stand as a motto for the spirit and substance of the musical world that has since become associated with Webern . . . Webern's conception is clear from his initial marking *durchwegs zart* (tenderly throughout) . . . Ending *so zart als möglich* (as tenderly as possible), the song has no instrumental postlude and dissolves with an up-sweep of the human voice . . . The conciseness of diction and the compression of form in this first song . . . foreshadows, and indeed already consummates, the stylistic ideal for which Webern was to become known.[51]

True as that is on the one hand, on the other it is open to question. Undeniably the 'spirit and substance' of this Avenarius setting, in particular, 'foreshadows' the characteristics of the later Webern. But that has less to do with the concept (and Moldenhauer's implication that it was intuitively clear to Webern himself from the first is only his own intuition) than with Webern's 'sensitivity to the form of the text as well as its content', on which Robert Schollum focuses in his consideration of 'Vorfrühling'.

Moldenhauer certainly goes too far in reading as much as he does of Webern's later development into the attenuated close of the song. The endings of these Avenarius settings, above all, show how far Webern still was in them from 'consummating' a stylistic ideal; if anything, they draw attention to his lack of certainty on this very point.

The close of 'Gebet', for instance, in its published form, might well suggest itself as an example of typically Webernian 'conciseness of diction', whereas Webern in fact decided on the form of the ending only at a very late

51 Moldenhauer, *Anton von Webern*, p. 60.

stage. In the sketches he had conceived this song with a six-bar postlude, which he at first retained even in the final draft, where it was notated clearly and given meticulous performance directions. Only later did he decide to end the song without a postlude (see Example 9).

**Example 9**

Conciseness was by no means Webern's sole and essential characteristic at this stage in his career. Schollum cites 'Freunde' as evidence of this:

> In its response to the text the song vacillates between Wagnerian chromaticism and Straussian tonal complexes, thereby producing a violent display of emotion, and an elevated vocal style [*Hymnik*] which is as unexpected in Webern as it is intense. That Webern had these expressive means at his disposal, even if they took the form of a cliché, should give us pause for thought, for these passages do not seem in the least inauthentic.[52]

The same is true of 'Gefunden'. Webern allows the song, at the words 'die Liebe schwebt über den Sternen her als Schöpfergeist', to culminate in a passionate, rich-textured C♯ postlude; in the sketch this outpouring gave way at the last to four bars dying away in silence, but – as in the case of 'Gebet' – Webern decided to dispense with these bars, so that the song ends on the climax with a sumptuous chord played ***fff***. As the sketches of the Avenarius songs demonstrate in numerous ways, it is no longer possible to speak of the young Webern as having received a revelation of a purely introverted stylistic ideal at the outset.

The Avenarius songs, to whatever extent they may be considered juvenilia, nevertheless show Webern's beginnings as a composer. Through

52 Schollum, 'Stilistische Elemente', p. 129.

them the poetry of Avenarius initiated in Webern far more than simply a creative process which on the surface remained within the lyricism that was typical of the turn of the century; it had a far-reaching effect on his maturing sensibility as well. On the one hand it helped him to elucidate his own creative character, since in addressing the specific lyrical forms as well as the more general cultural ideas of Avenarius he was able to crystallise an expression of his own world view. On the other hand his experience with it stimulated him to a style of text-setting that became increasingly subtle, and gradually achieved an independence in relation to the text that corresponded with Webern's achievement of an individual compositional style.

# 2 Gone with the summer wind; or, What Webern lost

## Nine variations on a ground

DERRICK PUFFETT

### I

One of the more intriguing 'might-have-beens' in music history is the thought that Webern, instead of studying with Schoenberg in Vienna, might have studied with Pfitzner in Berlin. According to Moldenhauer, Webern did actually travel to Berlin in 1904, together with Heinrich Jalowetz, for an audience with Pfitzner:

> At first, the master questioned the two young men on their knowledge of musical literature. However, when they mentioned the names of Mahler and Strauss, he made disparaging remarks. Webern, upon hearing his idols attacked, became so angry that he rose from his chair, took Jalowetz by the arm and stomped out of the room, abruptly ending the interview.[1]

Webern's own account of this incident, in a letter to Schoenberg of three years later, mentions the fact that in the 1903–4 concert season he had already heard the latter's *Verklärte Nacht*:

> The impression it made on me was one of the greatest I had ever experienced. The following year I wanted to go to Pfitzner, but I had hardly reached Berlin when it became fully clear to me that this was absurd and that I must return to Vienna in order to become your pupil.[2]

So Arnold Schoenberg gained a disciple.

[1] Hans and Rosaleen Moldenhauer, *Anton von Webern: a Chronicle of His Life and Work* (London: Gollancz, 1978), p. 71.

[2] Quoted in ibid, p. 72.

## II

There are passages in a well-known turn-of-the-century composition (not by Webern) which can compare in sheer beauty of sonority, and especially in the subtle relationship they display between voice and accompaniment, to anything by Strauss, Debussy or Hugo Wolf but which because of the way the composer has notated them are simply never heard.

Take that in Example 1.[3] In the third and fourth bars the texture is the characteristically Wagnerian one in which the voice is doubled by a rhythmic variation of itself in the orchestra. (Whether it is the orchestra or the voice that is really doing the doubling is an interesting question but not strictly the point.) This is not the case in the first two bars, where the voice merely projects two notes of the underlying B minor triad (or the augmented sixth chord on G: the F♮ should be read as E♯). Thereafter, however, the voice has the four pitches E♭–C♮–A♭–G♭ in semiquavers against the semiquaver-sextuplet motive that has dominated the immediately preceding passage. A similar example occurs seven bars later, when the 6/8 music in the orchestra is counterpointed against a 2/4 version of the same material in the voice. Here there is an additional point of interest in the voice's expressive high E, a note which is only fleetingly present in the orchestra.

**Example 1**

Shortly afterwards there is another very expressive passage, in which the voice picks out notes, or pairs of notes, from the 'accompanying' solo string lines. Especially striking is the B–A appoggiatura – *not* doubled in the

[3] Examples from this work are given in Berg's arrangement for voice and piano (vocal part minimally doctored, and words omitted, for present purposes). Some details have been omitted.

Example 2

orchestra – in the first bar[4] and the ascent to G in the second. In the fifth bar the voice is momentarily left exposed (see Example 2). Later still there is a passage in which the voice incorporates a rising phrase (A–B♭– B♮–C) within its general descent. Again, this phrase is *not* doubled in the orchestra (see Example 3).

Two more examples must suffice. In the first (Example 4) an especially beautiful effect is created by the appoggiaturas in the voice. And in the second (Example 5) the effect of the appoggiatura (C♯–B) is not only beautiful but motivic, since the B–C♯–B figure that the voice imitates (see brackets) refers back to an earlier song.[5] The last two bars of this latter example

[4] According to the orchestral score. Berg's arrangement has C–A here.
[5] Part I, b. 139.

Example 3

are also unusual, for the work in question, in that the voice sings phrases which are *entirely free* of the accompanying orchestral parts.

Why do all these wonderful effects go for nothing? Because the composer has stipulated that the notes in the vocal part are not sung but spoken; instead of noteheads he writes little crosses.[6] The composer of course is Schoenberg, and the work in question the *Gurrelieder*. The penultimate section of the work, from which my examples are taken, is a melodrama (entitled 'The summer wind's wild hunt'); it provides the first instance in Schoenberg's work of the device later known as *Sprechstimme*.

Historical antecedents for this practice are well known. One frequently cited is the early, melodrama-like version of Humperdinck's opera *Königskinder* (1896). When Humperdinck later revised his work he replaced the little crosses with real notes. Schoenberg never revised the *Gurrelieder* – and, presumably, never missed the notes he failed to hear. But there remains something quixotic, and mildly troubling, in the idea of a

6 Diamond-shaped open notes in Berg's arrangement.

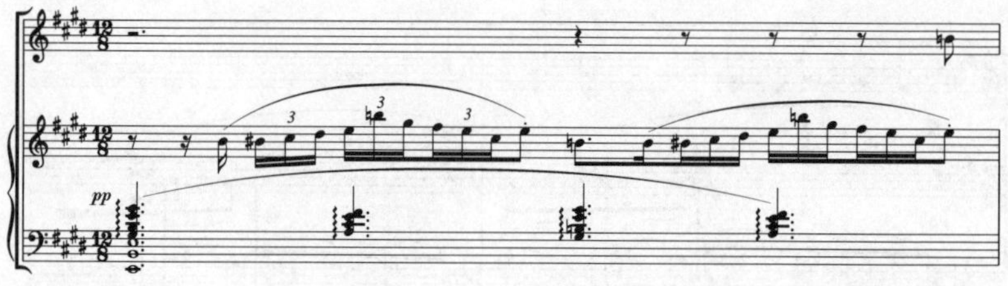

**Example 4**

composer writing an expressive and often beautiful vocal line, and then instructing that it be delivered in a manner which ensures that its beauties remain confined to the printed page.[7]

On another level this brings up the vexed question of what Schoenberg 'meant' by his *Sprechstimme* passages; whether he meant the same thing in some works and not others; why, in directing his own performances of *Pierrot lunaire*, he treated the vocal pitches in a manner that under another

7 This is perhaps too black and white a description of what actually happens in performance. Most Speakers (Schoenberg marks the part *Sprecher*) do make an attempt to hit some of the notes, especially in the more exposed places. But too often the result is an undifferentiated rant. It is fascinating, incidentally, to see how Hans Hotter, the most distinguished living exponent of the role, has varied his approach to it over the years: in his 1985 recording of the work under Riccardo Chailly (Decca 430 321–2) he was more attentive to exact pitch than he was in a BBC broadcast four years later under Simon Rattle; then, in a Promenade Concert performance of 1994 (this time under Andrew Davis), though his voice had almost gone (he was now eighty-five), he seemed more concerned again with exact pitch, at least in certain passages.

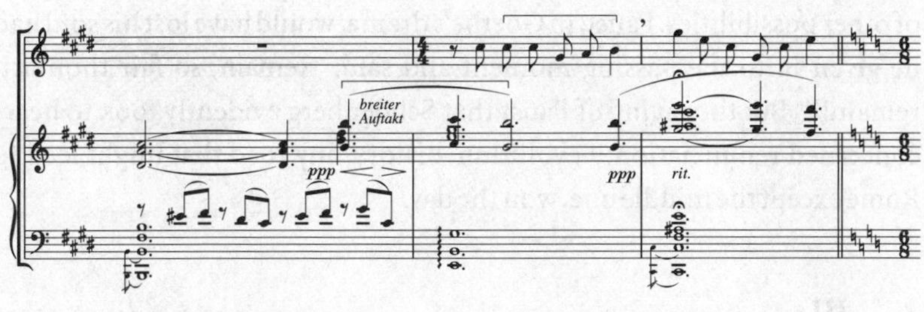

Example 5

conductor might seem cavalier;[8] and (on another level still) the whole matter of notation in the post-tonal works, why some pitches are written as sharps and others as flats etc. But for the moment it is enough to register a straightforward sense of loss. One does not have to be an arch-reactionary (of the sort castigated by Schoenberg himself[9]) to wish, not so much that he had continued composing for ever in the style of *Verklärte Nacht,* as that he had continued to explore the ramifications of his early manner for just a little longer than he did. It might be illuminating, in other words, to hear the Speaker's part in the *Gurrelieder* sung and not spoken once in a while.

Every artist's development carries with it a sense of paths *not* taken, of unfulfilled promise, of possibilities left untouched. No one can retrace these paths, and speculation is ultimately futile. But it can be done with more or less imagination, more or less tact. And it is all the more tempting

8 Cf. his famous recording of the work with Erika Stiedry-Wagner.

9 See, for example, the article 'How one becomes lonely', in *Style and Idea*, 2nd edn, ed. Leonard Stein (London: Faber, 1975), p. 30.

to speculate when the object of speculation is himself so sternly dismissive of other possibilities. Faust, in Goethe's drama, would have lost his soul had he given in to the passing moment and said: 'Remain, so fair thou art, remain!'[10] But the saying of Faust that Schoenberg evidently took to heart concerned renunciation;[11] evolution, history, any road that might lead to Rome except the middle one, won the day.

## III

Webern could not have known Schoenberg's evocation of the summer wind when he wrote his 'idyll for large orchestra', *Im Sommerwind*, in August 1904. He did not even meet Schoenberg until the autumn of that year, when he became his pupil, perhaps the first of Schoenberg's private pupils in Vienna. He had, as we know, however, heard some early Schoenberg scores, though not the *Gurrelieder*, which, having been composed for the most part in 1900–1, remained in draft until 1910. In that year, Webern, called upon, like most of Schoenberg's pupils, to help with the preparation of the latter's scores for performance, made an arrangement of the purely orchestral sections of the *Gurrelieder* for two pianos.[12] By that time his own style had moved far beyond the tentative late Romanticism of *Im Sommerwind*.

Discussions of *Im Sommerwind* do tend to get bogged down in style. Edward T. Cone, reviewing it along with other early works published in 1966, made the general point that

> It is impossible to listen with an unbiased ear to the juvenilia ... of a well-known composer. What we know of his mature production is bound to influence, favorably or unfavorably, our judgment of his early efforts. In particular, we are exposed by our prior knowledge to one of two

10 'Werd ich zum Augenblicke sagen: Verweile doch! du bist so schön!' Goethe, *Werke* (Berlin: Tempel-Verlag, 1963), vol.II, p. 935. Translation from Goethe, *Faust*, by Philip Wayne (Harmondsworth: Penguin, 1959), vol.I, p. 87. See also Wayne's Introduction to vol.II, p. 10.

11 'Entbehren sollst du! sollst entbehren! / Das ist der ewige Gesang ...' *Werke*, vol.II, p. 932. ('Renunciation!—Learn, man, to forgo! This is the lasting theme of themes ...' *Faust*, p. 82.) This was the motto used by Hugo Wolf for his early (and proto-Schoenbergian) D minor String Quartet.

12 See the entry for it in Moldenhauer's catalogue of Webern's compositions and arrangements: *Anton von Webern*, pp. 746–7.

> temptations – sometimes to both at once. On the one hand, since we cannot help remembering the superior works yet to come, it is hard not to look condescendingly upon compositions that, except in the case of a young Mozart, are bound to be imperfect copies; and it is great sport to point both to their imperfections and to their obvious models. On the other hand, it is even more amusing to find intimations of a style yet to be formed – occasional phrases or devices that seem to foreshadow the works of the composer's maturity. To be sure, both games, legitimately played, can lead to valuable insights. The one is a temptation only because it is so easy; it is usually safe. The other is challenging and potentially more rewarding – but accordingly more dangerous.[13]

While acknowledging the truth of all this, it is, however, possible to conceive of a third possibility (perhaps even more 'dangerous'): finding intimations of a style *not* later realised.

George Perle is at the mercy of a different ideology when he dismisses the work as of no aesthetic interest. (This is surely the implication of his assertion that in the case of Webern's juvenilia the legitimate interests of the scholar 'are the *only* legitimate interests'.[14]) Perle's concern is primarily with the editorial apparatus, or lack of it, which, as he rightly states, fails to 'meet the requirements of the more sophisticated and responsible performer, who wishes to know precisely what features of the text at hand are to be attributed to the editor rather than to the composer'.[15] One wonders,

13 'Webern's apprenticeship', *The Musical Quarterly* 53/1 (1967), p. 39.

14 'Webern's twelve-tone sketches', *The Musical Quarterly* 57/1 (January 1971), p. 2. My emphasis.

15 Ibid., p. 2. Perle continues in a footnote:

> From the recent publication (in Moldenhauer and [Demar] Irvine, eds., *Anton von Webern: Perspectives* (Seattle: [University of Washington Press], 1966), p. 34) of a single facsimile page . . . one can deduce that in this instance the attempt to present the piece in a performable version has led to nothing less than an unconscionable falsification. The editor, who has had the good judgment not to identify himself, has added every phrase and bowing indication, has transposed a number of passages to the lower octave in order to bring them within the range of the instruments, and has transferred to the appropriate clef a bar in which the French horn is called upon to read the tenor clef. This anonymous adaptation of a piece of juvenilia written when the composer was still ignorant of the most elementary principles of orchestration is offered not only in miniature score, but also in a recording by Ormandy and the Philadelphia Orchestra, issued by Columbia Masterworks as 'one of the few works by Webern that utilizes the full resources of a modern symphony orchestra.'

Perle is right, of course, but one wonders whether the apoplectic tone is fully justified.

nevertheless, whether the piece would have been so brusquely dismissed if it had shown more progressive tendencies. Perle's modernist stance causes him to be too harsh.

Perhaps it is better to be too harsh than to be too indulgent. Paul A. Pisk's evident affection for the work leads him to find in it

> a complete command of the technique of motivic development, an acute sense of formal balance, a masterful use of harmonic means, and a personal treatment of the orchestra. Furthermore, the problem of writing program music based on a poem and at the same time satisfying the requirements of absolute musical form is successfully solved.

Pisk even finds anticipations of

> the principle of *Klangfarbenmelodie* developed two decades later ... The sound of the orchestra is never conventional or dull, but always expressive, varied, and idiomatic for all instruments[!].[16]

There must be a balance between such extremes of view. The fact that the current (1995) CD catalogue lists four recordings of the work suggests that it is not quite as negligible as Perle makes out. At the same time one does not have to make grandiose claims for it in order to recognise its qualities. But this means looking at it for what it is and not for what it portends.

## IV

So what is it? It is Webern's longest orchestral composition – a point not without significance, given the importance of brevity for his later *œuvre* – and his only explicit piece of programme music.[17] 'Descriptive' music might actually be a better term. For the poem on which it is based, from the novel *Offenbarungen des Wachholderbaums* (Revelations of a juniper tree) by Webern's contemporary Bruno Wille,[18] is hardly more than

16 'Webern's early orchestral works', in *Anton von Webern: Perspectives*, pp. 44, 51.

17 I leave aside the implicit, or secret, programmes of later works such as the Quartet, Op.22, and the Concerto, Op.24, with their suggestive collocation of place-names in the sketches.

18 Wille's novel was written in 1895 and published in 1901; Webern owned the second edition, published in 1903. Pisk makes the point that Webern must have got the poem from the novel rather than from Wille's book of verse, *Der heilige Hain* (The Sacred Grove), which did not appear until 1908: 'Webern's early orchestral works', p. 44.

a series of moods and has little of the narrative content associated with programme music proper. The poem itself is reproduced in an Appendix below. The relationship between poem and music is fairly self-evident – not much scope for the New Musicology here – and it is enough to refer the reader to the description by Pisk, with the caveat that the poem actually consists of six extended stanzas or sections, rather than the seven Pisk claims.[19] This last point makes its detailed relation to the music a little problematical, since the music divides straightforwardly into seven sections. Relation of poem and piece can be seen at a glance from the following chart:

| Sections of piece | Stanzas of poem |
|---|---|
| I (bs 1–33) | 1 (lines 1–10) |
| II (bs 34–71) | 2 (lines 11–21) |
| III (bs 72–102) | 3 (lines 22–48) |
| IV (bs 103–?49) | 4 (lines 49–68) |
| V (bs ?150–75) | |
| VI (bs 176–218) | 5 (lines 69–87) |
| VII (bs 219–53) | 6 (lines 88–101) |

The only major discrepancy comes with the fourth stanza, which has to cover two sections of the musical structure. The musical structure itself is a little ambiguous here: section V could just as easily start at b. 143, with the change of time-signature to 6/8 – in which case the detached notes in the flute might be taken as a reference to the cricket (line 60 of the poem). Then again, the change of mood at b. 176 (*Aufjauchzend*), one of the most violent in the piece, is not prompted by any obvious change of mood in the poem.

These discrepancies, trivial as they might seem, are noticeable because the correspondence between music and poem has hitherto been so close. There is a vague but insistent alternation of mood between summery languor (heat haze, soft air etc.) and the more energetic spirit associated with the wind: sections I, III, V and VII are all summery languor, while II, IV and VI are energetic. (The contrasts are actually much more accentuated in the music than they are in the poem.) At times the references to the poem are quite specific: at bs 83ff, for example, which seem to correspond to the

[19] Ibid.

image of clouds billowing in lines 32–4, or bs 96–7, whose sudden unisons suggest the 'transfiguring flash of gold' in line 45. On a more general level, the correspondence of mood between Wille's stanza 4 and Webern's central section IV, with its evocation of the *sausender, brausender Wogewind*, is particularly close, though there are further incursions into a more direct pictorialism at bs 138–43 (the 'lauschige Stille' of line 59? – or does this come at b. 150?), b. 162 (the 'dreaming stream' of line 62) and bs 168–75 (the 'lark ascending', a solo violin in Webern as in Vaughan Williams, of lines 65–8). There is no direct counterpart in Webern for the exact repetition of lines from stanza 5 to stanza 6 (lines 82–7 = 96–101). But the attempt at a mood of religious calm (*Sehr ruhig und weihevoll*, bs 219ff), corresponding to the beginning of Wille's final stanza, is unmistakable.

The changes of mood are articulated through changes of tempo, texture and metre. There are also a number of characteristic/characterising themes: seven, to be precise. These do not quite correspond to the sections of the piece (in that more than one theme is sometimes introduced within a section) or to the seven 'motives' on Pisk's motive chart (these are really themes rather than motives, and Pisk's presentation of them is in any case designed to show similarities between them – motivic resemblances in the proper sense – rather than contrasts).[20] Their relation to the sectional divisions can be represented as follows:

| | |
|---|---|
| section I | theme 1 (which can be subdivided into 1a, first announced in bs 11–12, and 1b, stated in 21–2) |
| section II | theme 2 (*Lustig*, bs 34–5) |
| | theme 3 (*Sehr breit*, bs 65–6) |
| section III | theme 4 (bs 73ff) |
| | theme 5 (bs 83ff) |
| section IV | theme 6 (*Voll Schwung*, bs 107ff) |
| section V | theme 7 (bs 162ff) |

Some of these themes have the character of a leitmotive: for instance, theme 3, which seems to suggest the feeling of being overwhelmed by the beauty of nature. Others, such as theme 4, are more generally associative in character: here the chorale-like nature of the theme (sustained 3/2, low brass) actually tends to confuse the sectional organisation, since it seems to belong with

20 Ibid., p. 46.

the reference to an 'Orgelchor' in section IV. In certain cases it would be more appropriate to refer to 'thematic material' rather than themes proper, since the thematic profiling is so tenuous. But this only tends to confirm the relationships demonstrated in Pisk's chart.

The point about length is significant not so much for what it reveals about duration (clock time) as for what it reveals about time-scale. Just as the 'Eroica' marks an expansion in Beethoven's thinking not only in terms of duration but also in terms of pacing, complexity of relations between and among sections, and the sheer amount of musical material ('content', in Schenker's term) that needs to be generated – there is of course no question of aesthetic comparison here! – so Webern's early piece marks an extreme from which everything will subsequently contract. It helps to bear this in mind when contemplating the brevity of the Op.10 pieces, to cite only one example. The 'expansiveness' of the tone poem – not of *Eroica* dimensions, to be sure, but every breath is a novel in Webern – is expressed most obviously in the many passages built on pedals (especially tonic pedals), and also more generally in the homophonic textures, the latter sometimes enlivened by a counterpoint that is more ornamental in character (being related to the so-called 'false polyphony' of Wagner and Strauss, where the tendency to combine themes based on triads produces a textural activity which is not really contrapuntally generated) than the 'true' polyphony represented by the Brahms–Schoenberg tradition. Webern was shortly to embrace this tradition, wholeheartedly and with no turning back, in his Passacaglia, Op.1. Meanwhile the textures tend to look like those of a Strauss symphonic poem.[21]

As for the tonic pedals, these can most clearly be demonstrated by a bass graph. Example 6 shows the main tonal activity of the piece, together with its sectional divisions, changes of tempo and principal thematic statements (boxed); passages of thematic development are also shown. Below the graph, thick lines represent the musical space devoted to tonic pedals. These pedals can be seen to dominate the slow sections of the piece, in particular the outer sections. Section I begins with a fifteen-bar pedal on D, the

21 The passage quoted by James Beale is a good example: see 'Webern's musical estate', in *Anton von Webern: Perspectives*, p. 21. Beale writes under the mistaken impression that the work was composed under Schoenberg's tutelage.

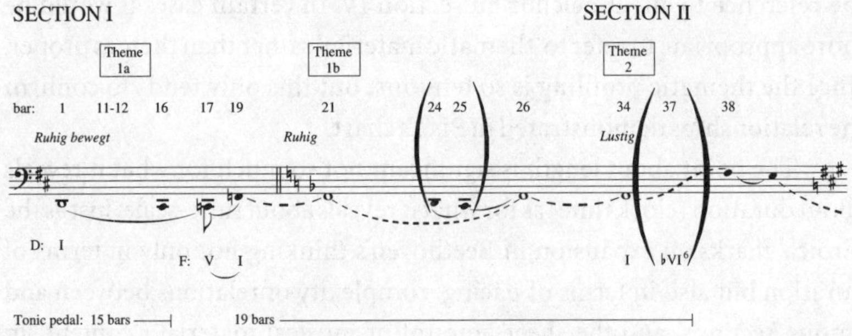
SECTION I
SECTION II
Theme 1a
Theme 1b
Theme 2
bar: 1 11-12 16 17 19 21 24 25 26 34 37 38
Ruhig bewegt
Ruhig
Lustig
D: I
F: V I
I ♭VI6
Tonic pedal: 15 bars
19 bars

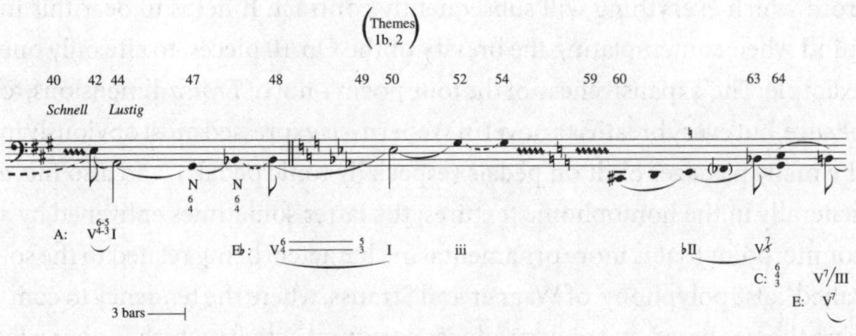
Themes 1b, 2
40 42 44 47 48 49 50 52 54 59 60 63 64
Schnell Lustig
N
N
A: V I
E♭: V I
iii
♭II
V
C:
V7/III
E: V7
3 bars

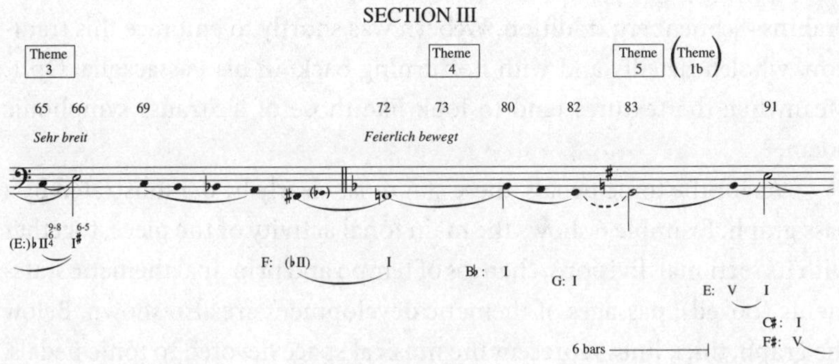
SECTION III
Theme 3
Theme 4
Theme 5
Theme 1b
65 66 69 72 73 80 82 83 91
Sehr breit
Feierlich bewegt
(E:)♭II I♯
F: (♭II) I
B♭: I
G: I
E: V I
C♯: I
F♯: V
6 bars

Example 6

SECTION IV

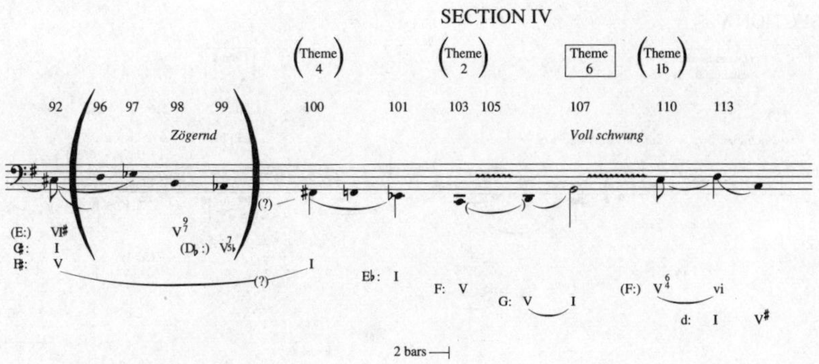


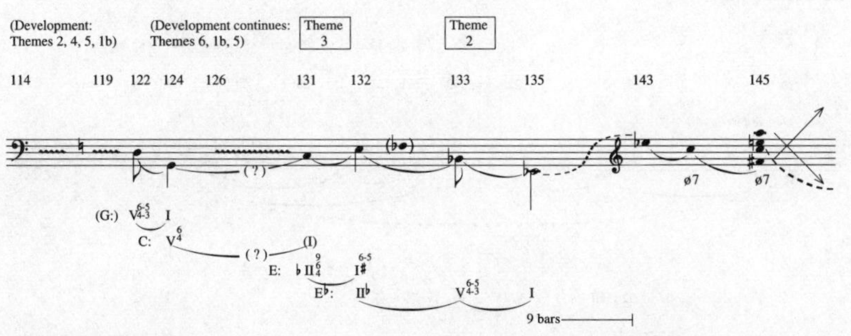


SECTION V

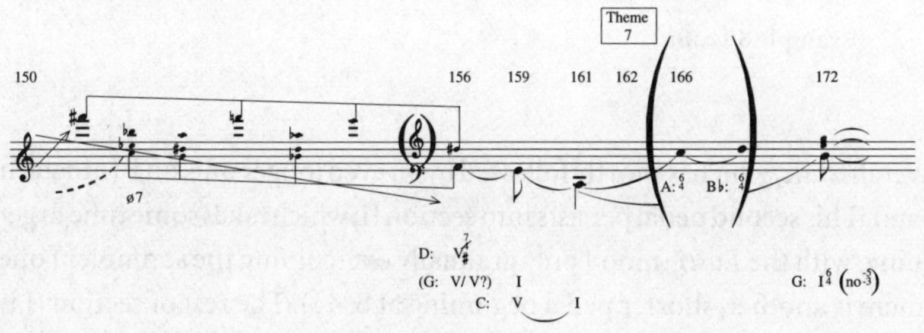


Example 6 (*cont.*)

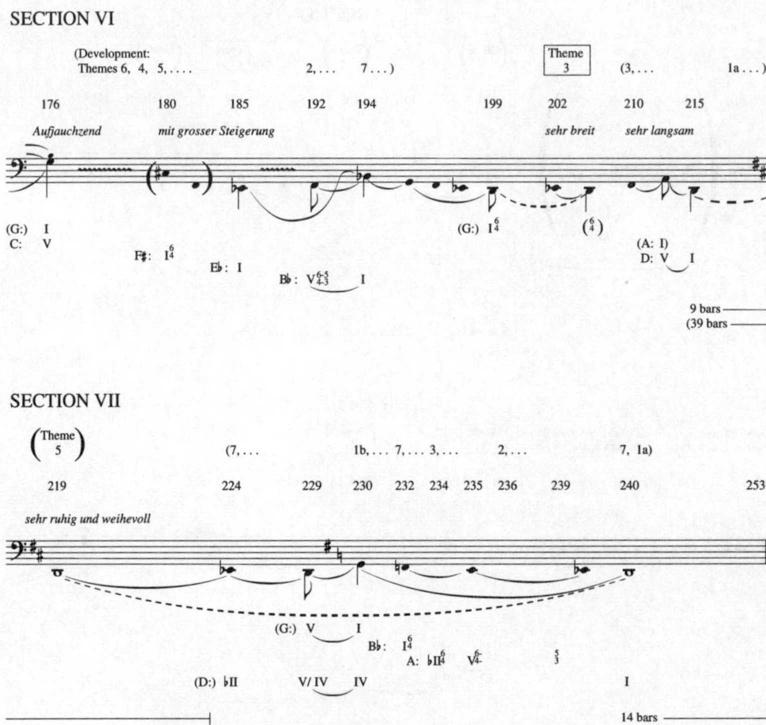


**Example 6** (*cont.*)

overall tonic, which is shortly followed by an even longer one, on F (nineteen bars). This second pedal persists into section II, which takes some time to get going, with the *Lustig* mood only gradually overcoming the somnolent one (there is another, shorter pedal beginning at b. 44). The rest of section II is much more active harmonically, with important cadences on E♭ (b. 50) and E♮ (b. 66): these are associated with major statements of themes 2 and 3 respectively. The slower section III, with its 'chorale' textures, includes a six-bar pedal on G beginning in b. 82 and a two-bar pedal beginning in 101. Section IV, the most extended evocation of the wind so far and the first extensive passage of development, has no time for pedals, but it does include another strong cadence on E♭ (b. 135); again, this is associated with theme 2.

A dramatic voice exchange (indicated by arrows on the graph), involving a chain of *Tristan* chords, dominant ninths and French sixths (of which more later), signals a move to the more lethargic section V. There are no pedals as such in this section, which is quite short, but towards the end a six-four sonority, one of many significant six-fours in the piece, acquires a tonic bass. The new chord marks the beginning of section VI. This section, another passage of development, contains further references to E♭ (b. 185) and B♭ (b. 194), the latter having taken over the 'climactic' function of theme 2, as well as a climactic (transposed) statement of theme 3 (b. 202), which has otherwise clung to its original (E-based) pitch throughout (cf. bs 65, 131). The last bars of this section initiate the longest tonic pedal in the piece, nine bars if 'tonic' is taken in its most literal sense but as many as thirty-nine if the final tonic prolongation, culminating in another, fourteen-bar pedal, is included.

This final tonic prolongation makes significant references to E♭ (♭II in D). Indeed the graph as a whole raises a question about musical quality. The capacity to write extended tonic pedals cannot of itself be taken, of course, as evidence of mastery: anyone can turn out interminable pedals on I. But there is enough interest in the balance between stable and unstable passages to suggest considerable sophistication. I am not suggesting a classical (Schenkerian) integration of foreground and background which would guarantee the young Webern admission to the Pantheon of masters. On the contrary, it would be easier to adduce evidence of tonal *incoherence*, of passages – like bs 66–72 – that suggest a clash of gears, a grating series of *non sequitur*s rather than the sweet hum of the tonal machine in perfect working order. (Even on this level, however, there are passages, like the transition from 143 to 161, that show great skill.) The point is rather that if an analysis of this sort were to be taken as evidence of quality, one would have to concede greater mastery to Webern's piece than to a work such as Schoenberg's *Pelleas und Melisande*, which makes similar (but less integrated) play with the neighbour-note ♭II–I motion[22] or, for that matter, to an acknowledged masterpiece such as *Verklärte Nacht*.

22 See the graphs of this work given in Derrick Puffett, '"Music that echoes within one" for a lifetime: Berg's reception of Schoenberg's *Pelleas und Melisande*', *Music and Letters* 76/2 (May 1995), pp. 236–7.

## V

One has to return to the question of style: this is, after all, the most interesting thing about the piece. James Beale, writing about the early Dehmel songs (1906–8), observes that 'Brought into a fluent idiom are all the advanced chords of the period: augmented chords, the French-sixth sound, freely inverted ninth chords [the influence of *Verklärte Nacht*?], and even chords built on the whole-tone scale.'[23] Whole-tone chords are also mentioned by Leonard Stein in his article on the same work.[24] This is interesting, because it points to a striking feature of *Im Sommerwind*. The use of augmented chords, including the French sixth, is no more than one would expect of a work written around the turn of the century: such sonorities had been common currency since Schubert. But the interest in whole-tone sonorities is a different matter.

At this point one has to distinguish between 'whole-tone sonorities' and 'chords built on the whole-tone scale'. I know of no evidence that in the period under discussion Webern had any clear conception of the whole-tone *scale* (though he must have heard of it). As a theoretical idea the whole-tone scale seems to have enjoyed something of the same status as the octatonic scale for German composers of this time: that is, whole-tone formations occur frequently in their music, just as octatonic ones do, but largely as a by-product of voice leading (especially voice leading involving chromatic alteration), not as the result of the conscious manipulation of a scale. This is a different situation from the one in, say, Russia, where, as Richard Taruskin has made clear, the octatonic scale was widely known and used (under the name the 'Rimsky-Korsakov scale') long before Stravinsky got his hands on it.[25] Similarly with the whole-tone scale: although this scale had been widely used and discussed in France,[26] there is no sign that it

23 'Webern's musical estate', p. 28.

24 'Webern's *Dehmel Lieder* of 1906–8: threshold of a new expression', in *Anton von Webern: Perspectives*, p. 58.

25 See Taruskin, 'Chernomor to Kastchei: harmonic sorcery; or, Stravinsky's "Angle"', *JAMS* 38 (1988), especially pp. 78, 99ff. [But see also chap. 3 below. –Ed.]

26 See, for instance, the discussion in René Lenormand, *Étude sur l'harmonie moderne* (Paris: Le monde musical, 1913); trans. Herbert Antcliffe as *A Study of Modern Harmony* (London: Joseph Williams, 1915), chap. 10. Lenormand cites examples from Koechlin, Bruneau and Saint-Saëns as well as Debussy.

had any influence whatever in Germany, *as a theoretical idea*, before Schoenberg discussed it in his *Harmonielehre* of 1911.[27]

But theory, as everyone knows, lags behind practice. Whole-tone formations, usually with a dominant function, are a regular feature of middle-period Mahler, and Schoenberg had toyed with them (notably in *Pelleas*) long before the whole-tone obsessions of his Chamber Symphony. And Berg's fascination with the French sixth, a subset of the whole-tone hexachord, is well known.[28] Such sonorities are commonly, and rightly, taken as a symptom of the preoccupation with symmetry (in the harmonic as in the formal sphere) which so fascinated the early atonalists and their contemporaries.[29] What interests me here is their prevalence in a work written *before* Webern came under Schoenberg's influence; their presence in the Dehmel songs, actually written under the latter's supervision, is less cause for surprise.

The 'prevalence' of whole-tone sonorities in the tone poem is demonstrated simply by listing them (see Example 7). The extracts are listed chronologically, with no regard for function. It will be seen that many of

27 The *Harmonielehre* by Rudolf Louis and Ludwig Thuille (1st edn 1907), for instance, a progressive book for its time, quotes examples of whole-tone writing from Liszt, Strauss and Pfitzner only to reject the concept of the whole-tone *scale* (*Ganztonleiter*) as 'totally impossible within our tonal system'. There is one further mention of the whole-tone scale in the chapter 'Über Kirchentonarten und Exotik', where whole-tone experiments (Debussy and Saint-Saëns are named) seem to be relegated to the realm of mood-painting: *Harmonielehre*, 8th edn (Stuttgart: Grüninger, n.d. [1913?]), pp.349, 416. Schoenberg discusses the whole-tone scale in chap.20 of *Harmonielehre* (1st edn, 1911); trans. Roy E. Carter as *Theory of Harmony* (London: Faber, 1978).

28 See, among other useful discussions, Craig Ayrey, 'Berg's "Scheideweg": analytical issues in Op.2/ii', *Music Analysis* 1/2 (July 1982).

29 Examples in Schoenberg, Berg and Webern are well known. Perhaps less well known are examples in Bruckner (for instance, the extended play with French sixths in the Adagio of Symphony No.9) and Strauss (the climactic chord of *Salome*). Even Schoenberg's more conservative contemporaries were affected by this concern: cf. the whole-tone mania of Pfitzner's song 'An den Mond' (1908), one of the examples in Louis and Thuille's *Harmonielehre*, and Othmar Schoeck's much later song 'Niagara' (1955). The origins of such passages in Liszt ('Der trauriger Mönch', the development section of the first movement of the *Faust* Symphony, etc.), whose experiments with other 'non-diatonic' modes, as well as with intervals such as fourths and tritones, are well known, are now generally acknowledged.

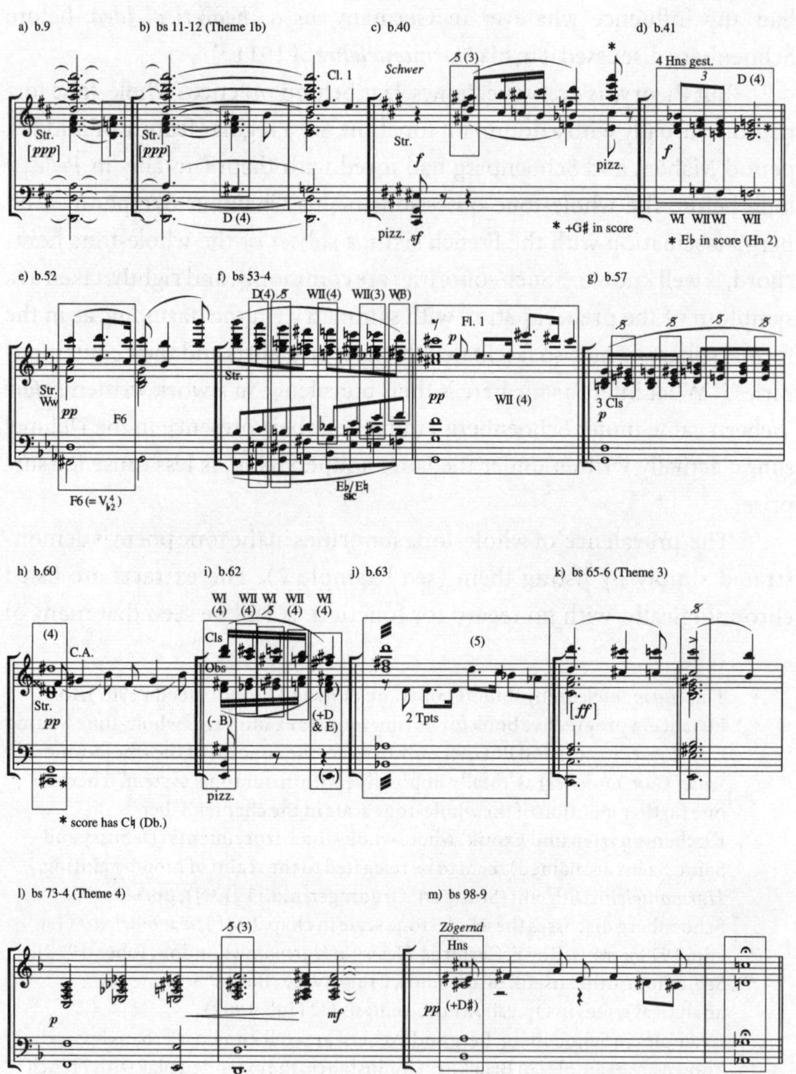
a) b.9
b) bs 11-12 (Theme 1b)
c) b.40
d) b.41
Str.
[ppp]
Cl. 1
D (4)
Schwer
5 (3)
Str.
f
pizz.
ff
* +G♯ in score
4 Hns gest.
3
D (4)
WI WIIWI WII
* E♭ in score (Hn 2)
e) b.52
f) bs 53-4
g) b.57
D(4) 5
WII(4)
WII(3) WB)
Ww
pp
F6
F6 (= $V^4_{\flat 2}$)
Str.
E♭/E♮
sic
Fl. 1
pp
WII (4)
3 Cls
p
h) b.60
i) b.62
j) b.63
k) bs 65-6 (Theme 3)
(4)
C.A.
Str.
pp
* score has C♮ (Db.)
WI (4)
WII (4)
WI 5
WII (4)
WI (4)
Cls
Obs
(- B)
(+D & E)
pizz.
(5)
2 Tpts
[ff]
l) bs 73-4 (Theme 4)
m) bs 98-9
5 (3)
p
mf
Zögernd
Hns
pp
(+D♯)
WI (5)
WI (4)

**Example 7**

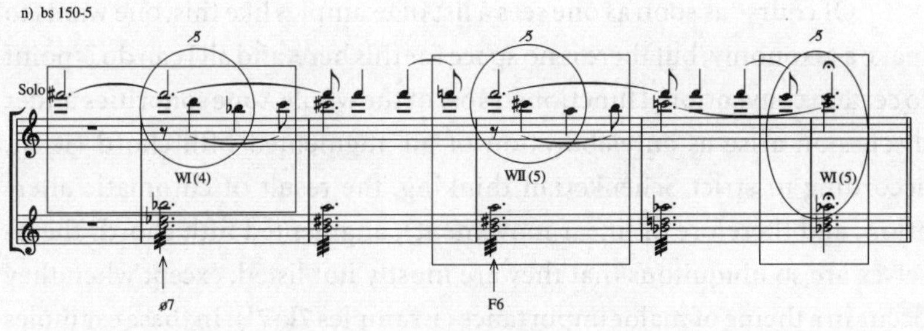

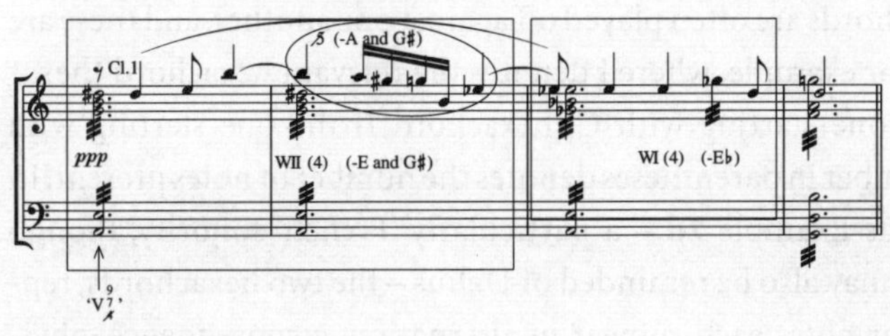


Key:
- augmented-fifth chord
- D 'Delius' sonority
- F6 French sixth
- WI, WII whole-tone hexachords I, II

Example 7 (*cont.*)

them arise contrapuntally, as a result of passing motion (Example **7b**, or theme 1a, which reads like a music example from Salzer's *Structural Hearing*; **7f**; **7i**) or neighbour-note movement (**7a**, the precursor of **7b**, with a true whole-tone chord being avoided by the continued presence of D, the tonic pedal, instead of C♯; **7g**). Others stem from chromatic alteration (**7j**, **7o**). Still others seem to exist as free-standing sonorities, not easily accounted for by linear means (**7c**, **7m**).

Of course as soon as one sees a list of examples like this, one wants to make a taxonomy; but there is no space for this here, and all I can do is point to certain conventional functions. Most of the whole-tone sonorities under discussion arise as an elaboration of an augmented-fifth chord (itself, according to strict Schenkerian thinking, the result of chromatic alteration, and therefore of linear movement); augmented fifth chords themselves are so ubiquitous that they are mostly not listed, except when they occur in a theme of major importance (Examples **7k**, **7l**). In these examples they are marked with a 5̸ sign. Other sonorities are more complex, involving four or five notes of the whole-tone hexachord. In such cases the two different hexachords are often played off against one another, and these are marked I (4), for example, where I denotes the relevant hexachord (hexachord I is the one starting with C, hexachord II the one starting with C♯) and the number in parentheses denotes the number of notes present. In passages such as Example **7d** – a particularly 'French' sonority, though British readers may also be reminded of Delius – the two hexachords, represented by four notes each, appear in alternation, a consequence, obviously, of the chromatic scale in the bass. Similarly Example **7m**. Example **7f**, on the other hand, combines chords drawn from the two hexachords with foreign notes, though one must be careful here about misprints.[30] A final example (Example **7n**), reminiscent of Wagner's Venusberg, shows the two hexachords (in their five-note forms) mediating between, and merging with, dominant ninths, a half-diminished seventh (the *Tristan* chord) and an extension of the French sixth which involves a fifth note (the C♯ in bs 152–3, the C♮ in bs 154–5) – this last creating a chord which sounds suspiciously like Scriabin.

The effect of this whole-tone thinking upon the larger structure is hard to determine, partly because there exists little theoretical framework for such a discussion. I should like to discuss two short passages, though, both of which seem to carry the idea through onto a larger scale. (Or perhaps the larger-scale organisation suggested the whole-tone details: it is impossible to say.) Example 8 shows the opening of section II, where the whole-tone interruptions have the effect of dispersing the mood of hazy languor and

30 Some of these are listed in Cone, 'Webern's apprenticeship', p. 51.

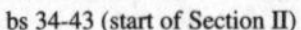


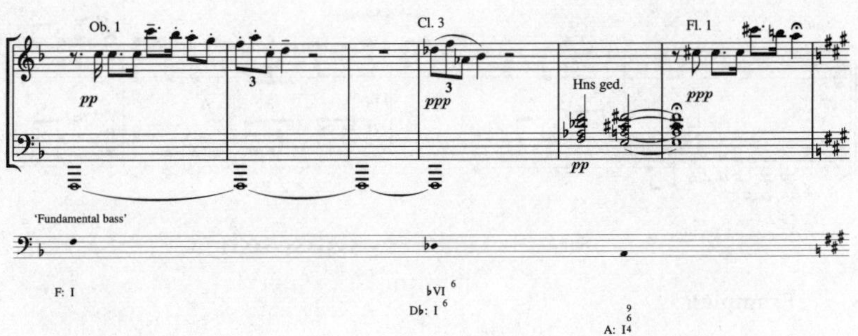


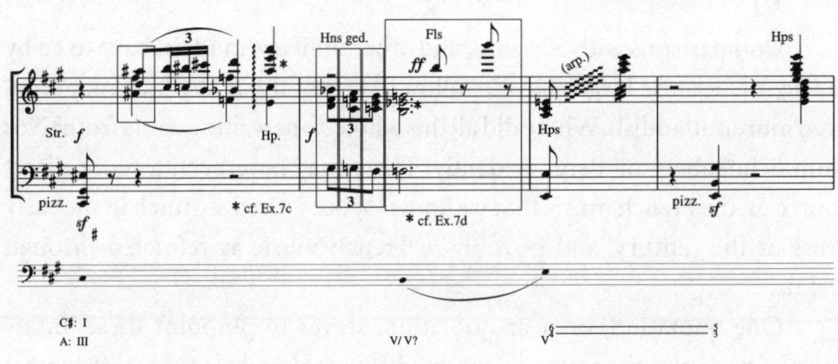


**Example 8**

initiating more energetic thoughts. The 'fundamental bass' line given beneath each system indicates that the passage is controlled by a pattern of descending major thirds, a pattern closely related to the whole-tone hexachord (in this case hexachord II). The bass movement gives way to more conventional fifth-relationships at the approach of the cadence. In Example 9 (the opening of section IV) the concern with symmetry that underlies Example 8 is made explicit by the movement of the bass note, in this case the dominant, on either side of the note that is eventually to prevail: first F major is hinted at, then G minor and finally A minor, before the bass note (after half a bar of impossible harp writing which Webern marks *Schnell*) settles on D.

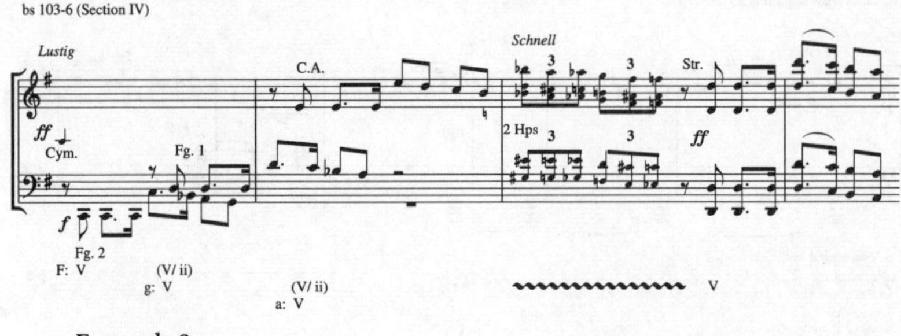


Example 9

## VI

Comparisons with Scriabin, and other unlikely 'models', have to go by the board, because I want now to follow a train of thought which may seem even more outlandish. Where did all this whole-tone writing come from? Not from Schoenberg or Berg, evidently. There may have been a more direct source: in the French music that we know Webern loved so much in the early years of the century, and possibly in French music as refracted through Delius.

One quotation, or near-quotation, serves to pinpoint these 'influences'. The *Lustig* oboe tune just quoted (Example 8, bs 34–5) starts with a dotted repeated-note motive which Webern must surely have got from Strauss's *Zarathustra* (1896). But one cock-crow is much like another. What is more interesting is the turn that the tune goes on to take, with an unresolved neighbour note, or 'added sixth', left hanging at the end of the phrase. This added sixth, especially when approached via an ascending octave (though in the Webern the tune returns to its original register before introducing the added sixth), is strongly reminiscent of the principal motive of Charpentier's *Louise*. This work had been a smash hit at the Paris Opéra-Comique in 1900 and, according to popular mythology, had made a strong impression on Delius, whose orchestral nocturne *Paris* (actually written the year before) is said to quote its melodies. These connections are represented in Example 10.

The quotation from the Delius (which is not, of course, a 'quotation' from the Charpentier at all) has been chosen more or less at random: there are other tunes in *Paris* that are built on an added sixth, and still others that come

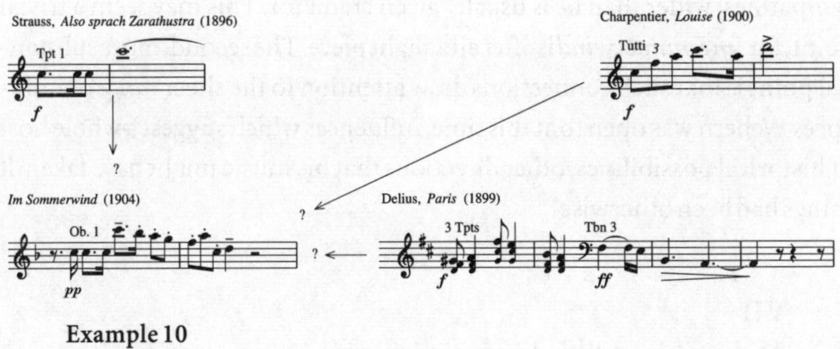


**Example 10**

closer to the general contour of the Charpentier melody. But the closeness of the connections is not the point. Nor is the point that Webern might have been specifically 'influenced' by one or another of these compositions – though he might well have been: *Louise* became familiar to German musicians soon after its first triumphs, and Delius's *Paris* had been played in several German cities, including Berlin, by 1904, partly because of the composer's energetic promotion of his music in Germany from 1900 onwards, partly on account of the interest taken in his music by German musicians such as Hans Haym and Julius Buths.[31] There are really two points at issue. The first is that the presence of such musical material in *Im Sommerwind*, whether Webern was actually 'influenced' by these particular pieces or not, indicates an expressive range, and a range of musical

[31] See Lionel Carley, *Delius: a Life in Letters 1862–1908* (London: Scolar Press, 1983), for information about Delius's early reception in Germany, especially the letters from Strauss (whose remark about the 'influence' of *Louise* on *Paris* was echoed by the publisher C.F. Kahnt, p. 199); from Humperdinck (p. 281); and from Schillings (p. 254). Delius studied in Leipzig in 1886–8 and travelled around Germany extensively in 1900 and 1901 trying to get his music performed. Major premières of his work in Germany, apart from *Paris* (1901), included *Koanga* (1904), *Lebenstanz* (1904), *Appallachia* (1904), *A Village Romeo and Juliet* (1907) and *A Mass of Life* (1908). [According to an entry in Webern's diary in which he lists all performances of the Vienna Hofoper during the 1902–3 season, *Louise* was performed there four times that year, probably in 1903. Although he does not specifically mention having heard it, it is very unlikely that he did not: it is clear from other diary entries that he was in the habit of attending all their productions. – Ed.]

sympathies, wider than he is usually given credit for. This may seem a trivial point, for *Im Sommerwind* is after all a slight piece. The second, more substantial point is that such connections draw attention to the sheer *range* of influences Webern was open to at this time, influences which suggest a whole host of historical possibilities, other directions that his music might have taken 'if things had been otherwise'.

## VII

At this point a little history is in order. Stravinsky's remark about Webern enjoying his *Pribaoutki*[32] has always seemed slightly jarring, something of a surprise to the reader brought up on the notion of 'Webern the Austrian provincial', the short-sighted Viennese, as impervious to the world outside his immediate circle as he was caught up in his study of plants and insects. Clearly the hermeticist image of the composer has been too important, not only for Webernians in particular but for the modernist mythology in general, to lose. Yet Moldenhauer provides ample evidence of how wide-ranging Webern's musical interests were when he was young.[33]

We learn, for instance, that in his late teens, at the time when he was studying with Edwin Komauer, Webern nurtured an admiration for Richard Strauss and a 'passion, bordering on idolatry', for Wagner (:38). This is unremarkable, as is his youthful enthusiasm for Beethoven's Ninth Symphony (:38–9). It is more surprising to read of his liking for Svendsen's 'magnificent' Cello Concerto (:39). The passion for Wagner continued into the new century, with a visit to Bayreuth in 1902; the music of Bruckner, Wolf and Mahler were also discoveries of this time (:39–40). In the same year Webern heard Liszt's *Christus* and wrote about it rapturously in his diary (:48–9). Horizons continued to broaden with an encounter with Berlioz's *Symphonie fantastique* (:55), followed by a production of Bizet's *Djamileh* (under Mahler) at the Vienna Court Opera: 'Music saturated with oriental ardour, full of ingenious rhythm, enchantingly orchestrated'

32 Igor Stravinsky, *Themes and Conclusions* (London: Faber, 1972), p. 95, note 1.

33 In the following paragraphs references to Moldenhauer, *Anton von Webern*, since they are so numerous, are given in the text.

(:56). (This was the same production that the thirty-year-old Heinrich Schenker had earlier reviewed in a Viennese periodical.[34])

The year 1903 reveals an interesting range of *dis*likes: Schumann's Fourth Symphony ('boring'), Weber's *Konzertstück* ('We probably are already past this music') and Scriabin ('languishing junk': 58). Webern was not unsympathetic to Glazunov's music, however, or to Rimsky-Korsakov's *Sheherazade.* Some disparaging remarks about Brahms's Third Symphony ('badly orchestrated – grey in grey': 58) ought not to be taken too seriously. But it is interesting to know he was already deeply fond of Schubert (:58). The great event of the following year, of course, was the meeting with Schoenberg: all other experiences are overshadowed by this.[35] And Webern's musical life must have been dominated by Schoenberg, as Berg's was, for the next few years. But in 1908 Webern is still open-minded enough to enjoy Debussy's *Pelléas,* which he heard in Berlin and raved about in a letter to Schoenberg (we are not told how the latter responded): 'O God, I cannot express how beautiful it was. I have surrendered unreservedly to this impression.' And in a second letter:

> The ending is one of the loveliest that exists. And the instrumentation – simply magnificent. I was entranced, for Maeterlinck's drama also possesses such unheard-of beauty – such atmosphere, such tenderness, then again so much passion.... The new stage art is something quite glorious, and therefore I must stay with the theatre. It is marvellous! Oh, how grateful I am that I may be occupied with these things, that I may sacrifice my life to them (:104).

Webern retained his adoration for the work as late as 1911 (:149); in the same year he also conducted some Debussy (:140–1). It is particularly intriguing to learn that around this time he was 'curious' about Delius and 'inquired about' that composer's *Mass of Life* (first given in Germany under Ludwig Hess) – with what results we do not know (:140).

Webern's 'lighter' repertory in these years (in 1910–11 he was assistant conductor at the Danzig Stadttheater) included Johann Strauss, Offenbach and Lehár (:141), not all of them composers he would later have been pleased

34 *Neue Revue,* 28 January 1898, pp. 143–4.

35 'Curiously enough, apart from [one] brief reference . . . , neither Schoenberg personally nor his music is ever mentioned in the diary.' Moldenhauer, *Anton von Webern,* p. 76.

to be associated with. We are told that he 'liked' Rossini's *Barber of Seville* (:141). It is impossible to know, of course, how much real affection went into the works he conducted, especially since the job of working in a theatre was so uncongenial to him. It would also be a mistake to attach too much importance to passing fancies. But it is surely significant that as late as 1912 he could still enjoy Richard Strauss (*Ariadne*: 659), surely a proscribed composer in the Schoenberg circle by this time, and that in the following year he found a 'new love', Verdi. In the same year, we learn, Charpentier's most recent work, *Julien* (a sequel to *Louise*), 'impressed him favourably' (:182). In 1914 Webern was 'drawn' to Schreker (:186). This would have been *after* Berg's trouble with that composer over the vocal score of *Der ferne Klang* and in the full knowledge of Schoenberg's disapproval of him. By this time Webern is beginning to appear in a new light, almost an eclectic in the manner of Berg himself.

1919 was the year of Webern's enthusiastic letter to Berg about Stravinsky (:229). In the following year the Society for Private Musical Performances gave its famous Ravel concert: Webern 'adored' that composer's Mallarmé Songs (which were not done on that occasion, however), especially the third (:236). From about this time onwards there are fewer effusive letters about other composers' music, a change no doubt related to the general change of aesthetic direction Webern's music took, along with that of so many other composers, just after the war.[36] But it is still illuminating to know that in 1929 he was fond of Eisler's music (:335) and that in the thirties he seems to have liked Janáček (:464). (The music of Bartók, however, was not to his liking: 464.) His tastes in his later years appear to have focused exclusively on German music, especially the music of Schubert and Mahler (:508). German here means of course the work of the Austro-German classical tradition, namely Haydn, Mozart and Beethoven, though exception could be made for specific modern works such as Strauss's *Salome* (:685). Hindemith, however, was a dead letter (:345). And in dismissing colleagues whose music he no longer found sympathetic, Webern now showed an intolerance bordering on contempt.[37]

[36] Ernest Ansermet said that when he conducted *Daphnis et Chloë* (presumably the complete ballet) in Vienna in 1940, Webern told him he had never heard it before: see Robert Craft, *Stravinsky: Chronicle of a Friendship*, 2nd edn (Nashville: Vanderbilt University Press, 1994), p. 109.

[37] The phrase is Moldenhauer's: *Anton von Webern*, p. 346.

## VIII

We begin to get a sense of what Webern 'lost'. It is not that the Austro-German tradition, inexhaustible supply of masterpieces that it is, was in any way 'restricted' or failed to give him what he wanted by way of example or inspiration. It is simply that, as he concentrated on one set of possibilities, other possibilities necessarily became excluded. This is no more than a truism which would apply to any composer. What makes it interesting, and even rather plangent, in Webern's case is the fact that the nature of his development always seemed so inevitable to him. And this theme of inevitability – the old Schoenbergian historicist cry, whether familiar in the name of 'evolution', 'tradition' or just plain 'history' – has been taken up and elaborated by many of Webern's followers.

Moldenhauer actually begins his book with the remark that 'my work was greatly aided by the fact that the composer seems to have been possessed by a profound sense of destiny as to his place in music history'.[38] This remark has to be read in its proper context, which is concerned with the preservation of documents, but there is a sense in which the 'critical' part of Moldenhauer's biography had already been written for him. Five hundred pages later he is quoting pupils of Webern from the 1930s who confirm his almost exclusive (by that time) dependence on the Austro-German tradition:

> Upon looking at my student efforts before I undertook work with him, [Arnold Elston writes] Webern noted certain French influences attributable to Debussy and Ravel. His reaction suprised me at the time. 'If we want to understand philosophy,' he said, 'we must turn to the ancient Greeks, and if we want to understand music we must turn to Mozart, Haydn, Beethoven, and the other great masters of the Austro-German tradition.' This meant, in effect, that all material for analysis and all models for the student-composer were exclusively drawn from the Austro-German classics. One may look upon this as a most confining attitude on Webern's part – not a single reference to Berlioz, to Verdi, to Mussorgsky, or even to the Liszt–Strauss vein in German music. But Webern's horizon was wholly filled by the music from Bach, through the Viennese classics to Wagner, Brahms, and Mahler; he found his complete personal affirmation as composer therein.

38 Ibid., p. 16.

And Elston adds: 'Occasionally he would analyse some early work of Schoenberg or Berg, always eager to point out their ties to tradition.'[39] Roland Leich, similarly:

> At an early lesson, Webern lectured at some length on the utter supremacy of German music, emphasizing that leading composers of other lands are but pale reflections of Germanic masters: Berlioz a French Beethoven, Tchaikovsky a Russian Schumann, Elgar an English Mendelssohn, etc. To me this was both shocking and amusing, but I was much too diffident to offer any comment.[40]

Friedrich Wildgans, in his book on Webern, develops the theme of 'inevitability', commenting (as if to trump his own argument): 'The observer may rightly assume that Webern's development as a composer was along an organic, logical and clear path.'[41] And Cesar Bresgen talks of Webern's 'conviction of [his] rightness'.[42] Even Cone's remarks about the 'dangers' of too close a study of a composer's juvenilia, for all Cone's sanity, assumes a teleological model of music history derived from Webern's own.

Of course history cannot be 'unmade'.[43] And there is obviously a sense in which Webern's restriction of his horizons, and of his aims, was necessary to his development as a composer. To posit an 'alternative' development for him, based on works he did not write, may therefore seem ridiculously misguided. But it is worth the risk, if only in order to remind ourselves, from another angle, what Webern 'lost'.

To start where we left off, with Charpentier and Delius: on the face of things, the idea of Webern as a composer of verismo opera, a German *Louise*, does not appear to have much mileage in it. On the other hand, we know that his appreciation of Debussy's *Pelléas*, and of 'the new stage art' underlying it, led him to toy for a while with the notion of an opera based on Maeterlinck. Moldenhauer writes of sketches, unfortunately no longer extant, for an

39 Arnold Elston, quoted in ibid, pp. 507–8.

40 Quoted in ibid, p. 510.

41 *Anton Webern*, trans. Edith Temple Roberts and Humphrey Searle (London: Calder and Boyars, 1966), p. 91.

42 'Webern's last months in Mittersill', in *Anton von Webern: Perspectives*, p. 115. The whole of Bresgen's last paragraph is worth studying.

43 *Pace* Hans Keller: see his three provocative articles 'Unmade history', *Music and Musicians* 23/10–12 (June–August 1975).

opera on *Les Sept Princesses* dating from 1910; and two years earlier Webern had planned to set the same playwright's *Alladine et Palomides.*[44] By 1913 he had developed an 'aversion' to Maeterlinck, a change exacerbated by the fiercely anti-German stance adopted by that writer at the outbreak of the First World War. Though the philosophical ideas expressed in *La Mort* (*Vom Tode*) had become repugnant to him, however, one is reminded that he had himself in 1913 written a play called *Tot.*[45] And many years later Webern considered writing an opera in collaboration with Hildegard Jone.[46]

Perhaps a little more credible is the idea of Webern as a composer of genre pieces *à la* Delius. What such pieces would have been like it is impossible to imagine in detail. But if we think of *Im Sommerwind* as a background against which the later orchestral works unfolded, their 'programmatic' elements become more comprehensible. It is also possible to identify certain musical gestures which may have their origins in the early descriptive piece. This is not a matter of uncovering 'anticipations'. Rather it is a matter of recognising that certain melodic, rhythmic or textural ideas which we now think of as quintessentially Webernian, that is, as being part of an abstract musical discourse fully in keeping with the rigorous modernist aesthetic that lay behind them, may have originated in music that was far more explicitly programmatic. The Op.6 Orchestral Pieces (1909) are probably the most fruitful area for such inquiry. (They are known, of course, to have been conceived in relation to certain poetic and autobiographical ideas, though characteristically Webern withheld these ideas from publication.[47]) Such musical gestures as the undulating figures at rehearsal number 2 in the last piece – scored, among other instruments, for six horns, the same number as are required in the tone poem and, perhaps significantly, the same number that Delius habitually wrote for in his larger orchestral pieces (and it is an unusual number, less commonly found than four or eight); the staccato figures for two horns shortly after rehearsal number 2 of the first piece; the chords for four muted horns at the start of No. 3; and the many fleeting passages for solo violin – all these strike a familiar chord with *Im*

44 Moldenhauer, *Anton von Webern*, pp. 113, 116.

45 Ibid., pp. 176, 199–203.

46 See his letters to her of 17 January and 8 September 1930, in *Anton Webern: Letters to Hildegard Jone and Josef Humplik*, ed. Josef Polnauer, trans. Cornelius Cardew (Bryn Mawr: Presser, 1967), pp. 14, 15.

47 See Moldenhauer, *Anton von Webern*, pp. 126–8.

*Sommerwind*.[48] Similarly, but at a further remove, the very short pieces of Op.10 (1911–13). One feels throughout this music that some private drama is being enacted. But the third piece, especially, with its cowbells and distant deep bells, is suggestive of not only the Mahler to which it is frequently compared but also, and more particularly, the Delius of the exactly contemporaneous *Song of the High Hills* (1911): Krenek, in commenting that 'Webern's music evokes the clear, thin air and the formidable tense silence of the very high mountain summits',[49] makes the similarity almost tangibly explicit.[50]

With Webern's two other works for full orchestra – the Passacaglia, Op.1 (1908), and the Variations, Op.30 (1940) – similarities with the early tone poem, let alone with Delius, become more fanciful. What these works do, rather, is call to our attention certain *absences* in the early work: the absence of Brahms, whose contrapuntal rigours and regular periodicity cast their unmistakable shadow over the Passacaglia, and, more surprisingly, given that Webern had discovered his music in 1902, the absence of Mahler. Give or take a few obvious Mahlerian fingerprints, such as the oscillating cello figure in bs 8ff or the harp open fifth towards the end (b. 215), I can find no sign whatever of the Mahlerian influence, and in particular the Mahlerian fragmentation, that was to become such a feature of Webern's later style.[51] It is perhaps the coming to terms with this influence, together with all the far-reaching consequences that this influence had for the Second Viennese School, that marks the greatest difference between

48 Cf. *Im Sommerwind* bs 162–71 (clarinets); b. 114; b.38; bs 168ff respectively.

49 'Anton von Webern: a profile', in *Anton von Webern: Perspectives*, p. 5.

50 It is possible that these pieces in their original versions, which are as yet unpublished, were even more overtly pictorial than they are in the versions in which we know them. Webern's policy, in preparing for publication in the 1920s works that had been conceived over a decade before, was to revise them in the light of his new, post-war aesthetic: see Felix Meyer and Anne C. Shreffler, 'Webern's revisions: some analytical implications', *Music Analysis* 12/3 (October 1993), especially p. 376. To this extent the Op.10 pieces may stand as a symbol of what Webern 'lost'.

51 Egon Wellesz reports that when he first met Webern, in October 1904, Webern preferred Strauss to Mahler: 'Anton von Webern: a great Austrian', in *Anton von Webern: Perspectives*, p. 108. Moldenhauer quotes a letter from about the same period in which Webern declares a preference for Strauss's themes: *Anton von Webern*, p. 40. The most blatant bit of Straussian writing in *Im Sommerwind* is the unison horn passages, and in particular the thumping cadences, at bs 135 and 194.

'early' and 'later' Webern. The cowbells, the mandolines, the muted brass, the E♭ clarinets – all these sonorities which seem so typical both of Mahler and of the later Webern were still in the future. (Some of them were still in the future for Mahler, too, in 1904: the Seventh Symphony, not to mention the very late works, had not yet been written.)

What expansive, explicitly programmatic works Webern might have gone on to write in the twenties, if his music had not taken the direction it did, is hard to imagine. But there are pointers. We know that in 1917 he was planning a number of Trakl settings with 'large orchestral ensemble', though when Moldenhauer goes on tell us that this ensemble involved trombone (*sic*), celesta, tamtam and timpani[52] one wonders if something has got lost in the translation. Then there is the sketch for the 'Piano Concerto' (later the Concerto for Nine Instruments, Op.24) which Moldenhauer describes in such tantalising detail. Although the list of instruments he gives hardly constitutes the 'opulent orchestral palette' he speaks of (shades of the large-orchestral version of *Les Noces*!), the imagination is whetted almost beyond endurance. What would such a Piano Concerto have been like? Fortunately another page of sketch, recently unearthed in Basel, enables us to answer this question. Though hardly of the grandiosity one had been led to expect – visions of Korngold or Rachmaninov – it is clear that the full orchestral setting allowed a clearer articulation of material, and a stronger contrast between opposing forces, than was possible in the chamber version. My reconstruction of this sketch, presented as Example 11, has also enabled me to solve a problem that has vexed two generations of Webern scholars: the mysterious inscription 'Tamb.' The new sketch reveals that the inscription is actually 'Tbe.', implying a quartet of Wagner tubas (here given in their conventional, 'Brucknerian' transpositions) whose quotation of a popular Viennese melody helps to make sense of the Austrian place-names scattered throughout the remaining sketches.

In the same spirit, and as my contribution to the Webern fiftieth-anniversary year, I offer my transcription (Example 12a; cf. beginning of *Im Sommerwind*, Example 12b) of the first page of a hitherto unknown tone poem from 1928, named *Der schöne Spiegel*, presumably after the Goethe

[52] Moldenhauer, *Anton von Webern*, pp. 275–6.

Etwas lebhaft
♩ = ca 80
8va
rit.
tempo
rit.
Kl.Fl.
Fl.
Flattzge
Ob.
Kl.
Hrn
Trp.
m.D.
Pos.
Tub. Ten. (B)
Tub. Bas. (F)
Mand.
Cel.
am Tisch
Hfe.
Glsp.
Klav. Solo
I. Vl.
II. Vl.
Br.
pizz.
Vlc.
pizz.


**Example 11**

poem that Webern would set two years later.[53] This is perhaps a little more than the *jeu d'esprit* it appears to be. The saturated string textures, resulting from a division into fifteen parts, show a continuation of the same harmonic/textural thinking that underpins the opening of *Im Sommerwind.* What was formerly a chord of D major, built up from the bottom like the prelude to *Das Rheingold*, is now a twelve-note chord *à la* Ligeti, arranged symmetrically ('mirror'-like) around the axis A – though it only takes a backward extension of the bass pedal note to produce the original chord of D. The first violin harmonics shimmer like the opening of Mahler's First Symphony. The canonic lines, also reminiscent of Mahler (the coda to the finale of the Sixth?), really call for four trombones, including the noble alto, but post-war economies have taken their toll. Tuned percussion – twenty years later Webern could have used a marimba – contribute to the canons. What all this is designed to show is that the composer of the Symphony, Op.21, was also the composer of *Im Sommerwind*, something some of his admirers seem to want to forget. It was only historical contingency, not the force of destiny, that prevented Webern turning out like Pfitzner or Franz Schmidt.

## IX

The reality was different: the years with Schoenberg, the adoption first of atonality and then of the twelve-note technique, the growing isolation, the picture of the lonely artist carving out his 'dazzling diamonds' for a hostile or indifferent public. And it is the reality that we must celebrate: Webern the master, the model for subsequent generations, the fantastic and inspired craftsman of Opp.6 and 10, the Trakl Songs, the String Trio and the Symphony. Yet there was a price to pay. And in calculating that price the name of Schoenberg must come into the reckoning. Obviously it would be absurd to 'blame' Schoenberg for everything that 'went wrong' in Webern's development after 1904 (just as he should not be given all the credit for what went 'right'). As with Berg, it is hard to imagine what Webern would have turned out like as a composer if he had *not* studied with Schoenberg; he might not even have gone on composing at all. Yet the fact

53 Item 307 in Moldenhauer's catalogue: see *Anton von Webern*, pp. 742–3.

Ruhig, schreitend
Kl.
Bkl.
Hr.
Pke.
Xyl.
(klingt wie notiert)
Cel.
(klingt 8va tiefer)
Git.
Mand.
Hfe.
I. Vl.
II. Vl.
Br.
Vlc.
Kb.
m.D.
mp
p
pp
ppp

**Example 12a**

[Some empty staves compressed; Moldenhauer's English directions translated into German]

Example 12b

remains that as Webern's compositional technique matured – largely under Schoenberg's guidance – so his expressive range, and range of musical sympathies, narrowed, leaving him with a set of relatively abstract preoccupations such as 'unity', 'synthesis' and 'logic'. Instead of the 'opulent' Piano Concerto we have the wiry reality and the inhibited reorchestration (most conductors prefer the original) of the Op.6 pieces. 'History' triumphed again.

In all this there is a curious parallel with the career of the Viennese theorist Heinrich Schenker. He too started out as a practical musician; in his youth, loved much music;[54] and, under the influence of a theory, saw his tastes narrow and narrow until, as with Webern, only a single tradition (much the same one) remained.[55] As with Webern, too, 'unity' and 'synthesis' became important concepts: the organicist metaphor, with Goethe at the centre, was of course common to both, though how different the results![56] With Schenker the road to the *Ursatz*, with Webern the path to modern music. And in each case the sense of mission, the conviction that the path chosen was the only possible one. (There is a nationalist dimension to all this too, though lack of space prevents consideration of it.[57])

[54] See the reviews translated in 'Three essays from *Neue Revue* (1894–7)', together with the accompanying article by Nicholas Rast, 'A checklist of essays and reviews by Heinrich Schenker', in *Music Analysis* 7/2 (July 1988).

[55] Nicholas Cook has made a similar point in *A Guide to Musical Analysis* (London: Dent, 1987), p. 58. On Schenker's 'aggressively German' sympathies, see also Ian Bent, 'Heinrich Schenker, Chopin and Domenico Scarlatti', *Music Analysis* 5/2–3 (July–October 1986), p. 132.

[56] Schenker left no comment on Webern as a composer. His reaction to Webern's conducting is recorded in Hellmut Federhofer, *Heinrich Schenker: Nach Tagebüchern und Briefen in der Oswald Jonas Memorial Collection* (Hildesheim: Olms, 1987), p. 266.

[57] The Webern–Schenker connection has been made before, in a rather unpleasant context: see Richard Taruskin, 'Back to whom? Neoclassicism as ideology', *19th-Century Music* 16/3 (1993), p. 299 and note. Taruskin's eagerness to overturn received opinion, in this case the Moldenhauers', leads him to talk of 'Webern's Nazism' as if this were established fact. But this is too delicate a matter to be treated so casually. The little evidence that is available suggests that Webern's nationalism was of the old-fashioned, First World War-generation kind (his roots in minor Austrian nobility are relevant here) rather than of the more modern, National Socialist variety. His hopes that the rise of Hitler might bring a greater public acceptance of his music are not so easily explained away, however.

With Webern the commitment to modernism – to Schoenberg, to being in the vanguard – meant giving up the delight in sound, so conspicuous a feature of the early tone poem, that could have been one of his most precious legacies. There is in the mature Webern none of the sheer delight in sound, let alone the idealisation of it – the cult of beauty – that we associate with Debussy, Delius or Schreker. Instead we have clarity, logic and functionality, the doctrine of *Fasslichkeit* that he had learned from Schoenberg and ultimately from Mahler. One might ask (and many have asked): what happened to the music? At what point did purely musical ideals get sacrificed to intellectual ones, not to mention (yet again) the historical ones?

Unanswerable questions. But it is possible to see in Webern a sort of split musical personality which was to become central to twentieth-century culture, or at least to that part of twentieth-century culture that remained in thrall to modernism. (Now that we live in a postmodern age, the idea of postulating 'alternative' histories is no longer as suspect as it used to be.) As he got older, his instinctive musicality seems to have been channelled more and more into conducting: one can see from photographs (especially the famous one of him rehearsing Mahler's Sixth, with his head thrown back like Karajan)[58] what an *emotional* experience this must have been for him, just as one can hear, in his recording of the Berg Violin Concerto,[59] a joy in the spontaneous aspects of music-making (and a breadth of tempo) that recalls Knappertsbusch. Composing, on the other hand, became more and more a matter of cerebration: the symmetries, the row tables and the fantastically complex formal schemes (which somehow fail to register emotionally, or to cohere with the evident emotion behind them, as they manifestly do in Berg) are part of a modernist tradition that continues with Boulez, Nono and Ferneyhough.

'Heart versus Brain' is of course an impossible distinction. We can no more visualise one without the other than we can unmake history. Yet Webern's loss is our loss too. The late cantatas, the projected large-scale works – even, perhaps, the hopelessly exaggerated durations that appear in

58 Reproduced in Moldenhauer, *Anton von Webern*, Plate IXc (following p. 320).

59 With Louis Krasner and the BBC Symphony Orchestra (1 May 1936), Testament SBT 1004.

the printed scores – are indications of a desire to compose longer pieces which might have been realised had he lived. To reduce this to the absurd would be to see Webern as the putative composer of *Licht* (but a *Licht* in which every second is a miracle of microstructure). But it is not totally implausible to imagine his career taking a similar direction to that of Pfitzner (with whom he nearly studied), Schmidt (from whom he did in fact take a few lessons) or Schoeck (one of whose vocal scores he prepared, a monstrous effort of forced labour, in the early 1940s).[60] And this raises a nice question of quality. Can anyone say, hand on heart, that the musical experience gleaned from a performance of the String Quartet, Op.28, or the Concerto, or the Saxophone Quartet, marvels of construction though they be, is *in any way comparable* to the experience afforded by Pfitzner's *Palestrina*, or Schmidt's Fourth Symphony, or one of the big Schoeck song cycles?

Had Webern's career indeed taken such a direction, it would have meant a total redefining of the twentieth-century musical canon.

## Appendix

### *Bruno Wille's poem 'Im Sommerwinde'*

from *Offenbarungen des Wachholderbaums: Roman eines Allsehers*, vol. II, 2nd edn (Leipzig: Eugen Diederichs, 1903), pp.70–3

Es wogt die laue Sommerluft.
Wachholderbüsche, Brombeerranken
Und Adlerfarren nicken, wanken.
Die struppigen Kiefernhäupter schwanken;
Rehbraune Äste knarren;
Von ihren zarten, schlanken,
Lichtgrünen Schossen stäubt
Der harzige Duft;
Und die weiche Luft
Wallt hin wie betäubt.

Auf einmal tut sich lächelnd auf
Die freie, sonnige Welt:

[60] The other side of the coin would be to recognise the modernist elements in Pfitzner's, Schmidt's or Schoeck's music.

Weithin blendendes Himmelblau;
Weithin heitre Wolken zu Hauf;
Weithin wogendes Ährenfeld
Und grüne, grüne Auen . . .
Hier an Kiefernwaldes Saum
Will ich weilen, will ich schauen—
Unter lichtem Akazienbaum,
Der, vom muntern Wind gerüttelt,
Süsse Blütentrauben schüttelt.

O Roggenhalme hin und her gebogen!
Wie sanft sie flüstern, wie sie endlos wogen
Zu blau verschwommenen Fernen!
Schon neigen sich und kernen
Viel Häupter silbergrün.
Andre blühn
Duftig wie frisches Brot.
Dazwischen glühn
Mohnblumen flammenrot,
Dunkelblaue Cyanen . . .
Doch droben wallen
Durch lichtes Blau
Wolkenballen,
Gebirgen gleich,
Halb golden und halb grau.
Und eia, schau,
Frau Sonne spreitet
Den Strahlenfächer von Silberseide
Kokett hernieder;
Dann taucht sie wieder
Aus schneeigem Wolkenkleide
Die blendenden Glieder
Und blitzt und sprüht
Verklärendes Goldgefunkel
Auf Auen—wo lachend blüht
Vergißmeinnicht und gelbe Ranunkel
Und Sauerampfer ziegelrot . . .

O du sausender, brausender Wogewind!
Wie Freiheitsjubel, wie Orgelchor
Umrauschest du mein durstiges Ohr

Und kühlst mein Haupt, umspülst die Gewandung,
Wie den Küstenfelsen die schäumende Brandung—
O du sausender, brausender Wogewind!
Nun ebbest du—so weich, so lind—
Ein Säuseln, Lispeln, Fächeln.
Bestrickte dich ein Sonnenlächeln?
Auch dein Gesäusel stirbt;
Dann—lauschige Stille!
Nur noch die Grille
Dengelt und zirpt
Im Erlengebüsch, wo das Wässerlein träumt,
Von Lilien gelb umsäumt.
Und droben, weltverloren, girrt
Inbrünstig die Lerche, schwirrt
Taumlig vor Wonne
Zu Wolken und Sonne
Und girrt und girrt.

Da wird mir leicht, so federleicht!
Die dumpfig alte Beklemmung weicht;
All meine Unrast, alle wirren
Gedanken sind im Lerchengirren—
Im süßen Jubelmeer—ertrunken!
Versunken
Die Stadt mit Staub und wüstem Schwindel!
Versunken
Das lästige Menschengesindel!
Begraben der Unrat, tief versenkt
Hinter blauendem Hügel,
Dort—wo hurtige Flügel
Die emsige Mühle schwenkt . . .
Friede, Friede
Im Lerchenliede,
In Windeswogen,
In Ährenwogen!
Unendliche Ruhe
Am umfassenden Himmelsbogen!—

Weisst du, sinnende Seele,
Was selig macht?
Unendliche Ruhe!

Nun bist du aufgewacht
Zu tiefer, heitrer Weisheit.
Gestern durchwühlte dein Herz ein Wurm,
Und heute lacht
Das freie Herz in den Sommersturm...
Friede, Friede
Im Lerchenliede,
In Windeswogen,
In Ährenwogen!
Unendliche Ruhe
Am umfassenden Himmelsbogen!

# 3 The golden thread: octatonic music in Anton Webern's early songs, with certain historical reflections

ALLEN FORTE

## Introduction

**Example 1** Five songs (Stefan George), Op.4 no.1

Example 1[1] shows the final vocal phrase of the first song ('Eingang') of Webern's remarkable early cycle, the Five Songs on Poems of Stefan George, Op.4 (1908–9).[2] The sequential melody of Example 1 divides the line into two patterns that correspond to the parallel imperatives of the poetic text: 'Traumfittich rausche! Traumharfe kling!' (Sigh, dream-wing. Ring, dream-harp.) By rhythm and contour the melody further splits into two vertical strands, the upper of which I have marked by asterisks on Example 1 to show the succession b$^1$–d♭$^2$–d$^2$–e$^2$. Now, to the sensitised analyst this tetrachord suggests a fragment of the octatonic scale, a suggestion that is enhanced when we realise that the entire melodic phrase consists of seven

[1] In the interest of graphical clarity, the musical examples do not include all the performance information on the printed score.

[2] The Moldenhauers refer to a 1939 letter to Berg student Willi Reich in which Webern lists Op.4 no.1 as one of the songs that he would recommend for performance in an ISCM concert of his music being planned in Basel for the following year. Hans and Rosaleen Moldenhauer, *Anton von Webern: a Chronicle of His Life and Work* (New York: Alfred Knopf, 1979), p. 122.

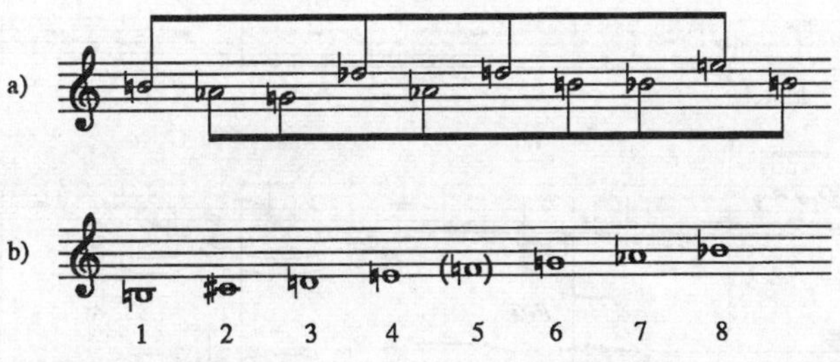


Example 2 Five songs, Op.4 no.1: octatonic parsing

notes drawn exclusively from that scale.[3] Inspired by this circumstance, Example 2 compares the octatonic scale beginning on $b^1$ and Webern's melody, which begins on the same pitch.

I have already pointed out the correspondence between the first four notes of the octatonic scale, shown in its complete ordered form in Example 2b, and the peak notes of Webern's melody, beamed in Example 2a. The remaining notes, those that comprise the lower strand of the melody, form the regular pattern of half-step dyads beamed in Example 2a for greater visibility. In the ordered scalar form of the octatonic (Example 2b) these dyads appear in positions 6 and 7 ($g^1$–$a\flat^1$) and positions 8 and

[3] The simplest designatum of the term 'octatonic', introduced by Arthur Berger, is the eight-note scale produced by alternating half and whole steps in the twelve-note chromatic scale: see Arthur Berger, 'Problems of pitch organization in Stravinsky', *Perspectives of New Music* 2 (1963), pp. 11–42. The octatonic scale is one of Messiaen's 'modes of limited transposition': see Olivier Messiaen, *Technique de mon langage musical* (Paris: A. Leduc, 1944). An earlier and little known theoretical study of the octatonic scale is Vito Frazzi, *Scale alternate per pianoforte con diteggiature di Ernesto Consolo* (Firenze: A Forlivesi & Co., 1930). I am indebted to Mauro Calcagno for bringing this book to my attention. The Russian manifestation of the octatonic scale is covered in Richard Taruskin, 'Chernomor to Kashchei: harmonic sorcery; or Stravinsky's "angle"', *JAMS* 38 (1985), pp. 72–142. See especially pp. 135ff on Rimsky's harmony textbook and its close approach to the octatonic scale. For convenience in referring to unordered pitch collections within the octatonic scale and 'unordered' octatonic collections I will use the hyphenated set names that are no doubt familiar to most readers [see Allen Forte, *The Structure of Atonal Music* (New Haven and London: Yale University Press, 1973) –Ed.]. This facilitates access to the complete array of forty set classes within the octatonic collection, 8-28, not merely to the seven set classes whose representatives are formed as contiguous elements of the octatonic scale.

Example 3 Five songs, Op.4 no.1

1 (b♭[1] and b), the latter 'wrapping around' from the tail to the head of the pitch-string. Two details are worth observing. First, the octatonic design takes precedence over the text, since the final single-syllable word, 'kling' (see Example 1) matches two notes, completing the regular pattern of the melody. Second, and more important from the theoretical standpoint, one note is required to complete the octatonic scale, an F.[4] The double-headed arrow on Example 3 marks the dramatic appearance of that note in the lowest register of the music. Example 3 also affords an opportunity for some brief comments on the octatonic features of the closing passage, which it depicts.

Letter A of Example 3 refers to the very low bass F, the note required to complete 8-28. Its connection with the vocal melody is made unequivocal:

[4] The incomplete octatonic scale here is an instance of 7-31, the set class to which any seven-note selection from the complete octatonic scale reduces. Although the complete octatonic *collection*, a term that describes any ordering of all the octatonic notes ('the octatonic'), not merely the scalar ordering, contains only one type of heptad, namely, 7-31, 7-31 itself is more gregarious; it belongs to four other octads: 8-12, 8-13, 8-18 and 8-27. Thus, although the affirmation of an octatonic presence in the absence of the complete octatonic (8-28) might seem problematic, it should be recalled that the subset *classes* of 7-31 are identical to those of 8-28, which is not true for the other octads listed above. Accordingly, heptad 7-31 possesses indefeasible credentials as 8-28's primary surrogate.

it corresponds temporally with the final melodic note b$^1$, as indicated by the double-headed arrow. And in the schematic scalar form of the octatonic (Example 2b) f$^1$ occupies a position exactly analogous to b$^1$, as the headnote of the second tetrachord (order position 5).

Readers may notice that the descant of the piano part in the closing music (Example 3) looks suspiciously octatonic, and, indeed, the four notes d$^1$–e$^1$–f$^1$–g$^1$ correspond exactly to those in successive positions 3, 4, 5 and 6 of the schematic octatonic scale, Example 2b. But letter B of Example 3 refers to the one note of the piano descant that does not fit that scalar pattern, d♯$^1$. In fact, D♯ (or any of its enharmonic equivalents) does not belong to this form of the octatonic at all, but to octatonic collection II or III.[5] Here, of necessity, we confront the unpleasant reality that not all of Webern's early songs fit the octatonic paradigm neatly – a considerable disappointment to the ever-hopeful analyst. But later in this article I will suggest ways in which various kinds of non-octatonic elements do relate perspicuously to the octatonic thread.

Returning now to the non-octatonic pitch d♯$^1$ at letter B of Example 3, I point out that the errant note contributes to a salient harmonic feature here: the exchange of dyads C–E and B–D♯ above the low bass F, fulfilling a local function. These dyads together form tetrachord 4-7, a member of one of the symmetric tetrachord classes that are such a pervasive feature of this early atonal music by Webern and which, as here, interrupt or otherwise 'interfere' with octatonic continuities, often creating an expressive aposiopesis. Indeed, one is tempted to say that these symmetric tetrachords may momentarily 'conceal' the golden octatonic thread, but, as I shall

[5] I follow Pieter van den Toorn's labelling, with reordering for mnemonic convenience, so that pitch class 1 begins Collection I, and so on: see van den Toorn, *The Music of Igor Stravinsky* (New Haven and London: Yale University Press, 1983). For each example, the relevant forms of the octatonic scale are reproduced in small notation so that the reader can locate the pitch configurations under discussion in the music, if he or she so desires.

Collection I (CI): 1, 2, 4, 5, 7, 8, 10, 11

Collection II (CII): 2, 3, 5, 6, 8, 9, 11, 0

Collection III (CIII): 3, 4, 6, 7, 9, 10, 0, 1

The abbreviated forms (CI, CII, CIII) will be used hereafter.

suggest later on, their constituent enantiomorphic dyads may often relate directly to an underlying structure that comprises more than one form of the octatonic.

In the music that begins at letter C of Example 3, however, the octatonic music returns to complete the song. Here, over low bass E, which strongly suggests a local E major tonic function (but one that would be difficult to verify in the song as a whole) are two changes of vertical harmony. The first of these (letter C) is an instance of octatonic pentad 5-32, while the second (letter D), corresponding to the change from $f^1$ to $g^1$ in the descant, is letter C's inversion, as $T_0I$, in John Rahn's notation. In terms of total sonority these bars produce octatonic hexachord 6-z49, a favourite of Debussy's, and the first hexachord of the subject of Webern's Passacaglia, Op.1.[6]

Before leaving this song, I should point out that the low bass succession shown in Example 3, F–E, completes a tetrachord that began in the extreme low register at the end of b. 9, with the onset of a new stanza of the poem ('Schauernde Kühle . . .'). The complete tetrachord is D–C♯–F–E, which, of course, is a fragment of octatonic collection I, shown in scalar form in Example 2b, where it occupies positions 3–2–5–4: the dyads remain intact, while their components exchange positions.[7]

In the remainder of this article I will illustrate and discuss other modes in which the octatonic thread pervades the early songs of Webern. At this juncture, however, it seems appropriate to enquire when the octatonic music first begins to appear in his songs. While I do not claim a definitive answer to this interesting and provocative question, I feel secure in stating that his song

6 See Allen Forte, 'Debussy and the octatonic', *Music Analysis* 10/1–2 (1991), pp. 125–69. The correspondence to the Passacaglia is interesting, but probably nugatory. Nor is my reference to Debussy intended to imply a historical connection.

7 Manipulations of this kind may remind the reader of Webern's serial music. It is with some reservations that I mention this, because efforts to relate this early music to twelve-note music have taken some unusual forms in the literature. See for example Elmar Budde, *Anton Weberns Lieder Op.3*: *Untersuchungen zur frühen Atonalität bei Webern* (Wiesbaden: Franz Steiner Verlag GMBH, 1971), pp. 68ff, where Budde illustrates the notion of *Klangzentrum* with the opening sonority of Op.3 no.4, octatonic pentad 5-19, a favourite of Webern's in these early songs.

'Ideale Landschaft', one of the five songs on texts by Richard Dehmel, composed between 1906 and 1908, is at least a very early instance of octatonic penetration, perhaps representing an effort by the fledgling composer to exert control over non-tonal pitch resources within an ostensibly tonal music.

## The Dehmel songs

'Ideale Landschaft', the earliest of the Dehmel songs, dating from spring of 1906, bears a key signature of one sharp and is presumably in E major/minor, judging from the final cadence. The song, over which loom heavily the shadows of Brahms and Wolf, is replete with those familiar standbys 'foreground chromaticism' and 'whole-tone' formations and exhibits clearly defined tonal progressions, as in bs 23–8, where the bass slowly ascends by step from dominant to tonic. For Webern, the generally tonal ambience apparently did not, however, rule out the inclusion of octatonic music, and although it is not abundantly represented it is certainly present in this early song.

In comparison to those in the later of the early songs, such as the passage discussed in connection with the preceding examples, the octatonic infusions of 'Ideale Landschaft' are deceptively 'naïve'. Example 4 shows a representative octatonic section in the piano part of bs 15–17.

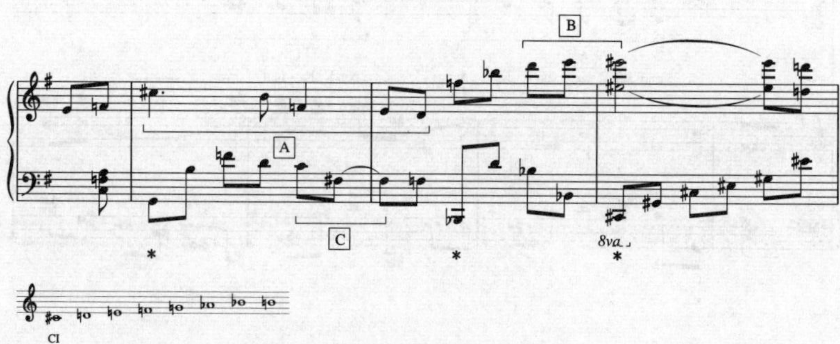


Example 4 'Ideale Landschaft' (Dehmel lieder)

Here (in Example 4) the descant is pure octatonic, presenting CI in its entirety, except for G♯/A♭. Only two segments of the melody are taken directly from the ordered octatonic scale: c♯¹–b¹ and f♯¹–e¹–d¹, which are adjacent in the melody (see letter A). The second of these segments is particularly prominent, occurring twice, in ascending and descending directions, at the end of the passage (letter B), with E♯ replacing F as the E major key orientation strongly suggests an altered submediant function (VI♯3).

In addition, the bass of the passage outlines a diminished triad, G–B♭–C♯, marked by asterisks, which also belongs to CI, and, in fact, only two notes in the entire passage are not members of that form of the octatonic: C and F♯ in the first bar of the left-hand figuration (letter C). This anomaly (if our octatonic perspective is viable) suggests a closer look. Accordingly, Example 5 reproduces the entire passage.

With the addition of the vocal line (see Example 5) we see that the octatonic passage sets a full line of the poem, undergirding the text 'und eine hohe Abendklarheit war' (and there was an elevated evening transparency). The vocal line is also octatonic, but in a more intricate way. Letter A applies to the bracketed melodic succession that ends on the peak note of the phrase, d² (setting the text vowel 'A'). This segment of the melody derives

Example 5 'Ideale Landschaft' (Dehmel lieder)

from adjacent positions 6, 7, 8 and 1 of CII, as can be seen by inspecting the scalar presentation of CII in small notation on the example. Letter C of Example 5 designates the final tetrachord of the phrase, which derives from positions 4, 5, 6 and 7 of CI, reordered as 7–4–5–6. This is a tetrachord of type 4-10, just as is the first tetrachord (at A). With regard to the scalar arrangement of the octatonic, tetrachord A preserves the dyads, but reverses the position of their elements, while tetrachord B is a circular permutation of its scalar model. The melodic segment designated by letter B of Example 5 incorporates the peak note $d^2$, which belongs both to CI and to CII, forming octatonic pentad 5-25. It is important to point out that 5-25 is not formed entirely from adjacent scalar elements, but incorporates one non-adjacent note, namely, $d^2$. Octatonic components of this type are called 'unordered', since not all of their notes are adjacent with reference to the scalar model.[8]

Finally, letter D of Example 5 delimits the configuration that incorporates the fractious $c^1$ and f♯ exposed earlier at letter C of Example 4. This, again, is an unordered subset of the octatonic. Since its notes can be located in CII in positions 1, 3, 4, 7 and 8, this part of the accompaniment groups harmonically with the first tetrachord of the vocal line, also drawn from CII. Together they form 6-z50, one of the more exotic of unordered octatonic hexachords.[9]

Thus Example 5 illustrates one way in which Webern combines components from two forms of the octatonic, in this case from Collections I and II. It also shows the role that unordered sets may play in his idiomatic exploitation of the special musical properties of the octatonic.

The octatonic music of Example 5 is by no means isolated in this early song. In Example 6, also drawn from 'Ideale Landschaft', we hear a four-bar melodic succession based entirely upon octatonic segments that set a complete line of the poem, 'und sahst nur immer weg von mir' (and you looked ever away from me) and the beginning of a short line that features the

[8] I have placed the commonly used term 'unordered' within single quotation marks here to remind myself and the reader that considerations of ordering are usually important to the analyses of the 'unordered' sets.

[9] Hexachord 6-z50, not one of the stellar subsets of the octatonic, does play a major role in Stravinsky's *Le Roi des Etoiles* (1912). In this connection, I should say that I rule Stravinsky out as a possible influence on Webern's octatonic usage. The musical differences are multiple and striking.

**Example 6** 'Ideale Landschaft' (Dehmel lieder)

keyword 'Licht' (light). This passage contains yet another subtlety of Webern's octatonic usage. The first melodic segment (letter A) projects an unordered pentad, 5-19 from CIII, but emphasises its contiguous subsets, c¹–c♯¹ and f♯¹–g–a¹. In contrast, the second segment (letter B), which is a form of hexachord 6-z23 from CI, occurs naturally as an *ordered* segment in the scalar octatonic. Webern's deployment of the hexachord, however, emphasises its symmetric design about the two trichords of type 3-2, b¹–c♯²–d² and g²–f²–e², but conceals, by inversion, the contiguity of its elements in the underlying scalar model. Moreover, the headnote of the second 3-2 trichord, g², sets 'Licht' and initiates the symmetric rhythmic pattern minim– crotchet–crotchet–minim that returns the line to its point of origin, b¹, thus lending a special weight to that pitch and suggesting further investigation of its melodic role in the context of a more extensive analysis.[10]

As will become evident in the context of the remainder of this article, the octatonic music in 'Ideale Landschaft' is not only strikingly original and interesting in itself but also stunningly proleptic. In the songs that Webern wrote after 'Ideale Landschaft' we hear more complex modes of octatonic infusion as he combines forms of the octatonic and introduces other sonic

[10] Hexachords of classes 6-z23 and 6-z13 are the only such that can occur as ordered subsets of six elements in the octatonic scale. Therefore, their presence in one of the songs may be a strong indication of an underlying scalar octatonic model. Like each of three other hexachordal subsets of octatonic octad 8-28, 6-z13 and 6-z23 occur four times as subsets. One hexachord, 6-27, enjoys a privileged relation with 8-28, occurring eight times as one of its subsets.

Example 7 'Helle Nacht' (Dehmel lieder)

domains, often proceeding directly from octatonic components. The piano introduction to the last and most complicated of the five Dehmel songs, 'Helle Nacht' (1908), illustrates.[11]

Item A of Example 7 is an unordered pentad from CIII, 5-16, within which is 4-17 (A'), about to become the first tetrachord of the vocal line (not shown). The configuration can also be parsed into two horizontal tetrachords, with 4-z29 on top and 4-12 on the bottom, the latter clearly derived from ordered positions in the scalar model. These too become important 'subjects' in the later contrapuntal music of the song, especially 4-z29.

Segment B of Example 7 is an ordered transposition of the music of A, thus a shift to CII. In the left-hand part of b. 1 of Example 7 (letter C) we find 4-z15 from CI, consisting of the dyad in scalar order-positions 5–4 above the dyad in scalar order-positions 7–8, thus revealing a close affinity to the

[11] The date of this song, 1908, suggests comparison with Schoenberg's lieder of the same period, notably those of Op. 15: see Allen Forte, 'Concepts of linearity in Schoenberg's atonal music: a study of the Opus 15 song cycle', *Journal of Music Theory* 36/2 (Fall 1992), pp. 285–382.

scalar model.[12] The letter D tetrachord transposes C to III. As a result of these combinations the introduction is something of an octatonic farrago, awaiting clarification in the main part of the song.

Finally, item E of Example 7 is an instance of tetrachord 4-8, a distinctly non-octatonic harmony. But its connection to the preceding octatonic material could not be clearer, since the upper dyad, f♯$^1$–d$^1$, repeats the preceding f♯$^2$–d$^2$ and the lower dyad, c♯–g, repeats the preceding c♯$^1$–g$^1$. Thus, non-octatonic tetrachord 4-8 partakes of two forms of the octatonic, CII and CIII.[13]

## Four George songs

In 1965 Hans Moldenhauer discovered four unpublished songs by Webern on texts by Stefan George that the composer had presumably intended to publish along with his Op.3 and Op.4 lieder. According to Moldenhauer Webern wrote out two of these in large notation for performance, indicating that he was completely satisfied with them. One of the two songs, 'Trauer I', is heavily, but by no means exclusively, octatonic.

The opening music of 'Trauer I' (see Example 8) engages two forms of the octatonic, CI and CII. Right at the outset two pentads from those model structures intertwine. Letter A of Example 8 designates pentad 5-19 of CII: the first vertical and the rest of the triplet figure, which is the most obvious octatonic scalar token. The other pentad, 5-28 of CI, consists of the upper two notes of the first chord, the second chord and the last two notes of the triplet. Pentad 5-19 then connects to the opening notes of the vocal line, which comprises tetrachord 4-3 (letter C), to complete 7-31 of CII on g♭$^1$, as marked by the down arrow. With the return of the opening configuration, yet another form of 5-19 materialises as $T_6$ of the first form, delimited by letter D of Example 8 (f$^1$–a♭$^1$–g♭$^1$–b–(f♯)–c). Letter E of Example 8 then identifies the completion of CI in the upper part of the accompaniment. Its

12 Of course here and elsewhere these order positions are not fixed, but are dependent upon the rotational arrangement of the scale the analyst uses as a model pattern. But the numeric positional relations hold, obviously.

13 The early songs contain many individual occurrences as well as clusters of symmetric tetrachords 4-7, 4-8 and octatonic 4-9. See, for example, Op.3 no.4, bs 6–7, the cascading interlocking forms of 4-8.

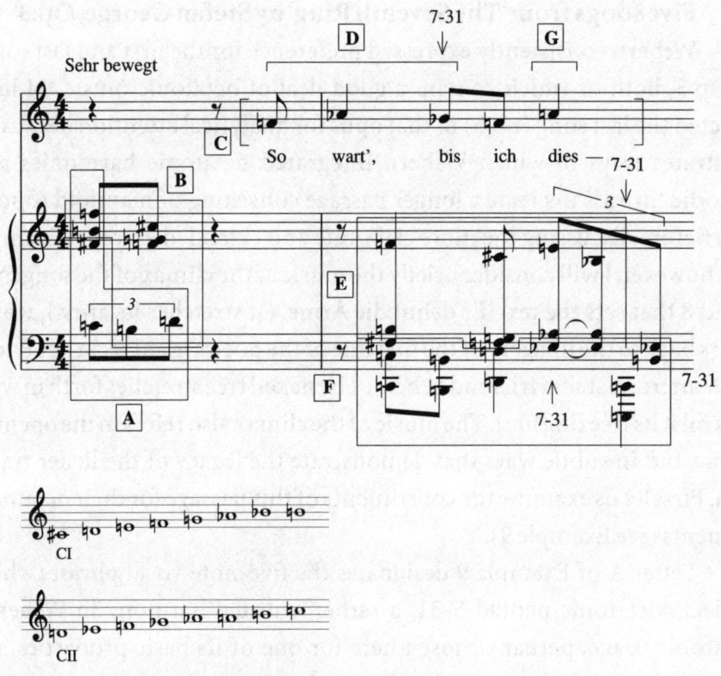


Example 8 'Trauer I' (four George songs)

last note is b♭, marked by the down arrow. Letter F is attached to the bracketed notes that continue CII in the lower parts and reach completion on e♭ and a♭, as marked by the up arrow.

Finally, letter G of Example 8 refers to the vertical form of 4-8 there, a collocation of CI and CII that momentarily interrupts the elaborate octatonic texture. With all this complexity, one might well ask: Where is the octatonic thread? Perhaps the most immediately audible octatonic trace is created by the left-hand triplet and its continuation in the voice part: octatonic 7-31 of CII: c¹–b–d¹–f¹–a♭¹–g♭¹–f¹–a¹. And another clearly scalar formation is in the bass alone, with C–B–D of b. 1 repeated in b. 2 and extending to E♭, completing tetrachord 4-3.

## Five songs from 'The Seventh Ring' by Stefan George, Op.3

Webern consistently expressed preference for the first and last songs of Op.3, both of which contain a good deal of octatonic music.[14] I have selected the last song (no.5) of that opus for analytical attention because it illustrates ways in which Webern integrated octatonic harmonies and melodic threads to create a longer passage consisting of manifold sonorities. Before discussing the more elaborate and extended excerpt (Example 10), however, I will consider briefly the music at the climax of the song in bs 7 and 8 that sets the text 'Er dehnt die Arme' (It stretches its arms), which refers back to the imagery of the first line of the poem: 'Kahl reckt der Baum im Winterdunst sein frierend Leben' (The naked tree stretches forth in winter's mist its freezing life). The music of the climax also refers to the opening music, but in subtle ways that demonstrate the legacy of the lieder tradition. First let us examine the constituents of this passage for their octatonic elements (see Example 9).

Letter A of Example 9 designates the five-note vocal phrase, which projects octatonic pentad 5-31, a rather unusual harmony in Webern's octatonic usage, perhaps chosen here for one of its basic properties, the exposed diminished seventh chord, tetrachord 4-28 ($e^2$–c♯$^2$–b♭$^1$–$g^1$), which dramatises the 'minor third', a basic motive in the song. Item C of Example 9 is an arpeggiation of hexachord 6-z13, which, it will be recalled (from note 10) is one of only two linear hexachords of the octatonic scale. In the scalar inset in small notation on Example 9 this form of 6-z13 can be located 'wrapped-around' in consecutive positions 7–8–1–2–3–4. Webern's considerable 'rearrangement' (with respect to the model scale) brings out the two diminished triads (e♭$^3$–$c^3$–f♯$^2$ and $e^2$–c♯$^2$–$g^1$) and within them the two minor thirds e♭$^3$–$c^3$ and $e^2$–c♯$^2$. The entire configuration is motivic: a horizontalisation of the opening chord of the song, shown in Example 10. With respect to pitch content, configurations A and C sum to octatonic 7-31, drawn from CIII. With the exception of its very first note, F, the three-note

14 See Moldenhauer, *Anton von Webern*, pp. 122 and 553. In Webern's letter to Willi Reich preceding the 1940 Basel ISCM concert, he expressed preference for Op.3 no.1, Op.3 no.5, Op.4 no.5 or Op.4 no.1, and Op.12 no.1 and Op.12 no.4, in that order. In a 1943 letter to Reich, the composer expressed preference for Op.3 nos. 1, 4 and 5. With the exception of Op.4 no.4, the Op.3 and Op.4 songs contain substantial amounts of octatonic material.

**Example 9** Five songs from *Der siebente Ring* by Stefan George, Op.3 no.5

chromatic figure, f³–e³–e♭³ (letter B), fits into CIII as well. As will be evident in Example 10, these three notes also come from the opening music: E and E♭ (as e² and e♭²) are in the descant of the opening chords, while F (as f) is the bass note. Moreover, the entire chromatic trichord, F–E–E♭, is heard as the long-range bass progression from b. 1 to b. 4 (see Example 10). In the melody of the song as a whole, F is reserved for special moments of contrasting poetic metaphors, setting the first syllable of 'Eise' (ice) and the second syllable of 'Frühling' (spring) in the last line of the poem, 'dass er im Eise noch Frühling hofft!' (that in ice it [the tree – and presumably, the poet!] still hopes for spring).

Example 10 reproduces the first six bars of the song. My translation of the relevant stanza follows the original, below.

Kahl reckt der Baum in Winterdunst
sein frierend Leben.
Lass deinen Traum auf stiller Reise
vor ihm sich heben!

**Example 10** Five songs from *Der siebente Ring*, Op.3 no.5

The barren tree stretches forth in winter's mist
its freezing life.
Let your dream, on tranquil journey,
revive before it!

Before discussing the octatonic organisation of this music, a few comments on some of its salient features, keyed to the large letters on Example 10, seem appropriate. The two chords of the introduction (letter A) coalesce into octatonic hexachord 6-z13 (CIII), with the first vertical a form of pentad 5-10, the second a form of 5-16. The two chords differ by only one note, since the 'minor thirds' on top and bottom exchange registral positions, a beautifully illusory 'motion', perhaps symbolic of the barren and motionless tree, so that the only real motion involves the change from f♯$^1$ to g$^1$ in the middle voice. (Compare the exchange in Example 3.)

Letter B of Example 10 points to the upper voice of the two chords, e♭$^2$–e$^2$, which repeats until letter E, where an ascending contour leads up to the peak note, c♯³, before descending directly to b♭¹ in b. 4, creating a musical delineation of the poem's tree imagery. This melody then sets the last two lines of the stanza, beginning at letter H, so that the melody of the first line of the poem is accompanied by the music of the second line's melody, in counterpoint, as it were – a most unusual circumstance in the German lied.

Even a brief hearing of the first phrase of the 'chromatic' vocal melody (letter D) – whose contours are so typical of Webern's music as well as that of his teacher – will alert the sensitive listener to an octatonic presence. Only the direct chromaticism (at letter F) interferes with that impression. And even the descending cadential motion at letter G ('Leben'), the largest interval in the line, occurs within an octatonic context.

At letter I, setting the poem's 'Traum', the bass reaches down to its lowest note, A♭, whose four manifestations in the vocal line begin with the second word, 'reckt' in b. 2, which has pictorial connotations of stretching. Again, the octatonic context of this low note is suggested by its immediately adjacent pitches, d and e. At the other registral extreme (letter J) the descant of the piano, doubling in octaves, imitates the vocal line's 'stiller Reise'.

Examples11–13 display the octatonic components of bs 1–6 of Webern's Op.3 no.5, beginning with CI. To make this accessible to the reader I have beamed together the stemmed notes that belong to CI, leaving the non-CI elements detached. For convenient reference, with each of the three examples a scalar ordering of the relevant form of the octatonic is supplied in small notation. Pitch-class set names are given here and there, and notes (represented as pitch-class numbers) required to complete the octatonic collection are indicated in parentheses. An additional symbol, the arrow, points to the note that completes the largest octatonic configuration, usually 7-31, but sometimes 8-28.[15]

Letter B in Example 11 shows a common feature of the octatonic in this music: each octatonic thread begins from a subset of the opening two-

15 As is often the case both in Webern's atonal and in his twelve-note music, the completion of a collection corresponds to a significant location in the music. Usually, the 'collection' is regarded by analysts as the complete chromatic aggregate. In the present study, I have taken the octatonic collection to be the 'universal' set. See Anne C. Shreffler, *Webern and the Lyric Impulse: Songs and Fragments on Poems of Georg Trakl* (Oxford: Clarendon Press, 1994), pp. 185ff, 'Chromatic circulation and form'.

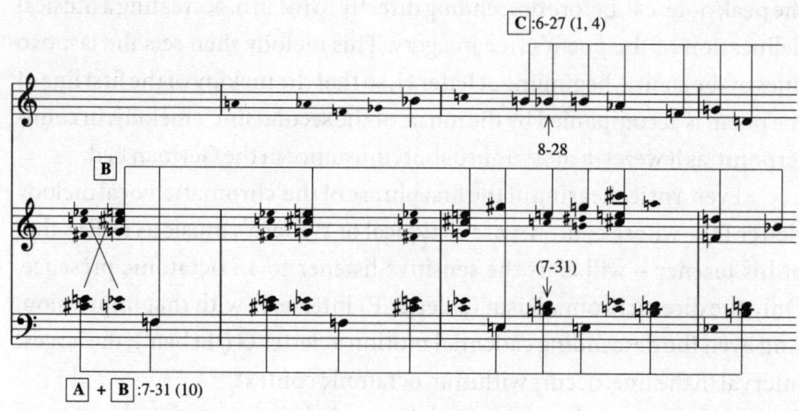


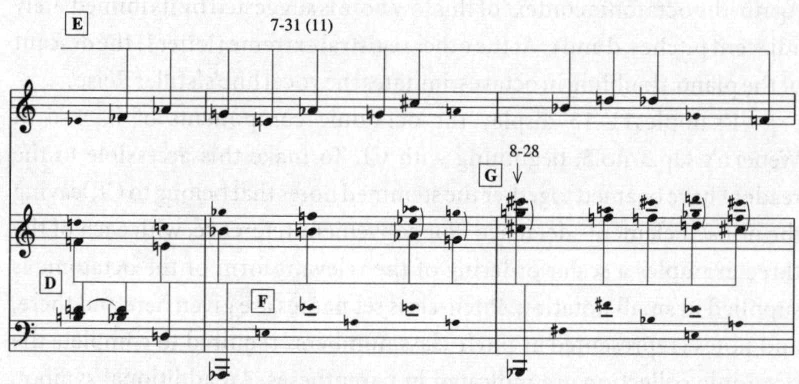


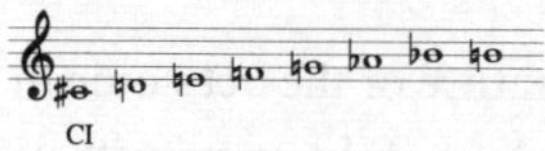


Example 11 Five songs from *Der siebente Ring*, Op. 3 no. 5: octatonic thread Collection I

chord harmony, here its diminished trichord G–C♯–E, which combines with bass f to maintain CI through the beginning of b. 3 as tetrachord 4-12. In b. 3, this tetrachord assimilates g♯², the first new note in the descant of the accompaniment, to complete pentad 5-16, which is inversionally equiv-

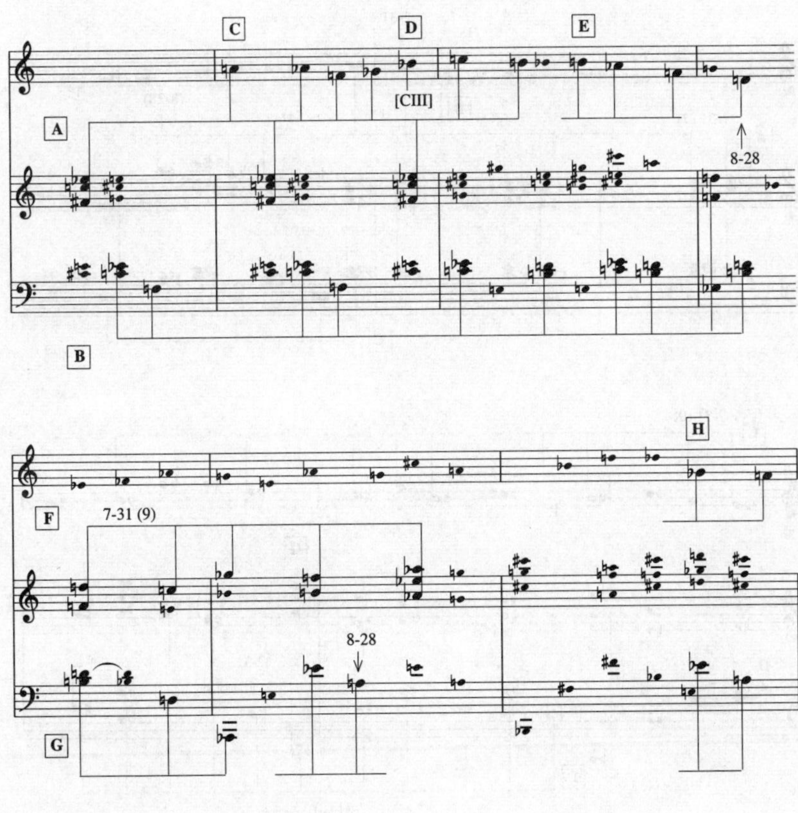


**Example 12** Five songs from *Der siebente Ring*, Op.3 no. 5: octatonic thread Collection II

alent to the entire second chord of b. 1. This strand of CI then finishes with an arpeggiation of the diminished triad with which it began: $e^2$–$g^2$–$c\sharp^3$, and arrival on the peak $c\sharp^3$ corresponds to the final statement of the second chord of b. 1, excluding G. Precisely on the final syllable of the text word 'Winterdunst' the left-hand minor third b–$d^1$ completes 7-31 of CI in the lower part and $b\flat^1$ in voice completes the entire collection.

Whereas CI in the piano accompaniment is interrupted by notes that belong to other octatonic constituents, the vocal segment that begins at

**Example 13** Five songs from *Der siebente Ring*, Op.3 no.5: octatonic thread Collection III

letter C of Example 11 proceeds, uninterrupted, to the end of the phrase. It begins with scalar pentad 5-10, which occupies positions 4 through 8; the final note of the phrase, $d^1$, then completes hexachord 6-27.

Exactly in the middle of b. 4, at the onset of the third line of the stanza, CI takes up residence in the inner parts and the bass (letter D). What is most remarkable here is the note-against-note counterpoint beginning on $f^1$ that the CI thread forms with CII, beginning on $d^2$ (see Example 12). This inner voice thread continues right up to the end of the section, doubling the descant of the accompaniment in the climactic motion to c♯³ (letter G of Example 11), which completes 8-28, and doubling again in the concluding motion d³–c♯³.

The five-note group at letter F of Example 11 is germane to the presence of CI in the music, for it points to the configuration above the bass that is unconnected to CI but that is distinct both registrally and notationally (Example 10), as well as theoretically distinct, by virtue of its membership in CIII (see Example 13).

Finally, letter E of Example 11 is attached to the beamed melodic configuration that is almost, but not quite, composed of elements of CI. I will return to this in connection with Example 14 below in order to present an alternative and non-octatonic reading.

Example 12 gives the somewhat meagre, but nonetheless interesting picture of CII's participation in this octatonic music. Indeed, the short fragments (eg. at letter D) are certainly overpowered by the longer threads that belong to another collection – in that case, CI. I have included them, however, for the sake of completeness.[16]

Like CI, CII's thread departs from the diminished trichord of the opening harmony (letter A). Beginning with b. 2, CII is right in the forefront as the melody of the vocal line (letter C), projecting linear hexachord 6-z13, a transposition ($T_5$) of the opening harmony in the piano, b. 1. This configuration, however, is interrupted by the dissonant b♭¹ (letter D), which represents CIII (to be discussed in connection with Example 13). After this, CI's presence in the vocal line becomes attenuated as it is interrupted again by b♭¹ in b. 3 and g¹ at b. 4. But linear pentad 5-10 (letter B) persistently represents CII in the left-hand piano part, especially in the minor thirds above the bass (octatonic tetrachord 4-3).

At letter F, the beginning of the second line of text, pentad 5-28 of CII unfolds without interruption in the descant of the piano part. With the additional notes of CII that accrue to it from the voice immediately below, the complete configuration sums to 7-31, lacking A (pc9). The missing note appears in b. 5 within the fragmented configuration that begins at letter G,

16 With one exception, d¹ in b.4, isolated single elements of CII are not stemmed and beamed. The same rule applies to the other readings of separate collections.

and at the tail of that lower constituent (repeated at the end of the excerpt) is the final occurrence of tritone e♭$^1$–a, which CI shares with CIII (see Example 13). This tritone pairs off with the final fragment of CII in the vocal line, g♭$^1$–f$^1$, which will be read analytically in a somewhat different way below, in Example 14.

Although, by virtue of its representation in the two-chord initial harmony (Example 13, letter A), CIII is the predominant octatonic collection at the beginning of the song, it appears in the vocal line only briefly, as the trichord g♭$^1$–b♭$^1$–c$^2$ (letter B), in the context of CII (see Example 12). Within that trichord (3-8) b♭$^1$ completes 7-31 of CIII. If the downstemmed a$^1$ of b. 2 in the voice part were to be included, violating the rule that excludes singletons from collection membership, a complete form of 8-28 would result.

At letter C of Example 13 the lower voice reiterates a trichord from the first vertical in the piano accompaniment, while the bass projects e–e♭, initially heard, reversed, as the upper voice of the opening chord succession. A fragment of CIII then appears at the end of b. 3 (letter D), ending on a$^2$, the note withheld from the collection in the descant of the accompaniment.

In the second part of Example 13, at the beginning of the third line of the text, CIII comes into its own in the vocal melodic line (letter E). Excluding a♭$^1$, d$^2$ and f$^1$, the line projects 7-31. These excluded notes, which could belong either to CI or to CII, cannot be effectively explained in isolation, but need to be integrated into the entire line. Two readings that do this are presented in Example 14 for the reader's consideration.

At letter F of Example 13 the lower parts are composed entirely of elements of CIII. From the full notation in Example 10 it is apparent that the lower parts above the bass comprise two strands, the upper of which projects e♭$^1$–e$^1$–f♯$^1$, a reference to the opening harmony of the song and one of the few 'motives' in this essentially athematic work.

In the climactic music at letter G of Example 13 CIII dominates the piano accompaniment, excluding only two notes, f$^2$ and g♭$^2$, which are the notes that set 'Leben' in the voice at the end of the phrase in b. 6.

Example 14 Five songs from *Der siebente Ring*, Op.3 no.5: voice bs 4–6

## An alternative reading

The parsing of the excerpt from Webern's Op.3 no.5 into octatonic strings ignores features of the melody that many readers might regard as 'obvious'. As the most salient instance, let us return to Example 10 to consider the hexachord (6-z43) that first occurs as the top line of the piano part, bs 1–3, and is then repeated verbatim (with two enharmonic spellings) an octave lower by the voice from the middle of b. 4 through the end of b. 5.[17] Examples 11 and 13 read this vocal line as a conflation of CI and CIII, thus masking its exact correspondence to the earlier line in the piano's descant.

In order to place this issue in better perspective, Example 14 parses the vocal line (Example 14a), including 6-z43, from the middle of b. 4 to the end of

[17] The early songs are replete with canonic passages, such as the canon shown in Ex.16 and the short double canon from b.6 in Op.4 no.1. Transferral of a long line from piano to voice is unusual, however. Webern returned to this procedure briefly later on. See Shreffler, *Lyric Impulse*, pp. 90–1, for an interesting description of this idea in the Trakl fragments of 1915.

b. 6 in two ways: first, Example 14b, as the interlocking octatonic strings that were shown separately in Examples 11 and 13 and, second, Example 14c, as successive forms of ubiquitous tetrachord 4-7, a reading that takes as its point of departure the first and last tetrachords in the melody, both of which are instances of that set class.[18] The second, alternative, reading has obvious virtues. Its basic component, tetrachord 4-7, is the only set class whose contiguous forms can account for all the notes in the line, in a manner analogous to that of the octatonic threads. And although it replaces the octatonic threads that account for much of the structure of this section of the song, its basic constituent, non-octatonic 4-7, is by no means foreign either to this music or to the early songs in general (see note 13). But while each of the octatonic threads unfolds a complete form of heptad 7-31, thus unifying the entire line within the octatonic palimpsest, the 4-7 tetrachordal collocation lacks an overriding unity, other than that based upon the transpositional sequence $T_0$, $T_6$ and $T_4$, which has no perceptible larger function – for example, the creation of a significant invariant subset projected linearly in a discontiguous fashion.

Nevertheless, from the analytical standpoint it is prudent to include the tetrachordal parsing in our study of the complete section, not only because it is interesting, but also because it is representative of Webern's multi-faceted musical designs in these singular lieder. For although the pure octatonic is often in the ascendant, octatonic components frequently interact with other pitch configurations to produce a variegated and complex universe that is not immediately accessible either to the casual or to the analytical listener.[19] In the remaining examples of this brief study, I will discuss several different kinds of such interactive designs, or modes of the octatonic, as well as contexts that integrate more than one of its forms.

[18] Heuristics for such parsings are given more rigorous attention in Forte, 'Concepts of linearity'.

[19] Among the small number of non-octatonic hexachords characteristic of these songs, non-symmetric 6-z43 and its complement, 6-z17, occupy prominent positions. And in Example 14's long melodic line the final hexachord is hypersymmetrical 6-20, which often materialises as a conflation of forms of 4-7, as here. Hexachord 6-20 is familiar to aficionados of Webern's twelve-note music, as it partitions the row of his Concerto, Op.24.

## Modes of the octatonic in the early songs

Example 15 involves an interplay of CI and CIII. This opening music, which sets the text 'Welt der Gestalten lang Lebewohl!' (World of forms, farewell for a long time!), first states octatonic pentad 5-16 of CI, designated by letter A of Example 15. Octatonic III (letter B) begins on g♭¹ ('Ge') outlining a G♭ triad over the still-sounding upper tetrachord of CI, which, as 4-17, contains two nicely old-fashioned triads that surely did not escape the composer's attention.[20] Unlike the CI music at letter A, the CIII music at

**Example 15** Five songs (George), Op.4 no.1

20 Nor, I suspect, was Webern unaware of the pun on G*es* (G♭) and '*Ges*talten'.

letter B represents all of 7-31, lacking E. CI music resumes at letter C, overlapping CIII (B) to complete hexachord 6-27, within which c♭$^1$ completes 7-31. Segment D, which introduces CIII on the second b♭$^1$ of the melody ('lang'), overlaps the letter C configuration of CI. Segment D consists of hexachord 6-30, which ends on c$^2$ over f♯$^1$, sounding against the lower parts. Finally, at letter E of Example 15 is a complete statement of linear pentad 5-10 of CI. I have shown only the descant of the piano part here in order to indicate the continuation of CI and to show the completion of 8-28 on d$^1$. Letter F at the end of Example 15 merely points out the repetition of trichord 3-2 (reordered) from the configuration at letter C.

The reading of the octatonic constituents of the beginning of Op.4 no.1 shown in Example 15 is not intended to be an analysis in any more extended respect, which would hardly be possible in any event without taking into account the rest of the song. It is intended to illustrate a particular mode of Webern's octatonic usage, however, one in which he draws configurations from more than one form of the octatonic collection to create a complex intertwining of elements.

Although the music in Example 16 probably represents an earlier mode of octatonic manipulation than that illustrated in Example 15, it presents its own idiosyncrasies and complications. First of all, and obviously, it is canonic. Each phrase of the canonic melody is an exemplar of the same set class, 5-z17, which is a 'classic' atonal set type.[21] Pentad 5-z17 is almost octatonic: of its five tetrachords, one is octatonic 4-3. It is this feature that we hear in each phrase of the canon, for the dyads of 4-3 occupy the outer positions in the motive, while the central and registrally distinct note completes 5-z17. On Example 16 I have this stemmed middle note in small notation. A brief glance will reveal that these notes sum to a diminished seventh chord. Indeed, only CI participates in the canon, but it participates completely: all of 8-28 is present, and the notes it excludes are precisely those of the diminished seventh chord, so that in this way 8-28 and its complement partition the total chromatic.

As in Example 15 (Op.4 no.1) the music in Example 17, from the beginning of the third song of Op.3, combines forms of the octatonic. In

[21] This is the pentad that Schoenberg developed canonically in the third of his Five Orchestral Pieces, Op.16 ('Farben'), adapted by Berg in Act I scene 2 of *Wozzeck* as one of the three chords upon which that scene is based.

**Example 16** 'Erwachen aus dem tiefsten Traumesschosse' (four George songs)

addition, it includes two 'wrong notes' (with reference to the prevailing octatonic collections) and its 'foreground' figures conflict with the large 'background' octatonic segments. Both these situations will be considered below, but first I draw the reader's attention to the three successive large segments at Example 17b.

The first of these large segments, letter A, consists of 7-31 drawn from CI; the second, letter E, is also 7-31, this time from CII; and the segment at letter F is CI in its entirety (8-28), with peak note $d^2$ completing the collection. Letter I designates the beginning of a complete statement of CIII, which sets the first part of the text 'die Hasel blühen' (the hazels blossom), following what appears to be Webern's consistent practice: to change the harmony with a new line of text. Thus, the octatonic organisation of the opening music of the song is relatively uncomplicated compared with the music of Example 16.

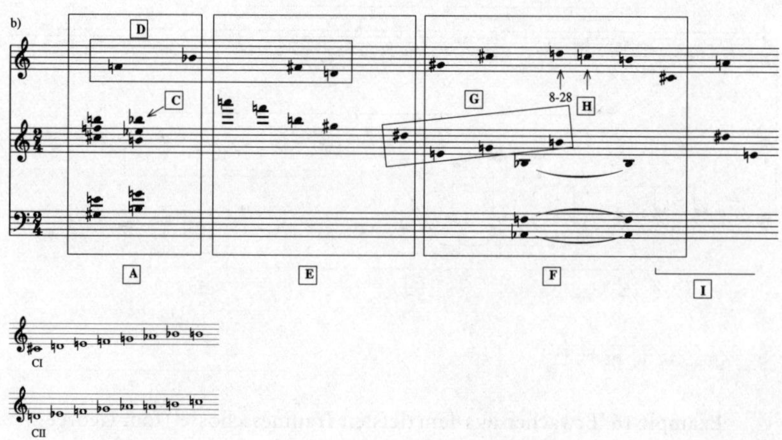


**Example 17** Five songs from *Der siebente Ring*, Op.3 no.3

Now to address the two issues mentioned above. At letter C of Example 17 the arrow points to e♭², which is not a member of the prevailing octatonic collection, CI. One explanation for its presence here is this: it is part of a form of 4-19, letter B, and thus relates directly to the melodic form of that tetrachord enclosed in the box labelled D. The two sets are related by transposition, the chordal version being $T_7$ of the melodic version, so that they share one pitch class, in this case represented by the B♭s in both parts. Tetrachord 4-19 is an important surface motive in this opening music, although it does not occur elsewhere in the song (except at the end of b. 2 and the beginning of b. 3 – not shown). The third occurrence here is marked on Example 17 by letter G, which is an inversional form of D ($T_9I$), considerably reordered. It does not belong to the octatonic collection, however, and thus does not conform to the large octatonic segments. This kind of discontinuity, between surface configurations and underlying octatonic formations, seems to be prevalent in Webern's early music. Indeed, he may have fostered this apparent conflict very consciously in an effort to avoid stereotyped melodic and even harmonic figures that would have exposed the underlying octatonic structure at every moment in the music. There is, after all, a world of difference between the musical aesthetics of a Webern and a Stravinsky.

Letter H of Example 17 points to the second 'wrong note', c². In this case, recourse to the vertical explanation offered for item C, e♭² in b. 1, is unproductive, and the horizontal setting of the contumacious note, within trichord 3-2, as d²–c²–b¹, invokes CII, so that c², especially in its trichordal context, might be construed as the note that completes CII in segment E.

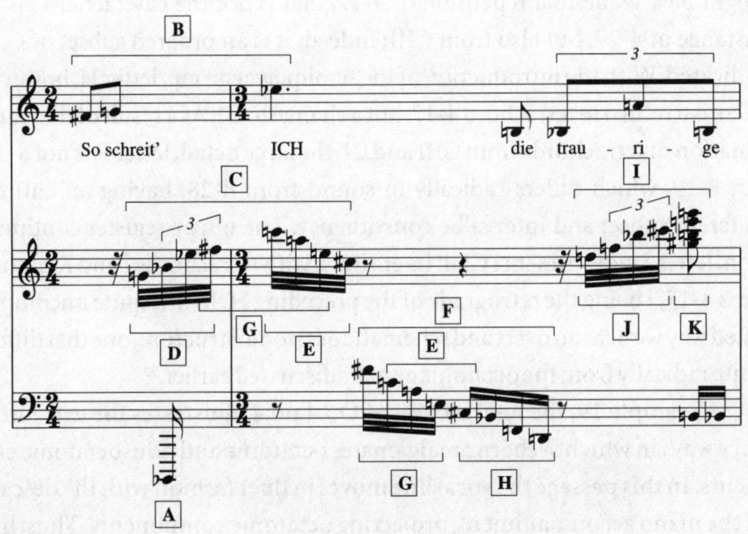


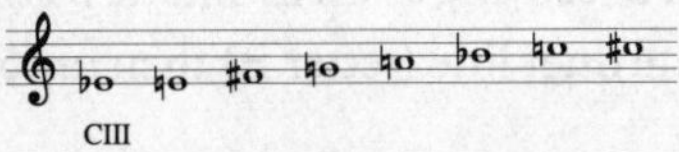


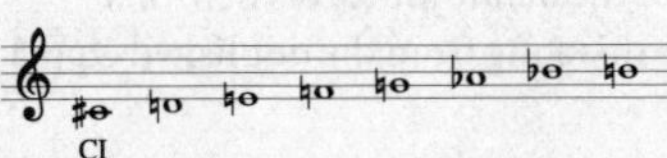


Example 18 'Trauer I' (four George songs)

Whether this is a better explanation than simply describing $c^2$ as a 'passing note' (see Example 19) I leave to the reader.

Example 18 is a relatively transparent octatonic excerpt from one of the early songs. Although at first glance the short excerpt seems to be a clear-cut octatonic passage, further hearing indicates some special aspects. Let us consider the lettered constituents from left to right, beginning with letters A and B. Letter A designates the low B♭, which is the lowest key but one on the standard piano (see note 26 below). This groups with voice trichord B to form 4-17 of CIII, the characteristic tetrachordal class for this passage. As suggested by the octatonic insets on Example 18, the music consists of elements of only two forms, CIII and CI, in that order, and at letter C CIII appears in its entirety, partitioned by contour into two forms of 4-17, at letters D and E. While the rhythmic pattern of the following group, letter G, suggests that this might be a sequential repetition of 4-17, that is not the case; letter G is an instance of 4-27, but also from CIII; indeed, it is an ordered subset of C, as indicated. With the introduction of the semiquaver group, letter H, however, there is a return to tetrachord 4-17, but a change to CI. As a result of this combination of tetrachords from CIII and CI, the large octad, letter F, is not 8-28, but 8-19, which differs radically in sound from 8-28, having an entirely different subset and intervallic constituency. The upper register continuation, letter I, now presents CI in its entirety, with tetrachords J and K both of class 4-17, J being the retrograde of the preceding H. In this quite uncomplicated way we hear an overt and schematic octatonic structure, one that differs quite radically from the octatonic gestalts discussed earlier.[22]

Example 19, the final section of Op.4 no.4, illustrates the extraordinary ways in which Webern amalgamates octatonic and non-octatonic elements. In this passage the vocal line moves in duet fashion with the descant of the piano accompaniment, projecting octatonic components. Thus, linear hexachord 6-z13 of CIII (letter A) sets the first part of the text line 'ferne singt sie nach' (she sings far away), with $b^1$ serving as a 'chromatic passing note'.[23] The second part of the composite duet line (letter B) then unfolds

[22] Perhaps it was the very overt statement of the octatonic forms here that influenced Webern's decision to exclude this song from the published Opp.3 and 4.

[23] In view of the pervasively octatonic organisation of these two upper voices I do not hesitate to relegate $b^1$ ('singt') to the lowly status of a passing note.

Example 19 Five songs, Op.4 no.4

the entirety of CIII, with 6-z13 (letter B') again setting the text. Here, although the scalar ordering of 6-z13 is not preserved, the trichords are reversals of those in the small reference inset of CIII on Example 19, once again suggesting the importance of the basic scalar forms of the octatonic and perhaps confirming Webern's awareness of them.

It is in the chord succession that the non-octatonic components of this music come into play. Yet, there is a continuing octatonic presence, as I will show. The first vertical in Example 19b, at letter D, is an instance of one of Webern's favoured hexachords, 6-z19.[24] Now, one of 6-z19's pentad subsets is 5-16, an octatonic item. In this case 5-16 is almost a contiguous subset of 6-z19, consisting of (from the bass up) E–B–F–G♯–G. But the octatonic 'infiltration' emanates not from CIII, but from CI, where it occupies positions 3, 4, 5, 6 and 8 in the small scalar arrangement on Example 19. When the descant of the piano part changes to f♯¹ (letter E), the harmony changes to a form of 6-z17, another of Webern's special hexachords. If we now read from the descant downward, octatonic pentad 5-19 materialises as f♯¹–c¹–g♯–f–b, an ordering that is a considerable disruption of the CII scalar arrangement, F–F♯–A♭–B–C. At letter F 6-z19 returns transformed by inversion ($T_4I$) relative to the first form of that hexachord at D. Its upper pentad is now octatonic 5-16, and this combines with 5-19 in 6-z17 to form hexachord 6-z13 of CII, shown in the small inset, Example 19c. Only the descant moves, from f♯¹ to a¹, and those notes, it will be recalled, belong to CIII.

Thus, all three octatonic collections have been activated in this final section. Of these, CII is the first to appear in the song – initially in the melody of bs 3 and 4, then in the melody and accompaniment of b. 5, including the last note of b. 4.[25] With the introduction of a new pitch in the accompaniment, c♯¹, CI now appears unconcealed at letter G, as tetrachord 4-18, just as the central tetrachord of the voice, with its special rhythmic pattern, descends in a traditional word-painting gesture, setting 'und minder wird mein Gram' (and my sorrow is lessened). Pentad 5-32 of CI, the tied minim chord, letter H, sounds until the end of the song. Against that chord, descant a¹, the final member of CIII forms a 'dissonance' with respect to the predominant CI. Together with the bass E, which has been in place since b. 13, the prominent 'E-major triad' within this final chord may cause some listeners to hear the final sonority as a quasi-tonic harmony. And the large-scale bass line from the beginning of the song to the end,

24 It is also, perhaps not surprisingly, a prominent hexachord in the atonal music of Schoenberg and Berg.

25 Like many other issues, the possible hegemony of one collection in a given song, although intriguing, must be placed on the shelf for later consideration.

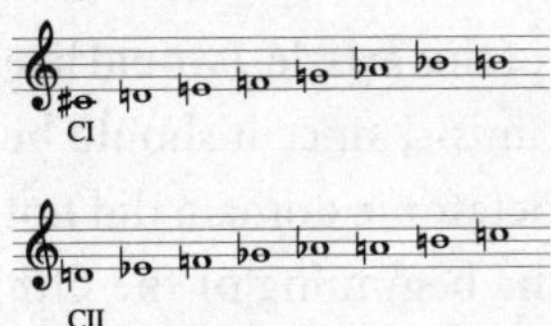


**Example 20** Five songs from *Der siebente Ring*, Op.3 no.1

G♯–F–F♯/G♭–F–E, which unfolds within the 'major third' G♯–E, may reinforce that interpretation.

In general, the bass lines of these early Webern songs are structurally significant over the complete span of the work: they project thematic pitch-class sets, and, more often than not, their pitch content is relevant to the octatonic dimension of the music. To illustrate, Example 20 displays the complete bass line of Op.3 no.1, a particularly fine instance.[26] As shown in Example 20a, the first bass segment derives pentad 5-28 from CI,

[26] Another remarkable instance: the entire bass of Op.3 no.5 forms octatonic hexachord 6-30 of CI. Webern's basses in these early songs often plumb the depths of the piano. For instance, the bass of b.10 of 'Trauer I' (Four George Songs, no.3) descends to its very lowest note, A, which is no doubt of autobiographical significance since the names Arnold, Alban and Anton begin with that letter.

preserving the scalar ordering in the inner 3-2 trichord, while the outer notes, E and d, are adjacent in the scale. From the middle of b. 4 until the end the bass projects linear hexachord 6-z13 of CII. In this succession only two notes are repeated, G♯ and D, which are two of the four notes that CII shares with CI and the two notes that end 5-28 in Example 20a. From the first D in 6-z13 to the end the bass unfolds linear 5-10, revealing the close connection of the bass to the scalar prototype. Example 20b reproduces the final music of the piano accompaniment, which unfolds a transposition ($T_6$) of 5-28 of the bass as shown in Example 20a. This connection, although remote, reflects Webern's well-known interest in replication, which is extended here to segments of the octatonic collection.

## Webern's later octatonic music

Although it is not within the main purview of this article, I would like at least to touch upon Webern's later octatonic music, since it should be emphasised that his compositional work in the octatonic domain did not end with the early songs.[27] Example 21 shows the beginning of the fifth movement of his Five Orchestral Pieces, Op.10, which date from 1911–13. According to the composer, the date of completion of the fifth movement is 6 October 1913.[28] The work is in the so-called aphoristic style: very few notes, very fast, with special orchestration and orchestral effects. This is evident at the very outset, where the opening melody is played by glockenspiel! As indicated on Example 21, this melodic line consists of three notes drawn from CII, letter A, and the remainder from CIII. The five-note figure beginning on $a^2$ is linear 5-10 (letter B), a pentad that should be familiar to readers who have come this far. CIII then continues with the vertical on the second crotchet beat of b. 3, interrupting CI. CI, at letter C, is introduced by trumpet in b. 2. Like the headnote of CIII ($a^2$ at letter B) the headnote of CI,

27 For a detailed study of an intricate octatonic essay dating from 1913, see Allen Forte, 'An octatonic essay by Webern: Opus 9/I of the *Six Bagatelles for String Quartet*', *Music Theory Spectrum* 16/2 (Fall 1994), pp. 171–95.

28 Moldenhauer, *Anton von Webern*, p. 194. In the manuscript of 'Op.6', an early version of Op.10 in the Pierpont Morgan Library, this movement is no.4. That version of the music differs in some significant details from the final version, one of which is relevant to the octatonic parsing of Example 21.

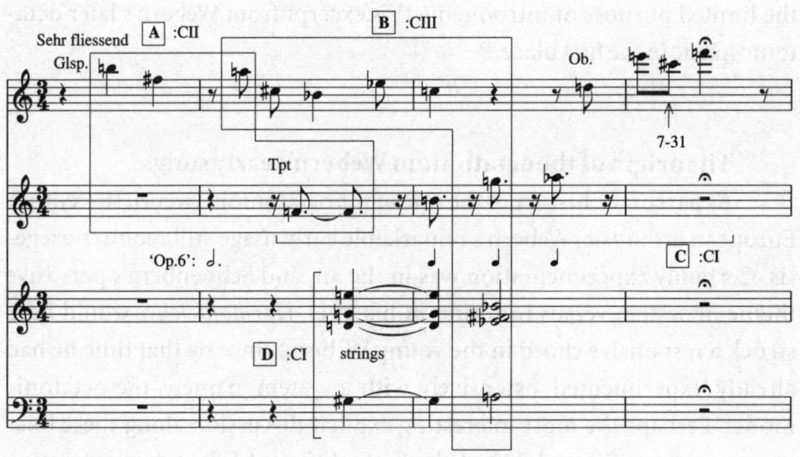


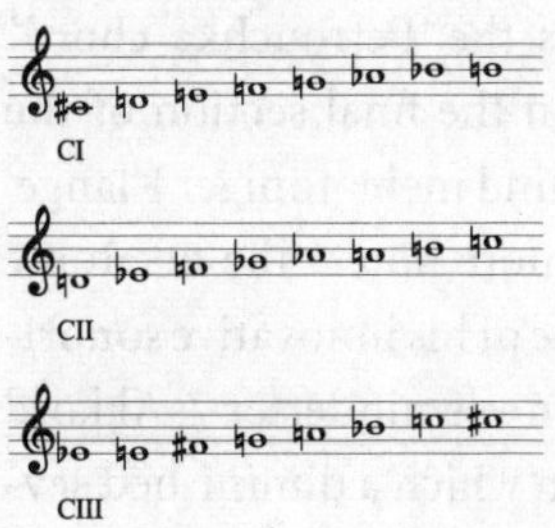


Example 21 Five pieces for orchestra, Op.10 no.5

$f^1$, also belongs to CII. In the Morgan Library version (see note 28) the placement and rhythm of the trumpet entrance is as shown in small notation below the second staff of Example 21: dotted minim followed by three crotchets. Thus, the trumpet's $f^1$ originally abutted f♯² of the glockenspiel, coming in before the glockenspiel's third note, $a^2$. Of the three statements of forms of the octatonic, only CI completes 7-31, on c♯³ in the last bar. Letter D of Example 21 designates tetrachord 4-z15, which is $T_1I$ of the tetrachord in CII labelled by letter A.

With the exception of bs 21–6, which include a complete statement of the diatonic collection 7-35(!), all of Op.10 no.5 is octatonic. Details of the section shown in Example 21 as well as the entire work obviously invite investigation much more extensive than it is possible to supply here, given the limited purpose of introducing this excerpt from Webern's later octatonic music in the first place.[29]

## The origin of the octatonic in Webern's early songs

As part of the history of the role of the octatonic in twentieth-century European art music, Webern's remarkable early usage still requires exegesis. Certainly experimentation was in the air, and Schoenberg's pervasive theme of system versus intuition in his 1911 *Harmonielehre* would have struck a responsive chord in the young Webern, since by that time he had already 'experimented' extensively with a system, namely, the octatonic model. Perhaps the most interesting explicit discussion along these lines appears on pp. 371 and 372 of the first edition of Schoenberg's treatise. Remarkably, his excerpt from Strauss on p. 372 (Example 235) is an octatonic harmony, hexachord 6-30, which, as the 'Petrouchka chord', attained notoriety about the same time. And in the final section of the *Harmonielehre*, 'Aesthetische Bewertung sechs- und mehr-töniger Klänge' (Aesthetic evaluation of sonorities of six and more notes) the octatonic is also prominent. Schoenberg even describes one of his innovative sonorities as 'Eine Addition zweier Akkorde, denen ein verminderter 7-Akkord gemeinsam ist . . .' (an addition of two chords in which a diminished seventh chord is common).[30] The 'addition' in question produces, once again, octatonic hexachord 6-30.

By 1911 Schoenberg had already had extensive experience composing with the octatonic in his own music, notably in the 1908–9 songs of Opus 15.[31] But these instances are not as complex and intricate as the

[29] In 'Octatonic essay' I hypothesised an intricate underlying octatonic design for the entire first piece of Webern's *Six Bagatelles for String Quartet*, Op.9 no.1. I believe that this is the first published study in which the octatonic is invoked to provide a structural model of a Webern work. Lest this sound too much like an instance of reflexive back-clapping, I hasten to add that at the time I wrote the Op.9 article I had not yet studied the early songs in any detail, and was therefore quite innocent concerning their octatonic constituents, an exiguity that detracts considerably from any claim to scholarly glory!

[30] Arnold Schoenberg, *Harmonielehre* (Leipzig/Vienna: Universal Edition, 1911), pp. 467–8.

[31] See Forte, 'Concepts of linearity'.

Webern passages discussed in the present article. Later on, Schoenberg incorporated the octatonic more extensively. An elaborate example is the Passacaglia (no.8) from *Pierrot Lunaire* (1912). And of course Berg is involved in this exploratory endeavour as well. For instance, the first hexachord of the tone row of the second movement of his *Lyric Suite* (violin I, b. 1) is linear 6-z13 – the same hexachord as the first hexachord of Schoenberg's *Die Jakobsleiter*, a work that played a pivotal role in the transition to twelve-note music. This observation raises the large issue of the proleptic role of the octatonic in what Schoenberg regarded as the ineluctable progression towards twelve-note music and system. Any worthwhile historiography of twentieth-century music will necessarily come to grips with this hypothesis when dealing with 'modernist' and 'post-modernist' phases, and, in so doing, will engage other angles and paths, such as those suggested by Busoni's scales, the writings of Capellen, which were influenced by the new field of ethnomusicology, and the innovative harmony treatise of Louis and Thuille.[32] It is a complex network.[33]

Meanwhile, we can speculate on the answer to another question. Why did Webern find the octatonic model so attractive? Clearly, his atonal apostasy must have occupied a central position in the decision to base significant portions of the music of his remarkable early songs on the intricate manipulations of octatonic materials such as those discussed in this essay. Therefore perhaps the answer is straightforward: the octatonic model and its resources seemed to offer a surrogate for the etiolated harmonies of the recently completed *Jahrhundert*'s crepuscular music. With few exceptions (for example, the 'half-diminished seventh' and the 'diminished seventh') the new resource supplied a large number of fresh melodic and harmonic

32 Two of the following three publications appeared in 1907, the year Webern composed his Dehmel songs, and the third was published a year earlier: Feruccio Busoni, *Entwurf einer neuen Aesthetic der Tonkunst* (Trieste, 1907); Georg Capellen, *Ein neuer Exotischer Musikstil* (Stuttgart: Carl Grüninger, 1906); Rudolf Louis and Ludwig Thuille, *Harmonielehre* (Stuttgart: Carl Grüninger, 1907).

33 In this larger context, other manifestations of the octatonic in European music, such as Debussy's idiomatic use of the octatonic fountainhead, necessarily play important roles in the study of historical aetiology: see Forte, 'Debussy', for speculations on the source of the octatonic in that composer's music.

configurations that were closely related, yet variegated – and we can hear those in the early songs. Webern may also have seized upon the new resource to assuage his concern that under Schoenberg's shadow his music might come to be regarded as epigonic.[34] Whatever motivations may have underlain his refulgent artistry, these early songs stand as an extraordinary corpus of music by any measure.[35] It is with this remarkable creative endeavour that the 25-year-old Webern first finds his place among the avant-garde composers of the opening years of the twentieth century, a group whose orientation, unique in music history, has been so eloquently characterised by Robert P. Morgan at the end of his essay on modernism in music:

> The composers of the first decade of the century sought to revive musical language by reinventing it. They tried to disengage musical sounds from their inherited attachments, to set them free from conventional associations in pursuit of what Schoenberg (along with Kandinsky) called the 'spiritual.' In sober retrospect, they may seem to have failed; yet theirs was a brave and exhilarating effort that fundamentally altered the nature of musical discourse.[36]

[34] This opinion is influenced by Shreffler's account of Webern's pursuit of small-scale works, compared with the large-scale endeavours of Schoenberg and Berg. See Shreffler, *Lyric Impulse*, pp. 7ff.

[35] The long delay in publication of these works is probably responsible for their failure to receive more contemporaneous attention. Op.3 was published only after the war, in 1921, and the publication of Op.4 occurred two years later, in 1923. The Dehmel songs as well as the four George songs were published in 1966 and 1970, respectively, after their discovery by Moldenhauer. For an informative discussion of changes Webern made in Opp.3 and 4 before publication see Reinhold Brinkmann, 'Die George-Lieder 1908/09 und 1919/23 – ein Kapitel Webern Philologie', in *Oesterreichische Gesellschaft für Musik, Beiträge* 1972–3: *Webern-Kongress* (Kassel, 1973), pp. 40–50.

[36] Robert P. Morgan, 'Secret languages: the roots of musical modernism', *Critical Inquiry* 10 (March 1984), p. 458.

# 4 A pitch-class motive in Webern's George Lieder, Op.3 [1]

ROBERT W. WASON

In tonal music, motivic events are generally regarded as intervallic relationships, whose actual pitch-class representations change with reference to a fixed-pitch background – the tonal centre itself, or a related tonal region that temporarily comes to the fore. In so-called 'atonal' music, that background is presumably absent, leaving us with only the intervallic relationships – the immediate object of most analytical investigations of this repertoire. Yet, even given the absence of *a priori* tonal considerations, there are 'atonal' pieces in which a particular pitch class or a collection of pitch classes is imbued contextually with greater significance than any transposition of it, tempting us to posit a favoured $T_0$ status. Throughout Webern's Op.3 a particular collection of pitch classes (*not* simply a collection type) recurs in a way that seems to give it special status, its contextual setting and larger meaning changing from one piece to the next, as we shall see.[2]

[1] The present essay contains detailed analytical remarks on all five songs of Webern's Op.3; the reader will need a score of the complete work to gain the most from this discussion. I wish to thank the John Simon Guggenheim Memorial Foundation, who generously supported the research and writing of the initial draft of this study.

[2] A number of pieces approximately contemporary with Webern's Op.3 come to mind in this regard. For example, the 'recapitulation' of Schoenberg's Op.11 no.1 reinstates the $T_0$ level of primary thematic material, as George Perle has noted: *Serial Composition and Atonality* (Berkeley and Los Angeles: University of California Press, 1963), p. 15. And a favoured transposition of the *Farben* chord acts as a quasi-tonic in Schoenberg's Op.16 no.3: see the analysis by John Rahn in *Basic Atonal Theory* (New York and London: Longman, 1980), pp. 59–73. This technique of early atonal music was recognised long ago by Hermann Erpf, who calls the quasi-tonic a *Klangzentrum* in his *Studien zur Harmonie- und Klangtechnik der neueren Musik* (Wiesbaden: Breitkopf und Härtel, 1929).

Reinhold Brinkmann has described the important role of these same pitch classes in Webern's revision of 'Ihr tratet zu dem Herde', the last song from the Op.4 George Lieder. Example 1a shows the last two bars in the earlier version of the song published in *Der blaue Reiter*;[3] Example 1b gives the version later published by Universal Edition incorporating Webern's changes. Concerning this music, Brinkmann says:

> In the later version the final bar of this song experiences a minimal, but utterly revealing correction. In [1a], there is a clear centralization of the close on the tone D, expressed in the soprano through an 'encircling' by the upper and lower minor second C♯ and E♭..., and by the contra-D in the piano, which ends a three-tone succession thoroughly in the sense of a tonal-pull in which the final D clarifies the C♯–E♭–D of the voice.[4]

Indeed, it might be added that both the existence of the same contra D in the previous bar and the D/E♭ exchange between bass and soprano at that point heighten the effect still further; and it is interesting that Webern continues to notate 'C♯' in the earlier version, instead of notating the second-to-last vocal note as D♭. Webern's revisions, on the other hand, essentially 'liquidate' (as Brinkmann would say) any potential fundamental D.

The present article focuses less on the general phenomenon of fundamentals and their mistreatment, and more on this specific example: D, 'encircled' by E♭ and C♯, which, as Brinkmann remarks, also exists in

Rudolf Stephan invokes Erpf's notion in an analysis of Webern's Op.4 no.4 in his *Neue Musik* (Göttingen: Vandenhoeck & Ruprecht, 1958), pp. 36–8). Elmar Budde finds a *Klangzentrum* in his analysis of Op.3 no.4: *Anton Weberns Lieder Op.3: Untersuchungen zur frühen Atonalität bei Webern* (Wiesbaden: Franz Steiner, 1971), pp. 68ff.

In the present analysis of Op.3 I have stopped short of the notion of a quasi-tonic, since the structural status of the preferred pitch classes is not uniform throughout the set of songs. (By the end of the fifth song such 'tonalistic' terminology seems not inappropriate, however.) The more neutral characterisation, 'pitch-class motive', is borrowed from Steven Laitz, who examines the use of fixed-pitch 'motives' in tonal music in his 'Pitch-class motive in the songs of Franz Schubert: the submediant complex' (Ph.D. dissertation, University of Rochester, 1992).

3 *Der blaue Reiter*, ed. Kandinsky and Marc, in a new documentary edition by Klaus Lankheit (Munich and Zürich: Piper, 1984).

4 Reinhold Brinkmann, 'Die George-Lieder 1908/9 und 1919/23 – ein Kapitel Webern-Philologie', in *Oesterreichische Gesellschaft für Musik, Beiträge 1972–73: Webern-Kongress* (Kassel/Basel: Bärenreiter, 1973), pp. 40–50; see pp. 44f.

a)

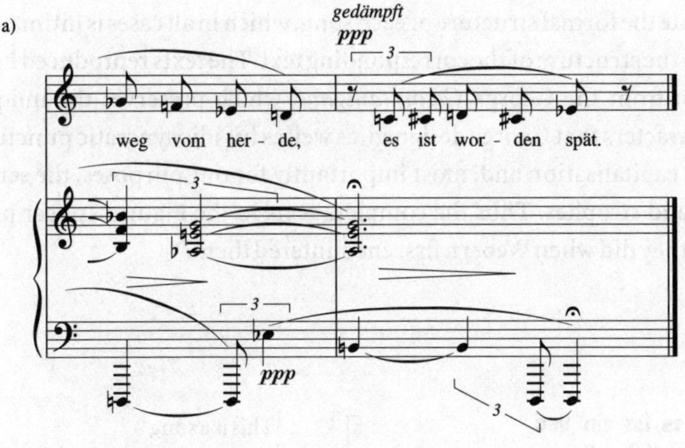


b)

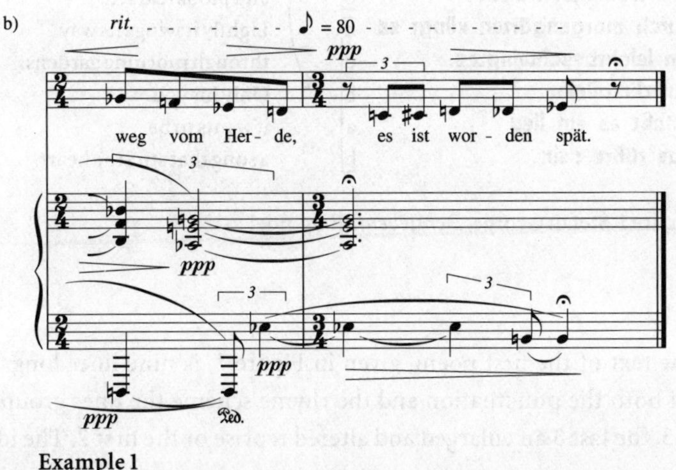


**Example 1**

Schoenberg's Op.11/2 and Op.15/14.[5] The list does not end there, however, for *encircled D*, as we shall refer to it, manifests itself in extraordinary ways throughout Webern's Op.3 George Lieder.

In order to appreciate the role of *encircled D* in this 'cycle' – a term I use advisedly at present, and one to which we shall return later – we must

[5] See Brinkmann's analysis of the latter in his 'Schönberg und George; Interpretation eines Liedes', *Archiv für Musikwissenschaft* 26 (1969), pp. 1–28.

investigate the formal structure of each song, which in all cases is intimately linked to the structure of the corresponding text. The texts reproduced here are taken from the George *Gesamtausgabe*, which preserves the unique print characters that George designed, as well as his idiosyncratic punctuation and capitalisation and, most importantly for our purposes, the setup of lines and strophes. Thus the complete texts in the Figures appear precisely as they did when Webern first encountered them.[6]

I

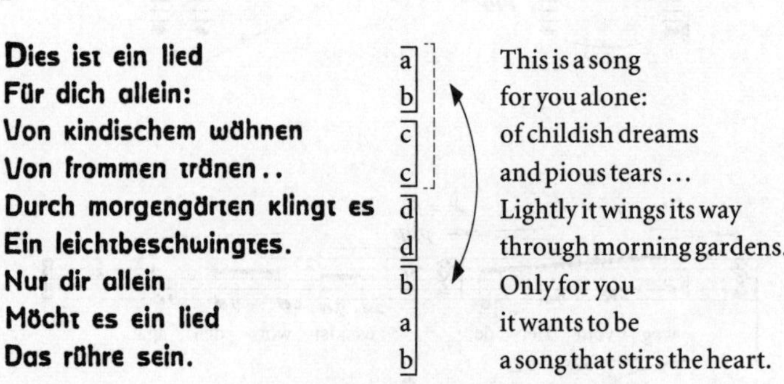


Figure 1 Stefan George, *Der siebente Ring*, no. 1

The text of the first poem, given in Figure 1, is nine lines long: by virtue of both the punctuation and the rhyme scheme the lines group as 2+2+2+3, the last 3 an enlarged and altered reprise of the first 2. The idea

6 *Stefan George: Gesamtausgabe der Werke*, vols VI–VII, pp. 157–61 (Berlin: Bondi, 1927–34). These idiosyncrasies were normalised in the publication of Webern's songs; text citations in the body of the present study follow the normalised texts. The translations are taken from the *Penguin Book of Lieder*, ed. and trans. S.S. Prawer (Baltimore: Penguin Books, 1984), the only generally available English translation that preserves the line and strophe setup of the original. (The reader should be warned that all of the texts of Webern's songs that accompany the Craft and Boulez recordings are unreliable.)

content of the poetry, however, leads to a three-part interpretation, in which the first 2+2 becomes the A section: first, the 'lied' and its description; next, a change of scene ('Durch Morgengärten klingt es / ein leichtbeschwingtes'); and finally a reprise of the opening idea, but this time with lines reversed so that the poet's intended is set out in front ('nur dir allein'). Webern's musical setting underscores the three-part interpretation.[7]

Upon turning to the score, we note that in b. 1, *encircled D* forms the head motive of the first phrase (consisting of two text lines). Beginning in b. 3, two rhyming lines ('von kindischem Wähnen / von frommen Tränen ...') are appropriately set in a modified sequence, rising by $T_2$. Upon returning to the first phrase, however, it becomes clear that the skeleton of this phrase – the tones that are emphasised textually, metrically, durationally or registrally (or a combination thereof): 'Dies', 'Lied', 'dich' – is preserved, transposed and, in effect, progressively 'revealed' in the next two phrases.

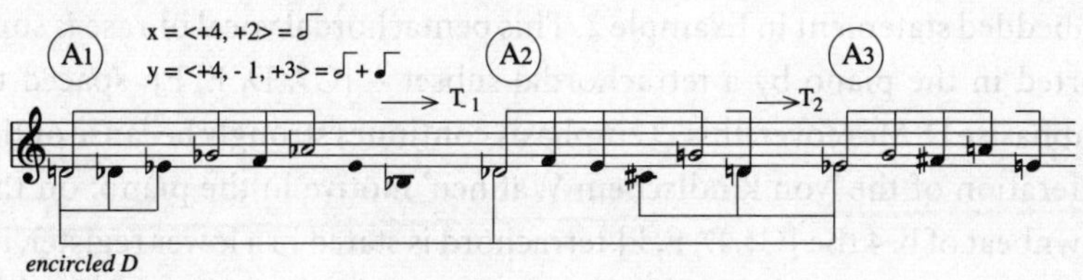


**Example 2**

Example 2 shows these three phrases, marked A1, A2 and A3. The primary skeletal three-note motive, x <+4,+2>, is marked by upward beamed and stemmed open notes, while its four-note 'embellishment', y <+4,–1,+3>, adds one solid note head (with upward stem) to each x. Note that the three phrases contain successively fewer pitches: eight, then six (with D♭/C♯ repeated), and finally five, of which four are motive segment y. Though obviously less important, we also note an embedded statement of *encircled D*, crossing the phrase boundary between A2 and A3. But most important, at the opening of bs 1, 3 and 4 a member of *encircled D* initiates

7 This analysis of text and form is heavily indebted to Budde, *Anton Weberns Lieder Op.3*, p. 41.

each of the phrases in *precisely* the order of b. 1, creating a quasi-'middleground' statement of D, D♭/C♯, E♭ (in beamed open notes, stems down), and determining the transposition network (–1,+2) of x and y. Thus the transposed replications of motives x and y may be heard as being supported by the longer-range statement of *encircled D*, a non-transposing phenomenon.

We now approach the piano part in these bars, noting that one of the most extraordinary features of the work is the extremely close relationship between voice and piano: indeed, the piano part is largely constructed of 'forecasts', or 'echoes', respectively, of the key vocal motives. For example, the soprano of the piano chords in the first bar obviously forecasts and supports the *encircled D* of the voice, while in b. 2 of the piano a canonic answer to the voice commences (embellished slightly by the G), reiterating *encircled D* at its outset.

Phrase A3 then begins in the voice – a passage which, in a tonal context, would most certainly point towards D minor; here it tends to emphasise C♯ and D from *encircled D*, as we might have noticed from the embedded statement in Example 2. This pentachordal vocal phrase is supported in the piano by a tetrachordal subset – {C♯, D, E, F}, spaced to emphasise D. Moreover, this D emphasis continues strongly because of the reiteration of the 'von kindischem Wähnen' motive in the piano: on the downbeat of b. 4 the {C♯, D, E, F} tetrachord is stated in a lower register, its spacing expanded and a doubled pitch class A added, all of which further emphasise D. Finally, at the end of the bar the complete 'von kindischem Wähnen' triplet vocal motive from b. 3 is now stated in piano, the bass supporting this with a partial *encircled D* – contra E♭ moving to d, this statement followed immediately by a truncated echo in the next bar.

We look now at the middle section: bs 6–7. At least three unique events articulate the arrival of this section: first, the lowest note of the piece occurs in piano; second, the echo and forecast technique becomes a near doubling of voice and piano for the first and only time;[8] and finally, the section starts with a retrograde of the first four pitch classes of section A1–D, D♭, E♭, G♭ – with the register of the two middle pcs changed (to produce an entirely new contour), all set in a rhythm such that the accent –

[8] This technique leads Adorno to speak of 'the inexact unison': see Theodor A. Adorno, *Der getreue Korrepetitor* (Frankfurt: Fischer Verlag, 1963), p. 105.

*Mor*gengärten – falls on *encircled D*. At this point, the piano left hand begins its most active passage of the composition, a rhythmic acceleration of the first vocal phrase of the middle section, in which *encircled D* is easily the most prominent element, reiterating its function as head motive of this section, just as it had been the *vocal* head motive in the opening section. Indeed, a look at the score will show that *encircled D* is repeated six times during this passage, its registration leading to the effect of the 'D pedal' throughout the section upon which Adorno has remarked.[9] Twice it is embellished with the neighbour note E, effectively expanding *encircled D* to {C♯, D, E♭, E}; this is also consistent with the vocal part, for when its second phrase (b. 7) – a truncated $T_1$ of the first phrase – is taken in combination with the first, the union of the two-line-register sighs yields the same tetrachord: compare 'Morgen-' in b. 6 with 'leichtbe-' in b. 7. Finally, the last repetition of *encircled D* in the piano ends on a chord containing doubled C♯ against D, which functions as the transition to the refrain, and can be heard as the completion of the piano's truncated 'kindischem Wähnen' echo of b. 5, which was the transition to the B section.

The role of *encircled D* in the refrain approximately parallels its role in the opening A section, although of course the piano now leads the canonic succession, and the 'pedal' G♯ is now subposed beneath the piano part. In essence then, *encircled D* begins life as a foreground detail, though, as head motive, it is certainly an immediately perceptible one. It then acquires quasi-'middleground' status as the generator of transpositional levels for the first-section phrases. In the middle section, it seems to penetrate yet deeper into the composition, as a 'pedal' and potential generator of harmony for a whole section. Yet it is undercut in the refrain by the G♯ pedal, and ultimately the notion of a 'D minor tonality' is problematic.

## II

Let us look now at the second song, in which *encircled D* is used quite differently.[10] In contrast to the reprise form of no. 1, this song, in its overall

[9] Ibid., p. 103.

[10] I have discussed this song in 'Remnants of tonality in Webern's Op.3/2', *Mitteilungen der Paul Sacher Stiftung* 4 (1991), pp. 27–30.

effect, is a single musical gesture of continuous, gathering intensity – what one commentator has aptly called a *Steigerungsform.*[11] This is most clearly evident in the use of dynamics (from the ***ppp*** of b. 1 to the ***ff*** of b. 10), the gradual expansion of register (culminating in the a$^2$ of the voice, and the piano's contra E in b. 9 and b♭$^3$ in b. 10), and in textural density, which again reaches its maximum in b. 9 with the piano's octaves: these enter here for the first and only time.

| | | |
|---|---|---|
| **Im windes-weben** | a | In the murmering wind |
| **War meine frage** | b | my question was but a dream |
| **Nur träumerei.** | c | Only a smile |
| **Nur lächeln war** | d | was what you gave me. |
| **Was du gegeben.** | a | From a damp night |
| **Aus nasser nacht** | e ? | radiance was kindled – |
| **Ein glanz entfacht –** | e | now May wakens desire. |
| **Nun drängt der mai.** | c | For your eyes and hair |
| **Nun muss ich gar** | d | I must now |
| **Um dein aug und haar** | d | live in longing |
| **Alle tage** | b | all my days. |
| **In sehnen leben.** | a | |

Figure 2 Stefan George, *Der siebente Ring*, no. 2

Despite its singularity of gesture, both the text (given in Figure 2) and the musical motivic structure may be seen to articulate a division into two parts, though the exact dividing point is not immediately clear. With respect to the idea content of the text, the first part of the poem is delicate and playful, while the second presses forward in earnest; moreover, while in the first part the poem is broken up by three marks of punctuation, the second is broken by only a single comma.[12] The first rhyming pair – 'Nacht' and '-facht' – articulates the midpoint, at which point George inserts the dash (and Webern inserts the *rit. . .accel. . .*: bs 6–7). But are we to divide the poem between seventh and eighth lines, sixth and seventh, or even fifth and sixth? Punctuation seems to suggest this last alternative, though the neater

11 Rolf Urs Ringger, *Anton Weberns Klavierlieder* (Zürich: Juris Druck Verlag, 1968), pp. 19ff.

12 Ibid., p. 20.

**Example 3**

division into halves yields an attractive free retrograde of end-rhymes. In the musical setting, Webern in fact divides the vocal line between the seventh and eighth lines, but the accompaniment presents the motivic material of the second section, in effect starting that section, while the voice is singing the seventh line. This use of phrase and section overlapping between voice and piano is utterly basic to Webern's compositional technique.

The *Hauptmotiv* of the first half of the piece, labelled *a* in Example 3, is a 'C♯ minor triad' in the directed-interval pattern <+9,–5>. It first enters with its $T_1$ imitation ('D minor') delayed by a semiquaver, a motivic complex we shall designate $a$+$T_1a$, which is shown in Example 3b. In b. 1, after the initial presentation, a variant occurs, whereupon the final semiquaver of the bar presents a 'chord' of four pitches (*in register*) extracted from the initial $a$+$T_1a$. Beginning on the second semiquaver of the second beat of b. 2, we find the complex transposed up a half step: $T_1(a+T_1a)$. Of course, this reading of the upper line assumes that we group the 'alto' F with the 'D minor triad' continuation: in that case the B♭ continues on to complete the 'E♭ minor triad'. Webern in fact stems the piano part according to this reading in an earlier version.[13] (In this version the passage begins up an octave on the second semiquaver of the first beat, where the right hand presents $T_1$ of the variant five-note figure from b. 1.)

In the opening bars, the voice is distinctly secondary to its accompaniment, *a* and its derivatives appearing only in the piano. But by b. 3 piano and voice begin to reverse roles, the piano right hand imitating the opening vocal line. In b. 4 the voice takes the new ('E♭ minor') transposition of *a* for the first time: <+9,–5>. It continues with <+5,–9> ('B minor') – an embellished (and transposed) retrograde, starting on the common f♯[1] (g♭[1]), while the piano left hand states *a* one last time at the *original* transposition: 'C♯ minor'.

13 Sacher Stiftung microfilm: 101–0097.

Example 4

The second section (end of b. 6ff) is articulated by the vocal cadence at the end of the bar – the only melodic appearance of *encircled D*. The *Hauptmotiv* (*b*) of this section, associated with the text 'nun drängt der Mai', is the appropriately pressing, upward motion shown in two forms (*b*1+*b*2) in Example 4a and b. In a composition hardly marked by repetition, the span comprising the last beat of b. 6 to the first two beats of b. 8 – relatively long, given the dimensions of the piece – is striking indeed: virtually the entire piano part is taken up with insistent repetitions of the complex *b*1+*b*2. From an intervallic point of view the relationship between *a* and *b*2 is clear: <+2,+7> fills in the +9 ascent of *a*. And, from the point of view of pitch class, if we were to ask just what this repeated pitch material might have to do with *a*, it is not difficult to hear the direct reference back to $T_1(a+T_1a)$ illustrated in Example 5.[14]

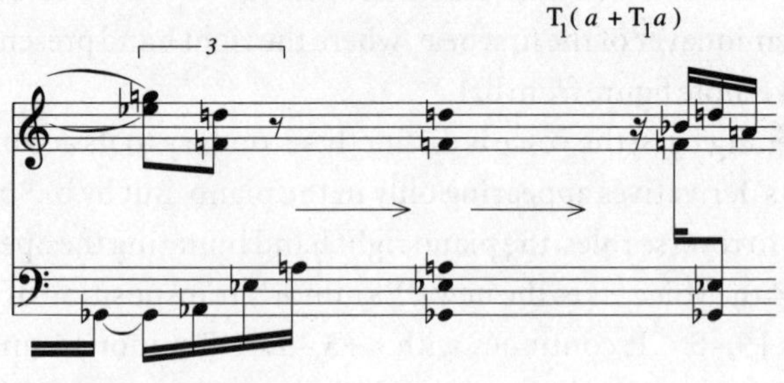


Example 5

[14] This hearing also explains the genesis of *b*'s <+2, +7> in *a*'s <+9>; in that case, *b*2 proves to be a 'filled out' version of *a*.

Noting the sequential transposition of *b*1 that characterises the piano part in b. 8, beats 2–4, we might also ask: why this *particular* transpositional network? After all, given the properties inherent in the [0136] tetrachordal type produced by *b*1's <+2,+7,+6>, a continuous $T_4$ network would have yielded all twelve notes – a typically 'Webernian' move, one might imagine. (Transposing the last four semiquavers in b. 8 down a semitone produces precisely this transpositional network, and hence all twelve pitch classes.) But the actual music uses the 'tonal' transposition network, $T_4$ to $T_5$, thus replicating the 'E♭ minor sixth chord' of $T_1(a+T_1a)$, and emphasising the motivic G♭–E♭. This also means that the last tetrachord repeats pitch classes E♭, C and F♯, placing the E♭ and F♯ in particularly emphasised rhythmic and registral positions, respectively.

Parts of b. 9 and all of 10 (in the piano) present various transpositions of the familiar *b*1. Why *these* transpositions? Indeed, an earlier version of the piece differs precisely on this point: the last three presentations of *b*1 occur at different transpositional levels from the final version.[15] Why might Webern have revised this ending? By now the question has become rhetorical: certainly the contra B♭, e♭$^1$, f♯$^2$ and b♭$^3$ in piano (all missing in the earlier version), together with the e♭$^2$, g♭$^1$, f$^1$ of the voice, reiterate one last time the importance of $T_1(a+T_1a)$.

In contrast to the first song, the second contains only one contiguous melodic statement of *encircled D* – an important one, to be sure, since it serves to articulate the two-part division in the vocal part. But more important still is the transformation of *encircled D* into a nearly ubiquitous 'harmonic' idea – a network of C♯, D and E♭ minor triads. The explanation of the workings of this network given here invokes transposition of hexachords that 'freeze' C♯ minor + D minor, and D minor + E♭ minor. In particular, the registral disposition of the D minor component of $T_1(a+T_1a)$ (in b. 2) seemed to call for such an explanation; moreover, transposition – and indeed transposition by T=1 – replicated the process by which $a+T_1a$ itself initially arose. Yet, at another level the work calls to mind a D minor centred between upper and lower minor seconds, recalling Lewin's description of 'inversional balance', a primary trait of Schoenberg's music and thought

15 This is presumably the 'korrigierte Frühfassung' mentioned briefly by Budde: see *Anton Weberns Lieder Op.3*, p. 14. It is now in the Sacher Stiftung (microfilm: 101–0129/31).

throughout his career.[16] An early example was certainly familiar to Webern in 1908: the recently composed *Kammersymphonie*, Op.9, in which such tonal centring is apparent in both local and long-range structure. But, again, to call *this* piece tonal certainly seems far-fetched.

## III

Let us now examine the role of *encircled D* in song 3.[17] Glancing at b. 6 to the beginning of 9 we note the analogy with the first song: once again it appears that the accompaniment gravitates to a D pedal (C♯/E♭ are in the alto) throughout what might appear to be a middle section. But things are not that simple: in contrast to the model of formal and structural clarity presented by the first song, the third is perhaps the most difficult of the five to interpret. No clear part-form emerges from the music, and at first glance the text likewise seems to yield no obvious grouping – at least by rhyme scheme (see the text in Figure 3).

| | | |
|---|---|---|
| An baches ranft | a | By the edge of the brook, |
| Die einzigen frühen | b | early, alone, |
| Die hasel blühen. | b | the hazels bloom. |
| Ein vogel pfeift | c | A bird whistles |
| In kühler au. | d | in the cool meadow. |
| Ein leuchten streift | c | Brightness touches us, |
| Erwärmt uns sanft | a | warms us gently, |
| Und zuckt und bleicht. | c | quivers and pales. |
| Das feld ist brach. | e | The field lies fallow, |
| Der baum noch grau . . | d | the tree is still grey . . . |
| Blumen streut vielleicht | c | Perhaps spring |
| Der lenz uns nach. | e | will strew flowers after us. |

Figure 3 Stefan George, *Der siebente Ring*, no. 3

16 David Lewin, 'Inversional balance as an organizing force in Schoenberg's music and thought', *Perspectives of New Music* 6/2 (1967/8), pp. 1–21.

17 Elizabeth West Marvin and I discuss this song from a somewhat different point of view in our article, 'On preparing Anton Webern's early songs for performance: a collaborators' dialogue', *Theory and Practice* (forthcoming).

Fortunately, George's punctuation – preserved in the published song – gives us an important clue. It clearly articulates an asymmetrical division of 3+2+3+4 lines: the first three divisions are marked by full stops, while the last four-line group may itself be divided further according to the lower-level comma and ellipsis. Moreover, the idea content of the poem seems to parallel this grouping, pointing to an overall division of the poem into two irregular parts, or 5+7 lines: in the objective first part, an anonymous narrative sets the bucolic scene, while the subjective second part concerns itself primarily with memories and hopes, expressed in the first person. Yet, lest we become over-confident, the last four lines seem to recapitulate the dualism, though it can be argued that once the protagonist enters the poem, he or she may well be the speaker of 'Das Feld ist brach' etc.

**Example 6**

Looking now at the music, we begin by noting the [0148] tetrachord-type that opens the vocal line {F, B♭, F♯, D}, an inverted form of which is immediately picked up and repeated in the piano – in this case, as {D♯, E, G, B}. The end of this repetition, in b. 3, coincides with the end of the third text line, and the first punctuation of the text: in fact, lines two and three are the only contiguous rhyming pair in the poem; of course, *that* is the point of the repeated piano right hand, which, together with the clear motivic reference shown in Example 6 – the motivic segment <+1,–2,–1,–10> in the voice ('die einzigen frühen / hasel blühen') is rhythmically altered and transposed by $T_{-1}$ – articulates this rhyme clearly.

'Ein Vogel pfeift' then picks up the exact three-note motive from the opening of the song to articulate the next two text lines, which cadence at 'kühler Au'. But, just as in the second song, the piano seems to overlap the vocal material, this time with far more ambiguous results. The crux of the problem is centred in b. 5: while the voice clearly starts the new section here, with its wide, sighing descents, the piano is ambivalent. Is b. 5 the cadence of the first section of the piece, or the beginning of the second? Both the

**Example 7**

very different texture in piano from the third beat of b. 3 to b. 5, and the close analogy between the piano chords in b. 5 and the last piano chord of the piece seem to articulate this as a section in the piano. Indeed, Example 7 shows an early draft of this same music, in which this structural articulation was even clearer: the bass notes (later liquidated) differentiated the piano music from previous material more radically, and the final chords of the piece were, except for the D♯, $T_{-7}$ of the b. 5 'half cadence'.[18] But, on the other hand, it is not difficult to hear the C♯–B soprano of b. 5 as the *opening* presentation of a motive that is continued and elaborated in b. 6, at which point *encircled D* arrives to define the next section more clearly.

Needless to say, much more might be said concerning the form of this piece, but this will have to suffice to introduce the music we are mainly concerned with in the present investigation: the piano part in b. 6 to the first part of 10. Example 8 attempts to show the workings of this passage in more detail.

[18] Brinkmann discusses this, and shows examples from the earlier versions in 'Die George-Lieder', pp. 48f.

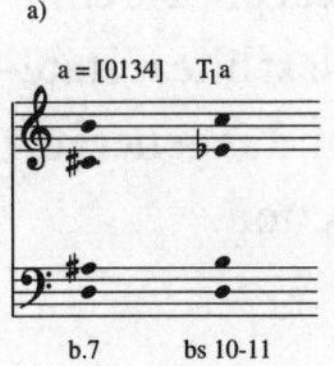


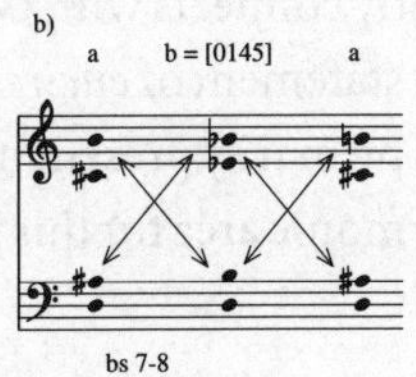


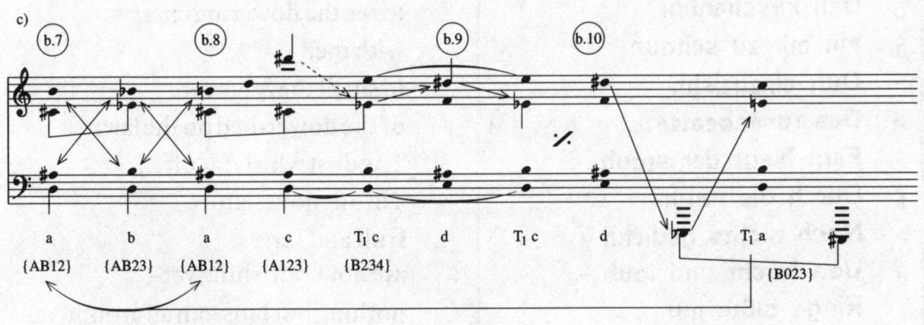


**Example 8**

Four tetrachordal types are involved, here labelled a to d. Example 8a shows that the passage as a whole can be regarded as a motion from an instance of tetrachord-type a [0134], here reified as D, A♯, C♯, B (spelling from bass upwards) to $T_1$ of this pitch-class collection, respaced of course to preserve the pedal D. Example 8b shows type a's initial move to type b, and thence back to a; the arrows show the characteristic Webern voice-exchanges, effectively confining change of pitch class to C♯–E♭–C♯. Example 8c shows that between the initial type a tetrachord and the final $T_1$a, type c [0125] plays the most important longer-range role: during b. 8, type c, reified as D, A♯, C♯, D♯, moves to $T_1$c, which then alternates with d [0127] in quasi neighbour-note fashion. The dominance of $T_1$c is not really in doubt, however, until d's 'deceptive' resolution to $T_1$a at the end of the passage. The stems show that through all of this, *encircled D* is divided between the bass and alto. While chords a and b were characterised by the C♯/E♭ motion, chord c contains all three components of *encircled D*; $T_1$c preserves pcs D and D♯, and part of d's neighbour effect is that it only preserves D♯, which is eventually transferred to the piano's lowest register, where it subsequently connects with C♯. Finally, the last vocal phrase commences with a clear statement of *encircled D*. Except for this last linear statement, *encircled D* is primarily present in the D pedal point, and as generator of a contrasting harmonic area for this part of the middle section.

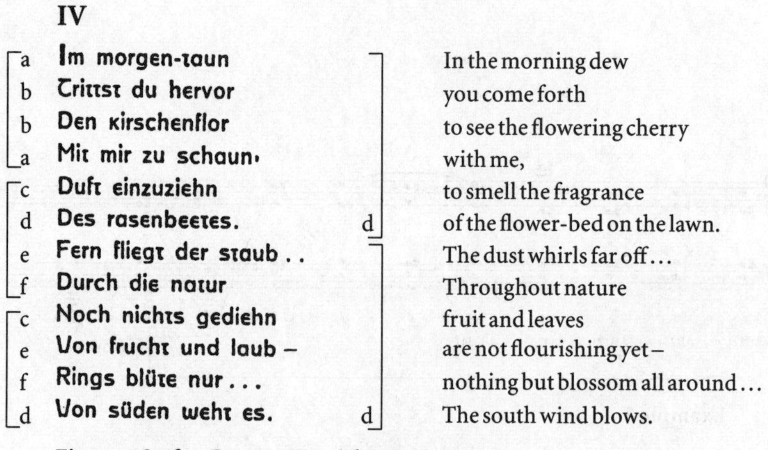

IV
a Im morgen-taun
b Trittst du hervor
b Den kirschenflor
a Mit mir zu schaun.
c Duft einzuziehn
d Des rasenbeetes. d
e Fern fliegt der staub . .
f Durch die natur
c Noch nichts gediehn
e Von frucht und laub –
f Rings blüte nur . . .
d Von süden weht es. d
In the morning dew
you come forth
to see the flowering cherry
with me,
to smell the fragrance
of the flower-bed on the lawn.
The dust whirls far off . . .
Throughout nature
fruit and leaves
are not flourishing yet –
nothing but blossom all around . . .
The south wind blows.


**Figure 4** Stefan George, *Der siebente Ring*, no. 4

In song 4, *encircled D* appears only linearly, and in only two places. These two appearances are extremely important, however, for they are crucial to the overall formal articulation of the piece. Figure 4 gives the text of this song, with analytical notes. As indicated, the structure of the text is unusually clear: by virtue of rhyme-scheme, the poem divides into three groups of four lines (abba, cdef, cefd – the last group permuting end-rhyme d of the second group). Yet the division by punctuation cuts across this, articulating two groups of six lines, a division further supported by the placement of end-rhyme d, and the precisely matching iambic dimetre of lines 6 ('Des Rasenbeetes') and 12 ('Von Süden weht es').

In approaching the form of the music, it appears that we might read it in three parts, which do not correspond at all to the three-part text reading: bs 0–4, 5–6 and 7–10.[19] The piano chords of the opening, which we shall

[19] Budde, *Anton Weberns Lieder Op.3*, pp. 69–70.

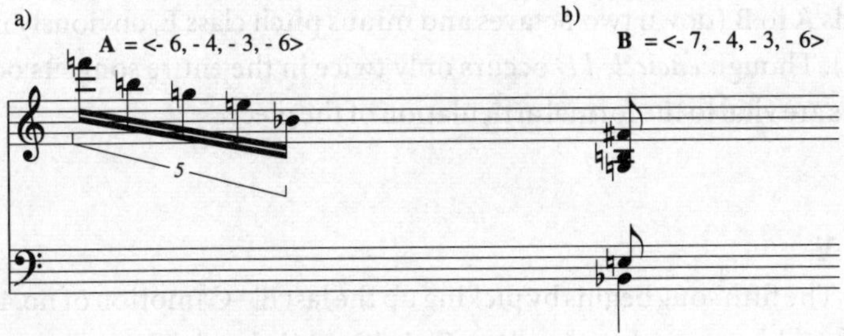


**Example 9**

label **A** (<–6,–4,–3,–6>) and **B** (<–7,–4,–3,–6>), respectively (see Example 9), turn out to be important formal markers. While the three sections are articulated reasonably clearly by the tempo indications *Fließend*, *Mäßig* and *Etwas langsamer als zu Beginn*, the exact onset of the second part remains problematic: the *ritard* in b. 3, together with the vocal fermata and piano arpeggio, tend towards closing this section, as does the subsequent descending arpeggiation in the voice, which brings back piano chord **B** at $T_1$ (up an octave). Moreover, the middle section is characterised by the piano's further accelerations of chords **A** and **B**, concatenated and overlapped, and these clearly begin in b. 4, not in b. 5.

Bar 4 is thus of extraordinary interest: the middle section begins here in the piano, but the voice seems to overlap with an ending to the first section. To complicate matters further, in b. 4 the music of 'Rasenbeetes' – directed intervals <–2,+1,–2> – at 'Fern fliegt der Staub' (bs 5–6) is transformed into <–1,+2,–1>; then the pitch content from this statement is retained, while the directed intervals return to <–2,+1> – the original form – with 'Durch die Na-', and finally '–tur' brings back the +5 of 'des Ras-' from the end of b. 3. All of this tends to articulate vocal bs 4–7 as a unified span cutting across the three-part form defined earlier.

By now the reader will have noticed that there are only two vocal bars in the entire piece characterised by *exact* repetition (bs 4 and 10, with their upbeats), and these actually *support* one of the formal readings we saw in our study of the text: composed of expanded *encircled D* (in *precisely* the form it took during the middle section of the first song), they articulate the division of the poem in halves through rhyming sixth and twelfth lines. To underscore this, the setting of line 12 brings back the succession of piano chords **A** to **B** (down two octaves and minus pitch class E, obviously in the voice). Though *encircled D* occurs only twice in the entire song, its occurrences are vital to the formal articulation of the piece.

## V

The fifth song begins by picking up the last E♭–C♯ motion of no. 4, this time 'reaching over' the C♯ with an E♮, in 'frozen', chordal form, in response to the text: 'Kahl reckt der baum / im Winterdunst / sein frierend Leben'. The frozen effect is that much more pronounced as a result of the voice exchanges that occur between the first two chords: a [01346]-type pentachord moves to a [01347]-type (here the literal chords happen to correspond to prime forms of set-types) through contrary motion exchange of four notes, while the lone F♯ of the inner voice moves to G, as is shown in Example 10a. Example 10b shows the four-note subset in common between the two pentachords, which is pitch-class symmetrical around D – and here registrally symmetrical around an (unstated) octave $d^1$ to $d^2$. We shall refer to this collection as chord **X**. The introduction of the bass F immediately after the two pentachords almost completes the filling of chromatic space from C to G, except for the missing pitch class D. Indeed, D is the last pitch class to enter the piece, and its first entrance in the piano in b. 3 is tentative – as a quasi neighbour, in an inner part. But in b. 4 D suddenly takes on extraordinary importance, appearing in no less than three registers, two of which might be taken as the 'fulfilment' of the registrally symmetrical chord **X**. Moreover, D is repeated in the piano, and is the melodic goal of both voice and piano. This 'putting-off' of D will have important implications later, as we shall see.

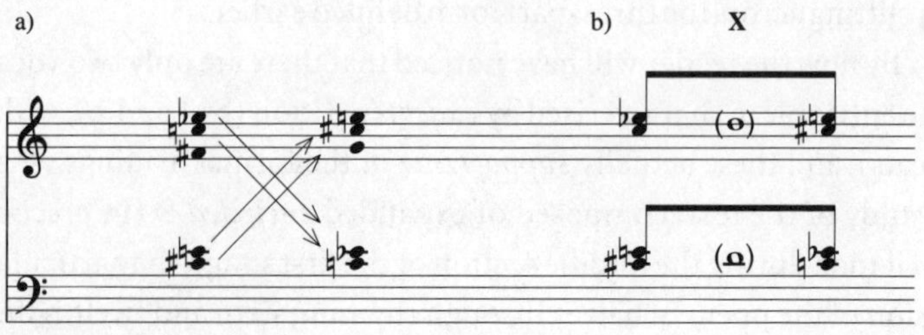


**Example 10**

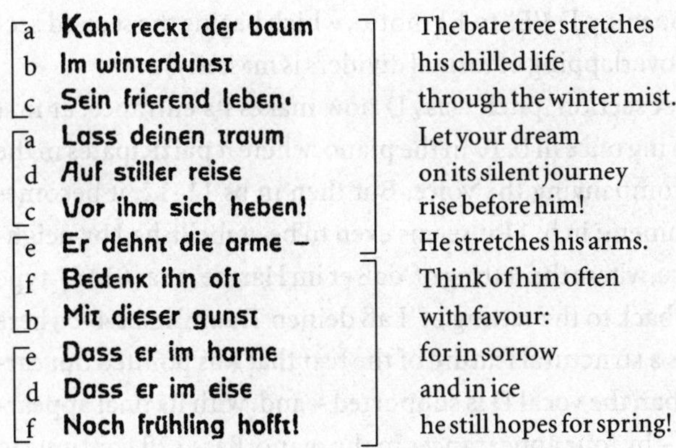

| | | |
|---|---|---|
| a | Kahl reckt der baum | The bare tree stretches |
| b | Im winterdunst | his chilled life |
| c | Sein frierend leben. | through the winter mist. |
| a | Lass deinen traum | Let your dream |
| d | Auf stiller reise | on its silent journey |
| c | Vor ihm sich heben! | rise before him! |
| e | Er dehnt die arme – | He stretches his arms. |
| f | Bedenk ihn oft | Think of him often |
| b | Mit dieser gunst | with favour: |
| e | Dass er im harme | for in sorrow |
| d | Dass er im eise | and in ice |
| f | Noch frühling hofft! | he still hopes for spring! |

Figure 5 Stefan George, *Der siebente Ring*, no.5

Once again we deal with the overall form of the piece, turning first to the text, given in Figure 5. Viewed in isolation, its form seems relatively clear: division into four groups of three lines, and thus into two halves of six lines each. Such a division is supported by end-rhyme scheme and punctuation in the first half, and in the second half by end rhymes and by the opening 'daß' of lines 9 and 10, which links with 'Laß' of line 4. Moreover, line 7, 'Er dehnt die Arme –', rephrases the content of line 1, 'Kahl reckt der Baum', creating a correspondence between the openings of the two sections.

Now let us return to the music and examine Webern's interpretation of the poem. Clearly, he also reads the poem in two large parts, but what we have taken to be the possible beginning of a B section, Webern transforms instead into the dramatic climax of the A section (in b. 8), and indeed of the piece as a whole. Chord X returns in b. 7, where it is embellished by neighbours, building to its *forte* statement at the climax in b. 8, together with bass F (from the opening), down two octaves, to produce the widest registral span of the piece, as the tree 'extends its arms'. (This lowest note of the piece will end the second section as well, with, however, important differences in effect.) The dissolution of the climax is then an arpeggiated statement of the complete pitch content of the first two pentachords (the C/F♯ tritone from the first, the C♯/G from the second), which also echoes the rhythm of 'Er dehnt die Arme' (moreover, the pitch-class material has four of five notes in common with 'Er dehnt die Arme,' permuted so that the piano seems to fill in the C–G space of 'Arme'). This dwindles down to the ***ppp*** statement of the opening D♯/E♭ to E♮ motto, which begins the second section (as usual, the overlapping of formal dividers is masterly).

As in the first section, pitch class D now makes its entrance, at first tentatively, appearing once in b. 10 in the piano, where it participates in the parallel sixths accompanying the voice. But then in bs 11–12, it becomes increasingly prominent: in b. 11 it seems even to be embellished by neighbour E♭ in the voice, where the setting of 'daß er im Harme', to a [0145]-type tetrachord, refers back to the setting of 'Laß deinen Traum' in bs 4–5 (here Webern reinforces a structural feature of the text that was pointed out earlier). In the same bar, the vocal D is supported – and, with its final appearance, even tripled – by four appearances in the piano. Bars 12ff continue to emphasise D: first, 'daß er im Eise / noch Frühling hofft!' repeats the previous 'daß er im' setting, but then goes on to extend the line past the previous E♭ neighbour, to F (which is embellished) and thence to A, yielding a full-blown D-minor arpeggiation. This, however, is undercut by the B♭/B♮ that begin and end the soprano in bs 11, 12 and 13. Moreover, that B♭ continues to be strong in the piano's tenor part from b. 12 to the end: though it seems to vacillate between upper and lower neighbours, B♭ ultimately prevails. At the same time, we observe that the piano's bass presents a strong D in b. 12 (echoed and supported by the piano right hand), and then arpeggiated motions of D–F in the remaining music.

A number of authors have noticed that this piece seems to be more tonal-sounding than other songs of Op.3, particularly towards the end. Before the publication of Webern's lieder without opus numbers, this apparently came as something of a shock. Indeed, Adorno,[20] convinced that the development towards modernity must proceed inexorably in an unbroken line, finds the 'negative highpoint' of Op.3 in the whisper at the close of the fourth song; thus the fifth marks a 'step backwards [and] could have been written earlier than the other songs', an opinion with which other progressive-minded authors, like Karkoschka, concur.[21] Ringger goes on to claim

[20] Adorno, *Der getreue Korrepetitor*, p. 114.

[21] In speculating about the possible chronology of composition, Erhard Karkoschka thinks that the last song was likely the first composed; he also places the first song near the beginning of composition, while the third and fourth he believes occurred nearer the end: Erhard Karkoschka, 'Studien zur Entwicklung der Kompositionstechnik im Frühwerk Anton Weberns' (Ph.D. dissertation, Tübingen, 1959), p. 45.

that it is the 'most traditionally structured of all twenty Lieder' that Webern wrote[22] (of course, the early works were unknown at the time this was written).

When it comes to describing just why the piece evokes tonal expectations, and just what those expectations are, however, there has been less than general agreement. 'With its unresolved suspension chord, [the piece] gets close to F major at the end', Adorno says,[23] but in making this remark, he, like others, has been drawn to the obvious foreground F major of b. 13, while missing the underlying implied tonality of the whole (which Ringger seems to have been the first to understand).[24] For that transitory bright spot – F major, which so beautifully coincides with the vocal high A, ***ppp*** – is the hope of spring, which, in the end, must inevitably sink back into the reality of winter: D minor, the strongly-implied harmonic context for this song, which in turn is present embryonically in *encircled D* throughout the opus. Thus, in the final harmony, the B♭ and E have the effect of unresolved suspensions, while the bass, F, acts just as it does at the beginning of this song, at the cadence in b. 8, and, we might add, as it did at the end of no.3: as a kind of scale-step III, a surrogate of the tonic, and in the present instance, a surrogate consonant bass.

## VI

Though the significance of D minor with respect to Webern's Op.3 may remain an object of some controversy, there is mounting evidence of the extraordinary importance of this tonality to the members of the Second Viennese School in general. The peculiarly large number of D minor, or at least 'D minorish', pieces has long been known – pieces such as the Webern Passacaglia, Schoenberg's *Pelleas*, *Verklärte Nacht* and First Quartet or, to move to less secure territory, Berg's *Der Wein*, or even the Schoenberg Fourth Quartet (at least, according to Sessions). Recently, David Schroeder has pointed to the connection with Strindberg, in whose works D minor

22 Ringger, *Klavierlieder*, p. 46.

23 Adorno, *Der getreue Korrepetitor*, p. 114.

24 Ringger, *Klavierlieder*, p. 46.

plays an important role,[25] and while, as mentioned, Reinhold Brinkmann has shown isolated instances of *encircled D* in Schoenberg's Op.11/2 and Op.15/13, Steve Larson has attempted to construct a D minor tonal model for the complete music of Op.15 no.2 – the opus which was very likely the direct inspiration of Webern's George Lieder.[26]

Besides this larger connection, *encircled D* and an implied D minor also bear on one of the perennial questions in the study of Webern's *Klavierlieder*: to what extent can any of these five collections be referred to as cycles? Webern, it seems, did not help the case for cyclic interpretation when, in a letter to Willi Reich, he suggested performing isolated songs extracted from three early opuses, recommending that Reich put together a programme for performance in Basel consisting of Op.3 nos.1 and 5, Op.4 no.4 *or* 1 and Op.12 nos.1 and 4.[27]

While all of the *Klavierlieder* offer problems with respect to this question, the George lieder, Opp.3 and 4, are particularly problematic. For one thing, it is impossible to know for sure that either opus was conceived as a group, or that the songs therein were composed in close proximity to one another. Though the manuscripts bear the date '1908–09', the individual songs are undated; we will know the chronology only when someone is able to date the manuscripts, and the chances of that occurring appear bleak, at best. Moreover, Moldenhauer's publication, in the early 1970s, of four additional George lieder along with Webern's other plans for grouping the total of fourteen songs, has made it seem that there is nothing sacrosanct about the internal ordering of these songs.[28] Apparently Webern at one point thought of publishing them in two groups of seven each as Opp.2 and 4. In fact this plan was only one of a number of projected groupings; the evidence of other groupings, however, is fragmentary, and thus it is impossible to reconstruct the complete evolution of the final ordering. Yet, it seems significant that of all the George lieder, the definitive ordering appeared in print

25 David Schroeder, 'Berg, Strindberg and D Minor', paper given at National Conference of the American Musicological Society, Austin, 1989.

26 Steve Larson, 'A tonal model of an "atonal" piece: Schoenberg's Opus 15, number 2', *Perspectives of New Music* 25 (1987), pp. 418–33.

27 Anton Webern, *The Path to the New Music*, ed. Willi Reich, trans. Leo Black (Bryn Mawr: Theodore Presser, 1963), p. 58.

28 Budde, *Anton Weberns Lieder Op.3*, pp. 12ff.

first with the five of Op.3: published in 1919 in the grouping we know now through the auspices of the Verein für musikalische Privataufführungen, Op.3 appeared two years before any of the early works published by Universal, and four years before Op.4. Might this mean that Webern was convinced earlier on that the five songs of Op.3 truly worked as a group?

I would answer a cautious yes, and despite apparently compelling evidence against conceiving of these pieces as cycles I would argue that the evidence in favour of such an interpretation is stronger in the case of Op.3 than in any of the other *Klavierlieder* of Webern before the Jone settings. The secondary literature generally agrees that the order of tempos – slow, fast, and then a gradual deceleration to a very slow ending – contributes greatly to this unified impression.[29] But while the unity of the text has also been recognised, it has been insufficiently emphasised: the textual sources of the fourteen songs are George's *Das Buch der Sagen und Sänge* (1895), *Das Jahr der Seele* (1897) and *Der siebente Ring* (1907). Op.4 contains songs from all three of these sources, and the order in which they occur is different from their ordering in George's works. The texts of Op.3, on the other hand, are all taken from *Der siebente Ring*, a work which had appeared very recently when Webern composed these pieces, and likely would have made a deep, and fresh, impression on the composer at this time. Furthermore, the order of songs in Op.3 corresponds *precisely* to the order of texts in *Der siebente Ring*: the five texts are the first five of a group of six, designated 'Lieder I–VI' by George.[30]

Now, could this parallel between George's ordering of the texts and their final ordering by Webern indicate close proximity for the composition of these songs? This time a more cautious yes; but after all, it seems likely that Webern would have set George's lieder in continuity; moreover, Webern may well have experimented with various orderings *later on*, after having composed all fourteen songs, only to return to his initial conception for publication.

[29] Karkoschka, 'Entwicklung der Kompositionstechnik', pp. 39–40; Ringger, *Klavierlieder*, p. 47.

[30] Stefan George, *Der siebente Ring* (Berlin: Georg Bondi, n.d. [1927]), pp. 157–62. It is unclear why Webern did not set the sixth poem, although it is interesting to note that this last poem, consisting of sixteen lines (as does the 'Vorklang' that precedes the six poems), departs from the structure of the others in the set.

Finally, it seems to me that the presence of *encircled D* gives additional evidence of closeness in compositional chronology for the songs of Op.3. While *encircled D* seems to play a negligible role in the other nine George lieder (with one possible exception), we have seen its strong presence in these five songs. Might it have been a subconscious musical idea – something that was just on Webern's compositional mind, so to speak, during the writing of these five songs? I leave this last question for the reader to ponder, but whether this is the case or not, the transformations of *encircled D* support the textual affinities and long-range tempo structure, helping to imbue this cycle with the greatest cohesiveness and unity of effect of any of Webern's pre-twelve-note works for voice and piano.

# 5 Performance and revision: the early history of Webern's Four Pieces for violin and piano, Op.7

FELIX MEYER AND ANNE SHREFFLER[1]

Webern's Four Pieces for violin and piano, Op.7, composed in 1910 and published in 1922, represent a radical re-thinking of the traditional violin sonata, transforming its form and structure as well as the usual relationships between the two instruments. Between the first sound, an unaccompanied harmonic e♭$^3$, and the final gesture of the fourth piece, which descends almost three octaves from d$^4$, *am Steg, wie ein Hauch*, the violin scarcely ever produces a 'normal' tone. The first and third pieces – static, slowly unfolding miniatures, saturated with ostinatos – are among the first of Webern's aphorisms; these continue the process of miniaturisation that began in 1909 (with Op.5 nos.2 and 4 and Op.6 no.3) and culminated five years later with the minute Three Pieces for violoncello and piano, Op.11. Yet Op.7 also contains two longer movements, whose densely motivic, athematic writing calls for a wide range of dynamics and playing techniques. These techniques – many of them quite new in 1910 – produce the variety of timbres that plays such a crucial role. As Theodor W. Adorno remarked: 'The guiding principle of interpretation is to develop the timbres from their structural function. This is complicated by Webern's confrontation with an openly unsatisfactory aspect of the entire tradition of chamber music with piano: the widely divergent sounds of piano and strings. Webern tries to correct this by making the usual violin and piano combinations exceptional.'[2]

[1] The authors collaborated on every aspect of the research and writing of this essay.

[2] 'Oberste Regel der Darstellung ist, die Koloristik aus der strukturellen Funktion zu entwickeln. Erschwerend tritt hinzu, daß Webern einem offen Unbefriedigenden der gesamten Tradition von Kammermusik mit Klavier sich

The fact that Adorno's comments on Op.7 take the form of performance notes reflects its status as one of Webern's most often-performed works. While Webern's music was played very little before the 1920s, the Four Pieces have enjoyed a continuous performance history which began soon after their composition in 1910. Perhaps because of this history, many sources for Op.7 have survived (again, exceptionally among Webern's works from this period), including two autograph violin parts, whose very existence is remarkable in a circle that later insisted on performing chamber music from score. After the first performance in 1911, Webern substantially revised the work, achieving what he called a definitive version in 1914. An early version of the first piece appeared in *Der Ruf* in March 1912; this was Webern's first publication. Later revisions coincided with a series of performances in the Verein für musikalische Privataufführungen between 1919 and 1921. Plans for the 1922 publication by Universal Edition brought on a final round of editing and polishing.

Webern regularly revised his works, especially those written before 1921, when regular publication of his music with Universal Edition began. In many cases, the long delay between composition and publication led to substantial changes. Elsewhere we have treated other aspects of Webern's revisions: their historical context and analytical implications, and the aesthetic shift that led him to make the changes.[3] Here we shall focus on the revisions that arose in the unusual case of an often-performed work.

While many of the revisions of Op.7 resemble those made in other works, Webern's practice is noteworthy here in several respects. First, there is a tendency to clarify 'noisy' or unpitched sounds; while this can be

stellt, der Divergenz zwischen dem Pianoforteklang und dem der Streicher. Webern sucht das zu korrigieren, indem er die herkömmlichen Kombinationstypen von Violine und Klavier zur Ausnahme macht.' Theodor W. Adorno, 'Anton Webern: Vier Stücke für Geige und Klavier op.7', in *Der getreue Korrepetitor* (Frankfurt a.M.: Fischer, 1963), p. 153.

3 Felix Meyer, 'Im Zeichen der Reduktion: Quellenkritische und analytische Bemerkungen zu Anton Weberns Rilke-Liedern op.8', in Hans Oesch, ed., *Quellenstudien I* (Winterthur: Amadeus Verlag, 1991), pp. 53–100; Felix Meyer and Anne C. Shreffler, 'Webern's revisions: some analytical implications', *Music Analysis* 12 (1993), pp. 355–80; Meyer and Shreffler, 'Rewriting history: Webern's revisions of his early works', read at the meeting of the International Musicological Society, Madrid, April 1992.

observed in other works as well, the fourth piece of Op.7 contains the most striking example of this kind of change in all of Webern's music.[4] Second, the relatively plentiful sources for Op.7 indicate a different, more practical type of revision than with other works; one finds layers of often contradictory markings indicating tempo, dynamics, character, articulation and playing technique, some of which appear to have been made during rehearsal. Third, whereas Webern revised most of his early works for publication during the 1920s, he began reworking Op.7 relatively early: many important changes were made in 1914 or before. This was only partly due to the fact that Webern tried several times to get his Violin Pieces published during this period (and therefore had to provide definitive clean copies of the work): just as important seem to have been his experiences in playing and hearing the work in performance.[5]

In this essay we offer new information about early performances of Webern's music, including a previously unknown letter from Webern to the American violinist Arthur Hartmann, in which the composer made unusually detailed comments about how to play an early version of Op.7. Then we attempt to untangle the complex layers of both 'desk revisions' and 'rehearsal revisions' found in the manuscript sources, providing a fuller picture of the work's long pre-publication history. Finally we address some of the revisions in detail, viewing them in an analytical context.

## Performance history

Webern's first piece to be played in public was the Piano Quintet (1907), which was performed in a concert of Schoenberg pupils. The Passacaglia, Op.1, was premièred on 4 November 1908 in another concert organised by Schoenberg for his pupils, with the hired Tonkünstler

4 There are also more revisions of pitch than usual; see Allen Forte, 'A major Webern revision and its implications for analysis', *Perspectives of New Music* 28/1 (1990), pp. 224–55.

5 Webern sent copies of Op.7 (together with other pieces) to the Dreililien Verlag in June 1911, and to Tischer & Jagenburg in October 1911, both of whom turned him down. In 1914 Emil Hertzka of Universal Edition showed an interest in several works of Webern, but these plans had to be postponed until after the war (in 1914 Webern specifically mentioned Op.7 as one of the pieces submitted; see postcard to Jalowetz, 28 June 1914, Sammlung Heinrich Jalowetz, Paul Sacher Stiftung).

Orchestra. Some songs from the later Op.3 and Op.4 and the Five Movements, Op.5, were performed in 1910, although the details are unknown. The most famous early Webern performance, though, is the so-called *Skandalkonzert* of 31 March 1913, at which his Six Pieces for large orchestra (later Op.6) were played to cheers and catcalls.[6]

In the twelve years between their composition and publication, Webern's violin pieces were played in public no less than ten times. This is an unusually large number in itself, but even more remarkable is the fact that two of these performances took place – and at least two further ones were planned – in the years before the First World War, at a time when Webern's public career as a composer was only just beginning. The other eight performances took place in quick succession between 1919 and 1921, and were all organised by the newly formed Verein. Details about the ten pre-publication performances are given in Table 1.[7]

**Table 1** Public performances of Webern's Op. 7 before 1922

<table>
<tr><th>before 1914</th><th>after 1918</th><th></th></tr>
<tr><td>24 April 1911 (Vienna):<br>Fritz Brunner,<br>Anton Webern (première)</td><td>21 November 1919 (Vienna):<br>Oskar Adler,<br>Eduard Steuermann</td><td></td></tr>
<tr><td rowspan="7">29 June 1912 (Vienna):<br>Arnold Rosé,<br>Anton Webern</td><td>23 October 1920 (Vienna)</td><td rowspan="7">Rudolph Kolisch,<br>Eduard Steuermann</td></tr>
<tr><td>6 December 1920 (Vienna)</td></tr>
<tr><td>20 December 1920 (Vienna)</td></tr>
<tr><td>18 April 1921 (Vienna)</td></tr>
<tr><td>2 May 1921 (Vienna)</td></tr>
<tr><td>6 June 1921 (Vienna)</td></tr>
<tr><td>27 November 1921 (Vienna)</td></tr>
</table>

[6] Concerts as reported by Hans and Rosaleen Moldenhauer in *Anton von Webern: a Chronicle of his Life and Work* (New York: Alfred A. Knopf, 1979), pp. 91, 97, 120.

[7] Most of this information is drawn from Moldenhauer, *Anton von Webern*; however, some erroneous dates ('October 23, 1919' and 'June 8, 1921') have been rectified, and two performances not recorded by Moldenhauer (21 November 1919 and 27 November 1921) have been added: see Walter Szmolyan, 'Die Konzerte des Wiener Schönberg-Vereins', in Heinz-Klaus Metzger and Rainer Riehn, eds., *Schönbergs Verein für musikalische Privataufführungen* (*Musik-Konzepte* 36, Munich, 1984), pp. 101–14.

The early performance history of this work comprises two distinct phases, separated by the First World War, which had brought performances of all Webern's works to a standstill. The later performances differed from the ones before the war in two important respects. First, all but the very first of the post-war performances were played by Rudolf Kolisch and Eduard Steuermann, two of the closest associates of the Schoenberg circle. The earlier performances, by contrast, had been given by well-known violinists who were also active outside the Schoenberg circle: Fritz Brunner of the Vienna Philharmonic and Arnold Rosé of the highly-regarded Rosé Quartet.[8] Others may have intended to play the piece, including Paul Hindemith, who copied out the first movement in 1915.[9]

Another violinist, the American Arthur Hartmann, an internationally known performer who is remembered today chiefly for his collaboration with Claude Debussy, was also interested in Webern's violin pieces. The circumstances surrounding the planned Hartmann performance were typical of the kinds of arrangements Webern had to make to get his music played in these years. Hartmann's association with Webern began when the violinist, who was living in Paris, wrote 'cold' to Schoenberg in search of new pieces for his instrument. Schoenberg replied that he had not written anything for solo violin and recommended that he consider Webern, who was 'surely the greatest talent of the younger generation'.[10] This Hartmann did,

[8] Rosé had intended to play Webern's violin pieces again on 20 November 1912, with Marietta (Erna) Jonasz Werndorff, but the performance was cancelled at short notice because the pianist fell ill: see the letter from Berg to Schoenberg of 23 November 1912 in Juliane Brand, Christopher Hailey and Donald Harris, eds., *The Berg–Schoenberg Correspondence* (New York and London: Norton, 1987), p. 130.

[9] See Giselher Schubert, 'Die Einsamkeit auf hohen Bergen: Aus der Webern-Rezeption der 20er Jahre', in Dieter Rexroth, ed., *Opus Anton Webern* (Berlin: Quadriga, 1983), pp. 156–61. Webern received another inquiry in late July 1914 from the Dutch violinist van den Henst; see his letter to Schoenberg of 25 July: 'Dank Deiner hat sich ein holländischer Musiker van den Henst aus Paris an mich gewendet. Ich werde ihm meine Violinstücke u. diese Violoncell-Stücke, die ich als letztes geschrieben habe [i.e. his later Op. 11], schicken.' (Quoted from the typescript of the Schoenberg–Berg–Webern correspondence at the Wiener Stadt- und Landesbibliothek.) However, in this case it is not even clear if he got round to responding before the outbreak of the war.

[10] 'Für Geige als Soloinstrument habe ich nichts geschrieben [...] aber mein Schüler Dr. Anton von Webern, sicher die allerstärkste Begabung der jungen

Klagenfurt in Kärnten
Schiffgasse 14
am 15. Juli 1914

Sehr geehrter Herr Hartmann!

Ich freue mich sehr darüber, daß Sie sich bereits so eingehend mit meinen Kompositionen beschäftigt haben. Das ist sehr lieb von Ihnen.
Als Antwort auf Ihre Anfragen:



(im IV. Stück) Ich meine ein mit der Bogenstange sehr scharf angegebenes sff [mit dem Holz angerissen, so zu sagen] Dieses sff muß sich aber gleich in ein ppp verlieren. Die Fermate so lange als eben das mit dem Holz hervorgebrachte Ton (ppp) noch hörbar ist. Es wird also keine lange Fermate sein. Vielleicht nehmen Sie zur Erhöhung der Deutlichkeit des Tones etwas von den Haaren dazu. Also eine Strichart halb „col legno" halb „arco" (mit Haaren). Ich glaube Rosé hat das auch so gemacht. Rosé spielte auch die col legno Stelle im III Stück:



in dieser gemischten Strichart.

Mit „leicht über die G-Saite rutschen" meine ich: es ist ein Seufzer ähnlicher Klang hervorzubringen. Ich möchte <u>nicht</u>, daß die beim leichten Berühren der Saite entstehenden Flageoletts <u>allzu deutlich hörbar werden</u>. Es sollen nicht deutliche Töne ~~hör~~ zu hören sein. Mehr ein Geräusch ähnlicher Klang. Das Rutschen hat von <u>oben nach unten</u> zu geschehen. Es muß beidemale genau ~~die~~ zwei Viertel des Zeitmaßes ausmachen. Also genau im Takt. Da es mir um einen

**Plate 1** Letter from Webern to Arthur Hartmann, 15 July 1914 (Special Collections, Sibley Music Library, Eastman School of Music, University of Rochester)

tieferen Klang zu thun ist, so bitte ich entsprechend nicht
zu nah beim Steg, vielleicht nur etwas über der Hälfte
der Saite mit dem Rutschen zu beginnen. Damit Sie jedesmal
bis ans Ende der Saite (beim Wirbel) kommen.
Das Rutschen ziemlich schnell, damit eben die Flageoletts
nicht zu deutlich werden.
Jedenfalls: äusserste Zartheit, ein kaum vernehmbarer
Laut muss entstehen.

Nochmals: <u>von der Höhe zur Tiefe rutschen.</u>

Hoffentlich habe ich mich verständlich gemacht.
Ich bitte Sie auch noch:
die „col legno"-Stelle im I. Stück ist ebenfalls kaum
hörbar, äusserst zart auszuführen. Ganz ruhig.

Seien Sie allerherzlichst und ergebenst gegrüsst.

Anton von Webern

Meine Orchesterstücke op. 4, die ich Ihnen schickte,
sollen im August von Wood mit dem Queens-Hall-
Orchester in London und kommenden Winter von
Dopper in Amsterdam mit dem Concertgebouw-Orchester
aufgeführt werden.
Schönberg hat die Stücke vergangenes Jahr in Wien
aufgeführt.

Plate 2 Letter from Webern to Arthur Hartmann (*cont.*)

and Webern thanked Schoenberg for the recommendation on 18 June 1914. Webern then had his violin pieces copied by Karl Kornfeld; he sent this copy, together with a print of his Six Pieces for orchestra (later Op.6) to Hartmann at the beginning of July.[11] The violinist responded with a friendly letter, expressing his interest and requesting information about two unfamiliar performance markings in the third and fourth pieces.[12] His letter prompted a quick reply from Webern (reproduced in Plates 1 and 2), in which he gave detailed instruction both on playing techniques and on the expressive character of several passages in his violin pieces. We shall return to this important letter, which gives a unique insight into Webern's ideas about performance matters. After this, there seems to have been no further communication between Webern and Hartmann. The planned performance almost certainly did not take place because of the outbreak of war in August 1914, and we do not know if Hartmann ever played this work later in his career.

Second, there was a marked difference between the two phases of the early performance history with regard to their institutional surroundings. Both pre-war performances had been organised by associations devoted to the cause of modern music: the première by the Verein für Kunst und Kultur (which was run by Webern, Heinrich Jalowetz and Karl Horwitz, among others), and the second performance by the Akademischer Verband für Literatur und Musik. Thus they took place somewhat apart from Vienna's 'official' concert life, but nevertheless received a fair amount of public attention. However, it was only partly the kind of attention the members of the Schoenberg circle had hoped for. Following the première

Generation, hat Geigenstücke geschrieben [. . .] wollen Sie ihm direkt schreiben?' Letter from Schoenberg to Arthur Hartmann, 9 June 1914 (Special Collections, Sibley Music Library, Eastman School of Music, University of Rochester; quoted with permission).

11 In the meantime Hartmann had complained to Schoenberg that he had not heard from Webern. When Schoenberg reproached Webern for this, the latter wrote a long letter of apology to his former teacher on 2 July 1914, explaining how the delay had come about, and adding: 'Sind vierzehn Tage wirklich so schlimm?' (Wiener Stadt- und Landesbibliothek).

12 We know this from Webern's report to Schoenberg of 16 July: 'Der Geiger Hartmann ist nicht mehr bös auf mich. Er hat mir einen sehr netten Brief geschrieben. Er interessiere sich sehr für meine Sachen. Er bat mich um Auskunft wegen zwei Stellen in den Violinstücken [. . .]' (Wiener Stadt- und Landesbibliothek).

of Webern's violin pieces (in the April 1911 concert, which also included his Op.5 and works by Berg and Horwitz), a nasty attack on Schoenberg appeared in the *Wiener Extrablatt*, as a result of which Schoenberg's followers felt compelled to write a letter of protest to the Viennese association of critics.[13] Even so, the day after the première Webern wrote to Jalowetz that the performance had gone quite well, and that the audience had at least remained quiet. Webern repeated this assessment a few days later in another letter to Jalowetz, but modified it when he later wrote to Berg (in a letter of 7 May) that the performance would have been better if Rosé had played, as was initially planned.[14]

Even worse, the second performance of Webern's work (which was programmed with pieces by Zemlinsky, Berg and Schoenberg) was interrupted by laughter; the offenders, according to Berg's report, were reprimanded by Rosé and were finally expelled from the hall by Adolf Loos. But Berg was still able to report that Webern's violin pieces had been '*very* effective'.[15] This opposition from part of the audience must have been none the less disappointing for the composers and performers, since they were convinced both of their artistic success and of the quality of the performances.

It was, among other things, this discrepancy between the modernist élite and the conservative part of the musical public that led Schoenberg, in 1918, to found the Verein für musikalische Privataufführungen, an institution whose concerts were open only to members of the society. Not only were all publicity and newspaper reports prohibited, but even the members of the Society were forbidden any expression of approval or disapproval at the concerts.[16] These prohibitions were intended to create a listening and rehearsal situation far removed from the normal concert atmosphere. Since no opposition was to be expected from the audience, and since there was no limit on rehearsal time, Schoenberg and his colleagues (who took an active part in the preparation of the concerts as rehearsal coaches (*Vortrags-Meister*)) had

13 See Moldenhauer, *Anton von Webern*, p. 143.

14 Postcard of 25 April 1911 to Heinrich Jalowetz and letter of 29 April 1911 (Paul Sacher Stiftung, Sammlung Heinrich Jalowetz). Letter to Berg in Moldenhauer, *Anton von Webern*, p. 143.

15 Postcard of 29 June 1912 from Alban Berg to Arnold Schoenberg; *The Berg–Schoenberg Correspondence*, p. 99.

16 See the official prospectus of the Verein (1919), in *Musik-Konzepte* 36, pp. 4–7.

almost total control over the performances. In view of the 'laboratory' character of these events, we can assume that the eight performances of Webern's violin pieces that took place here conformed closely to the composer's wishes, for Webern was not only served by two instrumentalists who were intimately familiar with the music of the Schoenberg school, but had supervised all the performances himself. The excitement of first public exposure that must have surrounded the first performances in 1911 and 1912 was thus followed, in the post-war years, by a series of private, composer-controlled performances of the kind that Webern himself praised as 'model, most exemplary, most carefully prepared performances'.[17]

## Sources for Op.7 and their relationship to the early performances

The manuscript sources for Op.7 consist mainly of ink fair copies originally made for colleagues, performers or publishers; typically for Webern's early works, very little sketch material has survived. At least four of the manuscripts, and possibly all of the completed ink scores, were used in performance. The most important sources for our purpose are the four autograph scores and the two autograph violin parts that were probably used in the first two performances and then as the basis for revisions: MSS 2, 4, 5, 7, 8 and 9. The 1912 publication of the first piece in *Der Ruf* (MS 6, reproduced in facsimile from Webern's autograph in Plate 3) provides a useful reference point, since it is the only source apart from the first and last (the Universal Edition publication) that can be precisely dated. An interesting, though only tangentially relevant, manuscript is a copy of the first piece by Paul Hindemith, which, although probably copied in 1915, reflects an earlier version.[18] MS 1 is a brief sketch page, which we shall not consider here because it does not figure in performance matters or the revision

17 'vorbildliche, mustergültigste, sorgfältigste Aufführungen': letter of 9 November 1918 to Heinrich Jalowetz (Paul Sacher Stiftung, Sammlung Heinrich Jalowetz).

18 This manuscript is reproduced in Schubert, 'Die Einsamkeit auf hohen Bergen', p. 160. Interestingly, the low bass note in bs 6–8 here is F♮ rather than F♯; this suggests that Hindemith copied the piece from an (unknown) early source, for Webern originally wrote F♮ (in MS 2) before adding the accidental, first in pencil and then in ink.

Plate 3 Webern, Four Pieces for violin and piano, Op. 7 no.3: MS 2, bottom layer (Sammlung Anton Webern, Paul Sacher Stiftung, Basel)

process.[19] We list MS 3, a fragmentary copy of the first piece, for the sake of completeness only. Table 2 shows the nine autograph sources for Op.7, listed in chronological order.[20] Although the ordering of the manuscripts themselves is beyond dispute, their precise dates can probably never be determined with certainty. It is also not possible to date each layer of revisions exactly, since several manuscripts were apparently in use at the same time. We do attempt, however, to present plausible hypotheses about the dating of the different manuscripts and their revisions. Our judgments about chronology are based on two types of evidence – first, and primarily, the content and appearance of the manuscripts themselves, and second, external events, such as performances and publication opportunities, that can be matched with specific sources.

As one might expect, the end of the story is clearer than the beginning. MS 7 contains markings by Steuermann, which indicates that it was used in at least some of the Verein performances after 1919, although it may have been copied before the war. MSS 8 and 9 were provided to Universal Edition as printer's copies for the edition in 1922, so they must have been written out before that time (and although there are few pencil markings, they could have been used in the later Verein performances as well).

Our decision to place the first five sources in 1912 or before might seem more controversial. The fact that the title page of the first fair copy bears the remark (in Webern's hand) 'endgiltige Fassung Sommer 1914' would seem to indicate that its top layer and all subsequent manuscripts date from *after* that time. Moreover, in other cases, we know that Webern revised his early works for the most part in the early 1920s, as he was preparing them for publication. Although we too began with the assumption that Webern must have revised Op.7 most substantially after 1918, the sequence of revisions, as well as other evidence such as the opus numbers on the title

19 This sketch was discussed by Forte, in 'A major Webern revision', pp. 232–7.

20 The correct title page for MS 4 is one that was grouped with MS 7; the paper matches MS 4 exactly, and the designation 'Op. 6, No. 1' is consistent with the earlier manuscript, not the later. Moreover, the title page currently with MS 4 clearly belongs to MS 7, on the basis of paper, handwriting and ink. Although the title pages are still separated (since the MSS are in different places), we have described them correctly in Table 2.

pages, the form of Webern's name used, and markings in other hands, clearly indicated that the first manuscripts, and possibly the bottom layer of MS 7, were originally written out before the war. This chronology is supported moreover by the readings in two firmly datable sources: the 1912 publication in *Der Ruf* and the musical examples in the letter to Hartmann of July 1914.

This proposed chronology also matches what we know about the early performances. MS 2, the first ink score, was created in June 1910 and must have been used at the première in April 1911. As in other early manuscripts, the title page gives 'Op. 6 No. 1' as the first opus number. The handwriting is much larger than usual, and Webern used paper with widely-spaced staves to facilitate reading. No violin part corresponding to this MS has survived, but since parts were used in performing Op.7 until its publication, it is safe to assume that one existed. (In the end it was decided to publish the work without a separate violin part.) In three of the pieces (I, III and IV), there are very few pencil markings. Only the second piece was heavily revised; these markings in red pencil reflect compositional decisions from a later stage, and could have been entered as late as 1919.

The first score, according to our scenario, quickly became useless, since Webern made substantial revisions after the first performance. The next two manuscripts, an ink score (MS 4) and a violin part (MS 5), reflect these revisions, and most likely were used in the second public performance of Op.7 in June 1912. Of MS 4 unfortunately only the last two pieces have survived. Comparison of MSS 4 and 5 (written on special 'part paper' with staves of alternating sizes for the main part and the cues) shows that they match in nearly every respect and could certainly be played together.[21]

Their chronology is supported by three pieces of evidence. First, MS 5 contains a reading of the first piece that clearly precedes that of the 1912 *Der Ruf* version, indicating that it (and, by extension, MS 4) originated in

[21] There is one apparent discrepancy: in the score of the fourth piece (MS 4) the violin's fifth harmonic in b. 8 is notated B–F [*sic*], without accidentals, while in the violin part (MS 5) it is notated B–F♯. This reading differs from the final version but, unlike the implausibly notated reading in MS 4, it is at least playable. Such an incorrectly notated harmonic in the violin line of the score could have been easily overlooked.

Table 2 Autograph sources for Webern's Op.7

| | Op. 7 no. 1 | Op. 7 no. 2 | Op. 7 no.3 | Op.7 no.4 |
|---|---|---|---|---|
| 1) | | sketches in pencil for bs 17–24, one page, PSS | | |
| 2) | 'Vier Stücke für Geige und Klavier / op. 6 No 1 / op 6 7 / Anton von Webern / *endgiltige Fassung Sommer 1914*': full score fair copy in ink, with corrections, ten pages, PSS | | | |
| 3) | full score fair copy in ink of bs 1–6, one page, PSS | | | |
| 4) | | | '4 Stücke für Geige und Klavier / op. 6, No 1 / op. 7 / Anton von Webern': full score fair copy in ink, with performance markings and corrections, five pages, PSS | |
| 5) | 'Vier Stücke für Geige und Klavier / op. 6 No 1 [corrected to] 7 / Anton von Webern / Geigenstimme': violin part with cue notes of piano part in ink, six pages; title page and performance markings in another hand, PSS | | | |

| | | | | |
|---|---|---|---|---|
| 6) | 'No 1 aus Vier Stücke für Geige und Klavier / Anton von Webern': full score fair copy in ink, one page (published in *Der Ruf*, March 1912) ÖNB (Nachlaß Ehrhard Buschbeck, Mus.Hs.37.097) | | | |
| 7) | '4 Stücke für Geige und Klavier / op. 7/ Anton von Webern': full score fair copy in ink, with performance markings and corrections, six pages, private collection, Basel (photocopy in PSS (Privatsammlung 1, Ref.-Nr.356)) | | | |
| 8) | 'Anton Webern / Vier Stücke für Geige [corrected in another hand to:] Violine / und Klavier / op. 7': full score fair copy in ink, seven pages, PML (Lehman Collection) | | | |
| 9) | 'Geigenstimme [corrected in another hand to:] Violine / Vier Stücke / für / Geige [corrected in another hand to:] Violine und Klavier / Anton Webern / op. 7': violin part in ink, five pages, PML (Lehman Collection) | | | |

ÖNB = Österreichische Nationalbibliothek, Vienna
PML = Pierpont Morgan Library, New York
PSS = Paul Sacher Stiftung, Basel

or before that year.[22] Second, both MSS 4 and 5 contain performance markings, those in the score in Webern's hand, and some of those in the violin part in another hand. At the piece's second performance, Webern played the piano and Rosé the violin (the markings in the violin part are therefore probably by Rosé). Finally, when Webern wrote to Hartmann during the summer of 1914, he quoted two short sections of music, one each from the third and fourth pieces, which match only MSS 4 and 5 (and later manuscripts). This proves beyond a doubt that MSS 4 and 5 were in use before the war.

Webern must have been satisfied with the version contained in the MS 4 score; since he cited it in his letter to Hartmann, we know that he considered it definitive for at least two years after the June 1912 performance. The 'endgiltige Fassung' of summer 1914 to which Webern referred on the title page of MS 2, then, concerns an already substantially revised version, preserved in the top layers of MSS 4 and 5. He would have written the note as a reminder to himself that there was now a better version, which in effect invalidated the first manuscript. It is moreover quite possible that this 'endgiltige Fassung' was also played in the Verein performances after the war. In a manuscript we know they played from (MS 7), many of the most substantial changes – the ones that essentially bring it up to the final version – were clearly made later, wedged in awkwardly and written in a different coloured ink. The bottom layer was probably very close to the 1914 version.

Webern's work on Op.7 therefore proceeded in three distinct stages, two of them before the war: a first version which he abandoned after the première; a revised version for the second performance (and further planned performances in 1912, 1914 and possibly even later), which he referred to as 'definitive'; then a later version that came about during or after the performances in the Verein. As we have noted, this intensive early revision was unusual for Webern and certainly reflects the fact that this work, unlike most of his others, was regularly rehearsed and performed. Even if we cannot always make a direct connection between a particular revision and a problem in performance, it is equally impossible to imagine what Webern would have done if he had never heard the piece played.

22 The version of the first piece in *Der Ruf* is *not* identical to the version in MS 2 (contrary to Forte, 'A major Webern revision', p. 225).

On the contrary, repeated encounters with the actual sounding work and an acute awareness of its performance problems led Webern to revise the work and refine his performance indications continuously.

## The main revisions in chronological order

Some of the divergent readings found in the early versions of Op.7 can be seen as compositional weaknesses that were later improved, while others reflect aesthetic choices, particularly Webern's earlier concern for timbral variety, even at the expense of pitch audibility. At all stages, Webern refined the tempo and performance indications, clarifying ambiguous markings and phrase divisions. Rather than providing an exhaustive catalogue of changes, we focus below on selected revisions made at three crucial junctures: first, revisions most likely made while copying out the score in 1910 (that is, before the first performance); second, revisions associated with the pre-war performances and publication plans (1911–14), and finally, those made during (or after) the Verein performances (1919–21). In some cases we present our observations about the revisions within a broader analytical context; this helps us to go beyond simple description and to hypothesise why the changes might have been made.

### Early revisions (1910)

The very earliest revisions concerned pitch changes above all, particularly in the first three pieces. We shall focus here on the first and third, since Allen Forte has already discussed the pitch revisions in the second.[23] These 'desk revisions' necessarily resulted from compositional, not performance, problems. Here we can see Webern balancing the demands of the new atonal language with the vestiges of tonality, which in 1910 still exerted a strong pull.

A puzzling example (because it seems to go in the 'wrong' direction) is found in the final chord of the first piece (b. 9); in the first ink score (MS 2), Webern changed the B♮ to B♭, resulting in the much commented-on final

[23] We believe that most, and probably all, of the numerous pitch revisions that Forte ('A major Webern revision') considers were made early, most likely before the first performance.

chord, which is a 6/4 inversion of the E♭ major triad. Why did Webern, having abandoned functional tonality in several previous works, use such a chord (whose 'tonal' sound is only slightly blurred by the E♮ in the bass) at the end of a clearly atonal piece? In particular, why did he do so when he had first used B♮, making the final chord an augmented triad? Perhaps we can best understand this revision if we look at the special role that pitch class E♭ plays in the piece. It not only appears much more frequently than any other pitch class, it also occurs in especially prominent places in the music (both vertically and horizontally),[24] thereby emphasising the large-scale contraction of textural space[25] shown in Example 1.

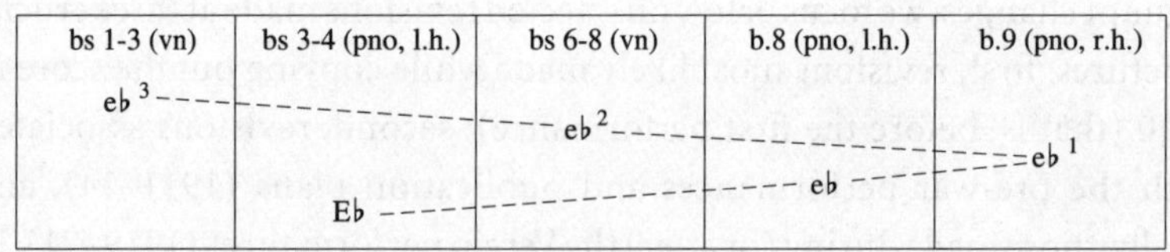


**Example 1** No. 1: important occurrences of the pitch class E♭

With his revision of the final chord, therefore, Webern strengthened the function of e♭[1] as the goal of this spatial contraction: by altering B♮ to B♭, he allowed for the chord to be heard 'tonally' (however briefly) with E♭ standing out as the 'root' tone. By contrast, the original version of this chord was less isolated in terms of sonority, since it was structured symmetrically both in itself and with the bass and the violin line – for the violin line in the original version is continued into the last bar, thus taking part in a five-note sonority symmetrically centred (in terms of interval classes) around e♭[1] (see Example 2). This was a particularly apt conclusion to the preceding bars (bs 6–8), which in the piano part contain another

24 The first note (e♭[3] in bs 1–3 of the violin part) is also the highest in the piece; and three times in the final version, new phrases in the bass line of the piano part begin with E♭ or e♭ (bs 3, 4 and 8). Moreover, in the ostinato c♯[2]–e♭[2] etc. (bs 5ff), the e♭[2] is emphasised by being placed on the strong beats.

25 See Wallace Berry, *Structural Functions in Music*, 2nd edn (New York: Dover, 1987), pp. 249–50.

**Example 2** No.1: pitch-class symmetry around E♭ in the original version (MS 2, bottom layer)

spatial contraction centred around the secondary axis a (as shown in Example 3).[26]

While the first version of the final chord is thus more in keeping with the harmonic structures that precede it, the definitive version gives the music a stronger tonal focus. This is even more evident when we consider the fact that the piece consists of two main parts of roughly equal length (the most obvious formal marker being the beginning of the violin ostinato (in b. 5), which spans virtually the whole second half), and that the exact midpoint (measured in crotchets) is marked by the chord F–B♭–B♮–D in b. 5. By changing the final chord Webern thus exactly resumed the 'midpoint chord', in which the 'root note' is transposed up a fifth (this is

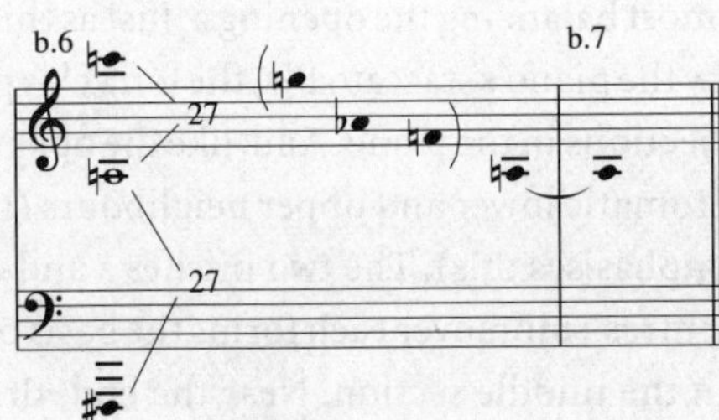


**Example 3** No.1, bs 5–7, pitch symmetry around a

26 Webern originally wrote F♮ in bs 6–7 (the accidental was added later, first in pencil, then in ink). He might have substituted F♯ in order to make the top and bottom notes equidistant from the centre pitch a, which is also the pitch that would follow next in the chromatic descent of the lowest piano right-hand notes (bs 4–6: $c^1$–b–b♭).

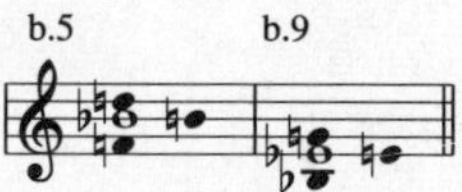


**Example 4** No.1: comparison of chords in bs 5 and 9

displayed in Example 4). Again, however, this hint at functional tonality (in this case a dominant–tonic relationship) is brought about at the expense of consistency in another area of pitch organisation. For while the 'midpoint chord' includes the last tone of the first twelve-note aggregate (B♭), in the original version the B♮ in the last chord completes the second one; in the final version, by contrast, the second aggregate remains uncompleted. Thus, chromatic saturation seems to have been less important to Webern as he revised the piece to strengthen its E♭–A centricity.

By contrast, a significant pitch change in the third piece suggests greater pitch symmetry (although it leaves a version that is still quite different from the final one). In altering the quintuplet figure in b. 4 as he was copying out MS 2, Webern kept an extra bar between what later became bs 4 and 5. The two early stages of this passage are displayed in Example5[27] (see also Plate 3). The original layer of the violin part in b. 4 immediately reiterates the first two pitches of the piece (a, b♭), then introduces a new pitch, $c^1$. In perhaps the most striking divergence from the final version, the $c^1$ returns at the end of b. 4, where it is sustained for the duration of seven quavers, almost balancing the opening a. Just as this sustained note was punctuated by the piano's staccato B♭s, the long $c^1$ is punctuated by three staccato interjections in the piano. And, like the opening a, the $c^1$ is surrounded by its chromatic lower and upper neighbours (b. 5 in MS 2: the original spelling emphasises this). The two pitches a and $c^1$ are thus established as parallel 'centres'; moreover each forms the basis of one of the two ostinato figures in the middle section. Near the end, the two pitches are juxtaposed (in bs 10–12, corresponding to bs 9–11 of the final version), the A displaced by an octave in the violin, and here they function again as static elements surrounded by chromatic neighbours.

27 The ink bottom layer was corrected with a paste-over; Webern generally made these kinds of corrections immediately. (Since Forte wrote in 1990 the Sacher Stiftung has had the manuscript treated so that the paste-overs can be lifted.)

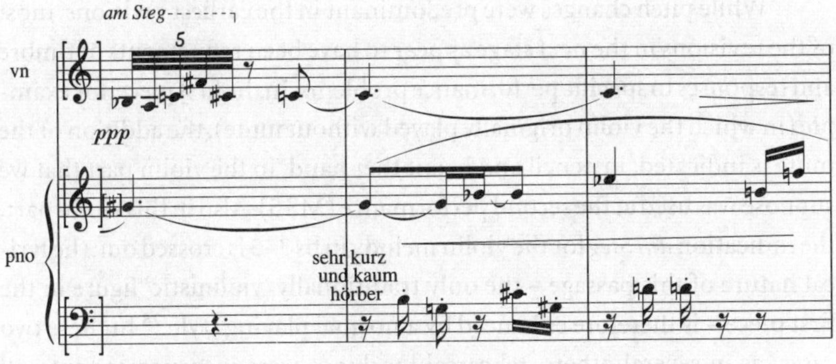

Example 5 No.3, bs 4–6

If the manuscript's original layer, with its emphasis on A and C, contains more pitch repetition, it also contains more interval repetition than the final version. With the f♯¹ and c♯¹ at the end of the quintuplet figure, two additional new pitches are presented which anticipate the perfect fourths of the ostinato. These initial fourths are echoed in subsequent bars: c♯¹–g♯ in b. 5 and b♭¹–e♭² in bs 5–6 (of which in the final version only the latter remains). The corrected quintuplet figure (shown in Example 5b) shifts the b♭ and a to the end of the figure, with b♭ emphasised rhythmically. The gesture moves downwards only, spanning the tritone e♭–a, which the sustained c¹ now symmetrically bisects.

## Second-stage revisions (1911–14)

While pitch changes were predominant in the earliest revisions, most of the revisions in the next stage appear to have been refinements of timbre and responses to specific performance problems. In the first piece, for example (in which the violin originally played without mute), the addition of the mute is indicated, in pencil and in another hand, in the violin part that we suppose was used at the second performance (MS 5). Also in this violin part, the indication *am Steg* for the violin melody in bs 3–5 is crossed out; the lyrical nature of this passage – the only traditionally 'violinistic' figure in the first piece – is therefore enhanced by a normal playing style.[28] In these two cases, as in several others, rehearsal markings were incorporated into all subsequent manuscripts and the published score. Other changes in the piece as a whole include the addition of expression and tempo markings and the modification of dynamics throughout (generally making them softer).[29] Such changes aim towards greater nuance and subtlety, perhaps carried out in reaction to performers' tendencies to overstate.

Webern took particular care with the *col legno* passages. In the quiet ostinatos of the first and third pieces (which can be seen as parallel in many ways), he added *weich gezogen* (gently drawn) to the *col legno* indications. In the loud *col legno* passages in the second piece (and in the first version of the fourth piece), where he clearly intended a 'noisy' effect, he added the modifiers *gerissen* (II, b. 9; IV, b. 9, first version) and *heftig* (II, b. 10). In his letter to Hartmann, Webern explains how he means the *col legno* (*gerissen*) to be played: 'I mean a very sharply attacked ***sff*** with the stick of the bow (struck with the wood, as it were). . . . You might use a little of the hair to make the pitch clearer. A kind of half "col legno", half "arco" bowing (with the hair). I think Rosé also did it that way.'[30] This technique of mixing *col*

28 In later manuscripts bs 3–5 of the first piece are marked *espress.*, a further step away from the altered sound of playing on the bridge.

29 Examples of expression markings added in MSS 4 and 5: II, b. 7, *langsamer* and *sehr zart*; III, b. 1, staccatos, b. 6, *weich gezogen*, bs 9–10, *kaum hörbar*; IV, b. 3, *rit.*, *molto espress.*, b. 5, *zart bewegt*, b. 7, *sehr zart*, b. 11, *langsam*. Dynamic markings: II, b. 16 violin, *crescendo* from ***f***; IV, b. 2 *piano*, ***pp***, b. 9 *piano*, ***f*** *crescendo*.

30 'Ich meine ein mit der Bogenstange sehr scharf angegebenes ***sff*** (mit dem Holz angerissen, so zu sagen). . . . Vielleicht nehmen Sie zur Erhöhung der Deutlichkeit des Tones etwas von den Haaren dazu. Also eine Strichart halb "col legno" halb "arco" (mit Haaren). Ich glaube Rosé hat das auch so gemacht.' (Sibley Music Library)

*legno* and arco is also recommended for the softer, *weich gezogen* passages: Webern continues, 'Rosé also played the col legno passage in the third piece [bs 6–9] with this mixed bowing.' [31] At the end of the letter, he adds with gentle urgency: 'the "col legno" passage in the first piece is likewise to be barely audible, played extremely delicately. Very quietly.' [32]

The balance between the altered tone colour desired and the audibility of the pitches must have been – and still is – hard to strike. Already in 1914, Webern showed a certain preference for pitch clarity, while at the same time not wanting to lose the special *col legno* sound quality. (In his performance notes, Adorno remarks that the violinist Christa Ruppert used a second bow, whose wood was rosined, for these passages. He observes, 'Ein prepared bow hat so gut sein Recht wie ein prepared piano', but fears that this might minimise the timbral distinction between *col legno* and normal playing.)[33]

The most significant second-stage revision, though, is found in the third piece: at some time between the first and second performances, the original bs 4–6 were compressed into two bars, eliminating several pitches

**Example 6** No.3, bs 4–5, MS 4, top layer

31 'Rosé spielte auch die col legno Stelle im III Stück in dieser gemischten Strichart.' (Sibley Music Library)

32 'die "col legno"-Stelle im I. Stück ist ebenfalls kaum hörbar, äußerst zart auszuführen. Ganz ruhig.' (Sibley Music Library)

33 Adorno, 'Anton Webern: Vier Stücke', p. 155.

in the process (see Example 6).[34] (While the omission of a handful of notes might not wreak much havoc in a longer, denser score, in a Webern miniature its consequences are enormous.) The revision, which occurs at the juncture between two static sections – the violin's sustained note punctuated by the piano at the opening, and the ostinato-based middle section – allows a more direct transition between the two sections as well as balancing the proportions of the piece. The pitch changes result in a feature for which this piece has been noted: the unfolding of a single twelve-note collection.[35]

Webern made two major changes in MS 4, both in bs 4–6: first, pitch changes in the piano left hand, and second, the elimination of the violin's c¹. As a result of the first change, the left-hand line presents itself as the continuation of the preceding violin figure, since it repeats – an octave higher – the violin's final pitch (a¹–a) and since, like the violin line, it is clearly downward-directed. The effect is a criss-cross movement between the ascending piano right-hand line and the descending violin/piano left-hand line, whose separateness is also emphasised by their distinct modes of articulation (legato vs *am Steg* and staccato). The revision also brings about a double confrontation of the two focal pitches E♭ and A in b. 4 (e♭¹ and a in the violin, e♭² and a¹ in the piano). This perceived 'line' between the descending violin figure and the piano's left hand is made even stronger by the second change, the omission of the violin's c¹; now its stasis cannot distract from the movement of the two contrasting lines.

There is also a tendency towards formal symmetry over the course of the revisions. One can perceive a development over the course of the piece's five sections. Initially, in section A, two distinct musical events are opposed in close proximity (sustained note in the violin, repeated staccato notes in the piano). Then there is an expansion of space in the piano in section B, b. 3 (first beat, piano; third beat, violin) to b. 5 (first beat), followed by a juxtaposition of three different types of lines spanning a range of almost five octaves. These widely spaced lines converge in section D (b. 9, piano–b. 11),

34 This change is documented in MS 4, where the correction is made on a paste-over. We believe this revision was made in or before 1912 because the later reading is found in the contemporaneous violin part (MS 5), which we know was copied before March 1912.

35 Arnold Whittall, 'Webern and atonality: the path from the old aesthetic', *The Musical Times* 124 (1983), p. 734.

and are reduced in section E (bs 12–14) to a densely-packed chord with a punctuating gesture in the left hand, whose texture and register are the exclusive domain of the piano.[36]

The revision of the piano left-hand line in bs 4–6 makes the transition between sections B and C much smoother, since the piano's low F in section C is now prepared by a series of increasing descending intervals in the bass (eight semitones, eleven and twenty-one). Moreover, by reducing the texture of section B to two parts, Webern integrates this section much more clearly into the overall density pattern of the piece, which progresses from one then two parts in section A to two parts in section B, three in section C, four in section D and finally to six parts in section E.[37] In this way, both the revision of the piano left hand and the elimination of the sustained $c^4$ increase the sense of forward propulsion in the music.

In the first version (MS 2), the formal proportions were still comparatively unequal, the durations of the five sections forming the following pattern:

(in quavers)

| Section | A | B | C | D | E |
|---|---|---|---|---|---|
| | 8 | 11 | 10½ | 8½ | 8 |

The compression of section B changes this formal pattern to the final, more balanced sequence:[38]

(in quavers)

| Section | A | B | C | D | E |
|---|---|---|---|---|---|
| | 8 | 8 | 9½ | 8½ | 8 |

Something similar can be observed with regard to the harmonic development of the piece. In the very first version (bottom layer of MS 2), aggregate completion occurs relatively early, with the entry of the pitch $e^3$ at the

36 See Jonathan Dunsby and Arnold Whittall, *Music Analysis in Theory and Practice* (London: Faber, 1988), pp. 173–5.

37 See Berry, *Structural Functions*, p. 212.

38 See Dunsby and Whittall, *Music Analysis*, pp. 181–3.

beginning of b. 7 (corresponding to b. 6 of the final version), whereas in the revised first version it occurs with the F♯ at the end of that bar; then a second twelve-note aggregate unfolds throughout the rest of the piece. In the later versions, however, chromatic completion is postponed until the very end of the piece (G in b. 12). The final section – the only formal segment that is preceded by a clear caesura – now not only brings to a culmination the textural density progression, but also the gradual process of chromatic unfolding.

Furthermore, Webern in the first version accentuated the exact midpoint of the piece by placing the aggregate-completing pitch (F♯ in b. 7, old numbering) on the twenty-third quaver of the first version's forty-five quaver duration (including final rests). This seems not to have been an accident, since in a later revision (MS 7), he shifted the climax of the central *crescendo–diminuendo* from the second quaver of b. 6 to the first quaver of b. 7, thus paralleling the shift of the midpoint of the piece with a shift of the dynamic climax that accompanies it.

•

## Later revisions (1919–22)

In accordance with the goals of the Verein, Webern aimed for greater clarity of pitch and more transparent textures in his later revisions of Op.7. To achieve this, he separated slurs (often turning them into staccatos), removed ties, further reduced the dynamics, and changed expression markings. These kinds of changes are especially typical of the first and second pieces. The biggest changes at this stage occur however in the fourth piece, where he completely rewrote the ending.

The ending of the first piece continued to occupy him. First he shortened the F♯ bass note in bs 6–7, which had been tied over through the first beat of b. 8. This change clarified the motivic correspondence between the ascending bass line in b. 3 and the descending one in bs 8–9, which contributes moreover to a larger formal symmetry (chord–ascending line–static chords + bass line–descending line–chord).[39]

[39] The formal symmetry is discussed by Erhard Karkoschka, in 'Studien zur Entwicklung der Kompositionstechnik im Frühwerk Anton Weberns' (diss., Tübingen, 1959), p. 107.

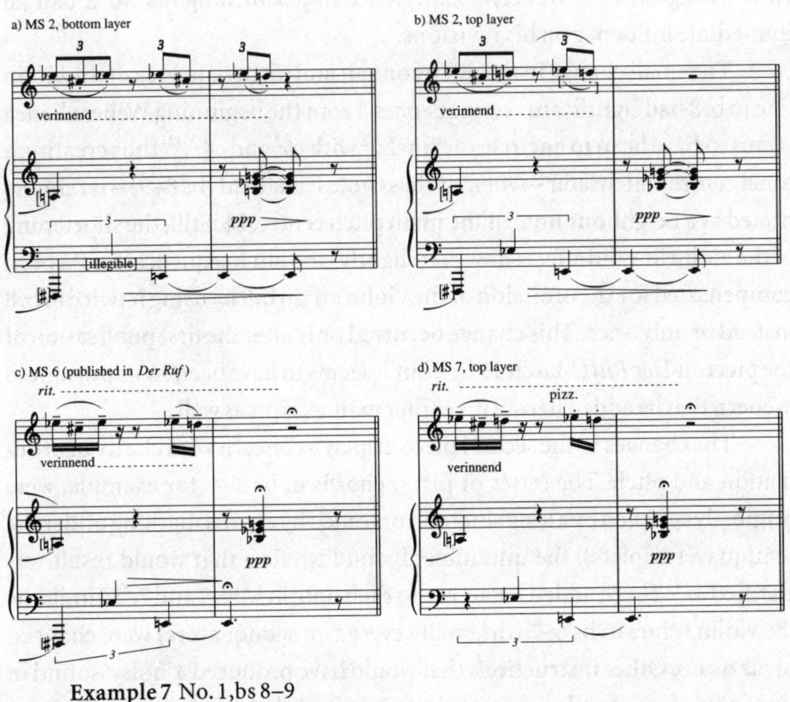


Example 7 No. 1, bs 8–9

The multiple alterations of the violin part in the final bars separate it timbrally even more from the piano (this is shown in Example 7). For one thing, the shorter violin line (which had continued to oscillate between C♯ and E♭ until halfway through b. 8) does not overlap with the piano chord any longer and contribute to its original pitch-class symmetry. For another, both its articulation and its rhythmic notation have been changed. The pizzicato indication for the last two-note group, added only in the final revision, immediately makes sense, as each of the violin phrases is now characterised by a different mode of attack (bs 1–3, harmonic; bs 3–5, *naturale, espress.*; bs 5–8, *col legno, weich gezogen*). The general tendency, now completed by pizzicato, is towards an ever 'noisier', less pitch-specific sound. By contrast, the change from a quaver triplet to a continuation of the semiquavers accompanied by a ritardando seems mainly to be a notational convenience, indicating to the performers that the ending of the piece should slow down very gradually. This is one of the changes which clearly suggests that Webern's experience in performing his work had an immediate influence on his revisions.

The small change in the pitch content and pitch sequence of the violin line in b. 8 had significant consequences. From the beginning Webern's idea seems to have been to encircle the final d² with e♭² and c♯²,[40] thus creating a tonal centre which later – when the bass note E is added (bs 8–9) – is reinterpreted as a neighbour note of the main pitch centre, E♭. Still, the shortening of the violin line did affect (however slightly) the pitch sequence: for Webern compensated for the omission of the violin's d² in b. 9 by using it twice in b. 8 instead of only once. This change occurred only after the first publication of the piece in *Der Ruf* (March 1912), but it seems to have been so important to Webern that he added it to all his earlier manuscripts as well.

The changes in the second piece display a concern with clarity of articulation and pitch. The series of piano chords in bs 3–4, for example, were originally spanned by a long slur (and preceded by a pedal marking under the semiquaver triplets); the undoubtedly muddy effect that would result was clarified as Webern added a staccato to each note in MSS 2 and 7.[41] Similarly, the violin's slurs in bs 6–7 (originally every two semiquavers) were changed to pizzicato. Other instructions that would have produced a 'noisy' sound in the violin – for example *am Steg* in bs 6–7, *heftig* in b. 10 and *roh* in b. 17 – were deleted. Even the designation 'G string' for the lyrical violin gesture in bs 2–3 was removed, perhaps because it might sound too romantic (see Example 8).

In the third piece a long slur in the piano's right hand extending from b. 3 to the beginning of b. 8 indicated one continuous melody spanning two sections of the piece. A separation into two slurs (with a breath mark in between) was made in b. 5 of MS 7 in another hand, possibly Steuermann's. In any case, Webern included this 'rehearsal change' in all later manuscripts of the piece.

The most striking and audible changes are found in the fourth piece. These changes, made at a crucial transition and at the end, affect the piece's overall registral shape, timbral progression and pitch structure. First Webern replaced the violin's fermata in bs 9–10 by extending the piano's

40 [For more on *encircled D* see Chapter 4 above. – Ed.]

41 For some reason, when Webern revised the second piece he went back to MS 2, making heavy corrections in red pencil; most of the same changes were more discreetly entered into MSS 7 (by erasures and additions in ink).

**Example 8** No.2, bs 2–4, MS 2, bottom layer

final chord in b. 9 (the two versions are compared in Example 9). This passage marks an important structural division: a loud, rhythmically articulated cadence-like ending to the first half of the piece which represents a turning point in the structure of the movement (the midpoint, measured in crotchets, occurs at the downbeat of b. 9).[42] The fermatas over bs 9 and 10 consisted originally of the violin's b, marked *sff* and *col legno* (*gerissen*). The piano rested during b. 10, its last chord in b. 9 was a crotchet instead of a quaver, and it was not tied over the bar. In all versions, the cadential quality is emphasised by a slowing of tempo (the conventionally violinistic grace notes on the last two attacks in b. 9 were removed after the first performance).

The section that begins in the second half of b. 5 and ends in b. 10 is parallel in many ways to the first section, bs 1–5$^1$. Both begin with a rising gesture (the first time in the violin, the next time in the piano); these gestures are closely related in terms of interval (both present interval classes 5, 1 and 3 in succession) and registral space (both span two octaves and a tritone: d$^1$–g♯$^3$ in bs 1 and 3, C♯–g$^1$ in bs 5 and 6). Both start rapidly and incisively, then slow down by means of written ritardandos and longer note values. The bass descent that began in the first phrase (contra-A, b. 2;

42 In Adorno's words, 'Hier wendet sich die Komposition und erzwingt jenen Doppelpunkt, nach dem das Ganze dann im Nachsatz sich löst': 'Anton Webern: Vier Stücke', p. 161.

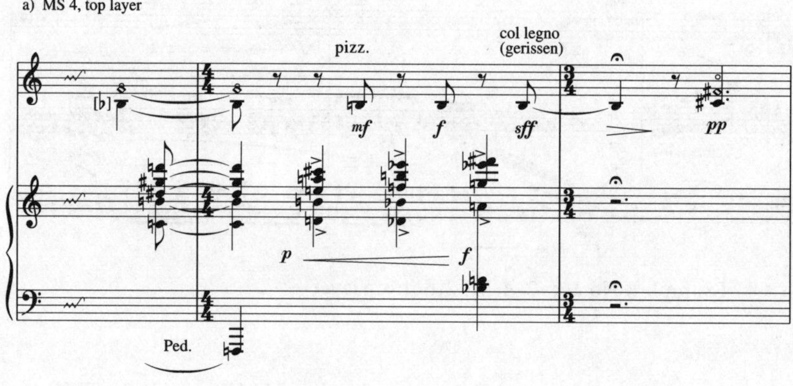


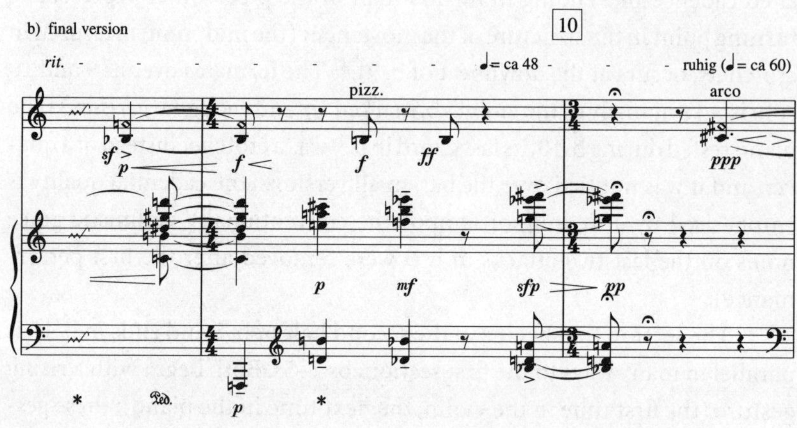


**Example 9** No.4, bs 9–10

contra-G, b. 4) is continued in the second (contra-F, b. 9).[43] The violin's registral shape spans the two phrases in an arch, first moving upwards from register 1 into register 3 (bs 1–3), while the second phrase picks up register 3

[43] In the fermata chords at the end of both phrases, Webern does not shy away from reinforcing possible tonal associations: the bass contra-G in bs 4–5 is accompanied by D a twelfth above, while the contra-F in b. 9 (also accompanied by its fifth, $c^1$) is followed by prominent B♭s in the following chords; moreover the bass F doubles the violin's harmonic (sounding) $f^2$.

**Plate 4** Webern, Four Pieces for violin and piano, Op. 7 no. 4: MS 2 (Sammlung Anton Webern, Paul Sacher Stiftung, Basel)

again, this time with harmonics (bs 7–8), and ends with an abrupt leap down into register 1.

Webern's revision of bs 9–10 strengthened the parallelism between the two phrases. First, the change of the piano's articulation in b. 5 to staccato emphasises this figure's resemblance to the accented opening gesture in the violin. In the revised version moreover, both fermatas (b. 5 and b. 10) are played by the piano alone. The revised phrase ending is also more 'solid' – that is, the pitches are more clearly audible – than the noisy, ephemeral sound quality of the violin playing *col legno*, *fortissimo*. In his letter to Hartmann, Webern cited just this passage to illustrate what he meant by a forceful *col legno* attack (as mentioned above). He then acknowledged that the fermata in bs 9–10 (of the early version) could not be held very long: 'This ***sff*** must fade immediately to ***pp***. The fermata as long as the tone produced with the wood (***ppp***) is still audible. It won't be a very long fermata then.'[44] Webern's comments indicate that the unstable and noisy quality of the tone was not something to be avoided, but was part of the effect he desired.

In the early version, the violin fermata, unaccompanied and wavering on the edge of audibility, cannot play a strong cadential role. What follows is even further removed from any kind of traditional closure. After a soft c♯³ harmonic, the piano, now reduced to two voices, outlines a four-bar melody that begins ***ppp*** and fades away (b. 14, *ganz verklingend*). Accompanying this are two remarkable violin gestures (bs 13–15): abandoning traditional notation, Webern simply indicates two descending wavy lines with the instruction 'über die ganze G-Saite leicht rutschen'. (Webern's original 'graphic notation' can be seen in Plate 4.)

This is indeed a bizarre ending for the entire set of four pieces, but one which deserves to be taken seriously, since it was hardly a passing fancy, but the version that was played for the first decade or so of the piece's existence. Indeed this passage and the preceding one in bs 9–10 appear to be among the very last things Webern changed before publication.[45] How carefully he

44 'Dieses ***sff*** muß sich aber gleich in ein ***pp*** verlieren. Die Fermate so lange als eben der mit dem Holz hervorgebrachte Ton (***pp***) noch hörbar ist. Es wird also keine lange Fermate sein.' (Sibley Music Library)

45 The revisions were made in the top layer in MS 7, which was probably added between 1919 and 1921.

thought about the particular effect he desired is clear from his instructions to Hartmann:

> With 'slide lightly over the G string' I mean that one should produce a sound like a sigh. I don't want the harmonics that result from lightly touching the string to be too clearly audible. One shouldn't hear distinct notes. A sound more like noise. The sliding goes from high to low. Both times it must take exactly two crotchets. Exactly in metre. Since I mean a lower sound, please don't start the sliding too close to the bridge, perhaps only over about half the string. So that you reach the end of the string every time (near the peg). The sliding [should be] fairly quick, so that the harmonics are not too distinct. In any case: the most extreme delicacy; a barely perceptible sound must be produced. Once again: slide from high to low. I hope I have made myself clear.[46]

Webern emphasises four things: first, that the sound should be extremely soft and gentle; second, that it should be closer to noise than to pitch; third, that its duration should be precisely two crotchets; and, finally, that the slide should descend into the violin's lowest register. Two of these characteristics are shared by the final version: the gentle quality (*wie ein Hauch* in the published score) and the metric placement. The 'noisy' quality and the low register, however, are unique to the early version.

The original ending can be heard as part of a process in which the usual role of the violin (and indeed of a 'fourth-and-final movement') is audibly subverted at every turn. Whereas the violin part begins with a pitched, traditionally virtuoso gesture (bs 1–4), it produces only altered

[46] 'Mit "leicht über die G-Saite rutschen" meine ich: es ist ein Seufzer ähnlicher Klang hervorzubringen. Ich möchte *nicht*, daß die beim leichtern Berühren der Saite entstehenden Flageoletts allzu deutlich hörbar werden. Es sollen nicht deutliche Töne zu hören sein. Mehr ein Geräusch ähnlicher Klang. Das Rutschen hat von oben nach unten zu geschehen. Es muß beidemale genau zwei Viertel des Zeitmaßes ausmachen. Also genau im Takt. Da es mir um einen tieferen Klang zu thun ist, so bitte ich entsprechend nicht zu nah beim Steg, vielleicht nur etwas über der Hälfte der Saite mit dem Rutschen zu beginnen. Damit Sie jedesmal bis ans Ende der Saite (beim Wirbel) kommen. Das Rutschen ziemlich schnell, damit eben die Flageoletts nicht zu deutlich werden. Jedenfalls: äußerste Zartheit, ein kaum vernehmbarer Laut muß entstehn ... Nochmals: von der Höhe zur Tiefe rutschen. Hoffentlich habe ich mich verständlich gemacht.' (Sibley Music Library)

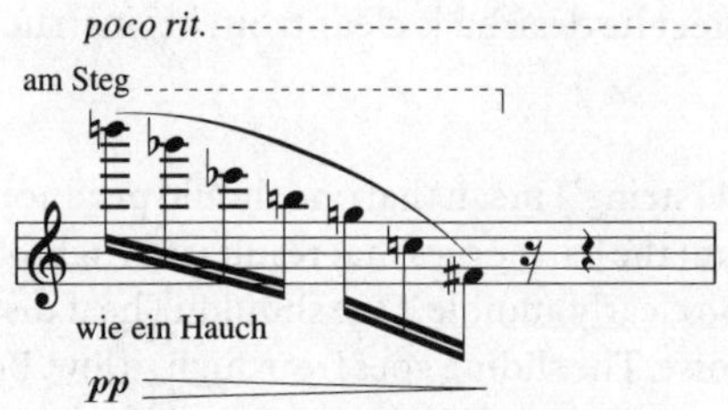


Example 10 No. 4, violin, b. 13 and bs 14–15

sounds after this point: harmonics (bs 7–9, 10–12), pizzicato (b. 9), *col legno* (bs 9–10) and unpitched sliding (bs 13–15). Except for the harmonic in bs 10–12 (which recalls the similar harmonic that begins the first piece), the violin's pitches become progressively less distinct. This progression from pitch to noise in the violin part is matched by a similar progression from metrical clarity to ambiguity. In piano and violin taken together, the decreasing density (from eight structural voices in b. 2 to one in b. 15) is accompanied by a large-scale diminuendo, from ***ff*** to ***ppp*** (*dim.*). As the piece literally unravels before our ears, it subverts our normal expectations of a final movement by denying any form of closure.

Webern's late revision of this passage, as Allen Forte has pointed out, is eminently sensible: the seven-note descending figure that replaced the slides shares many set classes with the rest of the piece (see Example10).[47] It also sums up in a single gesture the main registers in which the violin part has been active (although the $d^4$ is now the highest note in the four pieces). By substituting pitched for non-pitched sound and specific rhythms for an amorphous shape, Webern strengthens the sense of closure, appropriately enough for a passage that concludes a whole cycle as well as a single piece.

But although the revisions to the fourth piece might seem 'analytically unproblematic' from the pitch point of view,[48] they go a long way towards neutralising, or at least mitigating, the work's most radical features: its reinterpretation of form and closure, of the violin–piano relationship, and of the role of noise. The fact that these revisions were made during or after the Verein performances should not surprise us, since the guiding

[47] Forte, 'A major Webern revision', pp. 227–8.
[48] Forte, 'A major Webern revision', p. 225.

principles of the group emphasised just this kind of clarity and precision in composition and execution. The workshop environment moreover allowed Webern to work very closely with his performers. The input of musicians of the calibre of Kolisch and Steuermann was certainly crucial, just as Rosé's performance had helped Webern to form his own sense of the precise timbres he desired. The change in attitude that led him to place increased value on clarity of pitch and form can be seen in his revisions of other works as well; it represents part of a larger aesthetic shift (coinciding with the first steps towards twelve-note composition), which had deeper causes than mere practical experience. Even in its more pitch-oriented final version, however, the work's timbral features remain an integral part of its structure. As Adorno pointed out with regard to the printed version (the only one he could have known), the usual sonorities associated with this ensemble are here the exception rather than the rule: in sonic and formal terms, Webern's Op.7 must be considered a radically new realisation of the traditional violin–piano combination.

# 6 Webern's row tables

KATHRYN BAILEY

In the first chapter of this volume Susanne Rode-Breymann writes of Webern's affinity for turn-of-the-century lyric poetry and painting, and the fervour of his belief that art should be an expression only of that which moves the artist. She draws a portrait of a youth who is greatly affected, not by elegant mathematical solutions or number conundrums,[1] but by poetry about the night and the sea, who was moved to record at length in his diary his impassioned reaction to Schwind's painting of *Des Knaben Wunderhorn* and who longed, not for the sophistication of Vienna or the arcane refinements of its men of culture, but for a solitary life spent in the sight of 'glaciers, of eternal ice and snow, of the sombre mountain giants'.[2] The figure that emerges is oddly out of joint with the composer who, of the three Viennese, has traditionally been considered the most intellectual.

Webern's continued seeking after the sort of unity exemplified by Goethe's primeval plant surfaces repeatedly in his diaries and letters, and this quest has been put forward on many occasions as the reason for his employment of the twelve-note technique and his predilection for symmetrical patterns.[3] Yet this striving for a unity that was expressed by

1 Indeed, Webern's school records, which are in the Webern Nachlaß at the Paul Sacher Stiftung, show that as a boy he was not outstanding in mathematics: this is the only subject for which he was ever given the mark 'nicht genügend'. And it is not unusual to find errors in the calculations that occur occasionally in the margins of the sketchbooks.

2 From a diary entry dated 6 November 1904 (PSS).

3 See, for example, Ernst Krenek in his commentary in *Anton von Webern: Sketches (1926–1945): Facsimile Reproductions from the Composer's Autograph Sketchbooks in the Moldenhauer Archive*, compiled by Hans Moldenhauer (New York: Carl Fisher, 1968), p. 319: 'The *Farbenlehre* was very close to Webern, who found Goethe's idea that all organic life originated from one germinal nucleus to be a notion related to the basic concept of the twelve-tone technique.'

Goethe as a phenomenon of nature has often seemed in Webern's case to be a largely cerebral process – an intellectualisation of the proportions of nature in order that they might be expressed in music, along with an exploitation of the complex though not immediately apparent symmetries and other relationships inherent in groups of notes that have been ordered in very specific ways to very specific ends. It is difficult to reconcile the figure of abstract rationality who seems to hover behind works of such finely ordered complexity as the *Symphonie* and the Variations for Orchestra – and, indeed, all the other twelve-note works – with the young man who became so enraptured with Schwind's painting[4] or the slightly older one whose outlines of compositions to be written offered thematic descriptions such as 'coolness of early spring (Anninger, first flora, primroses, anemones, pasqueflowers)', 'cosy warm sphere of the highest meadows' and 'outlook into the highest region'.[5] Webern's row tables provide another view of this paradoxical figure and perhaps suggest a shift of perspective.

Webern's system of listing and numbering the permutations of his rows was until fairly recently a matter of conjecture. Although his row tables had been seen by both Luigi Rognoni and Friedrich Wildgans and were the source of the rows they gave in their writings about Webern in the 1960s,[6] in more recent years their whereabouts were not generally known. In fact they were in Wildgans' possession. After his death in 1988 they were recovered by Regina Busch and added to the Webern *Nachlass* at the Paul Sacher Stiftung in Basel,[7] where since that time they have been accessible to Webern scholars. The most basic of the questions raised in their absence was surely the very identity of the rows.

4 See pp. 14–16 of this volume.

5 From an outline of the proposed rondo movement of the Op.22 Quartet, in the Sacher Stiftung's Sketchbook I, p. 54. I have used Moldenhauer's translation (Hans and Rosaleen Moldenhauer, *Anton von Webern: a Chronicle of his Life and Work* (London: Gollancz, 1978), p. 423). The numbers assigned to the sketch books by the Sacher Stiftung will be used in this chapter.

6 See Rognoni, *La scuola musicale di Vienna* (Turin: Einaudi[?], 1966), pp. 335ff, and Wildgans, *Anton Webern – eine Studie* (Tübingen: Rainer Wunderlich Verlag, 1967), pp. 133–50.

7 See the announcement in *Tempo*, no.165 (June 1988), p. 58. Busch is currently preparing a facsimile edition of the row tables, with commentary and annotations, for publication by the Sacher Stiftung.

When the twelve-note sketchbooks were made available for scrutiny in 1986[8] the question of row identity was answered. But other questions arose. Webern identified the rows as he used them in his sketches, and it became clear that his system of organisation was neither consistent from one work to the next nor, apparently, entirely rational. It was possible to reconstruct most of the tables from the numbers that appeared in the sketches. Roger Smalley had in fact already done this for the Op.24 table in 1975, using just the pages of this work that were published in facsimile by Hans Moldenhauer in 1968,[9] and after seeing the sketchbooks in Basel for the first time in 1988 I did the same for the remaining twelve-note works.[10] But it was not possible to do the job with complete confidence from the sketches alone. In works where several of the possible row forms never appeared, the position on the table of these absent rows could only be extrapolated on the basis of the organisation of the other tables, and when I finally saw Webern's tables in 1989 I found that I had assumed more consistency than was warranted. This had resulted in two errors, in the tables for Opp.28 and 29. The work I had done, however, correct in other respects, revealed already several inconsistencies. In view of Webern's extreme care for detail in his music I found these inconsistencies intriguing, and I decided at that time to come back to the row tables at a later date and try to sort out the answers to some of the questions they posed. The following is the result of this return visit.

## Appearance

As a composer Webern was famously economical. In his music there is not a note too many; not a second is wasted. Several descriptive adjectives spring to mind: 'fastidious', 'meticulous', 'exacting'. Except for the occasional detail that has been deliberately altered in order to obscure a pattern of such flawlessness that it might otherwise be simply too much of a good thing,[11]

[8] Following their purchase by Paul Sacher in 1984.

[9] Smalley, 'Webern's Sketches (III)', *Tempo* 45/3 (1975), p. 15. This was the last in a series of articles written in response to Moldenhauer's publication of *Anton von Webern – Sketches (1926–1945)*.

[10] This was scheduled to appear in *Current Musicology*, but I withdrew it just before publication, when the tables were recovered.

[11] Such as the centre of the first movement of the *Symphonie*, where the axis of the palindrome is obscured by the use of grace notes.

his symmetrical constructions are perfect in every particular – apparently evidence of an unusually keen understanding of abstract relationships – and his canons are stunning in their intricacy, like those Chinese miniatures in which a series of nesting balls have been carved, one inside the other, from a single piece of ivory. It is therefore a considerable surprise to find the row tables from which he worked to be untidy, in both the physical sense and the technical, as well as uneconomical and in some respects confused. In these physical relics we catch an unfamiliar glimpse of the man Darmstadt has taught us to regard as the intellectual father of integral serialism. The man who made these tables seems perhaps not to have been so much a prodigy whose music was the result of reasoned calculations as a man who used his row tables as Stravinsky used his piano, to reveal wonderful surprises, not dissimilar to those unanticipated miracles he found on his walks in the Alps. An acquaintance with the row tables suggests that Webern's inspiration was at least as much visual (and, one supposes, aural) as it was intellectual, and that the amazing symmetries for which he has been celebrated were as often unexpected discoveries as inventions. Here, as in the mountains, the 'physical reality contains all the miracles'.[12]

The tables exhibit a certain physical economy. They are written on thirty-one small scraps of paper,[13] a few of which had been used previously and thus contain sketches or writing of some sort on the reverse side or on some portion of the page that was not required for the row table.[14] The tables for Opp.19, 23 and 25 are on single sheets; only those rows that are actually used in the music appear in these tables.[15] The tables for both Op.24 and Op.31 are on two sheets, each bearing twenty-four rows; each of the remaining tables (for Opp.20, 21, 22, 26, 27, 28, 29 and 30) occupies

12 See the Hochschwab letter quoted earlier in this volume (Moldenhauer, *Anton von Webern*, p. 231).

13 The largest pages used are half sheets of manuscript paper, but many pages are smaller than this. On the back of several is the trademark 'J.E.Protokoll Schutzmarke' and the size: 'No.105' (in the Op.31 table); 'No. 6, 20 linig.' (Opp.27–30); 'No. 8, 24 linig.' (Op.26); 'No.3, 14 linig.' (Op.25). The tables for Opp.19–24 are written on variously sized scraps of several sizes and grades of manuscript paper, with two types used for both the Op.20 and the Op. 2 tables.

14 This is true in the case of the Op.19 table and of p. 1 of the tables for Opp.20, 22 and 24.

15 Each of these works uses only the four untransposed rows and four others.

three pages, with sixteen rows to each page. It might be supposed that the number of pages, and thus the number of rows on each, was determined by the size of the scraps of paper available at the moment, but evidence argues against this.[16] There are no tables for any of the uncompleted, unpublished works, or for any of the other rows experimented with in the sketchbooks.

This economy does not however extend to the contents. Unlike Berg and Schoenberg, both of whom customarily wrote out only the forward-going rows – the prime and its inversion – on their row tables, since in doing this they had automatically produced the two retrograde forms as well,[17] Webern wrote out all four forms of each row at each level of transposition. This is not only an unnecessary duplication, but an unexpected extravagance in a composer whose music is so succinct. A similar prodigality seems to govern the handling of redundant row forms in the tables devoted to those rows that do not produce a full complement of discrete forms, and to the employment of colours in the early tables: we shall return to both of these questions in due course.

Just as surprising as the prolixity of the tables is the clumsy or careless physical appearance, particularly of the earlier ones – an untidiness which is difficult to reconcile with the meticulous attention to detail in the music generated from them. There seems to have been very little concern for making the pages match, either by using paper of the same type or by cutting the pages to the same size.[18]

16 The three pages of the Op.21 table, for example, were produced by tearing a single page of 24-stave manuscript paper into three (unequal) pieces; in this case, at least, three pages were clearly considered preferable to one or two.

17 See notes 56–9 below.

18 All the pages have been either torn or cut with scissors – in some cases both – from whole sheets of manuscript paper. While the tears have been folded first and are thus relatively straight, the scissor cuts have a certain infant-school character. Until Op.24 there appears to have been no attempt to cut the pages to the same dimensions, either horizontally or vertically. From Op.26 onwards pages are pretty well matched, until the table for Op.31, which consists of two strips taken from a large piece of manuscript paper with small staves very close together, the first page an entire width of the paper (although only the lefthand portion of it is written on), the second page cut untidily with scissors to a much narrower dimension. (About two or three inches of the righthand side of the first page have subsequently been folded back and under the second.)

**Plate 1** Anton Webern in his Mödling studio, summer 1930 (Sammlung Anton Webern, Paul Sacher Stiftung, Basel)

A well-known photograph of Webern in his studio (see Plate 1) shows the manner in which he mounted the row tables on his piano when he was composing. In this picture, which can be dated to the week of 20–7 August 1930, Sketchbook II is open on the piano music rack to pages devoted to work on a third movement of Op.22, which was never finished;[19] the Op.22 row table is tacked up on a board above. In this instance the three pages are in order from left to right, overlapping slightly and secured (precariously, one might think) with two thumbtacks at each join, one near the vertical centre and the other at the bottom. The fact that there are no tacks at the top, which would surely be the most obvious position to ensure stability,

[19] While the open pages of the sketchbook are not dated, p. 29 of the previous opening bears the date '20•VIII•1930' and p. 33 of the following opening the date '27•VIII•1930'. This photograph is printed backwards in Moldenhauer, *Anton von Webern* (between pp. 324 and 325). The date of this photograph was first established by Felix Meyer. See Markus Weber, 'Der Schaffensprozess im VI. Satz aus Anton Weberns *Zweiter Kantate* op.31: Versuch einer Rekonstruktion', in *Schweizer Jahrbuch für Musikwissenschaft* n.s.13/14 (1993–4), ed. Joseph Willimann (Bern: Paul Haupt, 1994), p. 100 note 14.

suggests that the board on which the pages were mounted probably did not extend upwards as far as the top of the row tables (the tables could not be placed lower than this and remain visible above the sketchbook). This does not explain, however, why there are no thumbtacks at the outer edges of pages 1 and 3. With four exceptions all of the tables have thumbtack holes and impressions in the same locations: none were secured at the top or at the outer edges. (In fact the whole arrangement seems awkward, particularly in the case of the tables for Opp.24 and 31, which consist of only two (thus longer) pages – these were overlapped slightly and secured with two tacks, one near the centre and the other at the bottom of the join: physical economy seems to have expressed itself also in the use of thumbtacks!) The exceptions are the short tables for Opp.19, 23 and 25, which were never mounted with tacks, and that for Op.20, of which only the first two pages appear to have been mounted side by side with edges overlapping at the top of the board, the third, with thumbtack holes in all four corners, probably having been pinned up below.[20] In fact the Op.22 table was the first to be pinned up in the way that was to be used thereafter: although the Op. 21 table was mounted in a very similar fashion, in this case p.1 was in the centre, with p. 2 to its left and p. 3 to its right.[21]

At some later time, perhaps even after Webern's death, though this seems unlikely, the pages of each table have been joined together with strips of sellotape on the left.[22]

20 Since this was the first of the tables to have been mounted vertically, Webern had apparently not yet found the most practicable position. On the other hand, it is possible that the constraints imposed by having the sketchbook on the music rack below the tables did not exist in the case of Op.20. The sketches for the Trio are not contained in any of the existing sketchbooks, and it is possible that they were not written in the same format as the other twelve-note sketches.

21 The relative positions occupied by the pages is clear, not only from the thumbtack holes, but from the colour of the paper: those portions that were exposed to the sunlight have browned, very badly in some cases (see for example p. 2 of the table in the photograph).

22 The last two tables, for Opp.30 and 31, remain connected in this fashion, while the tape used on all the earlier ones has perished, leaving only marks on the paper where it once was. This would seem to be an indication that Webern himself taped the pages of each table together to store it away when he had finished composing from it: in that case the ones that have survived are those made most recently.

The rows are written out on staves, in stemless black noteheads in close position (motion between adjacent notes is nearly always by the smallest interval possible, thus rarely exceeding a tritone[23]) and numbered consecutively, from one to forty-eight. The four row forms at each level of transposition are always kept together and treated as a unit. Within each of these groups the prime is followed by the retrograde on the same stave; the inversion and its retrograde are dealt with in the same way on the stave below. Thus the forward-going forms (P and I) alternate down the lefthand side of the page, the retrograde forms (R and RI) down the righthand side. A barline separates each row from its retrograde. For the most part the contour of each permutation reflects faithfully its relationship to the generating row. The retrograde forms are real retrogrades,[24] and the inversions are real inversions,[25] though the latter often begin an octave higher or lower than the original in order that they may lie within the stave.

On the first table, for Op.19, all the rows are carefully labelled: *Gr*[*undgestalt*], *Kr*[*ebs*], *U*[*mkehrung*], *U*[*mkehrung*]*Kr*[*ebs*]; *Transp*[*osition*], *Kr tr*, *U tr* and *Krebs U tr*. In the Op.20 table the first four forms are named; thereafter only the *Kr*, *U* and *UKr* are identified,[26] and in the table for Op.21 some of these are dispensed with as well (though somewhat erratically, as if through an oversight[27]). All such labels are dropped after Op.21.

23 The only exceptions are the minor sixth or augmented fifth between notes 8 and 9 of many of the forward-going rows and notes 4 and 5 of many of the retrograde rows on the Op.21 table, and the major seventh between notes 6 and 7 of some of the rows on the table for Op.30.

24 Exceptions to this, in which an interval in one row is answered by its octave complement going in the same direction in the retrograde of that row, occur in the following tables: Op.19 ($P_6$ and $R_6$); Op.21 ($I_0$ and $R_{10}$, $I_{10}$ and $RI_{10}$, $P_9$ and $R_9$, $P_8$ and $R_8$); Op.24 ($I_9$ and $RI_9$); and Op.30 ($P_4$ and $R_4$, $P_3$ and $R_3$).

25 Exceptions to this, in which an interval in one row is answered by its octave complement going in the same direction in the inversion of that row, occur in the following tables: Op.21 ($P_0$ and $I_0$, $P_1$ and $I_1$, $P_{11}$ and $I_{11}$, $P_2$ and $I_2$, $P_{10}$ and $I_{10}$, $P_7$ and $I_7$, $R_9$ and $RI_9$, $R_8$ and $RI_8$); Op.23 ($P_0$ and $I_0$, $R_0$ and $RI_0$, $P_6$ and $I_6$, $R_6$ and $RI_6$); Op.24 ($R_9$ and $RI_9$); and Op.27 (*all* P and I rows, and *all* R and RI rows, with the exception of those at $t_4$, $t_5$, $t_6$ and $t_7$).

26 The last two inversions, nos.43 and 47, in fact are not.

27 On p.1 row XVI, which is a retrograde inversion, is labelled *Kr* and there are no *Us* on p.1 after row III; all *Us*, *Krs* and *Ukrs* are identified on p. 2; the last two inversions on p. 3 are not labelled, or the first retrograde on that page (row 34) – the latter because there is no room to write at the top of the page.

Intervals of transposition are identified throughout in conventional (tonal) terms: *kleine* and *große Sekunden* and *Terzen, Quart, Quint, verminderte Quint.* No other intervals are named: the identification of transpositions as either upwards (*aufwärts*) or downwards (*abwärts*) obviates the necessity for any reference to intervals larger than a tritone, though transpositions of a fifth are indicated nonetheless in the tables for Opp.20, 21 and 26–29, and the $t_5$ rows in the Op.25 table are identified as *unter-Quint.* Octave equivalence is assumed: the beginning note of nearly half of the tritone transpositions is related to the beginning note of rows 1 and 3 as an augmented fourth rather than a diminished fifth,[28] and the *unter-Quint* rows of Op.25 begin on the note a fourth above.

The order in which the transpositions appear on the tables was continually evolving, but by the end of his life Webern appears to have arrived at an arrangement that he considered ideal. In the tables for Opp.30 and 31 the limits of the system ($t_0$ and $t_6$) are defined initially, with the remaining transpositions fanning out chromatically in both directions from $t_6$ – $t_5$, $t_7$, $t_4$, $t_8$, $t_3$, $t_9$, $t_2$, $t_{10}$ $t_1$, $t_{11}$ – to close the circle and complete the octave. Since the rows for Opp.30 and 31 are not similar, there is no reason to suppose that they should generate transpositions in the same order, so Webern's use of the same table for these two works would seem to be an indication of his satisfaction with this particular arrangement in general.[29] We shall return to this question later.

In all the tables the numbers 1–4 are assigned to the untransposed prime, retrograde, inversion and retrograde inversion, in that order. Since the ordering of transpositions varies from one table to another, the remaining numbers do not represent the distance of the transposition from the original, but only its position in the table. In those tables containing only eight rows the rows are numbered 1–8, even though they are not the same row forms in all three cases (Opp.19 and 23 use rows at $t_0$ and $t_6$, Op.25 at $t_0$ and $t_5$).

28 This is true of both the $P_0$–$P_6$ and the $I_0$–$I_6$ relationship in Opp.21, 27 and 28, and of one of the relationships in Opp.22, 26, 29, 30 and 31, in all of which either $P_0$ and $I_0$ or $P_6$ and $I_6$ begin in different octaves.

29 He had used nearly identical arrangements for two works in succession on two earlier occasions: the order of transpositions on the tables for Opp.21 and 22, and on those for Opp.28 and 29, were the same except for the relative position of the two fourth/fifth transpositions.

There is considerable confusion of arabic and roman numbers at the beginning; Webern appears to have started with arabic numbers, changed his mind in favour of roman, then subsequently returned to arabic. In the table for Op.19 the rows seem to have been given arabic numbers first, with roman equivalents added later. Some combination of roman and arabic numbers appears on the three tables for Opp.20–2, but the short table for Op.23 uses roman. Only arabic numbers are used from Op.24 onwards.

It is not only the order of transpositions and the vacillation between roman and arabic numbers that beg for explanation. The tables are written in several colours, which are used also to identify rows in the sketches, and these are enigmatic as well. At first four colours – red or orange, blue, purple and green – were used, in addition to ordinary lead pencil; purple does not appear after Op.21. Black ink, which is first seen on the table for Op.22, becomes increasingly important as the use of colours is reduced. A number of individual pencils can be identified. Most tables contain evidence of only one pencil of any colour; there are, however, a few exceptions to this, and these raise questions regarding dates and late additions (more about this presently). The tables for Opp.26 and 27 (both dating from 1935) use a green that is used nowhere else; it has weathered badly and is very faded. A green like one of those seen on the earlier tables reappears in its place in the last four tables, for Opp.28–31.

In the tables for Opp.19, 20 and 22 the rows themselves were written for the most part in lead pencil (this is now quite faded),[30] with most of the numbers and labels (*Krebs* and so on, and the intervals of transposition) in coloured pencils. In the Op.21 table the notes are written in coloured pencils as well throughout. From Op.24 onwards (with the exception of Op.25, which uses pencil) the notes are written in black ink.

The rationale governing the distribution of colours is even more difficult to perceive than that determining the ordering; indeed the two are closely related. Both are in transition until Op.30. In the beginning the colours seem to have had no purpose beyond that of differentiating between neighbouring row forms. In Opp.21 and 24 they are to some degree systematic, indicating relationships and similarities, but elsewhere

[30] On the Op.20 table the notes of rows 41–44 are written in blue pencil.

the use of colours, like the ordering of transpositions, appears to have been an abstract exercise.

The rows on the earlier tables are partitioned; this seems to mean various things. In Op.19 the row is partitioned into tetrachords and these are used in a way that is uncharacteristic of Webern's twelve-note writing generally.[31] This partitioning is suggested in the row table, in which dotted barlines divide all but the final row into tetrachords. The much more tightly constructed Op.20 row offers numerous tetrachordal and hexachordal identities.[32] In addition the introduction and coda of the second movement contain the last instances of segmental layering (again, of tetrachords) in Webern's music. All the rows on the Op.20 table are divided into tetrachords, once again by dotted barlines. Trichords are indicated also on this table, with slurs. This is curious, since the trichord is not a segment that is isolated in any way in Op.20. The hexachordal symmetry of the Op.21 row[33] is suggested only in the first row, in which a double bar separates the hexachords. The more subtle tetrachordal invariance[34] is only hinted at.[35] The obvious trichordal symmetry of the Op.24 row is reinforced with dotted barlines separating all rows on the table into trichords. There is very little partitioning after this: the more subtle symmetries of the Opp.28 and 29 rows are alluded to by barlines in the first row only, while that of Op.30 is ignored altogether.

## The tables

### *Op.19 (Two Songs on texts by Goethe)*

For the eight rows on the Op.19 table (see Figure 1) all four colours are used, a different colour being assigned to each pair of rows. While this use of colours is unique to this table (hereafter the same colour is used for all four row forms at the same level of transposition), one permanent

31 See especially b. 9 of the first song, where the three tetrachords of $I_6$ are layered and sung simultaneously by alto, tenor and bass in rhythmic unison.

32 Hexachords of rows related as $P_0$ and $RI_1$ have the same pc content, as do tetrachords of rows related as $P_0$ and $P_6$, $I_5$ or $I_{11}$.

33 Compare rows I and XIV ($P_0$=$R_6$) on Figure 3 below.

34 Compare rows I and XXXIX ($P_0$ and $I_9$) on Figure 3.

35 Tetrachords are separated by barlines in rows I, III, V–VII and VIII (see Figure 3). None of these particular rows are tetrachordally related, however.

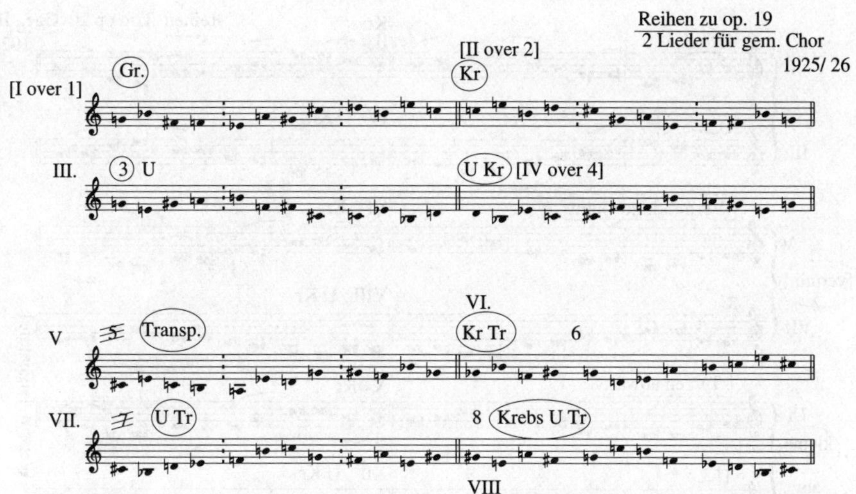


**Figure 1** Row table for Op.19 (Two songs on Goethe texts for mixed chorus and instruments)

feature of the tables is established here: the untransposed prime and retrograde are labelled in red. Red or orange is associated with the untransposed rows in all the tables: from Op.20 onwards this includes $I_0$ and $RI_0$ as well as $P_0$ and $R_0$. The remaining colour associations in the Op.19 table are: rows III and IV, blue; V and VI, purple; VII and VIII, green. The notes are in lead pencil, the heading 'Reihen zu op.19' and the title of the work are blue, and the row numbers, labels (*Gr.*, *Kr* etc.) and circles around the labels are in the appropriate colours (but see below).

The sequence of decisions regarding numbers on this table is not altogether clear, though it seems certain that the roman superseded the arabic. Roman I, II and IV have been heavily written over arabic 1, 2 and 4; arabic 5 and 7 have been shaded out with coloured pencil. Both numbers remain for rows 3, 6 and 8, though a circle has been drawn around the number 3 (in the sketches this is Webern's way of indicating something that is to be excised). Two things are puzzling: the position of arabic 6 makes it look like the afterthought rather than the original, and the row label *Gr.* (but *not* the circle around it) and roman I and II are all in a different red pencil, the same pencil in which the date was added (on this table and on most of the other early ones), almost certainly on a later occasion. Because the

Figure 2 Row table for Op.20 (String Trio), p. 1

appearances of this pencil are of particular interest and we shall refer to it on several later occasions, I should like to identify it as Red X.

*Op.20 (Trio for strings)*

The preference for roman numerals continues in the table for Op.20 (see Figure 2), though complete conviction seems to be lacking. In this case all the rows were given roman numbers, but arabic numbers have been added from 25 onwards (the arabic 25 is in fact written over roman XXV). The numbers 40, 47 and 48 have been encircled, and 44 is in round brackets.

The Op.20 table continues in the colourful tradition established by that for Op.19; in fact the next three tables, for Opp.20–2, induce a sense of chromatic overload. Although on the Op.20 table each colour is used for a full complement of four rows, no colour appears more than once (for row

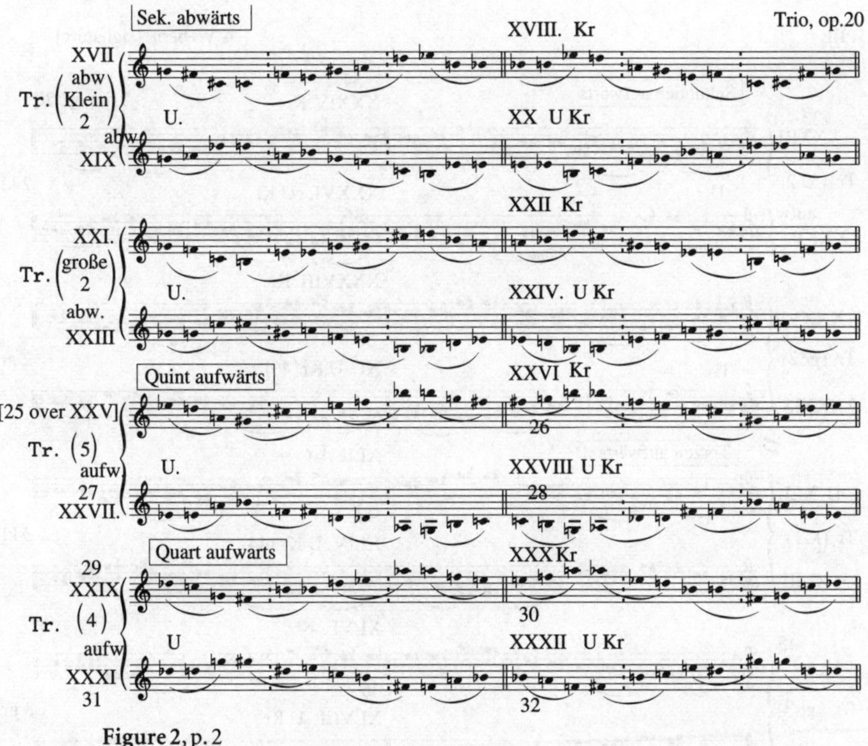


**Figure 2, p. 2**

numbers and labels) on any page. In this instance it would appear that the avoidance of colour repetition was a significant factor in Webern's choice of colours. The colours used for row numbers, curly brackets and labels (*U*, *Kr* and *U.Kr*) on p. 1 are respectively orange, green, blue and purple; on p. 2, a new green (chartreuse), lead pencil, blue and orange; and on p. 3, the new green, lead pencil, blue and orange.

A profusion of additional coloured items confuses the issue. Clefs, barlines and notes on this table are in lead pencil, with the following exceptions: the clefs for rows V–VIII are drawn in green and those for rows IX–XII in blue; the notes of rows XLI–XLIV are blue. Slurs used throughout to indicate trichords are now so badly faded – or erased – as to be nearly invisible on p. 1; on pp. 2 and 3 they are in the same colour as the labels and numbers except in rows XVII–XXIV and XLI–XLIV, where they are orange (the other indications are chartreuse in rows XVII–XX, in lead pencil in rows

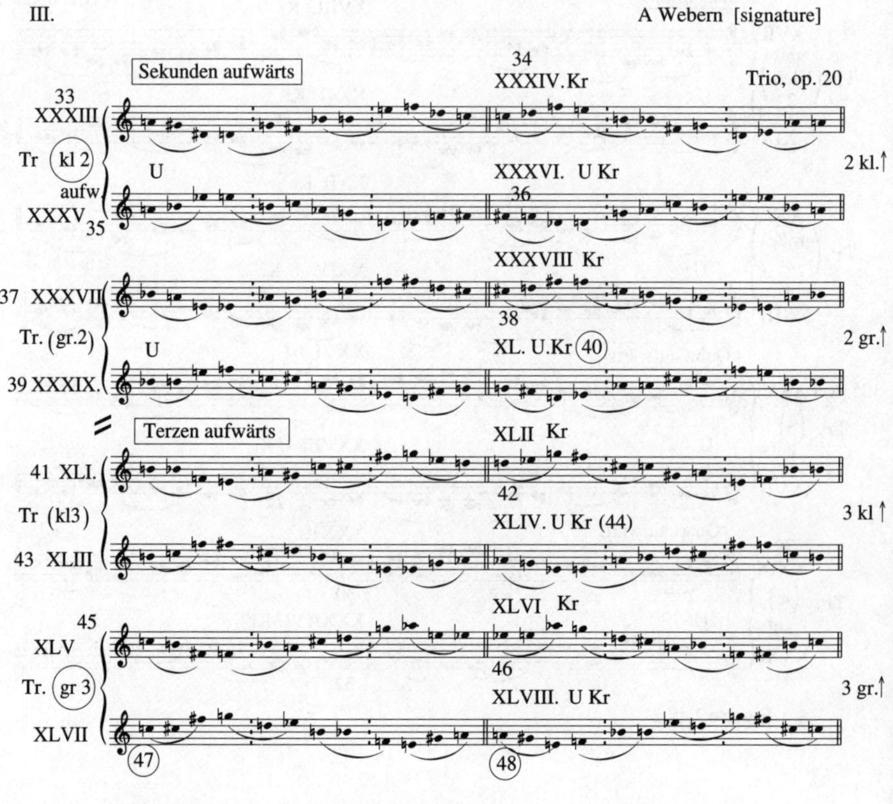


**Figure 2, p. 3**

XXI–XXIV and blue in XLI–XLIV); XXXVII–XL, where they are blue (the other indications are in lead pencil); and XLV–XLVIII, where they are in lead pencil (instead of the orange used for the numbers and labels).

Webern seems to have had bad luck with the pencils with which he started this table; both the original green and the purple (the same pencils used on the table for Op.19) appear to have given up before the end of the first page, the green just after rows V–VIII were numbered and labelled but before the interval of transposition was indicated, and the purple – already badly in need of sharpening at its first use – before its work for rows XIII–XVI was completed. Thus *Verminderte Quint* had to be written with a second green pencil. As this pencil is a lighter shade of green, it could not be used to write over the original green, so those bits of green writing that were illegible because of the advanced decrepitude of the original pencil were written over in lead pencil. The new green was used for all green indications on pp. 2 and 3. This green has also become illegible at the top of p. 2: *Tr. (abw Klein)* has been written over with lead pencil, and *abw* has been added again, below, in lead pencil only. While the purple pencil seems to have shared the fate of the original green, there was apparently no other purple at hand, so those purple indications that were illegible on p. 1 were written over also in lead pencil, and this pencil replaces the purple henceforth. Purple scribbles at the bottom of p. 3, of the sort one makes when trying out a pencil, support the theory that this instrument was giving trouble.

The transposition label (*Sek. abwärts*) at the top of p. 2 is orange (though badly faded); it is enclosed in a box, which was also orange but has been drawn over in blue. Except for the lead pencil over-writes just mentioned, all corrections and additions on pp. 2 and 3 of this table have been done with blue pencil, except where the original colour was blue: in these cases corrections are in lead pencil.

There is clearly an attempt to use the same colour for mod 12 complements; this is the rule from Op.21 onwards. But given the order of transpositions on the table it was impossible both to colour-code mod 12 complements *and* to avoid colour repetition (upward transpositions of a fourth and a fifth come on the same page, for example). However, to the extent to which it *is* possible to do so, complementary transpositions are numbered in the same colour.

### *Op.21 (Symphony)*

The indecision concerning roman and arabic numbers intensifies in the Op.21 table (see Figure 3). This is the first symmetrical row, and the clutter of numbers on the table is directly related to this fact, though the confusion of roman and arabic forms seems to result simply from Webern's tiring of the unwieldy roman numbers at some point (perhaps later than one might have expected him to) and switching to arabic instead.[36] The

[36] His method must have been to number the forward-going rows of each group first; his decision in favour of the more manageable arabic numbers was taken halfway through writing out the minor third transpositions on p. 3.

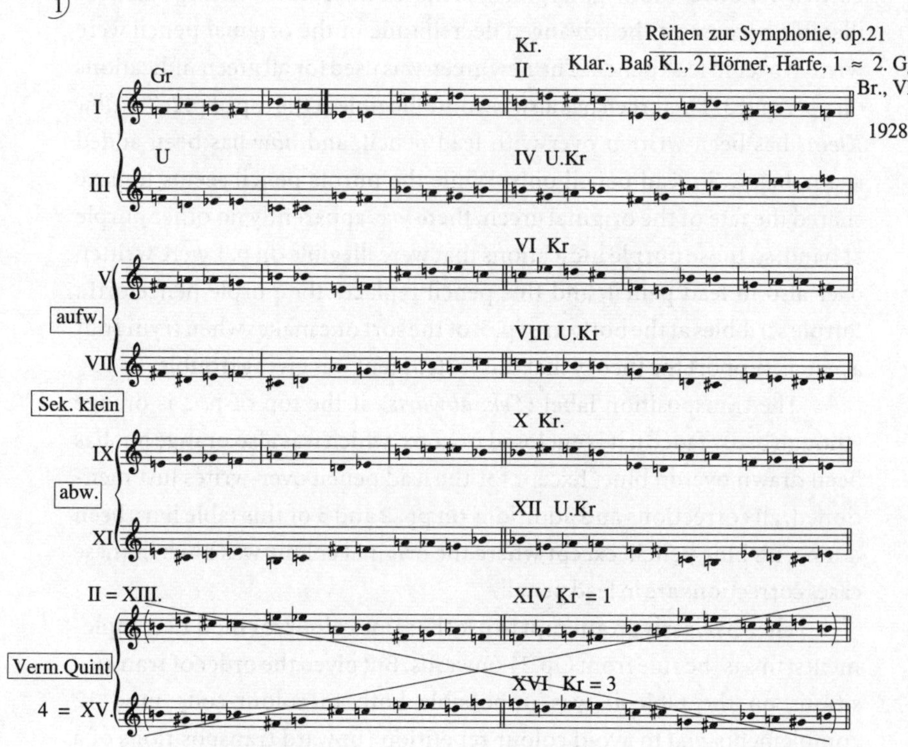


**Figure 3** Row table for Op.21 (Symphony), p. 1

Op.21 row yields only twenty-four discrete forms. Webern has identified most of the duplications, though curiously not all;[37] equivalent rows are identified with arabic numbers, regardless of the sort of numbers used *in situ.* This, as well as the position of the two numbers, would seem to indicate that the identification of the exact nature of redundancies was a later addition to the table.

The colours on the Op.21 table relate directly to the appearance of rows in the piece. The relationship between row table and music in this instance is intriguing, and reminds one more than a little of the chicken and egg conundrum. (Did Webern compose the piece following his table, or did

[37] He does not indicate the equivalents for rows XXV, XXVII, XXIX and XXXI, though he gives them for their retrogrades – XXVI, XXVIII, XXX and XXXII.

**Figure 3**, p. 2

he construct the table on the basis of what had already occurred in the piece? Or did table and music unfold simultaneously?) Except for the early appearance of the three fifth transpositions, the table describes a chromatically expanding interval series – an arrangement, one would suppose, chosen for its abstract logic. If the tritone and fourth/fifth transpositions, which replicate the first three groups on the table, had been placed at the end of the table, the interval series would have been perfect, and twenty-four discrete rows would have preceded their twenty-four duplications. This could not be done, however, without dividing one of the other transpositional groups between two pages, something which Webern was obviously loath to do (though there was nothing to prevent the fourth and fifth coming at the end of p. 3). As it is, new rows and duplications of those already presented alternate in an ultimately symmetrical arrangement: the

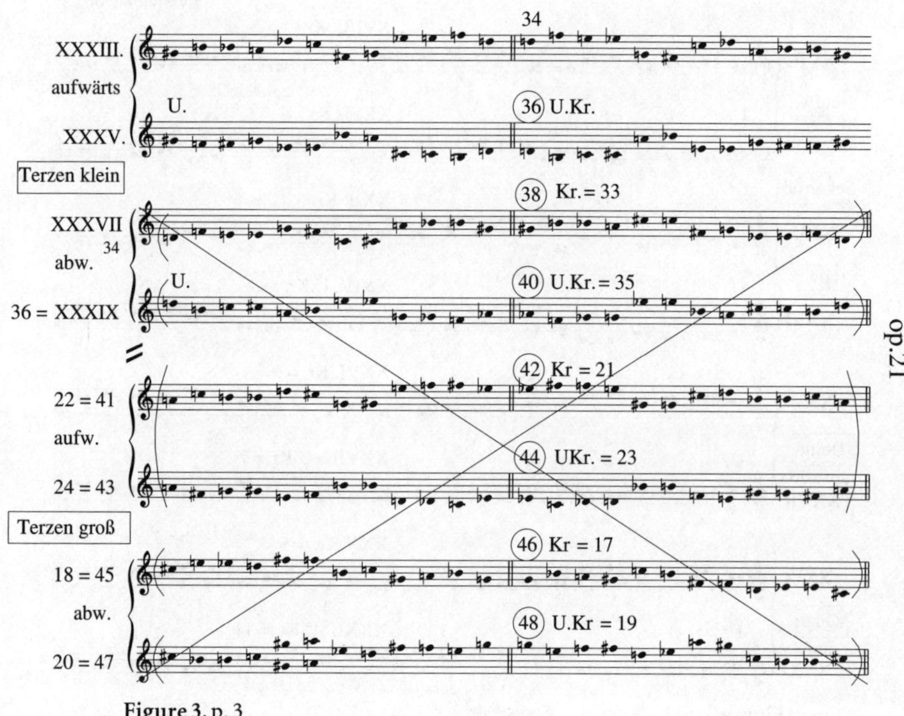


**Figure 3**, p. 3

first three groups of rows are followed by one group of redundant rows, then two more new groups are followed by two redundant groups, and the last new group is followed by the remaining three redundant groups. Given this alternating arrangement, the colours serve to sort out the new from the redundant, and to reflect the progress of the music (as shown presently), as well as the relationships inherent in this very special row.[38]

Two colours are associated with the first group of rows on this table (rows I–IV: $t_0$): the notes are written in purple pencil[39] and the bracket, barlines, row labels and numbers in the orange used on the Op.20 table. Only

[38] Because of the symmetry of this row, any rows related as $P_0$ and $R_6$ (or as $I_0$ and $RI_6$) are identical.

[39] I think. (It is very difficult to tell whether this is purple or ordinary lead pencil.)

rows from this group are used in the Theme of the Op.21 variations movement (the first movement of Op.21 to have been written). Both notes *and* numbers of the next two groups (V–XII: $t_1$ and $t_{11}$) are green.[40] These two groups contain all the rows that occur in Variation 1. The next group of rows (XIII–XVI: $t_6$) is redundant: it duplicates rows I–IV. In this group ordinary lead pencil has been used for everything: brackets, notes, labels, barlines, numbers. On this table lead pencil (and, later, purple) indicates redundancy: the precise nature of the redundancy is shown in this case by round brackets and numbers of the equivalent rows, both orange, the colour originally associated with those rows. The whole group is crossed out as a unit in purple. Everything in the next two groups (XVII–XXIV: $t_2$ and $t_{10}$) is blue.[41] All the new transpositions introduced in Variation 2 are from these groups. The next two groups (XXV–XXXII: $t_7$ and $t_5$) are again redundant, duplicating rows V–XII, and the treatment is essentially the same as in the earlier redundant group. XXV–XXVIII are in lead pencil and XXIX–XXXII are purple, now very badly faded. The equivalent row numbers, round brackets and this time also the lines crossing out each group are green, the colour of the groups that are duplicated.

The last page of this table is unique. It begins with the rows used in Variation 3. With this group of rows all the transpositions have been exposed (and used in the piece): the central variation of the movement combines rows from all groups, and subsequent variations simply regress back through the table. Predictably, this group of rows introduces a new colour. Surprisingly, this colour is Red X. It is used for *everything* on this page: clefs, brackets, notes, row numbers, labels, transposition labels for all sixteen rows. In all the row tables no other page is as uniform chromatically as this one. Only one other colour appears on this page: the purple that has identified all earlier redundant rows on this table figures also in the last three groups on this page. Here the equivalent numbers are written in purple (rather than in the colour of the originals, as previously), and the round brackets and crossing out are done in purple as well.

40 The box around *Sek klein* and the barlines separating the tetrachords in rows V–VII and IX are in lead pencil, as was all of row V originally. The latter has been written over in green.

41 Except for the *U.Kr* above row XXIV, which is in lead pencil.

The colour consistency of this page raises questions as to when it was written. It would be tempting to see it as a replacement page, written in haste throughout with whatever pencil happened to be at hand were it not for the fact that the thumbtack holes on its left side can be made to match those on the right side of p.1 of this table. But, whatever the reason, less time would appear to have been lavished on it than on the first two pages of this table, perhaps because all the rows after the first four have already appeared elsewhere.

A few details on this page have been corrected: the note (but not the sharp) of the G♯ in row 42 has been written over in purple, and the G♯ and A of row 47 have been written an octave lower, in blue.

The numbers used in the sketches for Op.21 add to the confusion. At first (in sketches for the Theme of the variation movement, where only the untransposed prime and retrograde are used) no row numbers are indicated, but beginning with sketches for Variation I each row is identified as it enters. All Webern's sketches are in pencil; much of the time the row numbers in working sketches are written in pencil as well, though at other times they are written in the colour in which they appear on the row table. Frequently the original pencilled number has been written over in the appropriate colour. Both roman and arabic numbers are used; those rows that bear roman numbers on the table are numbered – indiscriminately, it would seem – in both ways in the sketches.

The sketches for the early works are expansive; numerous working sketches of a section are followed by a 'good' version, in which details are more carefully and clearly presented than may have been the case in the previous sketches. In the case of the Op.21 variation movement, each section is labelled clearly in these 'good' sketches – 'Thema', 'I.Var.', 'II.Variation' and so on, in coloured pencil, and this title is usually enclosed in a box of a different colour. The sketch is sometimes labelled 'gilt'.[42] On these occasions care is taken that the row numbers are written clearly in the colours in which they appear on the row table: however, even here roman and arabic numbers seem to be used at random.[43]

42 Webern's way of distinguishing a 'final' version – one that he is satisfied with, though such versions are often superseded later.

43 Thus the 'best' versions of the various sections of this movement bear the following row numbers: Thema (Sketchbook I, p. 17) – I, II; Var.I (I/20, 22) – 25 o.[*oder*] 6, 26 o.5, 5≈6, 11≈12 (≈ indicates a row elision), 31 o.12, 32 o.11 (in the

The redundant rows on the Op.21 table are XIII–XVI, XXV–XXXII and XXXVII–48. Two of these rows, XXXVII and 38 (replications of rows 34 and 33), are not used in the *Symphonie.* Although all the other rows are used, most of them bear the number given at their first appearance on the table: thus the numbers XIII–XVI and 41–8 are not used in the Opus 21 sketches.

However, numbers from the remaining two redundant groups (XXV–XXVII and XXIX–XXXII) *do* occur in the sketches: rows 25, 26, 31, 32 and 39 are indicated in the variation movement, and 25 and 26 in the movement that became the first movement. In the case of the variation movement, all of these except row 39 are listed as alternatives (most often as the first, rather than the second, of the numbers given): thus 'XI o.32' but '25 o.6', '26 o.5' and '31 o.XII'. No alternative is given for 39, which in Variations III and V forms a palindromic canon with 35 and would thus have been more logically interpreted as 36. No alternatives are offered for rows 25 and 26 in the first movement. In fact, this sort of identification, like the absence generally of redundant row numbers in the sketches, would suggest that Webern *found* his symmetries on the row table rather than identifying them in advance on the basis of their abstract relationships to each other.

***Op. 22 (Quartet for violin, clarinet, saxophone and piano)***

Sensory overload continues on the table for Op.22, where colours are still used with apparent abandon, and once again there is a mixture of roman and arabic numbers (see Figure 4). In this case only the first twenty rows are given roman numbers, the remaining ones arabic. On the first page of this table the notes and barlines are not written in colours (I–XII are in pencil, XIII–XVI in black ink), but row numbers are written in orange

(*cont.*) sketch directly above this one, and in a subsequent version on p. 22, only the numbers V, VI, XI and XII are used); Var.II (I/25) – XXIII, XXIV, III, IX, XI, XVII, XVIII, with 17≈23 and 24≈18 indicated for elisions performed by the harp (sketches on pp.24–6 use the numbers III, IX, XI, 17, 18, 23 and 24); Var.III (I/27) – 35, 39, II, I; Var.IV (I/29) – VIII, XXI, 18, XII, II, 35 (sketch on p.30 uses same except for arabic 21); Var.V (I/29–32) – same as Var.III; Var.VI (I/34) – XXIII, XXIV, 10, 4, XVII, XVIII; Var.VII (I/37) – V, VI, XI, XII; Coda (I/36) – I, II. Sketches for the first movement contain the following row numbers: 24, I, 22, 20, VI, VII, 36, IX (exposition and recapitulation), 25, 35, IX, XI, 26, 36, X, XII (development).

**Figure 4** Row table for Op. 22 (Quartet for violin, clarinet, saxophone and piano), p. 1

(I–IV), green (V–XII) and lead pencil (XIII–XVI). This is the same colour scheme that was used for Op.21, though since this is not a symmetrical row the colours do not have the same significance here.

Notes and barlines are in pencil also on p. 2, except for the double barlines in the last two staves, which are blue. This page is on a rougher and more porous type of paper than was used for pp. 1 and 3, and it has become very brown from exposure to sunlight. (This can be seen in Plate 1 above.) Transposition labels on this page are in lead pencil, though the last two have been encircled in blue. The numbers of the first two groups on p. 2 are written in red, those of the last two are blue. Two blue pencils appear to have been used to make this table, as well as both red and orange (elsewhere these two colours do not appear together). Row numbers of the first two groups

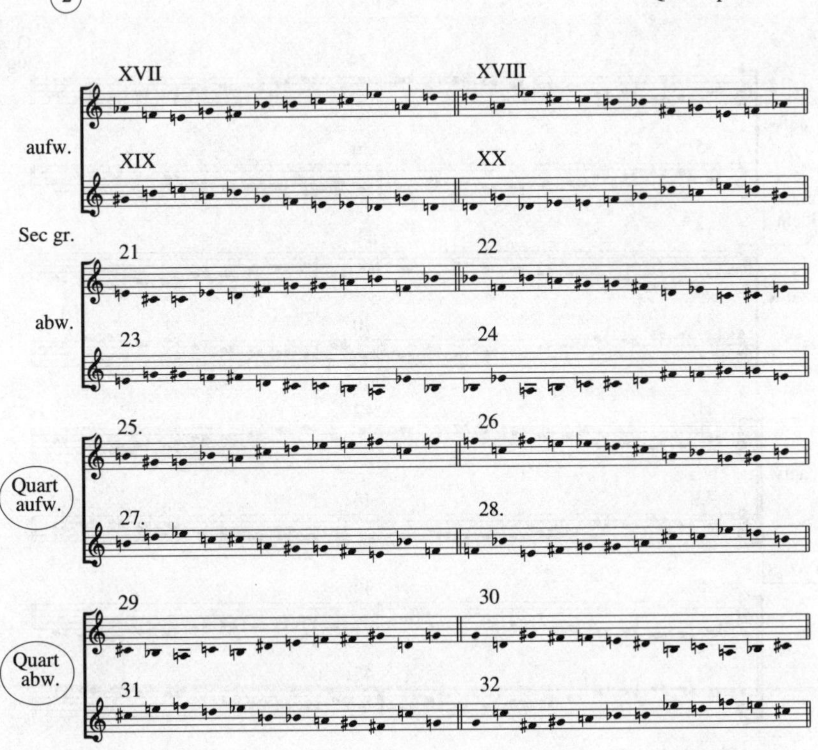


**Figure 4**, p. 2

at the top of p. 2 (rows XVII–24) are red, not orange, and the blue used on this page (for the numbers on rows 25–32) is not the same shade as that used on p. 3 (for rows 33–40). It could be argued that sunlight might affect colours differently on the very different paper used for these two pages, but the page numbers of all three pages remain orange (clearly the same shade used for the first group of rows on p. 1), and the more greenish blue used on p. 2 is not restricted to this page: the work title has been written at the top of all three pages in this colour. It is possible, of course, that the page numbers and work titles were later additions.

On the last page the notes themselves are in coloured pencil, blue for rows 33–40 and orange for rows 41–8. It must have been Webern's original intention that all the rows on this page should be blue: much of the preparation for the last eight rows – the transposition labels and many of the

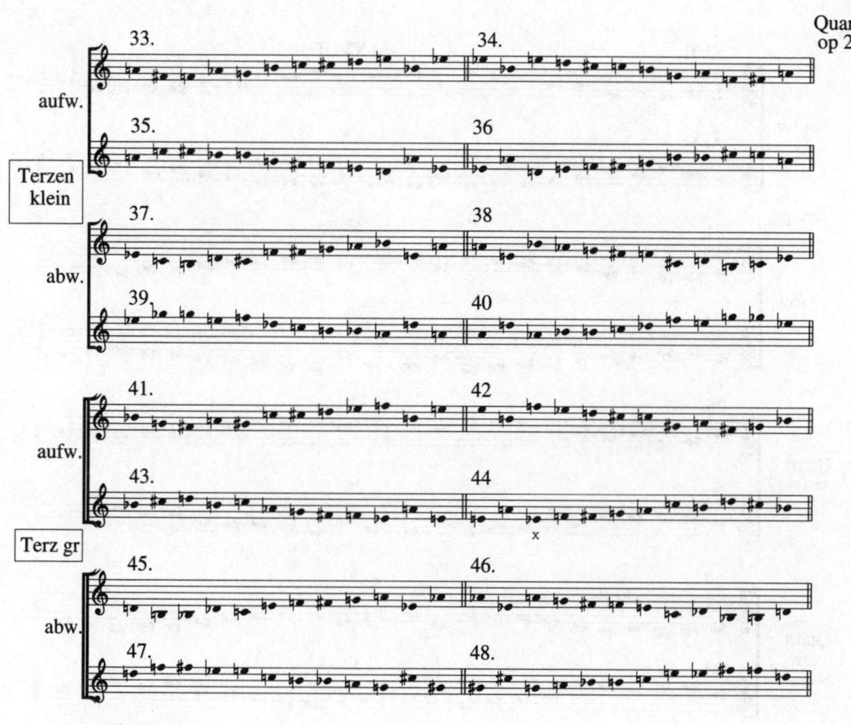


Figure 4, p. 3

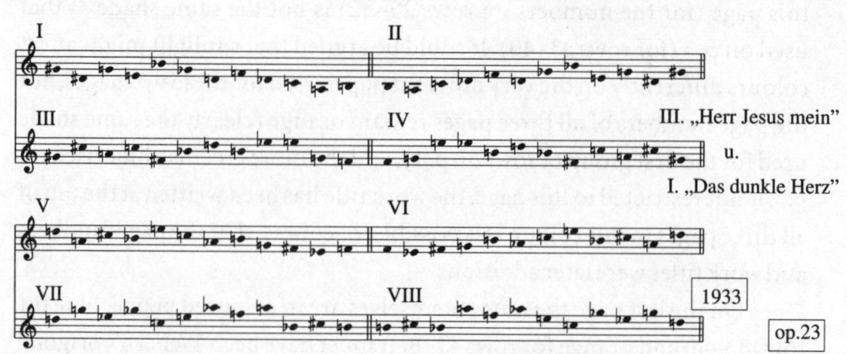


Figure 5 Row table for Op. 23 (Three songs from Hildegard Jone's *Viae invaie*)

barlines – are in that colour. Some of these have been written again in orange. Everything in the first eight rows is blue; the row numbers of the last eight are in lead pencil, the brackets match the notes, barlines are variously in orange, blue and lead pencil. The F♯ and A♮ of row 41 and the ♮ of G♮ have been written over in lead pencil. The paper used for this page was one stave short, and the last stave (containing rows 47 and 48) has been drawn in with lead pencil.

*Op.23 (Three Songs from Viae inviae)*

The abbreviated Op.23 table (see Figure 5) is written on the top section of a manuscript bifolio which has been cut neatly to size but from which, for some reason, the second folio was never removed. This seems a surprising extravagance after the scrappy bits of paper that have served for the tables of previous works. The notes, clefs and barlines are in lead pencil; row numbers are written in the same shade of red that was used for the last page of Op.21. This is the last table to use roman numerals.

*Op.24 (Concerto for nine instruments)*

The Op.24 table (see Figure 6) represents a considerable step in the direction of discipline and regularisation. Only arabic numbers are used on this table – and henceforth – and here for the first time all notes and transposition labels are in black ink, with only the brackets and row numbers in colours; the colour associations from this point on are simpler and more straightforward. Webern began writing this table in lead pencil as he had done before: the barlines on the first two staves were first written in pencil, then inked over. By the time he filled in the notes he had decided to do the whole thing in ink; with the exception of the short Op.25 table, this was his custom from this time forward. The transposition labels in the left margin, all written in black ink, are encircled in the appropriate colours, and the row numbers are coloured. The (red) row numbers for the first group of rows have been erased; the colours used on the remainder of this page are green for rows 5–12, blue for rows 13–20 and lead pencil for 21–4. On p. 2 rows 25–32 are written in red, 33–40 in blue and 41–8 in lead pencil. This is the first time that all the fourth/fifth transpositions take the same colour (in this case a non-colour); this will continue in subsequent tables. The only other groups to take the same colour are the major seconds (rows

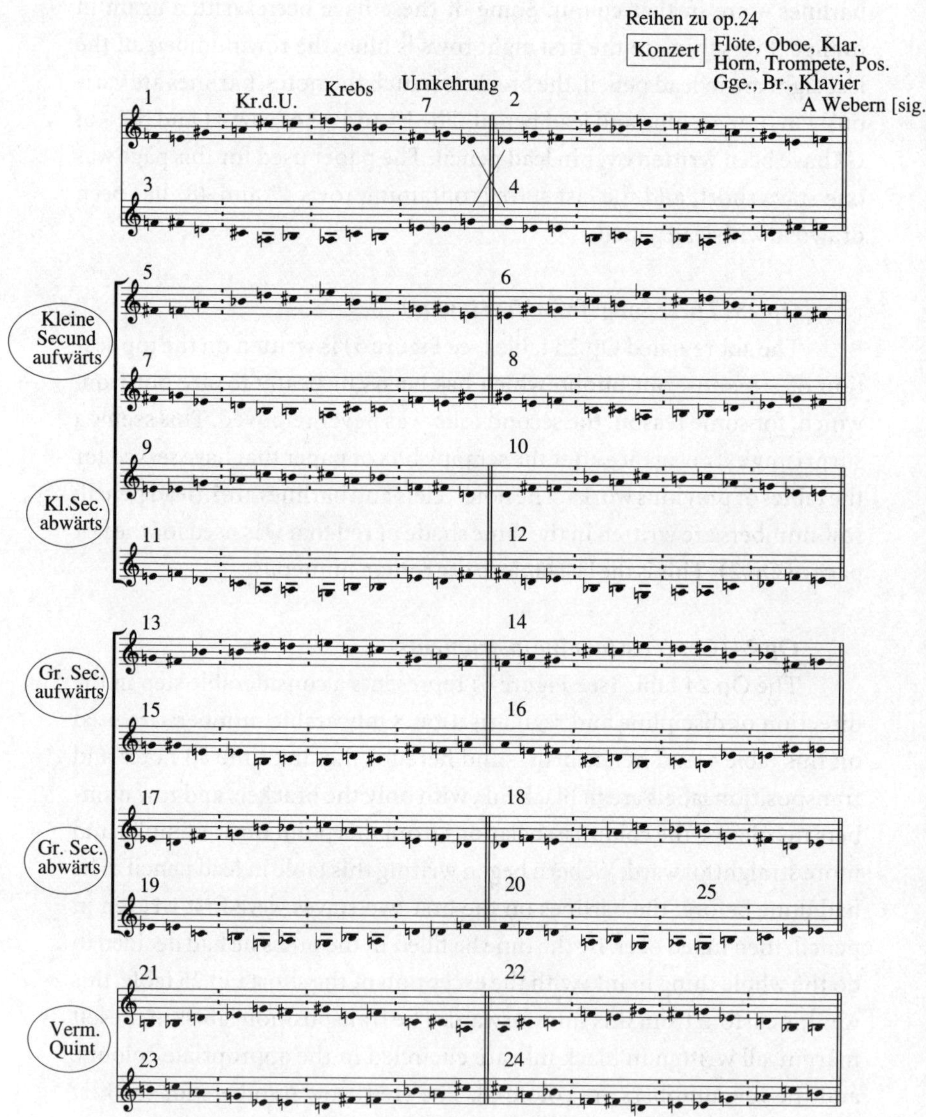


Figure 6 Row table for Op. 24 (Concerto for nine instruments), p. 1

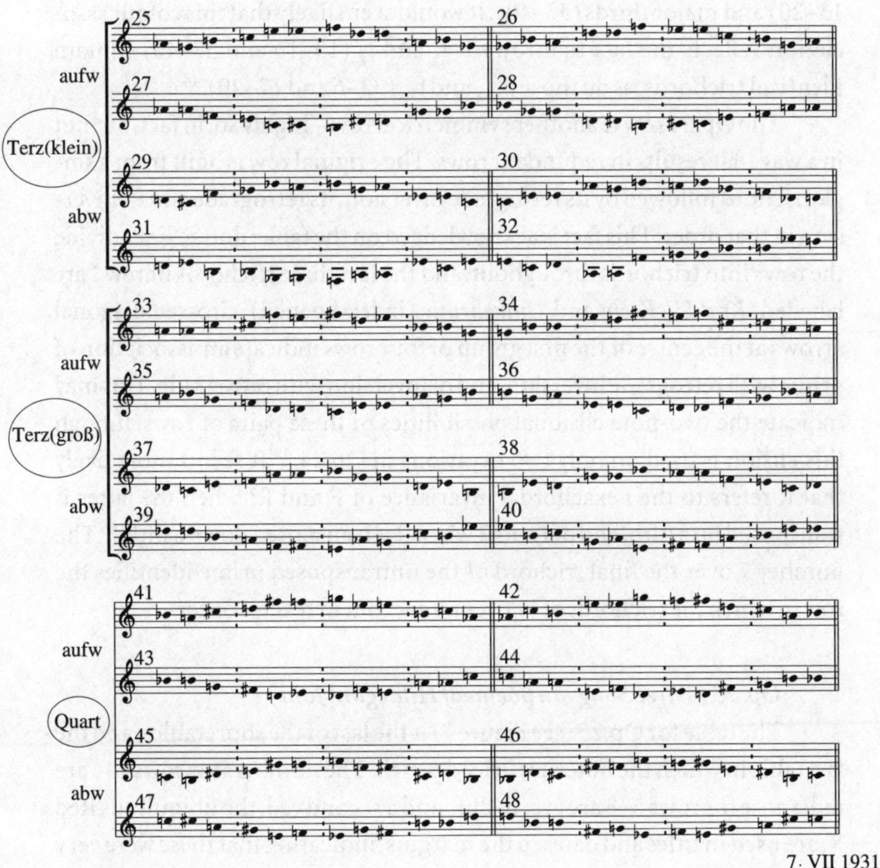
25
26
aufw
27
28
Terz(klein)
29
30
abw
31
32
33
34
aufw
35
36
Terz(groß)
37
38
abw
39
40
41
42
aufw
43
44
Quart
45
46
abw
47
48
7. VII 1931

**Figure 6**, p. 2

13–20) and major thirds (33–40). It would seem likely that this colour association reflects the fact that rows at $t_2$ and $t_8$ (13–16 and 37–40) contain identical trichords, as do those at $t_4$ and $t_{10}$ (33–6 and 17–20).[44]

The Op.24 row is another symmetrical row – highly so, in fact, but not in a way that results in redundant rows. The original row is built from a single trichord followed by its retrograde inversion, its retrograde and its inversion in that order. This fact is acknowledged on the table: dotted lines divide the rows into trichords throughout, and the last three trichords of row I are labelled, *Kr.d.U.*, *Krebs* and *Umkehrung* (in lead pencil). Crossed diagonal arrows at the centre of the first group of four rows indicate an association of prime with retrograde inversion, and of inversion with retrograde. This may indicate the two-note elisional possibilities of these pairs of rows, though this elision is used on only two occasions in Op.24.[45] It seems more likely that it refers to the hexachordal invariance of P and RI when the latter is transposed up a fifth, and of I and R when R is transposed down a fifth.[46] The number 7 over the final trichord of the untransposed prime identifies the row in which the trichords of $P_0$ occur intact but in reverse order.

*Op. 25 (Three Songs on poems of Hildegard Jone)*

The table for Op.25 (see Figure 7) is the last of the short tables, and the last table in which the notes are in lead pencil. The numbers for rows 1–4 are red; those for rows 5–8 are green. Blue and a second red, the ubiquitous Red X, are used in titles and dates in the margins, indicating that these were very

44 The same relationship occurs in other combinations, of course. In the case of $t_0$ and $t_6$ the numbers of rows 1–4 have been erased, but it is safe to assume that they were in lead pencil (the pencil used for the $t_6$ rows) originally. The rows $t_3$ and $t_9$ are coloured in the same way anyway, because both are minor third transpositions (rows 25–32). Only the rows at $t_1$ and $t_7$, and those at $t_{11}$ and $t_5$, are not colour-coded, presumably because Webern's decision to colour all the fourth/fifth transpositions in the same way took precedence.

45 In the first movement, $P_6$–$RI_6$ (rows 21, 24) in b.37; in the third movement, $P_{10}$–$RI_{10}$ (13, 16) in b.32.

46 Prominent use is made of this relationship in the outer movements: in the first movement, $R_1$ (row 6) and $I_8$ (39), $I_1$ (7) and $R_6$ (22) are hexachordally elided in bs 13–17 and 51–5, and $R_8$–$I_3$–$R_8$ (38–27–38) in bs 18–21 and 56–8. In the third movement $P_0$ (1) and $RI_7$ (48) in bs 56–60; $R_6$ (22) and $I_1$ (7) (*or* $I_7$ (47) and $R_0$ (2)) in bs 67–70.

Figure 7 Row table for Op. 25 (Three songs on poems of Hildegard Jone)

likely written on another occasion. One of these marginal additions, *2.Lied*, written beside the *Unter-Quint* transpositions, identifies the only place in Op.25 where these transpositions appear.

*Op. 26 (Das Augenlicht)*

On the table for Op.26 (see Figure 8), as on that for Op.24 (and henceforth), all clefs, barlines, notes and transposition labels are in black ink, the latter enclosed in boxes of the appropriate colours. On p.1 row numbers and barlines are red (rows 1–4), green (5–12) and blue (13–16); on p.2, red (17–24) and blue (25–32); on p.3, red (33–40) and green (41–8). (The latter is a very badly faded pencil used only for the tables of Opp. 26 and 27; it was originally chartreuse but now looks brown or even orange.) The red used throughout this table appears to be Red X; aside from the atypical p.3 of the Op.21 table, this is the only occasion on which Red X appears in the body of a table. It in fact makes only two more appearances after this, for the work title (but not for 'Reihen zu') at the top of the tables for Opp. 27 and 28. We shall return to this.

*Op. 27 (Variations for piano)*

In the table for Op.27 (see Figure 9) the fourth/fifth transpositions finally assume the positions in which they are to remain, directly after the tritone transpositions rows (thus, in the case of tables with three pages,

**Figure 8** Row table for Op. 26 (*Das Augenlicht*), p. 1

completing the first page), as well as the colour that was to be associated with them from this time onwards. The order on this table is otherwise anomalous: the order of the other intervals is altered so that all the minor intervals are on p. 2 and all their major counterparts on p. 3. Interval types are associated by colour rather than by proximity: all the seconds are blue and all the thirds are green. (The gathering used previously will be the rule again on the last four tables, where the seconds will fill one page and the thirds the next.) The colours used on p. 1 are orange (rows 1–4, badly faded) and green (5–16); on p. 2, blue (17–24) and orange (25–32); on p. 3, blue (33–40) and orange (41–8).

Although the Op.27 row is not a symmetrical one, the piece composed on it is one in which symmetry (as is well known) is very important. The hexachordal division which is such a prominent feature of the first movement of this work has been marked with particular determination on the row table: all the rows on either half of every page have been bisected with a single stroke of red pencil.

Figure 8, p. 2

*Op.28 (Quartet for strings)*

Here for the first time the intervals of transposition are placed in chromatically expanding order, uninterrupted by transpositions of a fourth or fifth (see Figure 10). The colours used on this table will remain in place for the last four tables, though the association of colours with intervals, the same here as in Op.27, will change on the last two tables when the interval series is reversed. The colours used on the tables for Opp.28–31 are red (1–4) and green (5–16) on p. 1; blue (17–32) on p. 2; and red (33–48) on p. 3.

The Op.28 row is again symmetrical, in such a way that only twenty-four discrete rows are produced. In fact this is true of the next three rows, for Opp.28, 29 and 30: in all cases this is the result of $P_0$=$RI_n$. Equivalents are noted on all three tables. On the table for Op.28 the transpositions are arranged in such a way that twenty-four discrete rows unfold in the first half

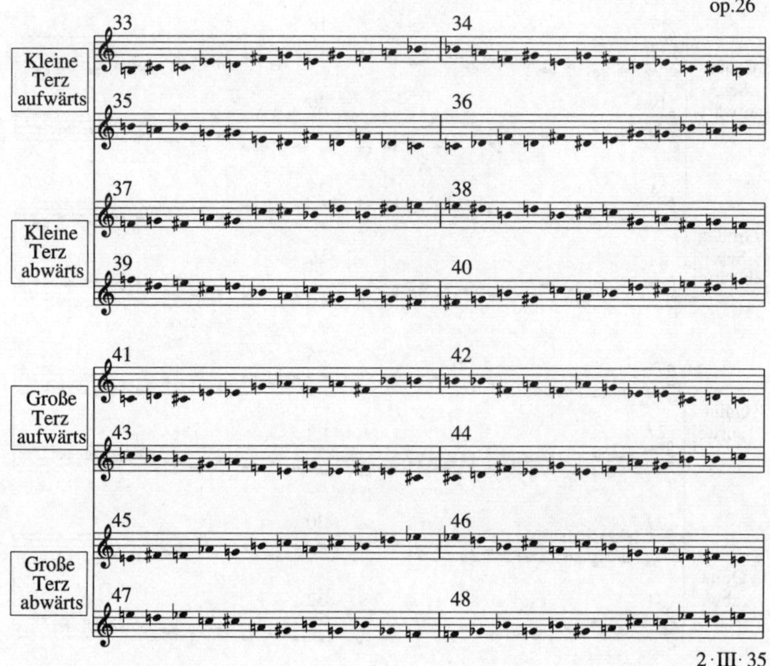


**Figure 8**, p. 3

of the table. Rows 25–32 have been written out but then boxed on three sides in red pencil, thus separating them from the rest of the rows on p. 2 and associating them instead with those on the following page (or those that would be on the following page, had they been written out) and thereby setting apart all the redundant rows. The third page has been prepared for the last sixteen rows, but these have not been notated. In the sketches for Op.28 Webern identifies all the rows with only the numbers 1–24.

*Op.29 (Cantata I)*

Though the transpositions are arranged in the same way in the table for Op.29, the interval of symmetry is not the same as it was in Op.28, and as a result redundant rows begin to occur as early as rows 9 and 10, which

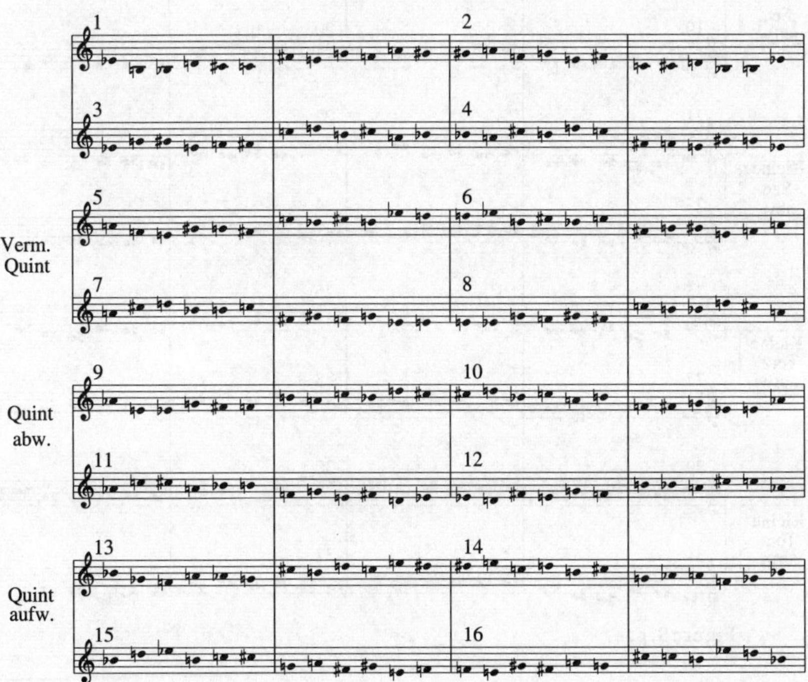


**Figure 9** Row table for Op. 27 (Variations for piano), p. 1

replicate rows 4 and 3 (see Figure 11).[47] Rows 9–10, 15–18, 23–26, 31–32, 35–38, 41–48 are redundant; this fact is indicated in a variety of ways. Rows 9–10, 15–16, 17–18, 23, 25 and 47–48 are enclosed in square brackets which are the same colour as the row numbers. None of the remaining redundant rows, except for 47 and 48, is written out. The empty staves where 41–46 should have been, along with rows 47 and 48, have been crossed out as a single unit in red. The numbers of all equivalent rows are indicated in the colours in which they appear elsewhere on the table. However, *all* equivalents are not noted. At first, on p. 1 and the upper half of p. 2, the numbers identifying

47 The interval of symmetry in the Op.29 row is such that it is impossible, keeping all four rows of each transposition together, to produce all twenty-four rows once before the repetitions begin.

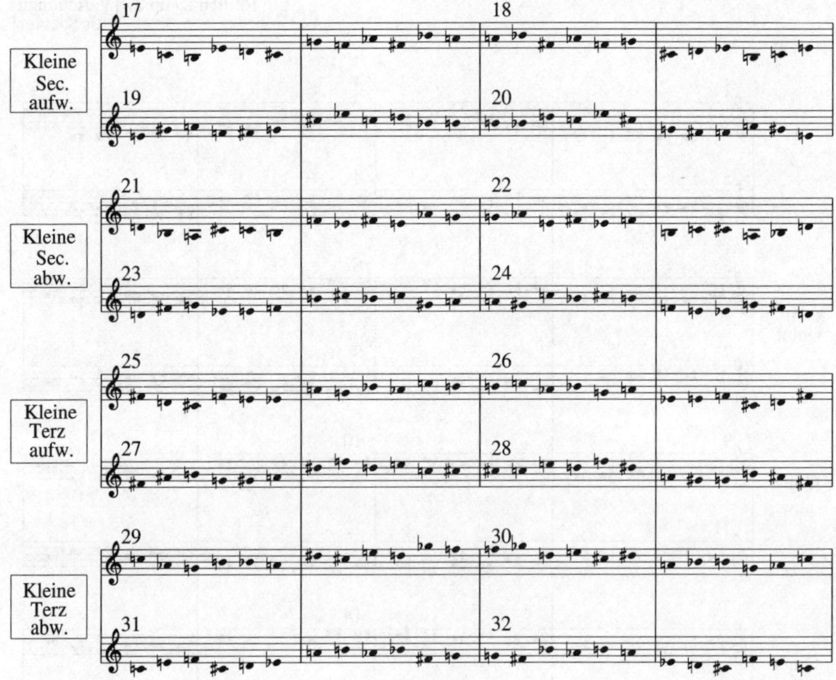


**Figure 9**, p. 2

equivalent rows have been added *before* row numbers on the left side of the page, *after* row numbers on the right side. The system changes with row 25: from this time on, whenever an equivalent is noted, it is written *after* the row number. This would seem to indicate that the equivalent numbers in rows 1–24 were later additions, while those in rows 25–48 were entered at the same time as the row number itself. Only the numbers of rows that are written out on the table are used in the sketches of Op.29.

### *Op. 30 (Variations for orchestra)*

It is with the Op.30 table that Webern seems finally to have found the ideal ordering of transpositions (see Figure 12). Here the series of seconds and thirds is reversed so that it describes a contracting, rather than an expanding, interval series. The colours retain the positions they occupied on the two previous tables; thus the seconds and thirds swap colours.

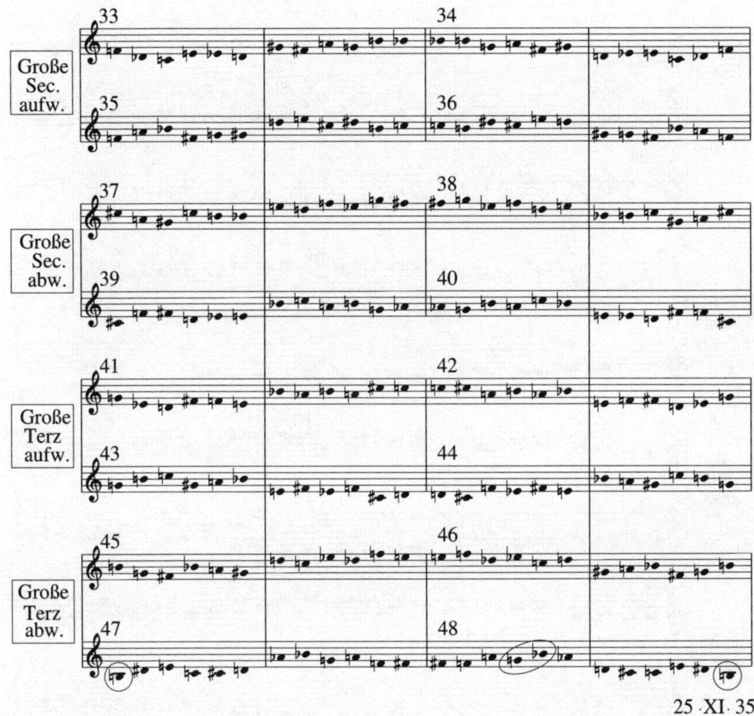


**Figure 9**, p. 3

Redundant rows begin to appear early again in the Op.30 table, but this time Webern seems to have been expecting them: none are written out, except for rows 45 and 46. As in both the Op.28 and the Op.29 tables, spaces have been prepared for all of the redundant rows; here each is represented by its first note only. Throughout, equivalents are noted in the way adopted with row 25 of Op.29.

In the Op.30 sketches Webern continues his practice of not using redundant row numbers, with one exception. In sketches for Variation 2 (Sketchbook IV, p. 61) the number 33 has been corrected twice, quite vigorously in red (the correct colour), to 35, the number of a redundant row (35=26), thus a row which does not appear on the row table.

### *Op.31 (Cantata II)*

The last table, for Op.31, is the simplest of the complete ones (see Figure 13). Row forms are not identified. This is not a symmetrical row; thus there are

**Figure 10** Row table for Op. 28 (Quartet for strings), p. 1

no redundancies to identify, and no equivalent numbers. There is no partitioning. Besides the notated rows themselves there are only row numbers and intervals of transposition, which are indicated in the left margin, in boxes. Like only Op.24 before it, this table is on just two sheets of paper. This affects neither the order in which transpositions are listed nor the assignment of colours, both of which remain exactly as in Op.30, which covered three pages.

## Order

And now to return to some of the questions raised by the tables. The constant peregrinations of transpositions was mentioned earlier and has been observed in the preceding examination. Table 1 (on p. 218) lists the order in which transpositions appear on all the tables.

**Figure 10**, p. 2

Similar transpositions were paired from the beginning, though the manner in which they are paired in the first full row table, that for Op.20, is different from that used consistently thereafter; here a transposition in one direction is followed immediately by one in the opposite direction at the same interval (thus pairing mod 12 complements – the order is usually ascending–descending). In the Op.20 table transpositions are paired instead according to interval type and direction: minor third down is followed by major third down, minor second up by major second up and so on. In a general way this first table is symmetrical: after the untransposed row and the transposition at the tritone, the intervals appear in the order descending thirds, descending seconds, descending fourth (though the fact that this is called an ascending fifth raises doubts that Webern thought in this way), ascending fourth, ascending seconds, ascending thirds. The

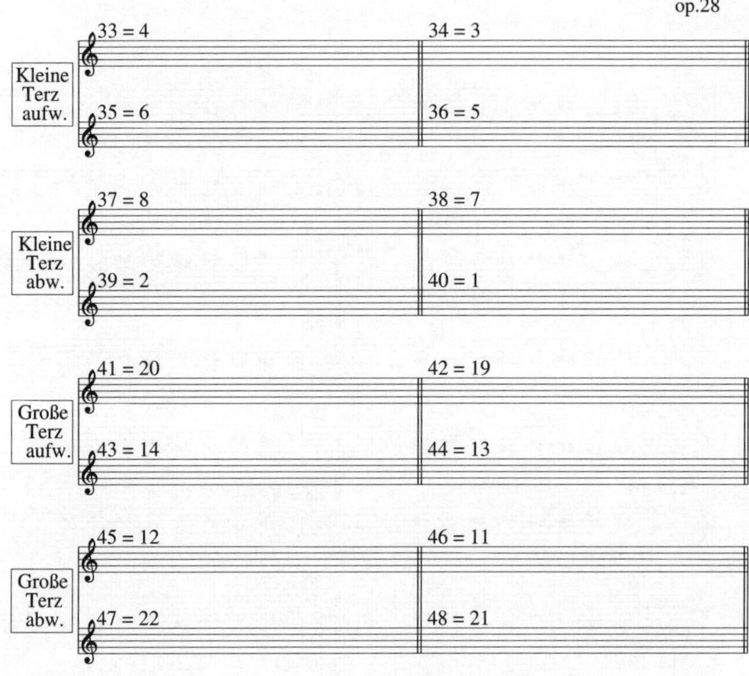


**Figure 10, p. 3**

symmetry is spoilt by the fact that in all cases, both before and after the centre, the minor version of an interval precedes the major. The reason for ordering the intervals in this way would seem to have nothing to do with either the nature of the row or the way it is used in Op.20.

In fact the ordering of the rows on the tables is not dissimilar to the ordering of books on the shelves of many libraries, where at least two determining factors – subject/author and height of book – operate concurrently. Because both the untransposed rows and the tritone transpositions consist of only four rows while eight rows are associated with each of the remaining intervals (four up, four down), because Webern seems to have been determined to keep all the rows at each interval of transposition together, and because he appears to have been equally determined that all the pages of a table should bear the same number of rows (thus either 3×8 or 2×12), the tritone transposition *must* occur on the first page of the table. Moreover, although his first impulse (in the Op.20 table) was to place it directly after the

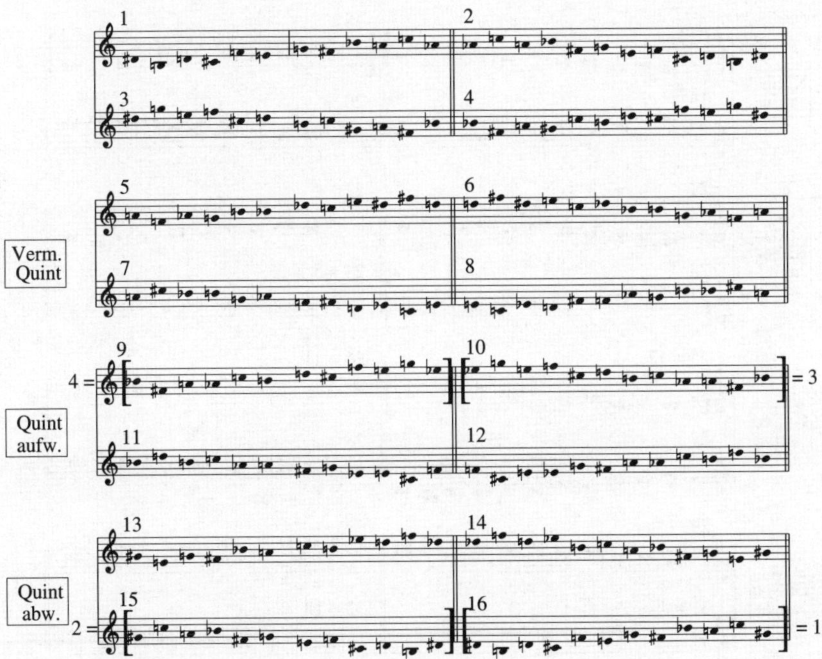


**Figure 11** Row table for Op.29 (Cantata no. 1), p. 1

untransposed rows, immediately thereafter (in Opp.20–6) he seems to have preferred it to be the last transposition on the first page; thus it does not occupy the same position in the series in the Op.24 table, which is written on two pages, and the remaining tables for Opp.21–6, which are on three. It resumes its original position directly following rows 1–4 on the Op.27 table (which is in other ways anomalous – see below), and here it remains.

Like the tritone, the transpositions of a fourth or fifth are slow to find their ideal position in the tables, and the question again appears to be governed by what might be thought a trivial requirement: Webern seems to have preferred these transpositions to come at the end of p. 2 of the table, as the tritone came at the end of p. 1. Thus while the fourth/fifths are the last

**Figure 11**, p. 2

thing on the Op.24 table they fall between the seconds and thirds elsewhere. But unlike the tritone these intervals are also subject to various interpretations. Identified as a fifth upwards followed by a fourth upwards in the tables for Opp.20 and 21, they have switched positions in the Op.22 table so that their treatment falls into line with that of the other intervals: here both are fourths, ascending and descending. In the Op.24 table they are again fourths, but in Op.26 they are identified as fifths. On the table for Op.27 these transpositions finally assume the position they will occupy in the remaining tables, though not yet the correct identification: here they are fifths, first falling, then rising (this descending–ascending sequence is unprecedented). In the Op.29 table the sequence is corrected, and finally, in the tables for Opp.30 and 31, the interval is a fourth as well.

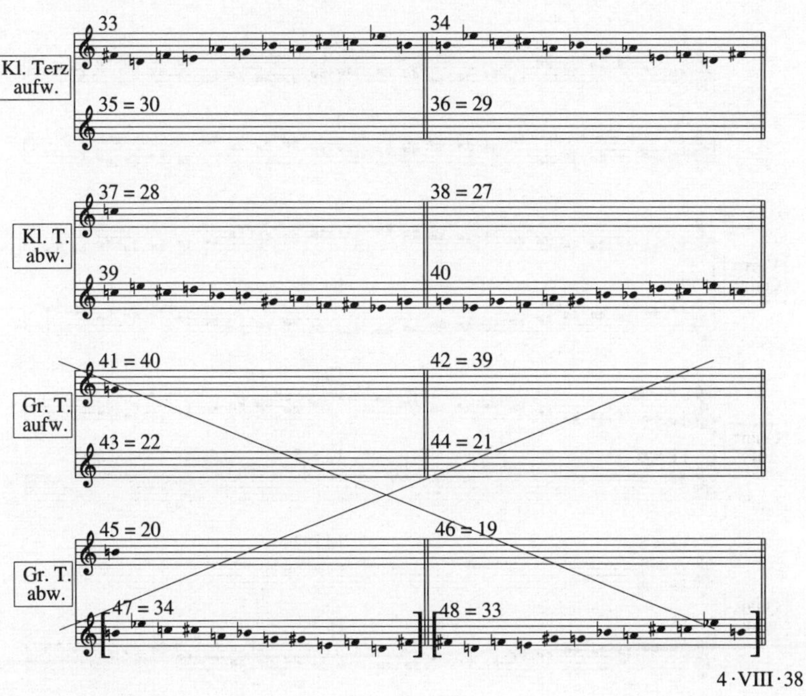


**Figure 11, p. 3**

In the Op.21 table the seconds and thirds have been shuffled so as to assume the pairings that they will maintain throughout the subsequent tables, and they appear in expanding order, which with a single exception is the order that is to be retained until Op.30; here this sequence is reversed. The one curious exception is Op.27, where the minor intervals are kept together and followed by the major: m2, m3, M2, M3. The three migrating fourth/fifth transpositions are the only variables in the tables for Opp.21–6 and 28–9; only in the last four tables, when these transpositions have found their best position, is the graduated interval series of seconds and thirds unbroken.

**Figure 12** Row table for Op.30 (Variations for orchestra), p. 1

## Spelling

The thorny problem of spelling is closely connected to Webern's interval nomenclature. Although the names used for intervals of transposition are the conventional ones, they do not have the conventional meaning: spelling discrepancies abound.[48] Far from indicating an indifference to

[48] In Op.20, between rows I and III, which begin on A♭, and the transpositions identified as *große 3 abw.* (rows XIII and XV, on E) and *kl3 aufwärts* (XLI and XLIII, on B); in Op.21, between I and III on F and the transpositions *Terzen klein aufwärts* (XXXIII and XXXV, on G♯) and *Terzen große abw.* (45 and 47, on C♯); in Op.26, between 1 and 3 on A♭ and *Große Sec. abwärts* (21 and 23, on F♯), *Kleine Terz aufwärts* (33 and 35, on B) and *Große Terz abwärts* (45 and 47, on E); in

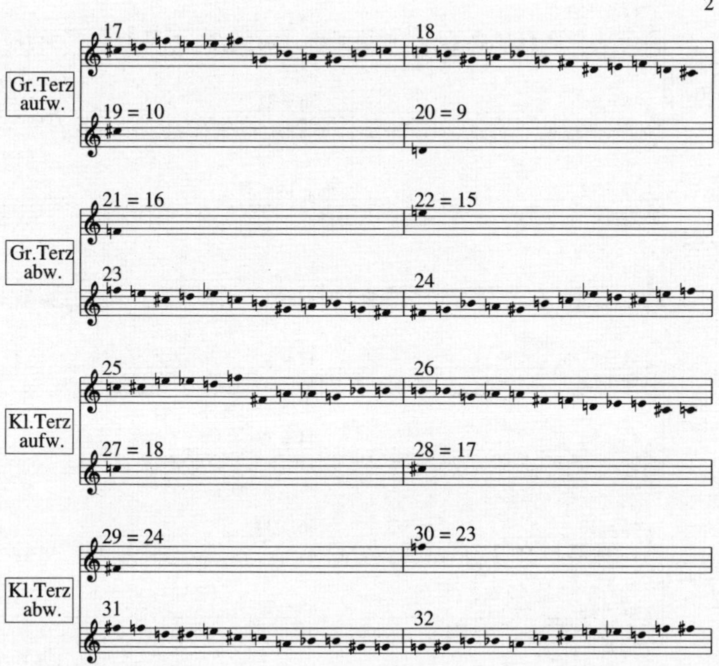


**Figure 12, p. 2**

*(cont.)* Op.27, between 1 and 3 on E♭ and *Kleine Terz aufw.* (25 and 27, on F♯), *Große Sec. abw.* (37 and 39, on C♯) and *Große Terz abw.* (45 and 47, on B); in Op.29, between 1 and 3 on D♯ and *Quint aufw.* (9 and 11, on B♭), *Gr.Sec. aufw.* (25 and 27, on F), *Kl.Terz abw.* (37 and 39, on C), *Gr.T. aufw.* (41, on G); in Op.31, between 1 and 3 on F♯ and *Gr.Terz aufw.* (17 and 19, on B♭) and *Kl.Terz abw.* (29 and 31, on E♭).

The situation is particularly complicated in Opp.22 and 28, where the first note of the original inversion is spelled differently from the first note of the original prime. If we consider the transpositions of prime and inversion separately in these two cases, in Op.22, where G♭ and F♯ are the first notes of the prime and inversion respectively, the following transpositions do not begin on the 'right' note: 21, 25, 29, 33, 39, 43, 45. In Op. 28, where prime and inversion begin on D♭ and C♯, the beginnings of transpositions 27 and 29 are misspelt.

These lists do not include those discrepancies concerning *kleine Sec.* transpositions, which are spelled as a second or a unison indiscriminately.

Figure 12, p. 3

convention, these seem in most cases to be the result of an attempt to satisfy the conditions of traditional voice leading: when the correct spelling of the first note of a transposition would have resulted in an awkward motion to the second note of the transposed row Webern preferred to misspell the transposition.[49] Matters are further complicated by the fact that he seems to have thought it important in most cases for the prime and inversion at any transposition to start on the same note, even in those cases (Opp.22 and 28) where $P_0$ and $I_0$ don't agree. (There are only three transpositions on these two tables – the Op.22 row at *Sec gr. aufw.* and the Op.28 row at *Quint*,

49 'Good' linear motion is constrained by Webern's decision never to use B♯, E♯, F♭, C♭ or double accidentals.

Table 1 Arrangements of transpositions in the row tables

| Op. no. | 20 | 21 | 22 | 24 | 26 | 27 | 28 | 29 | 30 | 31 |
|---|---|---|---|---|---|---|---|---|---|---|
| row nos. | | ($P_0$=$R_6$) | | | | | ($P_0$=$RI_9$) | ($P_0$=$RI_5$) | ($P_0$=$RI_{11}$) | |
| 1–4 | 0 | 0 | 0 | 0 | 0 | 0 | 0 | 0 | 0 | 0 |
| 5–8 | ∘5 | m2↑ | m2↑ | m2↑ | m2↑ | ∘5 | ∘5 | ∘5 | ∘5 | ∘5 |
| 9–12 | m3↓ | m2↓ | m2↓ | m2↓ | m2↓ | p5↓ | p5↓ | p5↑ | p4↑ | p4↑ |
| 13–16 | M3↓ | ∘5 | ∘5 | M2↑ | ∘5 | p5↑ | p5↑ | p5↓ | p4↓ | p4↓ |
| 17–20 | m2↓ | M2↑ | M2↑ | M2↓ | M2↑ | m2↑ | m2↑ | m2↑ | M3↑ | M3↑ |
| 21–4 | M2↓ | M2↓ | M2↓ | ∘5 | M2↓ | m2↓ | m2↓ | m2↓ | M3↓ | M3↓ |
| 25–8 | p5↑ | p5↑ | p4↑ | m3↑ | p5↑ | m3↑ | M2↑ | M2↑ | m3↑ | m3↑ |
| 29–32 | p4↑ | p4↑ | p4↓ | m3↓ | p5↓ | m3↓ | M2↓ | M2↓ | m3↓ | m3↓ |
| 33–6 | m2↑ | m3↑ | m3↑ | M3↑ | m3↑ | M2↑ | m3↑ | m3↑ | M2↑ | M2↑ |
| 37–40 | M2↑ | m3↓ | m3↓ | M3↓ | m3↓ | M2↓ | m3↓ | m3↓ | M2↓ | M2↓ |
| 41–4 | m3↑ | M3↑ | M3↑ | p4↑ | M3↑ | M3↑ | M3↑ | M3↑ | m2↑ | m2↑ |
| 45–8 | M3↑ | M3↓ | M3↓ | p4↓ | M3↓ | M3↓ | M3↓ | M3↓ | m2↓ | m2↓ |

*In this table* m *represents a minor interval,* M *a major and* ∘ *a diminished one.*

*abw.* and *aufw.* – that follow their progenitors in beginning on different notes. This does not happen on any of the other tables.)[50] Thus the spelling of the first notes of transpositions is governed by at least *four* considerations: the spelling of the original, the note to which the first note of the transposition must proceed, the spelling of the row's inversion at the same level of transposition, *and* an apparent preference for some spellings over

[50] More often the starting note of prime and inversion is determined by the motion to the second note of the prime (see Op.19, row VII; Op.21, row 47; Op.22, row 43; Op.26, rows 3, 27, 37; Op.27, row 39; Op.29, rows 3, 15, (31), 47; Op.31, rows 15, 35); however, in a few cases the prime is misspelt or begins awkwardly in order to cater to the requirements of the inversion (see Op.22, row 29; Op.26, rows 21, 31; Op.27, rows 1, 9; Op.29, row 9; Op.31, rows 29, 45).

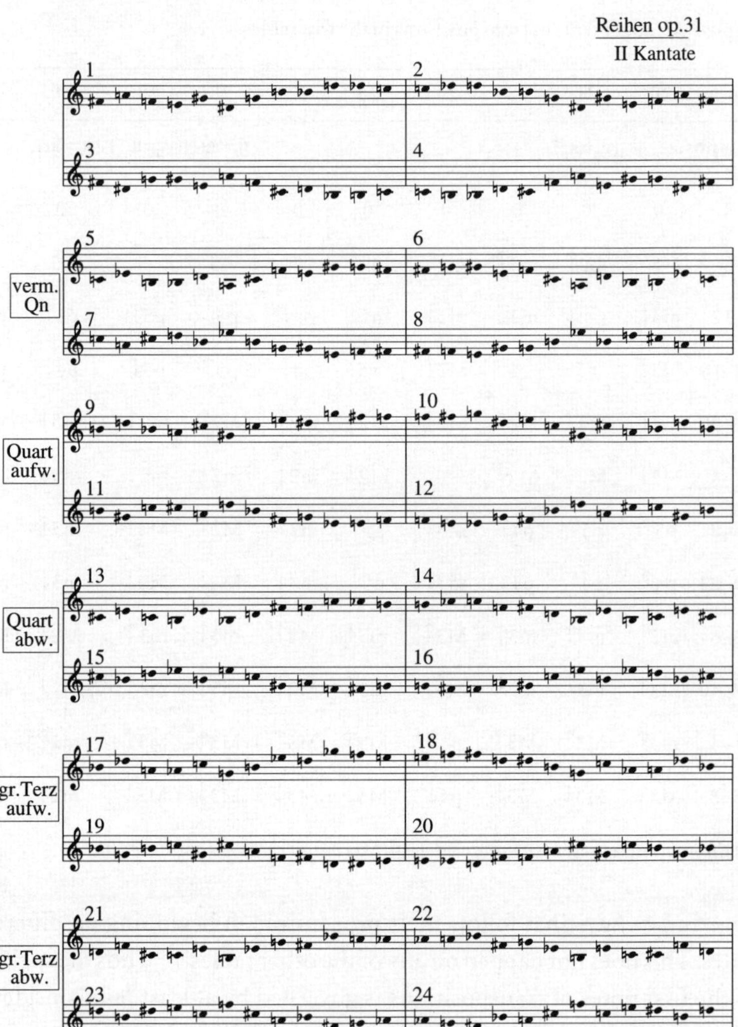


Figure 13 Row table for Op.31 (Cantata no. 2), p. 1

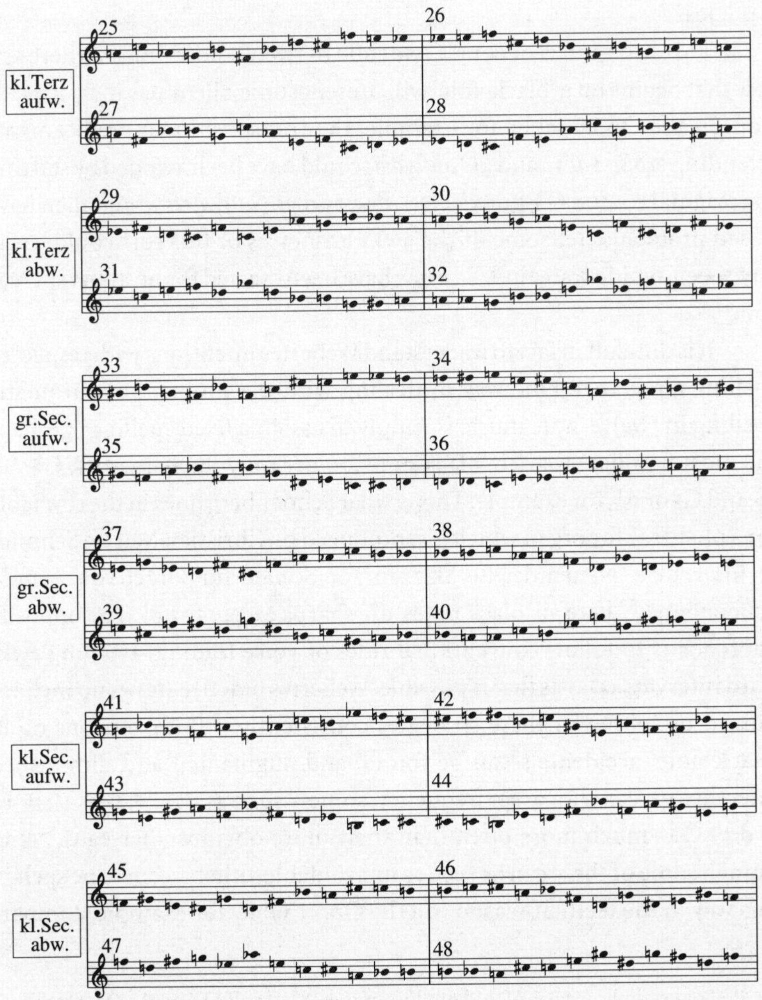
25
26
kl.Terz
aufw.
27
28
29
30
kl.Terz
abw.
31
32
33
34
gr.Sec.
aufw.
35
36
37
38
gr.Sec.
abw.
39
40
41
42
kl.Sec.
aufw.
43
44
45
46
kl.Sec.
abw.
47
48

**Figure 13**, p. 2

others regardless of context. The order of importance of these four factors is unclear.

This situation is of course endemic in twelve-note music, where any row that begins on a 'black note' will present some dilemmas in transposition. In the Op.20 table, for example, the transpositional predicaments attending *große 3 abw.* and *kl3 aufwärts* could have been avoided by starting the original row on G♯, but *kleine 3 abw.* and *gr3 aufwärts* would then have posed problems. Yet some of the awkwardnesses of this sort could easily have been avoided, and indeed a few have been created for no apparent reason.[51]

It is difficult in fact to understand Webern's intentions with respect to spelling altogether. One way of dealing with the problem of chromatic spelling in twelve-note music is simply to assign a fixed spelling (perhaps the most familiar) to each 'black note': to use only the names F♯, C♯, B♭, E♭ and G♯ or A♭, for example. This is what Schoenberg does in the row table for a phantasy for organ which is reproduced by Christian Martin Schmidt in his article 'Neuentdeckte Skizzen zur Sonate für Orgel von Arnold Schoenberg':[52] here all 'black notes' are sharps except for B♭. The opposite approach is to follow conventional rules of voice leading, avoiding awkward intervals as far as that is possible. Webern's practice shows no inclination to use either of these strategies consistently.[53] Both versions of all 'black note' accidentals can be found, and augmented and diminished intervals appear with great frequency, some – such as B♭–F♯, B♭–C♯, B–E♭ and F–C♯ – much more often than their more obvious alter-egos,[54] and though some of these can be seen as unavoidable, others seem to be spelt in this way in the teeth of reason (on the Op.21 table, for example, compare

51 For example, in view of the handling of rows XVII and XIX on the Op.22 table, how can one explain the opening of rows 29 and 43 (see Figure 4 above)?

52 In the *Journal of the Arnold Schoenberg Institute* 4 (1980), 138–51.

53 He seems to prefer not to use the less familiar spellings – D♭, D♯, G♭ etc. – thus the high frequency of such intervals as B♭–C♯, B♭–F♯, E♭–F♯, C♯–E♭ and B–E♭. Yet this was not a rule: how is one to explain the instances of A–D♭, F–D♯, G–D♯ (this last occurring twenty-two times)?

54 B♭–F♯ or its reverse occurs seventy-three times, B♭–G♭ thirty-one; B♭–C♯ occurs fifty-two times, B♭–D♭ fifteen; B–E♭ occurs sixty-five times, B–D♯ twenty-three, and F–C♯ occurs sixty-one times, F–D♭ twenty-eight. These are only the four such intervals that occur most often; the list continues.

C–C♯–B♭ in row IX and A–B♭–F♯ in row XIII – the rising semitone is treated differently in these two instances, and, it might seem, perversely so: no awkwardnesses would have occurred had the first been spelt C–D♭ and the second A–A♯.

## Dating

Each of the tables is dated, though all these dates do not give us the same sort of information. A precise date (day•month•year) appears at the end of the Op.24 table and each of those from Op.26 onwards, written in lead pencil or black ink, or, in the case of Op.26, the coloured pencil used for the last set of rows. It seems safe to assume that this is the date on which the row table was completed: when these dates are compared with those in the sketchbooks a logical sequence emerges, in which details of a row are worked out in the sketchbook, a separate table constructed once a satisfactory row has been arrived at, then sketches of music on this row begun (see Table 2 for a concordance of dates from the row tables with those from the sketchbooks). In several cases – Opp.21, 22, 24, 27, 30 and 31 – preliminary sketches of music predate the finalisation of the row and the formation of the row table.

The dates on the earlier row tables – those for Opp.19–23, and for Op.25 – are much less precise, and if the tables were in fact used as tools in the process of composition rather than retrospective records (and the photograph in Plate 1 would seem to be proof that they were) these dates were not written on the tables as they were constructed. Each consists of a year only, written in the top righthand margin of the first page of the table, in the manner of something recalled at a distance of some time; and, as we have seen, all are written in the same pencil, Red X, a pencil that was used on the body of only two tables, for the anomalous third page of the Op.21 table, and throughout the table of *Das Augenlicht*. All the information – titles and dates – on the Op.23 table is in Red X, as are the list of instruments just below the title (which is in pencil) on the table for Op.20 and the addition '3 Lieder' on the one for Op.25 (where the rest of the information is blue); the work title and/or opus number is written in Red X on all three pages of the Op.26 table; and the work title, enclosed in square brackets, has been added in this colour after the presumably original 'Reihen zu op.27' and 'Reihen

Table 2 Concordance of dates in the row tables and those in first sketches

| | *Row tables* | *Sketchbooks* | | |
|---|---|---|---|---|
| | | *dates* | *material* | *location* |
| Op.19 | 1925/26 (top righthand corner, in red pencil: probably added later) | | | |
| Op.20 | 1926/27 (top righthand margin, below instrumentation and in same red pencil; both probably added later) | | no sketches extant | |
| Op.21 | 1928 (top righthand margin, below instrumentation and in same red pencil; both probably added later) | Nov. Dec. 1927 | sketches of mvt 2 opening, a row | I/15 |
| | | January 1928 | another row, with its four permutations | I/16 |
| | | | the Op.21 row, Thema of mvt 2 | I/16 |
| Op.22 | 1929/30 | 14•IX•1928 | 'Concert für Geige, Klarinette, Horn, Klavier u Streichorchester' | I/54 |
| | (top righthand margin, below instrumentation; both in lead pencil and probably added later) | 6•V, 10•5 | several preliminary rows | I/54 |
| | | [n.d.] | several more rows | I/53, 56 |
| | | 27•V•1929 | another row, altered to become Op.22 row | I/56 |
| | | 28•V•1929 | first sketch of mvt 2 opening | I/58 |
| Op.23 | 1933 (at end, in same red pencil used for titles: probably written at the same time) | 1•II•33 | experiments with row and melody | II/52 |
| | | | correct row written out with other forms in the following order: IX, X ($P_9$–$R_9$);[a] I, II ($P_0$–$R_0$), III, IV ($I_0$–$RI_0$), V, VI ($P_6$–$R_6$), VII, VIII ($I_6$–$RI_6$) | II/52 |
| | | 4•IV•33 | sketch of opening of Op.23/iii | II/51–2 |
| Op.24 | 7•VII•1931 (at end, in lead pencil) | 16•I•1931 | outline of new work and row fragments | II/38 |
| | | 19•I | fragments of music, not using row; SATOR AREPO; *gilt* row and its retrograde, almost certainly added later | II/39 |
| | | 4•Febr•1931 | sketches of music, evolution of row | II/39–40 |

| | | | | |
|---|---|---|---|---|
| Op.25 | 1934 (at end, in same red pencil as titles, but different from red used for row nos; probably added later) | 4•VII•34 | experiments with (inv.) row; correct row with its permutations | II/75 |
| | | | sketch of no.1 opening | II/75 |
| Op.26 | 2•III•35 (at end, in green – same pencil used for last group of rows – badly faded) | 19•II•35 | a trial row, a melody, then opening melody of Op.26 | III/22 |
| | | 24•II | correct row and its permutations, labelled *gilt* | III/22 |
| | | 14•III•35 | short sketch of opening | III/22 |
| Op.27 | 25•XI•35 (at end, in black ink) | 14•X•35 | numerous experiments with row | III/43 |
| | | 16•X | page of sketches of mvt 3 opening, row changing | III/43 |
| | | undated | correct row and its permutations | III/44 |
| | | | sketches of Op.27/iii | III/44 |
| Op.28 | 23•I•37 (at end of p.2 (point at which he realised that he needn't write out any more rows), in lead pencil) | 17•XI•36 | title, outline of movements added later | III/57 |
| | | undated | $P_0$ and $R_0$ written out, symmetrical relationships noted | III/57 |
| | | 21•XI•36 | first sketch of mvt 3 opening | III/57 |
| Op.29 | 4•VIII•38 (at end of p.3, in ink) | 1•VII•38 | first work on row, sketches with 'wrong' versions | IV/2 |
| | | 3•VIII | *gilt* row boxed and labelled | IV/2 |
| | | 5•IX | first sketch for no.2 opening | IV/4 |
| Op.30 | 7•V•40 (at end, in ink) | 15•IV•40 | sketch of opening cello figure | IV/48 |
| | | 16•IV• | sketches of row | IV/48 |
| | | 17•IV | many sketches of opening figures | IV/48 |
| Op.31 | 14•VI•41 (at end, in ink) 3•XI•43 (in right margin at end, written vertically, in red pencil) | 7•V•41 | sketches of no.4 opening; sketch of row | IV/82 |

[a] *The appearance of these two rows is particularly interesting as they were not used in Op.23 and do not appear on the row table for that work.*

zu op.28' at the top of these two tables. It seems fairly certain that these dates, titles etc. were added later, and all at once. Work titles and lists of instruments on the other tables look like late additions as well: they are in various colours, frequently in pencils not used elsewhere on the tables in question. Were it not for the third page of the Op.21 table, which is in Red X throughout, it would seem fairly certain that Red X was a pencil in use in 1934–6, and that the retrospective dating was done at that time. But unless the Op.21 page replaced an earlier one or was written with a different pencil of the same colour, the use of Red X there complicates the issue, as this table dates from 1928.

In fact the tables just discussed do not comprise the whole of Webern's extant row tables. His first row table precedes sketches for a piano piece that was never finished. These sketches are on p. 17 of his first sketchbook, which is owned by the Pierpont Morgan Library in New York. The table gives the four untransposed row forms in the order that was to be used in all subsequent row tables; it is written in pencil, as are all the sketches in this book. A similar table appears at the top of p. 22 of this sketchbook, preceding sketches for the song 'Erlösung', Op.18 no. 2. (There is no table of rows for the first song of Op.18, as it uses the untransposed prime row only.) This table, like the one before it, contains the four untransposed rows and is written in pencil.

On p. 25 of this first sketchbook, at the head of the sketches for the third song of the Op.18 set, 'Ave, Regina coelorum', Webern used colours for the first time to distinguish between row forms, and the rows are identified in these colours as they are used in the sketches of the song which follow on this page and the one following. It is fairly clear that this table was made before composition of the song had begun: it contains tritone transpositions of the row and its retrograde, rows which were not used in the song. Here the label of the row itself ('Gr') is in red pencil, 'Kr.' is in blue, 'U.' in green and 'U.Kr.' in purple. The transpositions are in lead pencil on the staff below the inversion and its retrograde. Another table very like this one, though with the use of colours less well thought out, appears on p. 28, at the top of sketches for Op.19. In this case all four tritone transpositions are included. (They are used in Op.19.) As in the preceding table (and all the following ones), the row is red; in this case however the retrograde, which follows immediately, is in lead pencil. On the staff below, the tritone transpositions of these two rows are also in pencil. Below this the inversion, in green, is followed by its retrograde, in purple; and the tritone transpositions of these two rows, on the staff below, are in blue and lead pencil respectively. This arrangement has been tidied up in the separate Op.19 row table that now resides in the Sacher Stiftung.

Page 27 of the Morgan Library sketchbook also contains the first of Webern's set of separate row tables, a neatly prepared table on a small strip of paper which has been pasted into the sketchbook, over blank space following the sketches for 'Ave, Regina coelorum'. Both notes and labels of the four untransposed rows are in coloured pencil – red, blue, green and purple as in the earlier table for this row on p. 25 of the sketchbook. The two tritone transpositions, curiously still present, are in lead pencil; their presence suggests that this table too was prepared before composition of the song. This table was clearly intended to go with the others, now at the Sacher Stiftung, and its separation from them is apparently the result of an accident of history: this sketchbook – with Webern's first row table attached – was rescued from oblivion before the subsequent sketchbooks and row tables.

**Figure 14** Row table for Op.18 no.3, 'Ave, Regina coelorum'

The 'Ave Regina coelorum' table resembles the others in every respect but one, but this one difference is significant with reference to the question we have just examined in the text. The fact that this table bears no date would seem to be strong evidence that the dates written on the early tables in Red X were a later addition.

## Conclusion

It is surely of some interest to compare Webern's tables with those of Berg and Schoenberg. One might expect them to be rather similar, especially perhaps that the students might imitate the teacher, at least at the beginning. But this does not seem to be the case. In fact it is clear that the row tables were a more significant part of Schoenberg's creative process than they were for either Berg or Webern. Schoenberg, who publicly expressed such bitterness over the world's interest in the rows on which his works were based,[55] seems privately to have considered the row tables themselves as works of art. His tables were made in a wide variety of formats: cylinders, wheels, folded booklets, bound booklets, accordion-folded strips, two-colour grids which are to be read in all directions (rather like the puzzle canons of the Middle Ages), sets of cards containing selected pairs of row forms, cut-outs and overlays, slide rules, window devices, circular devices, Scrabble-like letter squares, dice and more.[56] All these devices were carefully handmade and are not only ingenious, but are interesting and pleasing artefacts in their own right.

Both Berg and Webern devoted much less energy than their teacher to the creation of row tables: it seems clear that for them the tables were simply a means to an end and held little interest independent of this. Berg wrote out only the prime and inverted rows in notation, ordered the transpositions chromatically and numbered them consecutively (I, II, III . . . XII).[57]

[55] See, for example, his letter to Kolisch dated 27 July 1932: 'I can't utter too many warnings against over-rating these [twelve-note] analyses, since after all they only lead to what I have always been dead against: seeing how it is *done*; whereas I have always helped people to see: what it *is*! . . . my works are twelve-note *compositions*, not *twelve-note* compositions . . . I can't refrain from speaking out against such an analysis . . .' (*Arnold Schoenberg Letters*, ed. Erwin Stein, trans. Eithne Wilkins and Ernst Kaiser (London: Faber and Faber, 1964), pp. 164–5).

[56] Schoenberg's twelve-note devices, which are held at the Arnold Schoenberg Institute in Los Angeles, were placed on display in a special exhibition there in July–December 1989. I am grateful to Archivist R. Wayne Shoaf for a photocopy of the catalogue, 'Schoenberg's Dodecaphonic Devices', which he prepared for this occasion with Assistant Archivist Susan L. Sloan. Photographs of three of these devices appeared as well in Sloan, 'Archival exhibit: Schoenberg's dodecaphonic devices', *Journal of the Arnold Schoenberg Institute* 12/2 (Nov. 1989), 202–5.

[57] The row tables for the basic set of *Lulu* are reproduced in facsimile in the Cambridge Opera Handbook by Douglas Jarman (Cambridge: Cambridge University Press, 1989), as plates 1a and 1b, between pp. 40 and 41, and in Thomas F. Ertelt, 'Alban Berg's *Lulu*' in *Quellenstudien und Beiträge zur Analyse*, Alban Berg Studien III (Vienna: Universal Edition, 1992), between pp. 40 and 41. I am indebted to Douglas Jarman for providing me with a photocopy of Berg's row tables for the Violin Concerto as well. The latter are reproduced in facsimile in the

Schoenberg also listed his rows in chromatically ascending and descending order in some of his tables, though, like Webern, he ordered them in other ways as well.[58] Unlike Berg, he labelled transpositions with the numbers –3, +3, –6, +6 etc., which, like Webern's *kleine* and *große Terz*, translate into English as minor third, major third, minor sixth, major sixth and so on.[59]

In view of his apparent fascination with palindromes, and particularly with the letter matrix SATOR AREPO TENET OPERA ROTAS, it is curious that Webern seems never to have used a matrix (as Schoenberg did on occasion[60]) in mapping out his rows. But perhaps this is not just a subject for idle curiosity. Can it be that this strikes at the very source of half a century's misunderstanding of Webern's compositional process?

Many things about the row tables are disquieting. To begin with small things: the untidiness and inconsistencies (in ordering, spelling, use of colours) seem at variance with the meticulous exactness of his published scores. So too the frequent intrusion of trivial (imposed) physical constraints upon designs that would otherwise have been clearly explicative. A concern over these details seems often to have taken precedence over the desire to represent situations in the clearest way. Or is this putting the wrong slant on things? Is it possible, rather, that Webern was concerned with the immediate physical format but unaware of the specifics of the (e.g. symmetrical) situation they represented?

In some ways the tables do not give evidence of the sort of organised mind that we assume to be behind the works. This is true for example of spelling, which seems neither to reflect an attempt to express accurately the

*Katalog Musikhandschriften, Schriften und Studien Alban Bergs im Fond Alban Berg und der weiteren Handschriftlichen Quellen im Besitz der Österreichischen Nationalbibliothek*, ed. Franz Grasberger and Rudolf Stephan and published as Alban Berg Studien I/1 (Vienna: Universal Edition, 1981), pp. 178–9, where they are given the wrong caption ('Tonreihen zu "Lulu"'). The row tables for *Der Wein* are published in Herwig Knaus, 'Alben Bergs Skizzen und Vorarbeiten zur Konzertarie "Der Wein"', in *Festschrift Othmar Wessely* (Vienna, 1982), pp. 355ff. I wish also to thank Regina Busch for sending me the transcript of her paper 'Einige Bemerkungen zur Zwölftonkomposition bei Schönberg, Berg und Webern', in which she describes selected row tables of Schoenberg, Berg and Webern.

58 Several of Schoenberg's row tables are reproduced in volumes of the B Series of the *Sämtliche Werke* (Mainz: B. Schott's Söhne/Vienna: Universal Edition, 1984).

59 Shoaf and Sloan, 'Schoenberg's Dodecaphonic Devices' (no p. nos.).

60 In his multicoloured grid tables; see ibid.

relationships of the row forms (inversion, retrograde) nor to indicate a decision to use a limited number of spellings consistently. Equally Webern seems little concerned to follow conventional practice.

Why did Webern write out the retrograde forms of all his rows when his two friends found this unnecessary? And, having decided to write them out, why did he not make all the inversions and retrogrades exact? The way he went about things suggests not so much a determination to outline fully the symmetries of the rows he had devised as a need to *see* all the row forms individually, in order to *visualise* the relationships at his disposal. It is unarguable that he was fond of symmetrical rows which restricted his field in some way (witness the rows used in Opp.21, 24, 28, 29 and 30). Yet his tabulation of these is clumsy and imperfect. On the table for Op.21 we can almost sense his surprise when the rows begin to repeat themselves. He must have known when he put this row together that this would happen; but had he known exactly *where* it would happen, would he have ordered the transpositions in the way that he did? His arrangement of this table is neither completely logical in an abstract sense *nor* entirely faithful to the succession of row forms in the work (though it is sufficiently nearly both of these to make us suppose that they interested him). *Nor* does it handle the hexachordal symmetry in an elegant way: there is never any evidence, here or elsewhere, that he was concerned with doing this. As it happens, if this table had answered any one of these conditions it would have fulfilled all three: the most logical arrangement, of *all* the transpositions in an expanding series with the three fourth/fifth transpositions last, would also have reflected the progress of the piece without the necessity of qualifying colours, and, in addition, rows 1–24 would have presented no redundancies. Yet Webern did not order the transpositions in this way, apparently because he was tied to a physical format of three pages with transposition groups undivided across page breaks. This seems a trivial reason for which to forfeit the most lucid expression of an innovative and brilliant idea.

Only once, with the Op.28 table, did he happen upon an order that would allow all twenty-four rows to emerge once before repetitions began to appear. But even this 'perfect' table seems to have been an accident. It was apparently not until he had written in eight redundant rows that he realised that all the rows had already been exposed; at this point he wrote the date on the table and stopped writing rows, even though he had prepared the next page in advance. (Surely the preparation of this page is proof that the outcome of this arrangement had not been foreseen.) Having found a satisfactory arrangement, however, he proceeded to use it again for the hexachordally symmetrical Op.29 row, presumably expecting similar results. This of course did not happen. Again he appears to have been taken by surprise. Row 24, which was the last 'new' row stated on the Op.28 table, is not the first redundant row here, but it *is* the first one that he doesn't write in: it is as if he noticed only at this point that the table for Op.29 was not yielding results similar to those on the previous table. Upon making this discovery, he appears to have gone back over what he had written, identified redundant rows and put brackets around them, adding equivalent row numbers; having been alerted to the situation, he subsequently noted the numbers of equivalent rows as he came to redundancies, and did not write out the rows themselves. He changed the pattern for Op.30: in this case again he could have found an order of transpositions that would have allowed all the rows to unfold once before redundancies began. But he didn't. He *did*, however, know what to expect this time and was not caught off guard: this is the only table for a symmetrical row in which no redundant rows are notated.

These tergiversations seem to me to indicate much less familiarity on Webern's part with the particulars of row symmetry in the abstract than it has been traditional to assume. Certainly it fascinated him, and I have no doubt that he saw it as akin to the unity so admired by Goethe (and others), but it would appear that the palindromes and reflections that are such a characteristic feature of his music were patterns that he *noticed* once the rows had been written down, rather than something that he calculated in advance. At least some of his symmetrical rows were the fruits of a long series of trial-and-error operations,[61] and it seems fairly certain that he did not realise the full potential of what he had created until he saw the possibilities on the row table before him.

61 The row for the Concerto, Op.24, for example. See my article, 'Symmetry as nemesis: Webern and the first movement of the Concerto, Opus 24', in *JMT* 40/2(1996).

It is not my intention to belittle either Webern's achievement or his mental acuity. Nor do I wish to suggest that his remarkable symmetries were either unconscious or accidental. What I do suggest is that a closer acquaintance with his sketches and the row tables from which he worked may cause Webern scholars – and, through them, others – to alter their view of the way in which he approached and used the twelve-note method, and perhaps of the nature of his inspiration as well. That the man who expected to find the mysteries of life answered in the beauties of nature should have found solutions to the problems of musical unity in the configurations of his row tables seems to me entirely consistent. Seeing and experiencing may have been more significant aspects of his apprehension of the secrets of serial technique than were intellectual abstractions – an order of priorities which was in complete harmony with his views of life in general.

# 7 Webern's lyric character[1]

CHRISTOPHER WINTLE

## I

*The lyric quality of his music distinguishes Webern from Schoenberg whose faithful disciple he was. Schoenberg covers a far wider field, while Webern thoroughly explores a corner of it.*

Thus Erwin Stein, in his obituary of Anton Webern for *The Musical Times* of January 1946.[2] The need to preserve public decorum and the dignifying effects of private loss would not have kept Stein from an important recognition: that his words concealed as much as they revealed. Stein, of course, had been an intimate of Schoenberg's circle for almost fifty years.[3] He had published on the composer from 1912 until 1958 (as editor of the posthumous letters[4]); he had been deemed loyal until almost the last (in 1950 the dying Schoenberg feared he might 'become my enemy'[5]); and, on 2 October 1942, after thirty years of friendship, he was even allowed to address his former teacher as *du*.[6] Therefore he would have known all too well what ambivalence lay in his seemingly innocuous testimonial to Schoenberg's 'faithful disciple'. For it was Stein himself who was cited as

[1] The material for this chapter was first presented to a meeting of the Institute of Advanced Musical Studies at King's College London chaired by Arnold Whittall on 23 January 1995. I am grateful to Irene Auerbach for advice over the German translations.

[2] Erwin Stein, *Orpheus in New Guises* (London: Rockliff, 1953), pp. 99–102 (p. 100).

[3] The interweaving of the lives of Stein and Schoenberg is described in H. H. Stuckenschmidt, *Arnold Schoenberg: His Life, World and Work*, trans. Humphrey Searle (London: John Calder, 1977).

[4] *Arnold Schoenberg: Ausgewählte Briefe* (Mainz: B. Schott's Söhne, 1958); English translation by Eithne Wilkins and Ernst Kaiser (London: Faber & Faber, 1964).

[5] Stuckenschmidt, *Arnold Schoenberg*, p. 512.

[6] Ibid., p. 455.

witness for the prosecution in Schoenberg's notorious attack on his former pupil, penned as one of a series of 'memorials' in the summer of 1940:

> 1907 new style. Told Webern about short pieces. One of the piano pieces should consist of only three to four measures.—Webern starts writing shorter and shorter pieces—follows all my developments. Always tries to surpass everything (exaggerates)...
>
> After 1915: Webern seems to have used twelve notes in some of his compositions—without telling me...
>
> 1921... Started twelve tone composition. Told Erwin Stein. I had now... wanted to keep all my imitators at a distance because I am annoyed by them: I even do not know any more what is mine and what is theirs—Webern jealous about Berg, had suggested to me to tell Berg he (in about 1908 or 9) should not write in the new style—he has no right to do it—it does not fit to his style—but it fitted to Webern's!!!
>
> Webern committed at this period (1908–18) many acts of infidelity with the intention of making himself the innovator.[7]

What the trusty Stein learnt through Schoenberg, then, was of a fidelity so intense as to be indistinguishable from a rapacious infidelity, and of a corresponding exaggeration of creative focus necessary to achieve 'thorough' domination of (apparently) the most fertile corner of the newly constituted musical field. The tenacity of Webern's predatory discipleship, moreover, was testament to its central position within his creative character. What Stein could have said, but did not say, was that Schoenberg was the indispensable, provident father-figure, *retained* by flattering devotion, but *repelled* by the destructive zeal with which those devotions were ministered. (Schoenberg, needless to add, was quickly filled with remorse for what he had written: 'It looks awful and throws a bad light on me, especially if one compares Webern's letters to me with these.'[8])

But Stein also refers to another trait of Webern's, the one which distinguishes his music from Schoenberg's: the exclusive pursuit of 'lyric quality'. Although elsewhere in the obituary Stein writes, 'Webern was primarily

[7] Ibid., pp. 442–3.
[8] Ibid., p. 444.

a lyricist in the same sense as Schubert and Debussy were', he recognised that he was so in a special way: 'Ecstasy was his natural state of mind: his compositions should be understood as musical visions.' His melodies, furthermore, 'move in wide intervals, and the frequent use of extreme ranges increases the intensity of the exalted expression'. And there was a quasi-religious source to his inspiration, nurtured with typically unflagging devotion: 'An intense love of the Austrian mountains remained throughout his life.'

But once more, in his apparently unmitigated praise, Stein was wielding a two-edged sword. For the isolation of 'lyric quality' implies a creative restriction, an ability to use just one element of a partnership which properly deployed marked the boundaries of rounded musical expression, and hence of creative capacity. This partnership, of *the lyric and the dramatic in music*, was described in general terms by Hegel (1770–1831) in his *Aesthetik* (the italics are mine):

> *Lyric music*... expresses individual moods of the soul melodically. It must above all maintain its independence of what is merely descriptive and declamatory, although it may also further portray the specific content of a text whether that content is of a religious or any other character. However, *dramatic music* is much more appropriate to emotions of a tempestuous or unrequited character, to unresolved emotional conflicts or to tensions within us; these are less suited to independent lyric treatment and serve effectively as integral parts of a dramatic design.[9]

Here the definition of lyric character (or tone) is clear enough: expressive of a particular mood, melodic and self-sufficient, and possibly tied to certain kinds of text. Carl Dahlhaus draws a further contrast between lied, which for him entails specifically *lyric* expression, and sung narrative (or ballad), which does not.[10] The contrast lies in the different relationship with the listener that the two types imply:

[9] Trans. in Peter le Huray and James Day, *Music and Aesthetics in the Eighteenth and Early-Nineteenth Centuries* (Cambridge: Cambridge University Press, 1981), pp. 349–50. For further discussion of 'lyrical stasis and dramatic motion', see Stephen Downes, *Szymanowski as Post-Wagnerian* (London and New York: Garland, 1994), pp. 55ff.

[10] Carl Dahlhaus, *Nineteenth-Century Music*, trans. J. Bradford Robinson (Berkeley and Los Angeles: University of California Press, 1989), pp. 104–5.

> [I]n a lied, it is the composer who is speaking, not as himself but as a 'lyric ego' beyond the grasp of fact-hungry biographers. Unlike sung narrative, a lied is an utterance that is not directed ostentatiously at an audience but, in a manner of speaking, is overheard by the audience. Listeners are essential to the ballad, but incidental to the lied.

Lyric character, in other words, denotes a certain preoccupation of the 'lyric ego' with itself, which is (apparently) unmodified by awareness of an attentive other. Dahlhaus also notes that lyric tone entails no formal obligations: 'Unlike the sonata, lyrical genres are left unaffected when a "disintegrated" – meaning through-composed – form is used in lieu of a schematic one.' For the lyricist the manipulation of narrative and time is not of the essence.

By contrast, dramatic music is hard to define without drawing three further subdivisions: *the operatic, the theatrical* and *the symphonic.* The operatic explores the interplay of passions within a narrative context, and embraces the effects of time and place (the nocturnal storm in the final act of *Rigoletto,* for example); the theatrical also depends upon a narrative, though not one necessarily unfolded in a theatre or opera house (the rending of the temple curtain towards the close of J. S. Bach's Matthew Passion, for instance); the symphonic, on the other hand, sublimates drama into absolute music, and finds its *locus classicus* in those sonata forms that integrate radical contrasts (as in the first three movements, and to a slightly lesser extent the fourth, of Schubert's (Fantasy) Sonata in G major Op.78 / D 894 for piano).

Hegel speaks of conflict and tension, the unresolved and unrequited. Since these raise the prospect of release, fulfilment and resolution, formal strategy, conceived in terms of beginning, middle and end, is paramount. Since contrast presupposes strong differentiations of character, the *dramatic,* unlike the *lyric,* addresses the problems posed by the presence of 'another' (the psychoanalytic 'object'); in the theatre or opera house that 'other' may be human, natural or even supernatural; in abstract music it has to be represented in all the ways described by countless analysts: through contrasts of motives, themes, statements and developments, chromatic and diatonic elements, dynamics, articulation, instrumentation and so forth.[11]

[11] Donald Francis Tovey especially drew on the distinctions between the lyric and dramatic in music. See his entry on Haydn in Cobbett's *Cyclopædia of Chamber*

And when Hegel speaks of tensions 'within ourselves', he recognises that members of the audience are no longer observers – Dahlhaus's eavesdroppers – but participants of a kind in the action. As W. H. Auden once wrote,

> Drama began as the act of a whole community. Ideally there would be no spectators. In practice every member of the audience should feel like an understudy.[12]

Since theory is famously stricter than reality, there can be no surprise that these categories sometimes cross or overlap. In the first movement of Beethoven's Sonata in D major for piano Op.28 ('Pastorale'), for instance, the high drama released by the opening $D_7$ chord (it returns as augmented sixth in the transition) is contradicted by the 'lyrical' manner of the melodic writing. Similarly the Adagio from Haydn's String Quartet Op.20 no.2 can be heard only against the background of *opera seria* accompanied recitative. And of course there are truly lyric aspects to opera, oratorio and symphonic music.

So how did Schoenberg, mentor of Stein and Webern, view these distinctions? A striking essay on 'Problems in teaching art' from as early as 1911 finds him racked with guilt:

> it can be superfluous or downright dangerous to force someone to compose symphonic [viz. dramatic] forms if his expressive needs are later going to seek out the path of lyricism.[13]

Indeed, these words are doubly striking because they are in no way clarified by their context. Why 'downright dangerous'? And who is the 'someone'

*Music* (London: Oxford University Press, 1929). In 'Introduction: operatic music and Britten', in *The Operas of Benjamin Britten*, ed. David Herbert (London: Hamish Hamilton, 1979), pp. xiii–xiv, Hans Keller writes:

> it is the field of instrumental music pure and complex which, just because it has absorbed musical drama in its sonata thought, seems furthest removed from stage drama – and within that field, it is, of course, the string quartet and its relatives (such as the string quintet) which, *ceteris paribus*, present the richest and subtlest expression of sheer musical drama.

On the operatic side, Debussy, of course, blended opposites by describing *Pelléas et Mélisande* as *drame lyrique*.

12 W. H. Auden, *The English Auden*, ed. Edward Mendelson (London: Faber & Faber, 1977), p. 273.

13 Arnold Schoenberg, *Style and Idea*, ed. Leonard Stein with translations by Leo Black (London: Faber & Faber, 1975), p. 366.

that, consciously or preconsciously, Schoenberg had in mind in talking about misplaced force? Berg, the composer of *Lulu*, the greatest symphonic drama of the twentieth century? Hardly. Webern? In the light of Stein's remarks, more likely.

Schoenberg's later writings deem further that the requirements of melody and the 'lyric' are less strenuous, less demanding psychologically, than those of symphonic thematicism.

> Since rhythmic characteristics are less decisive in a melody, it could be called two-dimensional, comprising chiefly interval and latent harmony. On the other hand, the importance of rhythmic development makes the problem of the theme three-dimensional.[14]

And in his now politically incorrect essay 'The blessing of the dressing' (1948), Schoenberg also described the capacity to think 'of the whole destiny of the idea' as 'masculine', and 'the other manner', which 'takes into account with good understanding the nearest consequences of a problem, but misses preparing for the more remote events', as 'feminine'.[15] (Schoenberg's valuation, of course, represents a reversal in the history of musical ideas: a century earlier, in *Opera and Drama*, Wagner had warned that masculine intellectualism departed from feminine lyricism at its peril.[16])

Rhythmically less decisive, lacking the ability to sustain long-term development, two-dimensional, womanly: these, then, are Schoenberg's pejoratives which lurk behind Stein's decorous delimitation of Webern's creative character. Nor have they dissolved with time. Commemorating

[14] Arnold Schoenberg, *Fundamentals of Musical Composition*, ed. Gerald Strang (London: Faber & Faber, 1967), p. 102.

[15] Schoenberg, *Style and Idea*, p. 385.

[16] Richard Wagner, *Opera and Drama* (1851, rev. 1868), trans. Edwin Evans, 2 vols., (London: Reeves, [ca1910]). See Part III, chap. 3, pp. 503–8. Speaking of 'maternal primitive melody' (p. 503), Wagner writes:

> The more the faculty of instinctive emotion became compressed into that of the arbitrary understanding, and the more lyrical contents became accordingly changed from emotional to intellectual (as happened in the course of human development) the more evident became the removal from the literary poem of its original consistency with primitive articulate melody; which it now only continued to use, so to speak, as a mode of delivery and merely for the purpose of rendering its more callous, didactical contents as acceptable to the ancient habits of Feeling as possible. (p. 504)

Schoenberg's centenary in 1974, Hans Keller wrote pointedly, though without using Hegel's terms,

> Webern never was a symphonist anyway: not only did he renounce extended structure, but he was a stater and varier rather than a contraster and developer – which is one of the reasons for the temporary popularity of this considerable minor master amongst composers whose own symphonic impotence needed a father figure to hide behind.[17]

'Impotence . . . father figure to hide behind': the failure of masculinity speaks for itself. Still more recently, Alexander Goehr has pitted Webern's strength as a lyricist and composer of variations – a natural extended form for short-breathed composers – against his relative lack of strength as a 'symphonist':

> I love particularly the middle-period songs, and then again the Cantatas. But . . . I do not find that he always succeeds in sonata-fugue syntheses as well as in the variation forms. It is difficult for me to keep the material in mind when it is so miniscule.[18]

Goehr's 'love' of the vocal music, however, returns us, as Keller's strictures could never do, to Webern's virtues. For Stein also speaks of 'ecstasy' as a mental set, of musical visions, of wide melodic intervals and the pursuit of extremities (a hallmark of almost every aspect of composition), of intense, 'exalted' expression and of a fascination with nature and the Austrian landscape. The conclusion seems ineluctable. If we cross these familiar virtues with a musical understanding of how Webern turned his limitations *qua* lyricist to advantage, we shall surely be taken to the heart of his creative enterprise.

Nothing shows this understanding to greater advantage than the last of the three songs of Op.25, written in 1934 (see Example 1). This sets words by Hildegarde Jone drawn from the cycle *Die Freunde*.[19] The fact that Jone was both a woman and a devoted friend was undoubtedly of supreme

[17] Hans Keller, 'Schoenberg: the future of symphonic thought' (1974), in *Essays on Music*, ed. Christopher Wintle (Cambridge: Cambridge University Press, 1994), p. 186.

[18] Alexander Goehr and Christopher Wintle, 'The composer and his idea of theory: a dialogue', *Music Analysis* 11/2–3 (July–October 1992), p. 167.

[19] Hans and Rosaleen Moldenhauer, *Anton von Webern: A Chronicle of his Life and Work* (London: Gollancz, 1978), p. 439. Webern did not live to hear the Op.25

**Example 1** Op.25 no.3, 'Sterne, ihr silbernen Bienen der Nacht'

songs, which were first performed seven years after his death in New York on 16 March 1952 by Bethany Beardslee and Jacques Monod. Moldenhauer writes:

> *(cont.)* [Webern] had busied himself with this text already in August [1934], as is indicated by some initial formulations of the melody line appearing amidst the Concerto sketches. However, that earlier approach differed substantially from the definitive concept now taking shape. The draft (Sketchbook IV, pages 9–14) – disclosing several beginnings, various alternatives, and repeated changes in tempo – was finished on 8 October.

Example 1 (*cont.*)

creative importance to Webern; yet to modern tastes the appeal of her text is not immediately obvious (the following literal translation differs slightly from the singing version).

> Stars, you silver bees of night around the flower of love! Truly, the honey from it hangs on you shimmering. Let it then drip into your heart, into the golden comb of honey, [and] fill up the comb to the brim. Ah!, already the heart overflows, blissful and for ever saturated with eternal sweetness.

**Example 1** (*cont.*)

Yet seen from the perspective of Webern's personality – and there is no need to distinguish here between his actual and creative characters – this saccharine nocturne assumes dimensions Jone may never have intended. The poem's metaphorical world is formed from those objects in nature (Webern's lifelong love) that offer the least threat: stars, bees, honeycombs. Hence its eroticism is solitary, or at least without challenge. Even more, its psycho-sexual climax, the 'filling to the brim' which is matched by overflowing music, pinpoints Webern's predilection for the 'ecstasy' described by Stein, and its transcendent overtones accord this fleeting moment of bliss the status of an eternal 'vision'. Reinforced in the music by an increasingly intense, exalted, widely-leaping melody, it allows the 'lyric ego' to gather itself into an assertion of overwhelming and single-minded vehemence. It is an epiphany which shows in art the trait identical to that which in life Schoenberg had found so irksome.

At this point in the argument a contradiction emerges: where previously Webern was cast as 'feminine' lyricist, contenting himself with the pleasures of the moment, he is now shown to have sequestered Jone's lyricism to pursue goal-oriented 'masculine' domination. Is Stein in part wrong? Or is the contradiction merely a result of misapplied metaphor? Before we turn to the music for an answer, we need first to resolve these contradictions, and to do so in such a way that the resulting aesthetic categories may prove useful as analytical precepts. Our best starting-point will again be Stein's obituary, this time his comparison of Webern's lyricism with that of Schubert and Debussy.

## II

Example 2 reproduces 'Die Liebe hat gelogen' (ca1822), a lied of Schubert's which casts its two verses of text into three sections of music:

(A, v.1) Love has told a lie,
care weighs heavily [upon me],
[I am] betrayed, ah betrayed,
by everything around me.

(B, v.2) Hot drops flow
ceaselessly down my cheek,
let go of your pounding, my heart,
you poor heart, let go.

(A1, v.3) [as verse 1]

If we look at the rhythm of the melody alone, we may understand Schoenberg's remark that lyric concerns are essentially *local.* In bs 3–6, the four lines of verse 1 occupy just one bar each. In the first of these, at b. 3, Schubert observes the stress patterns of the poem, introduces a 'pathetic' dotted figure into each of the first two beats, and stretches a three-stress line into quadruple metre (the emphasis is thrown onto the third):

poem: Die Liebe hat gelogen
/ / /

music: Die Liebe hat gelo - gen
/ / / (/)

The resulting bar-length 'motive' is stated and repeated three times, with a modification for the cadence in b. 6: importantly, there is neither contrast nor development (by liquidation, for example). Here, *lyric concentration is achieved by repetition alone.* The same is true of verse 3.

When Schoenberg defined 'lyric theme', he was describing a subsidiary contrast within the drama of sonata form. Now, conversely, in the central part of Schubert's lyric, we can see six bars of subsidiary 'dramatic'

**Example 2** Schubert, Op.23 no.1, 'Die Liebe hat gelogen'

tonal instability. This leads to the climactic plea, where, the 'lyric ego' typically admits the 'other' by *splitting* into 'self' and 'heart': 'you poor heart, let go'. Yet despite the drama, Schubert changes his lyric procedures as little as possible. In b. 8 he constructs a bar-length 'motive of development'; to create a sense of forward movement, he shifts the first accent to the second beat, so that the anacrusis now follows rather than precedes the first beat.

The principal stress in the bar, therefore, is left empty. This motive of development is repeated with minor modification in b. 9, and the two bs 8—9 are 'sequenced' in bs 10–11. In bs 12–13, the goal of his 'dramatic' development, Schubert plays a trump card by reintroducing the music from the A section recast in light of the B section. The intensified return forms a metaphor for the relentless misery which attends betrayal; the line repeats the previous high point, but does not extend it.

So much then for Schubert and lyric repetition. Although, as we shall see in due course, Webern was heir to this procedure, he was also heir to its contradiction. By harnessing Schoenberg's principle of developing variation, he was able to amplify the central, 'unstable' part of the song. Of course, the term 'development' here does not necessarily imply the dramatic contrasts of symphonic thought, although Schoenberg, like Keller after him, used the principle to demonstrate the unity of the contrasting themes. Rather, developing variation is used in the familiar way defined by Severine Neff in the introduction to Schoenberg's recently edited *ZKIF*: 'varied in the sense of the motive itself, "developing" in the sense of creating a progression of logical and comprehensible connections'. For 'developing variation has a profound effect on articulating larger segments of a musical form: for example the introduction of "new" motives can characterise and hence differentiate the main and subordinate features of phrases or even sections of a piece'.[20] In the sketchy *ZKIF* itself, Schoenberg offers his 'most detailed explication' of the principle in relation to the first movement of Mozart's 'Dissonance' Quartet, K.465, where 'the changes proceed more or less directly toward the goal of allowing new ideas to arise. (To liquidate, unravelling)'. In other words, progression and comprehensible connections stand at the service of novelty. It is this principle – of Goethean, plant-like metamorphosis – which, as we shall again see, Webern harnesses in order, not to replace Schubert's kind of instability, but to enrich it.

At this point, we can draw together our first pair of contradictions into

[20] Arnold Schoenberg, *ZKIF (Zusammenhang, Kontrapunkt, Instrumentation, Formenlehre (Coherence, Counterpoint, Instrumentation, Instruction in Form)*, translated by Charlotte M. Cross and Severine Neff, edited with an introduction by Severine Neff (Lincoln and London: University of Nebraska Press, 1994), pp. lxii–iv and 38–43.

the aesthetic category of *developmental lyricism*: Webern, in other words, is looking for constant evolution while preserving a context that traditionally favours simple repetition. This category, moreover, leads to another pair of contradictions, the source of which again lies in Schubert's song.

The accompaniment reinforces two extreme kinds of utterance: at the beginning, the pianissimo expression of betrayal is supported by the halting, desolate rhythmic figure which is now known best from Schubert's string quartet, *Death and the Maiden*: its numbness, furthermore, is offset by resentful, stabbing dislocations in both harmony and dynamics. By contrast, the central section of the song introduces a syncopated palpitating figure, again reinforced by 'pathetic' accents. This figure comes into its own, so to speak, at the song's climax when the lyric ego splits to address its heart. The impassioned rhetoric of these bars (12–13) is a kind of declamation, an address to an 'other' which expects no reply; although it uses the music of the opening, it invests it with a taut, charged mode of delivery.

Once again, we shall see that Webern polarises and develops Schubert's extremes of *expression* and *declamation*. To heighten *espressivo*, he introduces the labile tempos and dynamics increasingly characteristic of Austro-German music since Wagner. The first page of Berg's Sonata for piano, Op.1, could serve as an example of this style. Apart from the two uses of the term *espressivo* itself, all other instructions in these nineteen bars refer to fluctuations of tempo within the framework of *mäßig bewegt*. These fluctuations are sometimes supported by sympathetic dynamic change: *accelerando* (starting already with the third beat of the piece), *ritardando, a tempo; accelerando e crescendo*, *stringendo*, *molto ritardando* (with a crescendo), *ritardando e diminuendo* and so forth throughout the piece.[21] By contrast Webern's intensified *declamation* crosses the pointillism induced by his own refined deployment of twelve notes with a principle familiar from tonal music: that legato is best sustained by introducing periodically short breaks in attention. These breaks are effected by staccato

[21] This aspect of Berg's sonata will be discussed more fully in a forthcoming paper by Susan Bradshaw. For a preliminary account of this, see Christopher Wintle, 'A bridge too far?', *The Musical Times* 135/1820 (October 1994), pp. 612–21. This essay also discusses a paper by Boján Bujić, in which he contrasts the global structures of Pierre Boulez with the moment forms of Karlheinz Stockhausen.

notes or chords, with or without accents.[22] In Webern's Op.25 song, the principle pervades the accompaniment. However, although the taut dessication of the piano part stands in marked contrast to the flexible legato of the vocal line, the wide melodic intervals themselves also represent a kind of declamation. Here the line is obviously heir to the tradition of Wagner, Strauss and Schoenberg himself.

This contradiction yields our second aesthetic category, *declamatory espressivo.* Equipped with this, and the previous category, *developmental lyricism*, we may now turn directly to Webern's song.

## III

Example 3 lays out the vocal line of the piece on seven systems. It is essential to see that Webern's metre is rewritten here to show the underlying temporal unit, not as his single bar of 2/4, but as a group of three such bars. This group thus makes a macro-unit (or 'hypermeasure') of 3/2; and the figures at the beginning of each system show that all the proportions of the music are multiples of three. (There are two macro-units of 4/2; but these are quickly balanced by bars of 2/4.) To the limited extent that they may be gathered into a three-part form, the proportions read: 24+(12+9+6+9)+(9+9). Without this rebarring, it would not be possible to grasp the organisation of the line at both local and global levels.

Let us look at each system in turn, concentrating at this stage mainly on rhythmic features.

In system i, our pairs of contradictions are immediately visible. The line comprises two motives. The first, A, projects, as *declamation*, two keywords, 'Sterne' and 'Liebe' at its beginning and end (element 'A'). These are cast in identical rhythm but accorded opposite articulation: *forte* and *sehr rasch* in the high register for 'Sterne', *pianissimo* and *viel mäßiger* (with a doting *ritardando*) in the lower register for 'Liebe'. This treatment reinforces an observation of Goehr's:

[22] The use of isolated chords as 'fillers' in sostenuto music, creating momentary breaks of tension to regenerate the lyricism, is a commonplace in, for example, Verdi (see the introductory chorus to Act II of *Luisa Miller*) and Stravinsky (the first movement of the Symphony of Psalms); it has furthermore become part of the *lingua franca* of post-Webern contemporary music.

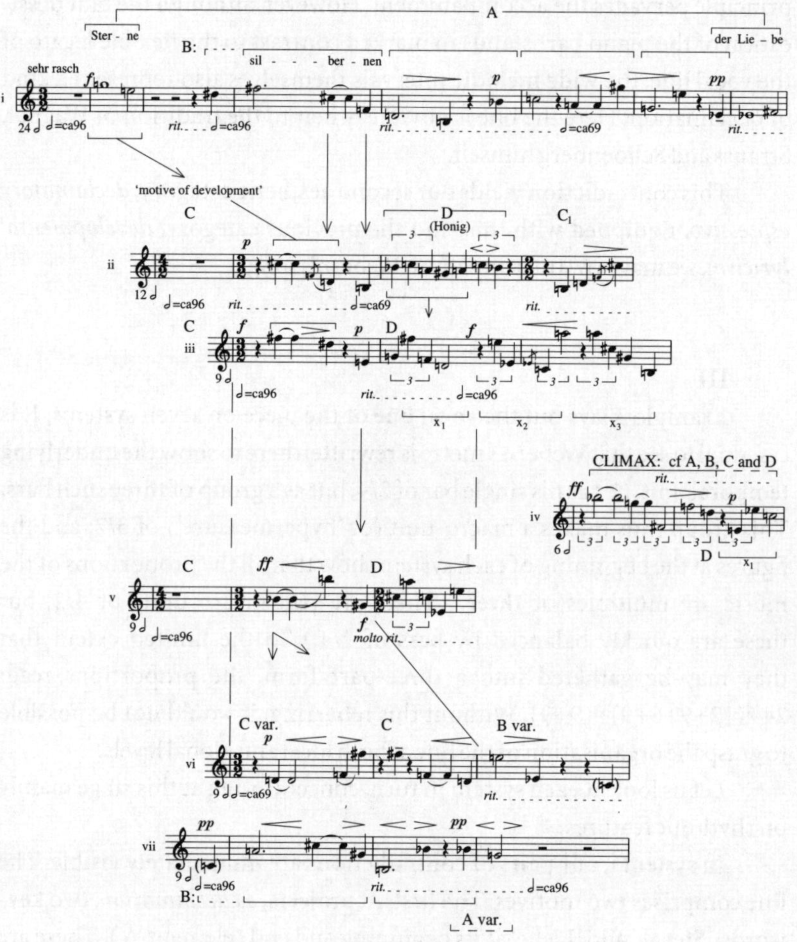


**Example 3** Op.25 no.3, chart of the vocal line

> I... admire the way the word functions in his music, as a kind of object separated from its syntactic context by the technique (derived from his earlier work) of isolating sounds through rhythmic and dynamic articulation as well as octave displacement.[23]

Motive B, by contrast, is stated and repeated three times, in the *lyric* manner. Like Schubert, Webern generates his bar-length motive by enlarging

[23] Goehr and Wintle, 'The composer and his idea of theory', p. 167.

the stress of the poetic metre, elongating the first (strong) syllable, and progressively shortening the second and third (weak) ones:

| | | | |
|---|---|---|---|
| | sil-bernen | | sil- ber- nen |
| poem 2: | — / / | music 3: | — — — |
| | | crotchets: | 3 2 1 |

However, the repetitions of the B motive are varied with respect to the actual durations of the notes: the phrases are once again segmented, to throw into relief individual words such as 'der Nacht'. The changes of tempo are indicated immediately below the system. These changes create the *espressivo* quality and mark the boundaries between declamation (*sehr rasch*) and expressive introspection (*viel mäßiger*). Hence the fluctuations during the four statements of the B motive accompany the overall drop in dynamic level from *forte* to *pianissimo*.

As in the Schubert song, the opening material is reconstructed in system ii to form a motive of *development*, which similarly includes a silent downbeat. Although described as motive C, it blends the declamatory and lyric elements – motives A and B – of the first system. But between the two statements of this new motive, C and C1, yet another figure emerges, motive D. This depiction of the shimmering, hanging honey introduces triplets into the melody; in system iii – a loosely sequential expansion of the second – their development by liquidation (marked $x_1$, $x_2$ and $x_3$) represents the principal action of the poem, the mellifluous infusion of the heart. The intensified dynamics of this system prepare for the culminating *fortissimo* of the next. This climax of system iv, indeed, effortlessly blends the *declamatory* falling 'minor third' of motive A, the *lyric syncopations* of motive B, the *developmental* empty downbeat of motive C and triplets of motive D to create an image of utmost intensity, whose forthrightness quickly yields to an *espressivo* dissipation of energy: in the second bar of this system there is a sudden ritardando and decrescendo, and a fragmentary reintroduction of the liquidated version of motive D, $x_1$.

The remaining three systems retrace the path of the song, more as a kind of foreshortened palindrome than as the third section of a Schubertian A–B–A1 form. (The foreshortening seems calculated: systems ii–iv and v–vii equally occupy twenty-seven minims.) System v reclaims the rhythm of systems ii and iii, while returning to the climactic ***ff*** (although the B is the highest note, it is not the structural climax, a point to be discussed in due course); system vi presents two versions of motive C, which prepare for the return of motive B by abandoning the triplets (of motive D); and system vii reestablishes lyric equanimity with two statements of motive B. The declamatory isolation of the last two notes, furthermore, carries with it some memory of the very opening motive A, albeit ***pp*** and rhythmically withheld.

## IV

At the first *Music Analysis* conference held in London in 1984 Allen Forte made a telling aside. Referring to his table of 'prime forms and vectors of pitch-class sets' published at the back of *The Structure of Atonal Music*, he described set 6-2 (012346) as 'redundant': it should be removed, he joked, for it was of no use to man or beast.[24] There was much formalist truth in his jest. As Example 4 shows, the twelve-note row of the Op.25 songs falls into two 6-2 hexachords, which, in terms of pitch content, are necessarily related by inversion; hence these hexachords *nearly, but not quite* fall into two complementary chromatic segments. What is included in the first hexachord is a C♯ rather than a D, which means that both 6-2 hexachords contain a tritone: G–C♯ and G♯–D respectively. Example 4 shows furthermore that there are *nearly, but not quite*, four (014) trichords in the particular ordering Webern has selected. On the face of it, then, this set, *qua* set, has nothing like the elegance of the trichordally derived set of the Concerto Op.24, or even some putative set rearranged from it in which the trichordally derived sets would fall into two chromatic hexachords.[25] Yet there is an irony to this inelegance. For if (for the sake of argument) Forte did wish to dismiss both the hexachord 6-2 and the row of this song for their lack of formalist allure, it is just that attribute which might have pleased Keller. For what he attacked in Webern and his followers was the fetishism of the 'structural' row, the set which had not been derived from a concrete basic idea (or *Einfall*):

[24] Allen Forte, *The Structure of Atonal Music* (London: Yale University Press, 1973), pp. 179–81.

[25] This is fully discussed in Christopher Wintle, 'Analysis and performance: Webern's Concerto Op. 24/II', *Music Analysis* 1/1 (March 1982), pp. 73–99.

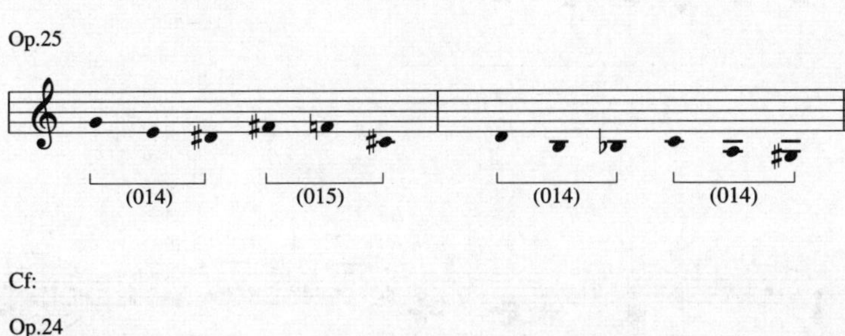


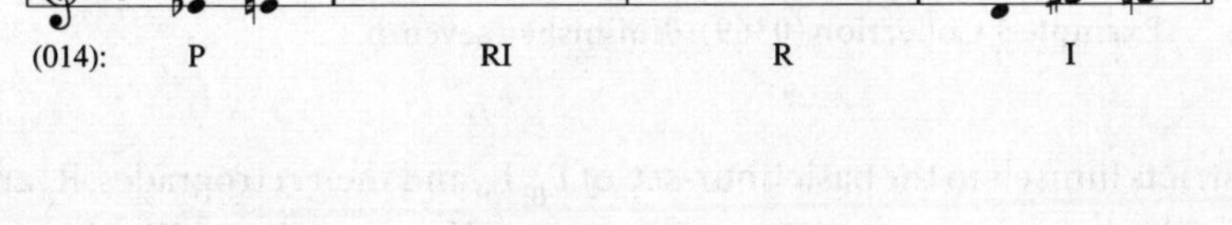


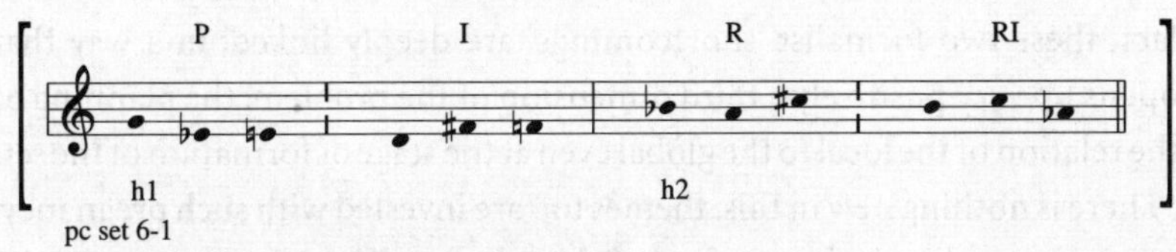

**Example 4** Pitch class set 6–2

> While for Webern the tone-row is usually abstract, which is to say that it does not readily crystallize into something of melodic significance and therefore remains largely inaudible, the Schoenbergian tone-row is *abstracted from a melodic idea*, an initial inspiration[.][26]

What is of even less formalist interest about this set, moreover, is the apparent lack of adventure in its use. For, as Example 5 demonstrates, Webern

[26] Hans Keller and Milein Cosman, *Stravinsky Seen and Heard* (London: Toccata Press, 1982), p. 27.

Ex. 5

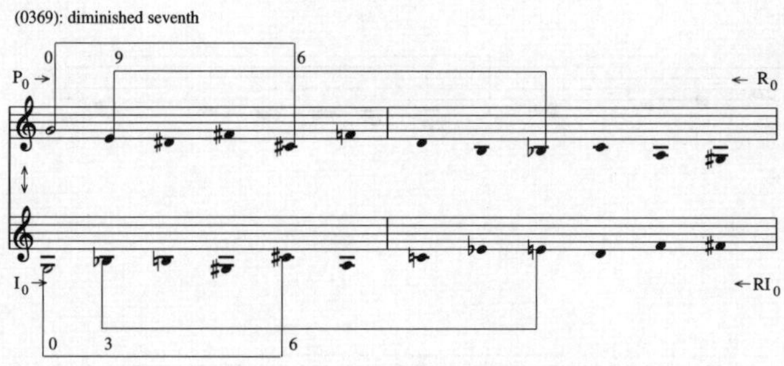


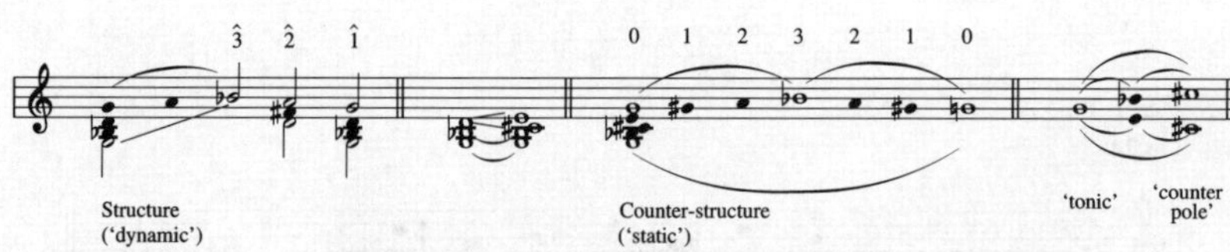


**Example 5** Collection (0369): diminished seventh

restricts himself to the basic 'four-set' of $P_0$, $I_0$, and their retrogrades, $R_0$ and $RI_0$. There are no transpositions of the row, and hence no 'instability' here. In fact, these two formalist 'shortcomings' are deeply linked, in a way that opens up very positively a third dimension of the problem: the planning of the relation of the local to the global even at the stage of formation of the set. (There is nothing new in this: themes too are invested with such pregnancy, as we have already learnt from Schoenberg.) The issue turns on the rearrangement of the first hexachord of the basic set to include C♯, the note that stands at a tritone (6) from the starting-point G (0). The capacity of the tritone to form a counterpole (or substitute dominant) to the first note (or substitute tonic) was emphasised by Webern himself:

> Considerations of symmetry . . . are now to the fore . . . For this reason the middle of the octave – the diminished fifth – is now most important. For the rest, one works as before.[27]

[27] Anton Webern, *The Path to the New Music*, ed. Willi Reich (Vienna: Universal, 1960); trans. Leo Black (Bryn Mawr: Theodore Presser, 1963), p. 54.

Example 5 shows that in the alignment of the $P_0$ and $I_0$ forms, G and C♯ necessarily occupy the same position (or order number) in each set; that the first dyads present 'minor thirds', G–E in the P form and G–B♭ in the I form; and that all these notes taken together represent a diminished seventh. It will be argued that the expansion of this diminished seventh forms a deep (or background) structure (what Keller used to call *die große Linie*), and that against this are projected the sets of the surface (or foreground). Since the entire song represents a single arch, the reason for sticking scrupulously to the four basic sets is now clear. Webern is creating what is for him a larger and more daring stable area than anything he aimed for in, for example, the Concerto.

Example 5 also draws the consequences of Webern's comparisons of tonal and twelve-note composition. The dynamic model of the (tonal) *Ursatz*, with ascent and descent in the upper voice counterpointed by arpeggiation in the bass, gives way to a monodic situation, once the triad has been 'bent' into a diminished seventh. Whereas there may still be arpeggiation of diminished sevenths, and filling-out of 'minor thirds' by chromatic voice leading (or by a 'modal' mixture of whole and half steps) there is no counterpoint between upper and lower voices, for the simple reason that the bass has nothing independent to do. Nor is it even able to define any more the local function of a melodic note as either structural pitch or embellishment (appoggiatura, suspension and so forth): clearly, one does not 'work as before'. This means that the style of twelve-note music is what was adumbrated in the earliest days of atonality: that of refracted monody, of monody which attracts concurrent layers of activity, but which is not essentially dependent on any of them for definition.

Although Example 6, therefore, may have the appearance of a (Schenkerian) tonal graph, it is in fact very different from one. Neither the 'deep line' of level 1, nor the detailed set workings of level 2, is accompanied by a bass (derived from the piano part), as would be the case with Schubert. Rather, the analysis of the accompaniment, which creates a sonic 'penumbra' around the voice, belongs to a later stage of enquiry. (This analytic procedure in fact reflects priorities in the act of composition: Schoenberg himself famously wrote the entire violin part of his twelve-note Fantasy, Op.47, first; the piano part was added later.) Only at two points in the piece is the piano directly implicated in the organisation

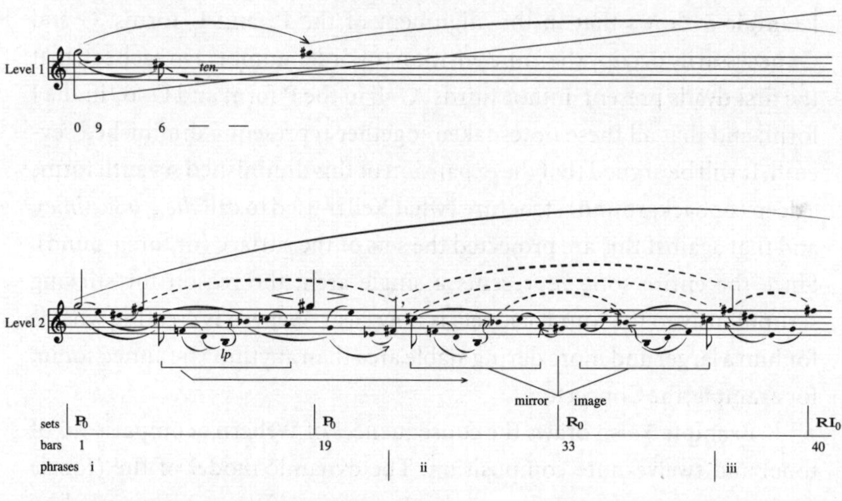


Example 6 Op.25 no.3, voice-leading graph

of the monody. At b. 48 in level 2, the first hexachord of the retrograde inversion occurs in the voice and the second hexachord is consigned to the accompaniment. Similarly the first note, the 'tonic' G, of the following inversion form is moved into the piano. The reasons for these changes will be discussed shortly.

Level 1 is predicated on three assumptions: first, that by starting and ending on the same note, G, the piece is establishing a 'tonic' of a kind; secondly that the climactic B♭ is heard as a kind of 'third degree', and is approached and quitted by chromatic stepwise movement; and thirdly, that because there is a transfer of the closing G to a lower register, this G is reached by downward arpeggiation of a diminished seventh which spans the entire song. This arpeggiation thus turns level 1 into a compound line. The analytical justification for this description lies in Webern's handling of registration. As can be seen from level 2, during the song each of the twelve notes occurs in two registers. This is even true of the note B: it marks the extremes of the vocal part (as low point (lp) and high point (hp)) but is not heard in the middle of its range. Significantly, the only exception is the note C♯, the diminished fifth counterpole to G. As level 1 shows, this C♯ is held fast in its register, mediating between the G and E above it at the opening, and the B♭ and G below it at the close.

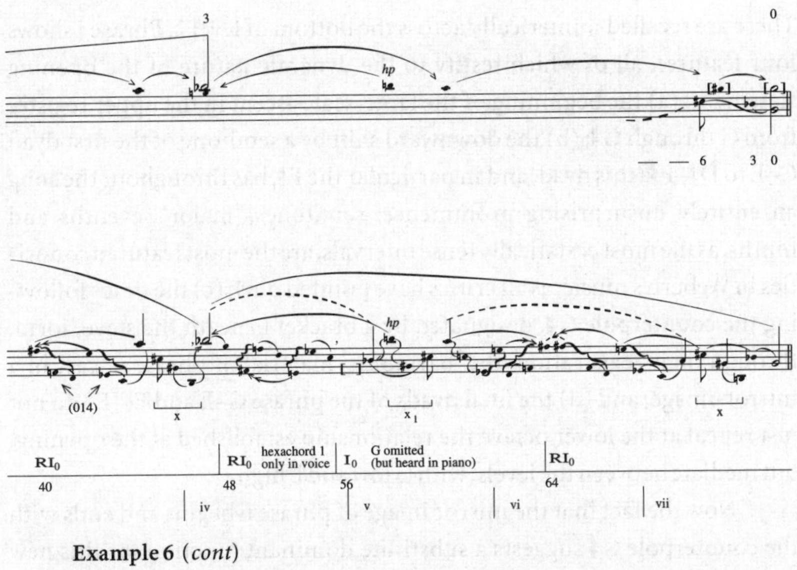


**Example 6** (*cont*)

In level 2, the symbols explain how the sets may be heard to elaborate the background. 'Minor thirds' are consistently articulated by slurs, as are pairs of thirds forming a tritone. Dotted slurs (indicating the retention of a pitch), and the relative weight of the note heads (with longer values indicating hierarchic supremacy) carry their familiar Schenkerian connotations. The dependency of one pitch upon another is indicated by a slur culminating in an arrow. When the arrow has a single head, the relation of the two notes is a semitone; when it has a double head, it is a tone. Usually this dependency is that of a note which is *not* part of the source diminished seventh (0369) upon one which is. But this is not always the case. At two points F♯ establishes a local supremacy, drawing the tonic G into it: this is true at bs 19–24, and again at bs 37–40. The large brackets, used in pairs four times during the song, show recurrent motivic formations. These articulate the pairs of (014) trichords from the I and RI set forms; their registration on the first and last occasions is identical, but is different on the second and third. The remaining intervals, which are not associated by slurs, of course, are not 'dead' ones: their identity and recurrence is guaranteed by the serial manipulations.

What, though, does this level tell us musically? Let us follow the argument according to the melodic phrases defined in the previous example.

These are recalled numerically across the bottom of level 2. Phrase i shows four features, all of which testify to the dynamic nature of the opening statement: (a) the beginning of the large-scale ascent in the upper register from G through G♯; (b) the downward shift by a semitone of the first dyad G–E to D♯–F♯ (this dyad, and in particular the F♯, has throughout the song an entirely unsurprising prominence: semitones, 'major' sevenths and ninths, as the most ecstatically tense intervals, are the most featured sonorities in Webern's music, as all critics have pointed out); (c) the notes following the counterpole C♯, designated by a bracket beneath the stave, form, through their registration, the 'harmonic' material of phrase ii, cast in a mirror-image; and (d) the final dyads of the phrase G–E and E♭–F♯ do not just repeat at the lower octave the relationship established at the opening, but mediate between the levels, with G low and E high.

Now the fact that the mirror image of phrase ii begins and ends with the counterpole C♯ suggests a substitute dominant function for this new part of the song. Phrase iii, by contrast, resumes F♯, unfolds above it a 'minor third' A (a deep passing note), and in the process introduces the bracketed (014) trichords. The phrase also ends with the downward unfolding of the trichord marked x, which awesomely places the lowest note, B, immediately before the ensuing structural climax, B♭. (In the music the treatment of bs 43–4 is especially interesting, because the A is broken by a rest in the middle of the word 'goldene': this may be to help the singer, as well as to avoid pre-empting the long phrase at the point of climax.)

Strikingly, phrase iii has introduced the RI form of the set. This, together with the I form, provides the sole vocal material for the rest of the song; hence the phrases from here to the end redispose the same groups of notes, with differences governed solely by the demands of the *große Linie.* In phrase iv, the climactic B♭ and G are followed by the return of the two (014) trichords, redisposed registrally to retain the generally high climactic tessitura with F–D and E♭–C dyads. The omission of the second RI hexachord may have been necessitated by a need to delimit the number of notes in use – Webern's text setting eschews word-repetitions and is predominantly syllabic (small exceptions occur in bs 30, 36, 43 and 57) – but the absence of the hexachord, together with the omission of the first note of $I_0$, brings the B♭ rapidly back into focus. This B♭ begins phrase v transferred to the lower register, which, in this post-climactic final part of the song, comes increasingly to the fore; but, unexpectedly, the B♭ leaps to B in the upper register (b. 57). This B is in fact the highest point in the song, and the point of greatest dynamic intensity (crescendo following ***ff***). Yet it is important for the sense of the song to understand that it *overshoots the limits of the structurally highest B♭* (b. 46) from the previous phrase: the singer is now exclaiming ('Ach!') how the heart is overflowing, exceeding its prescribed limits.

At the end of phrase v, and at the beginning of phrase vi, the almost complete return to the original registration of the two (014) trichords means that the A–F♯ dyad is once again unfolded in the upper register. Yet, in phrase vii, the A is transferred to a lower register like the climactic B♭ before it; here it sinks through G♯ and comes to rest on the 'tonic' G. When, gratefully, we reach this close, we realise how meaningfully this note G has been withheld from the line since the climax (bs 46–7).

## V

With the piano part we come face to face with the deepest paradox of all. On the one hand, the self-denying sparseness of the instrumental writing stands in obvious contradiction to the gratifying fullness of the vocal writing in its pursuit of 'ecstatic vision'. Indeed, the accompaniment is striking for all the things it never offers: a counterpointing bass line, a cushioning texture and a 'narrative' character of any independence. Rather, the pointillistic texture restricts all note values to crotchets, and even eschews triplets. On the other hand, the contradiction permits an exceptional identification of pitch and rhythmic material between the two parties. The sharing of the same set forms fulfils, by loose analogy, the Brahmsian ideal of deriving the material of the accompaniment from the melody, whether by diminution or canon (as in, for example, 'Wir wandelten, wir zwei zusammen', Op.96 no.2); and the rhythm of the motive of the accompaniment (bs 1–3) 'derives from' that of phrase ii of the voice (bs 29–31), thus anticipating the 'developmental' stage of the song at the outset.

Beyond this, the piano supports the voice in traditional ways. It adds discreet word-painting for the bee-like stars (the pointillistic pin-pricks), the flower (a tender moment of legato), the overflowing (the piano gathers up the momentum, the voice releases it), and the sweetness of love (the

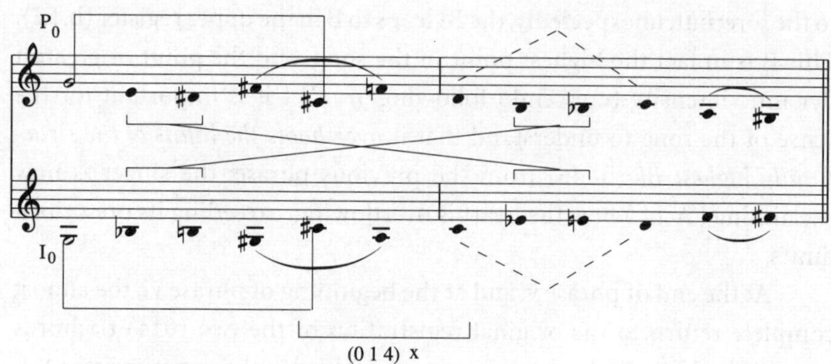


**Example 7** Sets, including motive x

pedal sustains the lowest note); it reinforces the declamation with staccatos, *sforzandos* and chords, which are sometimes spread or preceded by grace notes; it creates a fuller texture through the use of the sustaining pedal both at the climax (bs 45–6) and at the close where energy is dissipated (bs 73–8); and it supports the *espressivo* with slurs, arpeggios (30–1, 37–8, 45–6) and, finally, weighted chords. Its tempo fluctuations and dynamics broadly follow and support those of the line. Moreover, it provides an introduction, two brief interludes and a postlude in the normal way.

Before pursuing these details, however, we must again consider the properties of the sets. These are reproduced in Example 7. We have already seen how the tonic (G) and substitute dominant (C♯) occupy the same order positions in both P and I forms, and how there is an exchange between E and B♭ in the Prime and B♭ and E in the Inversion (the second and ninth positions in their respective sets). But the new relations described here are the semitone adjacencies which create 'major sevenths' (or, by inversion, 'minor ninths') or 'minor sevenths' (or 'major ninths'). In $P_0$ the descending dyad formed by the second and third notes E–D♯ is matched by another, the eighth and ninth notes, B–B♭; in $I_0$, in the same order positions, the corresponding dyads are B♭–B and E♭–E. In other words, the pitch content of the two dyads remains the same, though their internal order is reversed. With the final dyad of $P_0$, A–G♯, the case is slightly different: it again recurs reversed in $I_0$, but only as an unadjacent dyad in the fourth and sixth positions. Correspondingly, the final dyad of $I_0$, F–F♯, recurs reversed in $P_0$ in the fourth and sixth positions. The two notes not described hitherto form the 'minor seventh' dyad, and occur in the seventh and tenth order positions respectively as D–C in $P_0$, and C–D in $I_0$.

**Figure 1** Op.25 no.3, the piano sets

| set | bar | notes |
|---|---|---|
| $R_0$ | 1–6 | |
| $RI_0$ | 7–13 | |
| $P_0$ | 13–16 | B♭–C is taken by the voice (bs 15–16) |
| $RI_0$ | 17–21 | |
| $R_0$ | 22–6 | F♯ is taken by the voice (b.24) |
| $RI_0$ | 27–31 | |
| $P_0$ | 31–6 | |
| $I_0$ | 37–41 | D is taken by the voice (b.41) |
| $R_0$ | 42–6 | |
| $I_0$ | $46^2$–$52^1$ | |
| $R_0$ | $52^2$–6 | This is interspersed with the residue of $RI_0$ from the voice:<br>$R_0$: $52^2$, G♯–A; $53^1$, C; $53^2$, B♭–B; 54, D–F–C♯<br>$RI_0$: $52^2$, A–C♯–G♯; $53^3$, B–B♭–G |
| $RI_0$ | 57–60 | |
| $R_0$ | 61–4 | F–F♯ is taken by the voice (b.63) |
| $I_0$ | 65–9 | |
| $R_0$ | 70–3 | C♯ is taken by the voice (bs 71–2) |
| $I_0$ | 74–8 | |

These sets are grouped to show the periodic return of the opening set in the piano part, $R_0$. There is a regular alternation of P or R with I or RI sets throughout.

As we shall see, Webern exploits all these correspondences with just the thoroughness Stein described. Figure 1 lays out the sets of the accompaniment, and details the points where notes in the piano part are taken by the voice, and vice versa. What is immediately significant is how the sets regularly alternate a Prime (or Retrograde) form with an Inversion (or Retrograde Inversion) form throughout. It is as if Webern wishes to maximise the opportunity for drawing upon the kinds of P/I relations that have just been described.

We are now ready to examine the accompaniment.

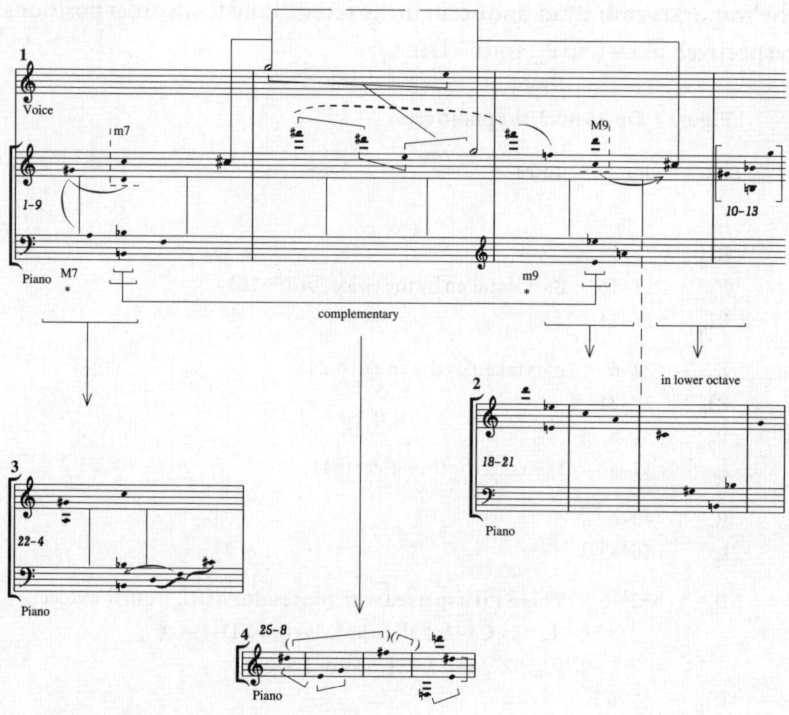


Example 8 Registration of bs 1–28

*(i) bars 1–28*

The first system of Example 8 shows the interaction of voice and piano at the opening. The choice of $R_0$ means that its last pair of notes, E–G, overlap the first pair, G–E, in the voice: hence they are placed in the same register. The notes F♯ and D♯ are placed in an octave higher still, thus importantly preserving their 'minor third' character; the dyad D♯–E thus sounds as a 'major seventh'. This E–D♯ (or E♭–E), as we have seen, is a shared (conjunct) dyad between the P and I set forms, and indeed *will always be articulated as a 'major seventh' throughout, as will its complementary dyad, B♭–B (or B–B♭).* This complementariness emerges if next one compares the registrations in bs 1–3 with those of the answering phrase in bs 7–9. There are two groups: the opening 'major seventh' G♯–A (the beginning of $R_0$) is answered by the 'minor ninth' F♯–F (the beginning of $RI_0$); and, in b. 2, the B♭–B 'major seventh' includes an F within it and supports a 'minor seventh', C–D; whereas in b. 8 the 'major seventh' is the (complementary) E–E♭, the note within it is an A, and the dyad it supports is now a 'major ninth', D–C. Moreover, the final note of the piano introduction is the counterpole, C♯, which significantly precedes the 'tonic' G in the voice.

Within the general framework of bs 1–9 (three three-bar units), this complementariness of the sets is reinforced in the actual music by the metric complementation of bs 1–3 and 7–9, where the upbeats in one become the downbeats in the other and vice versa. Bars 4–6, on the other hand, fuse the downbeating of the voice motive (G–E) with the upbeats in the piano. *Sforzato* appears to be used as a mode of attack, and not, as in Haydn or Beethoven, as an indication that a principal accent has been displaced; and the introduction of the *piano* dynamic at b. 8 (rather than at the beginning of the third unit at b. 7) is intended to support the *ritardando*. The C♯ in b. 9 loses its *sforzando* also on account of the drained momentum.

How much do these local early registrations establish principles which will be exploited globally? Although $R_0$ recurs five times in the piece, it is only at b. 61 that the first dyad G♯–A returns in the same registration, slurred (though even so without a staccato on the A); on the other hand this dyad reappears in the same register, but staccato, at bs 22, 42 and 52. The dyad B♭–B migrates registrally through three different levels which are determined locally: the boundaries of the first part of the song are fixed by its appearance in a low register at bs 2, 20 and 23, with other intervening appearances in the middle register, where it interacts with the voice in bs 12 and 15. Similarly, C♯ is almost entirely fixed throughout in the same register as in the voice part: the three exceptions (bs 20, 24, 49) also respond to pressing local demands.

The second system of Example 8 shows that the piano part at bs 18–21 reproduces the registration of bs 8–13, though with bs 20–1 transposed into a lower register to accord with the overall descending profile of this section. Similarly, system 3 shows that the opening registration is reproduced in bs 22–4, with D and C♯ dropped into the lower register. System 4 represents the piano interlude between the opening and central part of the song, and demonstrates that registrally it acts as a postlude to the first section: the D♯–F♯ and E–G dyads are preserved, again in a lower octave, although the D♯–F♯ relations are created from unadjacent members of their respective sets. For this reason the F in b. 28 is dropped two octaves, where it is able to form a 'major seventh' with the E (rather than a 'minor second' as would otherwise be the case).

### *(ii) bars 29–52*

Example 9 shows the close registral integration of voice and piano in the 'developmental' part of the song (systems 2 to 4 in Example 3). The beamed notes show the progress of the 'deep line' of Example 6; x denotes the (014) trichords marked in Example 8 (the fifth, sixth and seventh order numbers in the P and I forms); the lines connecting bracketed dyads or trichords show the shared registrations; and the three encircled arpeggios mark the declamatory beginning of each system (2, 3 and 4), with the boundary notes G♯/G in the first, G/G♯ in the second and F♯/G in the third making a circumlocution of the 'tonic'. In the music itself, the rhythms of the piano part for the most part complement those of the voice to create a continuum of regular attacks: significantly, only after the vocal climax (b. 46), from bs 47–51, is this principle relaxed.

### *(iii) bars 52–60*

We have already seen that Example 8 catalogues the integration of piano and residual vocal sets in bs $52^2$–6. Although these bars prepare for the cry 'Ach' at 56–7, with the upbeating (014) trichords preparing for the 'sensational' syncopated G/B♭/B at bs 56–7, they also set up the piano registration of bs 57–60. This may be seen by comparing the trichord D/F/F♯ in bs 52 and 57, the dyad C♯-C in bs 52–3 and 58, and the positioning of G♯, B and B♭ in bs 52–3 and 59. Once again the relative harmonic stability of the piano writing throws into relief the all-important activity in the upper part of the voice.

### *(iv) bars 61–78*

The typically withheld, *morendo* character of the final section is reinforced registrally in a number of ways. First, Webern continues to match voice and piano as before (v. 65–6/pf. 69; v. 69–70/pf. 71; v.73–6/pf. 74). Secondly, when he touches the lowest point in b. 73 with the piano F♯ (to lend gravity to 'Süsse'), he sounds the octave below the F♯ heard in the cli-

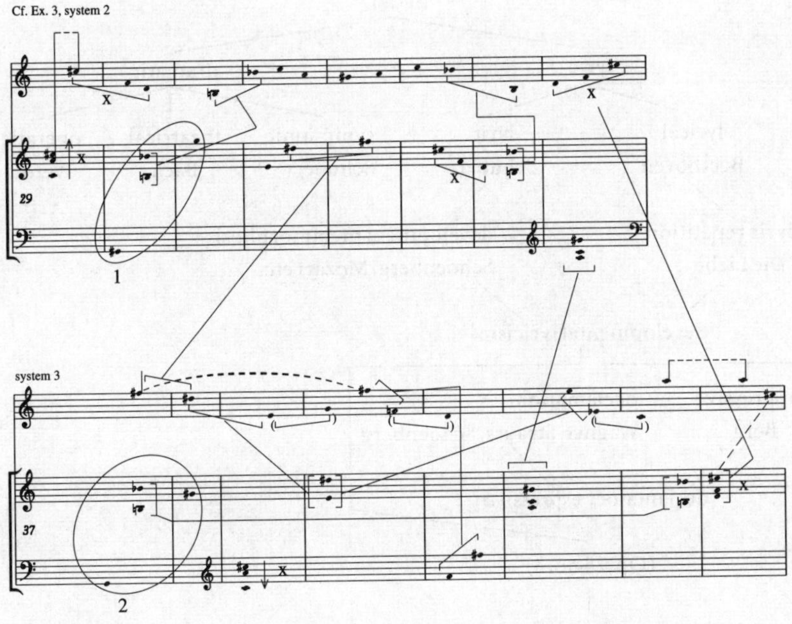


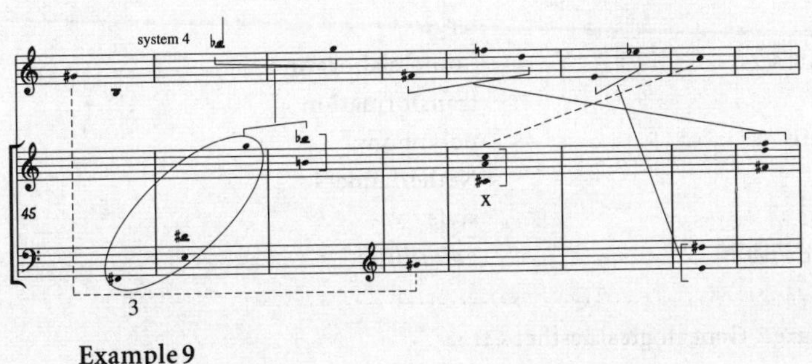


Example 9

mactic bs 45–6. Thirdly, as we have already noticed, he reintroduces the slurred G♯–A from bs 1–2 *in situ*, though now quietly and smoothly downbeating – a token of recapitulation within admittedly a generally palindromic context: the G♯s at bs 65 and 74 are also bound by a slur. Fourthly, some of his registrations appear to look back nostalgically to the more charged situations earlier in the song: for example, the high left-hand D in b. 71 recalls the Ds in bs 8 and 28. Most remarkably, because the trichords in

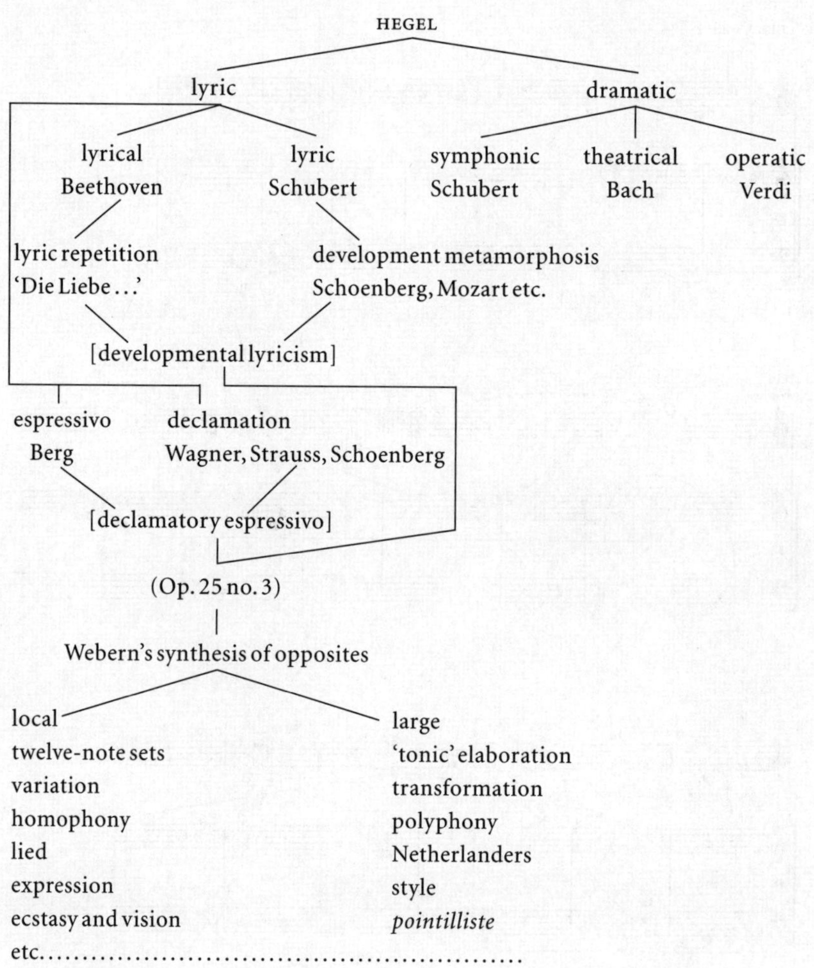


**Figure 2** Genealogical aesthetic tree

bs 77 and 78 appear to refer to those in bs 57–8, and the *sf* A in b. 76 to that in b. 59, the postlude encaptures the spirit of the text in 56–60: we are left with the congealed memory of the overflowing heart. In the music itself, the rhythm is continuous, with the exception of three vocal ligatures, which are left dotingly unsupported at bs 62, 66 and 72. The postlude recalls the upbeating momentum of bs 1–3, 25–7 and (for reasons just given) most particularly 53–5.

## VI

Where, then, has the investigation of Stein's 'lyric quality' taken us? Figure 2 sums up the aesthetic argument, leading from the broad definitions of Hegel to the more detailed ones of Schoenberg and his school. Importantly, the subdivisions necessarily reflect the evolution of music from the time of Schubert to that of Webern: obviously, it would be hard to apply the precepts of the 1830s to the music of the 1930s without some kind of reconstruction. Indeed, the genealogical tree includes a final principle which holds the key to any further elaboration of Webern's creative character: the synthesis of clearly-defined opposites. Such opposites (*developmental lyricism* and *declamatory espressivo*) already inform the analysis of the melodic line, and are again in evidence in the discussion of the accompaniment: the Brahmsian integration of the musical material offsets the textural opposition of full, ecstatic legato in the voice, and sparse, dessicated staccato in the piano. Earlier in this chapter, moreover, Goehr's definition of 'sonata-fugue synthesis' (in, for example, the first movement of the Symphony) signalled a fusion of classical homophonic symphonism with Netherlandish polyphony – a more remote 'background' than any Schoenberg could claim. The 'middle period songs' he cited similarly review the (homophonic) lied in the light of accompanying counterpoint. Others, too, have explored Webern's typical fusion of variation (changing restatement) and symphonic metamorphosis (constant development).[28]

The aesthetic summary also polarises the demands of the local and the global, something which would not have occurred with music of the two preceding centuries. In itself, the dichotomy reflects a recent difference of critical view. On the one hand, Keller claimed that [hierarchical] tonal thought persisted into Schoenberg's twelve-note music, and that in the first movement of the Fourth String Quartet, for example, he could amplify the first subject with 'harmonic resolutions' that 'took an eternity' to play.[29] Arnold Whittall challenged this kind of claim, demanding evidence in the form of voice-leading graphs.[30] These Keller declined to provide. Instead

[28] See, for example, Arnold Whittall's essay in this volume (p. 264).
[29] 'Schoenberg: the future of symphonic thought', p. 260, note 15.
[30] Arnold Whittall, 'Schoenberg and the English: notes for a documentary', *Journal of the Arnold Schoenberg Institute* 4/1 (June 1980), p. 29.

he insisted that, when he wrote, the 'foreground is atonal' but 'the background isn't', he was not using Schenkerian terms in their original sense. Rather, in his own two-dimensional theory of music, he implied by 'background' the 'sum total' of expectations generated by precedent (what had been achieved in prior works), and by 'foreground' what the composer, writing against this background, had done instead.

However, the difference has been implicitly resolved in this essay. Example 6 sets the (Schenkerian) foreground of sets against the background of a symmetrical structure, the diminished seventh, which here assumes a referential status in lieu of the triad; on the other hand the (Kellerian) foreground of rhythm and phrasing in Example 3 has been projected against the background of a Schubert song and the tradition of thought between Schubert and itself. The two lines of argument are obviously linked, especially in relation to the design of the whole.

This resolution, however, raises yet a further issue: what analytic judgment can be passed on the song? To answer this question, we need first to ask another: in Example 6, do the notes of level 1 – the G and its counterpole C♯, as well as the E and B♭ – exert sufficient authority as 'deep' structure for the listener to be able to sense the depth that Webern himself claimed as his goal? Certainly, at the beginning and end, the metric positioning of the 'tonic' G as downbeat enhances its status for just the reasons described by Edward T. Cone:

> By structural downbeat, of course, I do not mean the arbitrary accentuation of the first beat of every measure; I mean rather phenomena like the articulation by which the cadential chord of a phrase is identified, the weight by which the second phrase of a period is felt as resolving the first, the release of tension with which the tonic of a recapitulation enters. (In [the third movement of Webern's Variations for piano Op.27], I hear the downbeat as the E♭ at the beginning of measure 12; and I consider it no accident that it occurs at the beginning of a measure, preceded by a *ritardando*.)
>
> It is just here that the importance of the rhythm to the establishment of tonality emerges, for the cadence is the point in the phrase at which rhythmic emphasis and harmonic function coincide.[31]

[31] Edward T. Cone, 'Analysis today', in *Problems of Modern Music*, ed. Paul Henry Lang (New York: W.W. Norton), pp. 44–5.

In a complementary way, the positioning of both the counterpole C♯ at the beginning of the 'development' and the B♭ at its climax on upbeats, articulates their relatively unstable character. But beyond this it may still be felt that the constant rotation of all twelve notes in voice and piano militates against anything more than a token feeling of large-scale structural control. Is this what Webern intended? Or did he hope for a more equal balance between his opposites? (One may even ask, does the analysis itself distort his priorities?) And what sort of challenge does his example pose for composers who still seek to relate the local to the global?

The challenge of projecting the *große Linie* is obviously of greatest concern to performers. But how many actually tackle this music? Its sheer difficulty means that it will probably always be better known from recordings than recitals. Hence the discs are bound to attract close scrutiny. Currently, the songs are available in the collection of Webern's 'complete works [with opus numbers]' issued in the name of Pierre Boulez; the Op.25 collection is sung and played by two undeniably gifted artists, Halina Lukomska and Charles Rosen.[32] Among many merits of the performance of the challenging third song is Rosen's ever alert critical intelligence. This is in evidence in his controversial decision not to pedal the last three bars (it is possible to argue that the pedal contradicts the staccato of the second chord and hence goes awkwardly against the grain). Yet it does not take an armchair Beckmesser to point out that Lukomska's singing of phrase i (bs 1–23) neither observes the performing instructions, nor meaningfully contradicts them. The crucial opening dyad ('Sterne') is sung as a falling 'second' and not a 'minor third'; there is neither a *ritardando* from b. 13 nor a *viel mäßiger* from b. 17; and there is very little overall drop in dynamics or change of tone. Most disconcertingly, the closing 'der Liebe' is marked by a poco *ritardando* only: it is certainly not an extreme pianissimo *espressivo* contrast to the forthright *declamatory* opening. As a whole, indeed, the performance lacks the sense of analytically-inspired overall shaping which, as has been shown elsewhere, was Webern's own priority as a performer.[33]

How curious that, fifty years after the appearance of Stein's obituary, we have still to get the measure of Webern's lyric character!

32 *Webern Complete Works Opp. 1-31*, Sony SM3K 45845, 3CDs ADD. The Op.25 songs were recorded in London on 5 September 1970.

33 See Wintle, 'Analysis and performance'.

# 8 Music – discourse – dialogue: Webern's Variations, Op.30

ARNOLD WHITTALL

*I have been to the Hochschwab. It was glorious, because this is not sport for me, not amusement, but something quite different: it is a search for the highest, a discovery of correspondence in nature for everything that serves me as a model, a model for all that I would like to have within myself. . . . It is not the beautiful landscape, the beautiful flowers in the usual romantic sense that move me. My objective is the deep, unfathomable, inexhaustible meaning in everything, especially in these manifestations of nature. All nature is dear to me, but that which expresses itself 'up there' is dearest of all.* Webern to Berg, 1 August 1919[1]

## I

In a letter to Hildegard Jone of 22 December 1940, Webern transcribed the second bar of his Variations, Op.30, explaining that 'I am now making the fair copy of the score'. After the quotation he declared: 'That's one of the germ cells. It is a Variation movement (Metamorphoses).'[2] A few months later, in May 1941, he provided Jone with further comments on Op.30, invoking his favourite Goethean imagery:

> Imagine this: 6 notes are given, in a *shape* [*Gestalt*] determined by the sequence [*Folge*] and the rhythm, and what follows . . . is nothing other than this shape over and over again!!! Naturally in continual 'Metamorphosis' (in musical terms this process is called 'Variation')—
> —but it is nevertheless the same every time.
> Goethe says of the 'Prime Phenomenon' [*Urphänomen*]:
> 'ideal as the ultimate recognizable thing,
> real when recognized*,
> symbolic, since it embraces every case,
> identical with every case**'.

[1] Hans Moldenhauer (in collaboration with Rosaleen Moldenhauer), *Anton von Webern: a Chronicle of his Life and Work* (London: Victor Gollancz, 1978), p. 231.

[2] Anton Webern, *Letters to Hildegard Jone and Josef Humplik*, ed. Josef Polnauer, trans. Cornelius Cardew (Bryn Mawr: Presser, 1967), p. 42.

* In my piece that is what it is, *namely the shape mentioned above*! (The comparison serves only to clarify the *process*).
** Namely in my piece! That is what it does![3]

Given the clarity with which Webern proclaimed the Goethean analogy, and sought to persuade Jone of its validity, it might be regretted that he did not give his Op.30 the explicitly Goethean title of *Metamorphosen*. The composer who did adopt that title four years later, Richard Strauss, has recently had the possible Goethean connections of his work explored in a remarkable analysis which seeks to demonstrate not only that the 'study for 23 solo strings' evolved through transformations of a sketch for a setting of Goethe's poem *Niemand wird sich selber kennen,* but also that the meaning of the completed work engages with – if only to invert – the Goethean precept that through the pursuit of self-knowledge human beings can discover the spark of divinity within themselves.[4] Timothy L. Jackson argues that

> the motivic link with the *Niemand wird sich selber kennen* sketch suggests that the adagio was probably conceived as a Goethean work from the outset. Only when Strauss had perceived the composition in its entirety, with its peculiar physiognomy of obsessive foreground motives superimposed on continuous middleground transformation, could he associate the idea of 'Erkenne dich selbst' in *Niemand wird sich selber kennen* with the concept of 'Metamorphose' presented in *Die Metamorphose der Pflanzen* and *Die Metamorphose der Tiere.*

Jackson then goes on to argue that, whereas

> Goethe's view of metamorphosis, like the classical notion, is essentially optimistic; it is a view of 'order in motion' . . . in Strauss's instrumental meditation, Goethe's concept is violently inverted; through self-knowledge, man regresses from the divine to the bestial.[5]

This startling claim serves to reinforce Jackson's main thesis, viz. that 'the fundamental theme . . . of the *Metamorphosen* is . . . poetic, philosophical,

[3] Ibid., p. 44. Webern refers to no.1369 of Goethe's *Maximen und Reflexionen.*

[4] Timothy L. Jackson, 'The metamorphosis of the *Metamorphosen*: new analytical and source-critical discoveries', in *Richard Strauss: New Perspectives on the Composer and his Work*, ed. Bryan Gilliam (Durham, N.C. and London: Duke University Press, 1992), pp. 193–241.

[5] Ibid., p. 201.

and possibly autobiographical: the negation of the traditional affirmation of self-knowledge as a means of discovering the divine within'.[6]

The present essay will in due course come to consider the extent to which Webern's Variations might also be interpreted in the light of Goethe's concept of metamorphosis, and also of his understanding of self-knowledge, which might be linked with Webern's 'search for the highest', and 'the deep, unfathomable meaning in everything'. In these terms, the Variations might be understood as a religious text, a musical consequence of the composer's belief that the pursuit of self-knowledge, and the overcoming of one's human vulnerability to doubt and despair, is 'a means of discovering the divine within'. On the other hand, it might be argued that the very reason why Webern did not call Op.30 *Metamorphosen* was that he had no desire to create expectations that this non-texted work was in any way a parallel text to writings of Goethe which did more than state the essential structural principle that he quoted in his letter to Jone.

This essay will explore the middle path between those alternatives: the hypothesis is that Op.30 not only 'composes out' that structural principle, but also attempts to express an engagement with Goethe's philosophical ideas. The conclusion will be that the attempt was unsuccessful, to the extent that the 'classical' continuities of the philosopher metamorphose into the irresolvable ambiguities of the post-tonal composer. This interpretation will be offered, not because it can be shown to expose any conscious or unconscious intention of the composer's, but because it is an interesting possibility, responding to and – it is to be hoped – not demeaning the perceived aesthetic power of the music.

The analysis that follows will centre on the nature and presentation of those 'irresolvable ambiguities' inherent in Webern's post-tonal musical language, and these will be interpreted both structurally and semantically. The interaction of textural connection and fragmentation is complemented by the alternation of expressive states to be characterised primarily by the terms 'vulnerable' and 'assertive'. The use of such terms inevitably casts a hermeneutic haze over the music, since they are shorthand sketches for much more subtle and diverse ranges of expressive nuance. Since 'vulnerable' is normally used in the sense of 'liable to damage or harm' (*Shorter*

6 Ibid., p. 200.

*OED*), the implication is of music expressing a state of weakness and instability, just as 'assertive' implies confidence and decisiveness. As the narrative that follows makes clear, any such pairs of opposed terms – lyric/dramatic, weak/strong, feminine/masculine – are meaningful as much for their tendency to move towards common ground as for reinforcing their opposition. They enrich musical expressiveness while resisting simple semantic constraints.

The hazards of reducing shades of musical meaning to single pairs of opposed terms are not lessened by the fact that such states are likely to occur in most compositions. Since most music ebbs and flows, tenses and relaxes, it is not surprising that analysts who wish to deal with musical meaning in other than purely structural terms should seek for more specific differentiating topics as a way of illuminating the particular expressive qualities of any work of substance. In the case of Op.30, those essentially optimistic ideas that Webern found in Goethe (and Jone) might be proposed as such a topical matrix. Yet it might rather be that the 'particular' in Op.30 is the primarily musical – the motivic, collectional matrix – and the 'general' is the semantic context which Webern's work shares, in outline, with so many other compositions. Structure and semantics intersect with special power in Op.30 because Webern's strategy of sustained dialogue stemming from the interaction of motives, tempos and expressive states is ideologically resonant, aspiring to bear witness to his Goethean convictions yet generating an essentially unstable structure. Reading Op.30 as a dialogue between degrees of vulnerability and assertiveness calls into question the extent to which Webern was able to 'work as before'.[7] Before addressing this subject in detail, however, it is important to consider the basis on which the claim can be made that a non-texted composition can serve as a discourse, and not just as a structure in which a 'purely musical' shape is presented 'over and over again'.

[7] 'Considerations of symmetry, regularity are now to the fore, as against the emphasis formerly laid on the principal intervals – dominant, subdominant, mediant, etc. For this reason the middle of the octave – the diminished fifth – is now most important. For the rest, one works as before. The original form and pitch of the row occupy a position akin to that of the "main key" in earlier music.' Anton Webern, *The Path to the New Music*, ed. Willi Reich, trans. Leo Black (Bryn Mawr: Presser, 1963), p. 54.

## II

No recent writer has wrestled more intensely with the abiding ambiguity of the relation between music and language than Robert Hatten, and part of his definition of 'discourse' is useful at this point: 'for music, loose term describing the strategic or thematic/topical flow of ideas in a musical work, as in "musical discourse" or "thematic discourse"'.[8] It is not my intention here to predicate close parallels between literary studies and musicology in the way they enquire into the nature of artistic communication. In its complexity and pioneering spirit, Hatten's work demonstrates how far musicology remains from an analytical practice that can treat of musical meaning – the 'thematic/topical flow' – as confidently as it does of musical structure, even when its subject matter is the familiar ground of Beethoven's late masterworks. My concern is less with general issues in interpreting the expressive signification of post-tonal music than with the interpretation of possible parallels between verbal texts (with associated concepts acknowledged by the composer) and a musical work: and even this modest enterprise is likely to reinforce the eternal ambiguity of the relation between word and tone. As a 'loose term' relating to a 'flow of ideas', 'discourse' is an embodiment of that ambiguity rather than a resolution of it.

The immense growth and development of music analysis since the 1950s has not significantly reduced the analyst's dependence on words as a means of communication. Even when it is an article of faith that the essence of an analysis can be conveyed non-verbally, through graphs, tables or charts, the interpretation of that essence is likely to require verbal definitions, statements and arguments, and words become even more vital when an analysis attempts to consider matters of musical meaning and signification.

Webern's most extended discussion of one of his own works, the String Quartet, Op.28, can be held to focus extensively on matters of structure and technical procedure, and it may be the source of some critical regret that it contains no reference to those extra-musical elements, both personal and topographical, that appear on the work's sketches.[9] There seems to have

[8] Robert S. Hatten, *Musical Meaning in Beethoven. Markedness, Correlation, and Interpretation* (Bloomington and Indianapolis: Indiana University Press, 1994), p. 289.

[9] For Webern's essay on Op.28, see Moldenhauer, *Webern*, Appendix 2, pp. 751–6. For the composer's annotations to the Op.28 drafts, see pp. 486–92.

been a distinction in Webern's mind between aspects of the work that might be of public concern and those that were entirely private. The discipline of musicology, dedicated as it is to the full exposure and interpretation of facts and information, requires that both public and private materials be identified and discussed. At the same time, however, the recent impact of literary theory on musicology has helped to call into question the treatment of the associated texts of any composition – whether words on sketches or poems set to music – as elements that are magically absorbed through translation into a musical language. Rather as Bakhtin enriched the concept of dialogue, turning it from a straightforward binary alternation or exchange into an asymmetric dualism – 'a process in which different modes of expression at once presuppose, question, and interpret each other'[10] – so the 'new', interpretative musicology sees music and any associated text as joint participants in a heterogeneous discourse, a 'heteroglossia' which embodies 'a plurality of relations, not just a cacophony of different voices'.[11]

All metaphors concerning what music 'says' may merely be strategies designed to circumvent the inherent and ultimately unsurmountable speechlessness of art, as Adorno for one defined it.[12] Yet such metaphors continue to provide worthwhile ways of exploring the dialogue between that 'speechlessness' and a cultural tradition that cannot keep words and music apart. After all, even Hatten's notion of musical discourse as a 'flow of ideas' does not simply offer the choice of 'flow' as succession or as superimposition: it suggests a process involving musical statements whose contours give them identities which can be thought analogous to the identities of verbal propositions. Musical ideas are not translations of verbal propositions, but they are, to an extent, equivalent to verbal propositions. They can therefore form the basic material of the kind of musical structures that may be categorised as 'dialogues'.

10 Lawrence Kramer, 'Music and representation: the instance of Haydn's *Creation*', in *Music and Text: Critical Inquiries*, ed. Steven Paul Scher (Cambridge: Cambridge University Press, 1992), p. 141, note 8.

11 Michael Holquist, *Dialogism: Bakhtin and his World* (London and New York: Routledge, 1990), p. 89.

12 T. W. Adorno, *Aesthetic Theory*, ed. Gretel Adorno and Rolf Tiedemann, trans. Christian Lenhardt (London: Routledge & Kegan Paul, 1984), p. 164: 'the true language of art is speechless'.

There is always the possibility that a composer may establish some degree of connection between a personal experience and the music written at the same time, so that, when the Moldenhauers report that Webern's sketches for Op.30 'were interspersed', as usual, 'with sundry diary notes of family happenings',[13] we might seek to establish direct parallels between the two. Webern's own argument in his lectures – 'Music is language. A human being wants to express ideas in this language, but not ideas that can be translated into concepts – *musical* ideas'[14] – is a classic autonomist warning against incautious attempts at simple translation. But this cannot preclude the possibility that there can be an association – for example, between the strong, affirmative ending of Op.30 and Webern's joy at the recent birth of a granddaughter, or even at Germany's defeat of France. Associations between musical character and verbal concepts become even more contingent where matters of the composer's beliefs are concerned. If, as Anne Shreffler has argued, it is correct to speak of 'the vocal origins of Webern's twelve-tone composition',[15] it is no less important to acknowledge that his twelve-note technique was sustained and enriched by ideas that emerge consistently in the texts he chose for his vocal works.

It is possible to use 'dialogue' in music analysis as a term whose meaning is exclusively formal: for example, to speak of the dialogue between a theme and its accompaniment may serve to introduce an account of the ways in which an accompaniment realises the harmonic implications of the theme, underpins it texturally, complements it rhythmically. In such contexts the dialogue may promote the idea that the accompaniment, even if its textural identity is clear and consistent, is somehow subordinate to the theme, simply through its lack of thematic substance although, at the same time, the theme might well appear incomplete without it. In circumstances where a theme for variations is so homogeneous in texture and integrated in character that no effective element of dialogue can be teased out of the theme itself, the analyst may seek to transfer the term to relations between theme and variations, encouraged by the fact that proper verbal dialogues

13 Moldenhauer, *Anton von Webern*, p. 568.

14 Webern, *Path*, pp. 42–3.

15 See Anne C. Shreffler, '"*Mein Weg geht jetzt vorüber*": the vocal origins of Webern's twelve-tone composition', *Journal of the American Musicological Society* 47/2 (Summer 1994), pp. 275–339.

involve successive exchanges rather than simultaneous statements. Yet the analytical relevance of dialogue may be called into question if there is only a gradual, graded, evolutionary change of mood and texture in the variations. It is rather when changes are dramatically extreme, leading to a sense of different textures and moods being juxtaposed without transition, like the opposing elements of an argument in which the extremism of one side fuels greater extravagance and exaggeration on the other, that the dialogue metaphor will seem more convincing: that is, when exclusively formal considerations begin to interact with matters of mood and tone.

As already suggested, musical dialogue may be at its purest, and its most remote from verbal dialogue, when 'voices' are combined or superimposed. Canon, as practised by composers who preserve the distinction between consonance and dissonance, is the most explicit display of variety in unity, of separation enhancing interdependence. At the opposite extreme (within the spectrum of tonal practice) is that vocal, dramatic circumstance associated pre-eminently with Wagner, in which the dialogue of voice and orchestra is not so much one of melody and countermelody as one between fully realised melody and less continuously realised melodic material. When the orchestral melody is more continuous and the vocal melody relatively fragmented, this may serve to represent a character's vulnerability in relation to the more confident orchestral 'chorus': and while a fully realised vocal melody cannot by definition save the character from vulnerability when the 'accompaniment' is that of a large, turbulent, orchestral 'web', the Wagnerian dialogue at its most resonant often seems to involve the challenge to the character's knowledge and experience which the collective, fully realised orchestral material can suggest. This is, it might appear, a dialogue between solo lyricism and collective symphonism, a musical prose that comes fully to life only when the musical discourse preserves the tension between its constituent elements even as it strives to resolve that tension.[16]

[16] In Wagner's 'monologues' there is often the sense of a fully formed, appropriately harmonised, orchestral melody in which salient motives are explicitly represented, stimulating dialogue with a vocal line which may seem to resist the orchestra's dominating clarity as much as to embrace it. This interplay of acceptance and resistance contributes greatly to the sense of nobility tinged with fatalism that often arises with particular intensity in these contexts, as at the start of Marke's solo in Act II of *Tristan und Isolde*, or of Hans Sachs's 'Wahn! Wahn!' in Act III of *Die Meistersinger*.

Once the move has been made to characterise the musical components of a discourse in terms of an opposition – as here, between lyric and dramatic, reflective and assertive, vulnerable and confident elements – it is tempting to seek to refine and elaborate the interpretation in relation to more specific topical categories with suitably wide cultural significance. Given Webern's Goethean concern to associate the natural with the spiritual, it might seem attractive to propose categories that also serve to create a Beethovenian connection. After all, as Robert Hatten has observed, 'in the works of Beethoven ... the pastoral ... involves the poetic conceit of feelings inspired by Nature, either in the secular sense of a grounding in the "Natural" (Rousseau) or in the pantheistic sense of God in Nature'; and Hatten's analysis of the first movement of Beethoven's Sonata, Op.101 – 'the mixing of tragic elements endows the pastoral with greater seriousness and the elevation of style in turn supports the interpretation of the pastoral as a poetic conceit for a spiritual state of innocence (or serenity) subject to the disturbances of tragic experience (or remembrance)'[17] – might seem to offer a possible model for the expressive world of Webern's Op.30. Yet, given the difficulty of translating Hatten's concretely defined topics of pastoral and tragic into Webern's twentieth-century vocabulary, and of equating Beethoven's tonal world with Webern's post-tonal context, the enterprise must inevitably appear problematic. Despite Webern's own association of the first movement of Op.28 (with which Op.30 has much in common) with the slow movement of Beethoven's last string quartet,[18] it is undoubtedly the case that what, in Beethoven, is relatively stable and specific is, in Webern, more allusive and ambiguous. I do not wish to exclude all possibility of interpreting Op.30 as a pastoral/tragic discourse, as one way of preserving the link with Goethe and the cultural values embodied in Webern's celebration of Goethe. Nevertheless, as with the idea of Op.30 as an

17 Hatten, *Meaning*, pp. 92–6.

18 See Moldenhauer, *Anton von Webern*, p. 752. In a letter to Reich (3 March 1941) about Op.30, Webern affirmed that 'my "Overture" is basically an "Adagio" form', and noted that 'Beethoven's "Prometheus" and Brahms's "Tragic" are other overtures in adagio-forms' (Webern, *Path*, p. 60). It is tempting to speculate on whether or not Webern knew of Max Kalbeck's claim that the *Tragic* Overture (along with the middle movements of the Symphony No. 3) used material which Brahms had first conceived in association with Goethe's *Faust*.

optimistic religious text, it is unwise to assume before fuller analysis that any such interpretation can be anything other than vulnerable and unstable.

## III

Kathryn Bailey has provided an admirable account of the incompatibilities between the traditional concept of variation form and the possibilities of twelve-note composition. Since Webern worked with motives, not themes, and motives which are 'too short and elementary to function as a theme'[19] tend to be developed rather than varied, Webern's so-called variation forms are at worst a 'sham', at best an 'irony'.[20]

Webern's own awareness of the problem may have triggered his increasing tendency to exploit the kind of formal duality that he found in the slow movement of Beethoven's last quartet: 'a theme and variations but at the same time, and for him more importantly, a three-part song form'.[21] Bailey, in tune with Webern's own arguments, speaks in terms of the unity and synthesis of these different formal models. With reference to the first movements of Op.28 and Op.30, she comments that 'both works represent the union of two theoretically antithetical forms: variation, which is reiterative and essentially linear, and ternary form, which is circular with a reprise'.[22] She also claims that Op.30 was 'his most ambitious attempt at synthesis, setting out to unite not only two homophonic structures based on essentially opposed principles, but two very different traditions as well: the complex rhythmic and metric procedures of the Netherlanders and the formal conventions of the nineteenth century'. At the same time, Bailey suggests that 'Webern's predilection for synthesis places him directly in the Austro-German tradition that he inherited from Beethoven and Brahms'.[23]

A 'predilection for synthesis', by all means. But are the 'theoretically antithetical' forms synthesised in practice? It is perhaps only possible for two distinct formal principles, deployed simultaneously, to achieve

19 Kathryn Bailey, *The Twelve-Note Music of Anton Webern* (Cambridge: Cambridge University Press, 1991), p. 197.
20 Ibid., p. 196.
21 Ibid., p. 198.
22 Ibid.
23 Ibid., p. 199.

synthesis if each acknowledges a higher structural force – tonality – as Beethoven does in the finales of the third and ninth symphonies, and Brahms in the finale of his fourth. Even if we allow that Webern achieves a striking degree of 'harmonic' consistency, what most musicologists would regard as an absence of tonality[24] also creates an absence of that 'background' to which the distinct formal principles could both refer, and for which the 'higher authority' of twelve-note technique is no substitute. This is not to say that all elements of higher structural levels are absent in serial Webern, but to draw a distinction between tonal and post-tonal strategies. Christopher Wintle's conclusion about the second movement of the Concerto, Op.24 is relevant:

> While there *is* a parallel here between the larger deployment of a single hexachord to embrace an entire section, and the concept of *Stufen*, and while there is also a pattern of (set-)substitutions, there is more significantly no sense of motion towards a cadence *per se*, no *Auskomponierung*, and no voice-leading by stepwise movement. And it is part of the aesthetic of Webern's twelve-note music that the expressive power is achieved precisely by denying the assurances that these conventional tonal means offer.[25]

Some readers may be impatient with the argument that there is a real distinction to be made between the claim that variation and adagio forms are synthesised in Op.30 – that is, that the work's clear sectional divisions allude to both types simultaneously – and the counter-claim that there is at best co-existence: both are alluded to distinctly, in such a way that competing claims and tensions are acknowledged. In practice, after all, the 'synthesis' claim tends to imply that the problematic variation concept is absorbed into the acceptable ternary concept. Yet surely the 'ternary concept' is no less problematic, since what Bailey defines as 'circular with a reprise' is, in Op.30 at least, nothing of the kind. The 'reprise' offers not only further motivic transformation, but also significant structural and textural

24 Graham Phipps has recently attempted (unsuccessfully, in my view) to analyse Op.30 in terms of tonally-rooted chordal structures. See his 'Harmony as a determinant of structure in Webern's Variations for Orchestra', in *Music Theory and the Exploration of the Past*, ed. Christopher Hatch and David W. Bernstein (Chicago and London: Chicago University Press, 1993), pp. 473–504.

25 Christopher Wintle, 'Analysis and performance: Webern's Concerto Op.24/II', *Music Analysis* I/1 (March 1982), p. 98.

variation of the motivic and topical matrix which, if only metaphorically, can be regarded as providing Op.30's theme. It is not, then, that variation is absorbed into ternary form. Rather, the two schemes challenge each other, by means of a rich dialogue between developmental and variational strategies, applied not so much to abstract pitch-class elements as to actual, characterised motivic components. What might have remained an 'irony' is transformed by Webern into an intense – in his terms spiritual – musical discourse: one to which the Goethean title *Maximen und Reflexionen* is far from inappropriate.

The obvious similarities of technique and texture between Op.30 and the two cantatas that frame it might even provoke the question: Is it a cantata in disguise? The initial double-bass tetrachord (Example 1) certainly recalls the rhythm and general contour (deriving from the [0,1,3,4] collection) of Webern's setting of Jone's words 'Wie bin ich froh' (Op.25 no.1). Yet this does not lead on to the disclosure of a hidden song of some kind, comparable to the Baudelaire setting that lies submerged in the finale of Berg's *Lyric Suite*. Even so, the music of Op.30 is sufficiently similar in character to that of the later vocal works to indicate that it might validly be regarded as connected, though less explicitly, to Webern's preferred poetic and philosophical topics.

Anne Shreffler has produced powerful arguments to support the view that Webern's adoption of the twelve-note method arose primarily 'from a personal desire . . . to reflect Nature's order in music',[26] and if, as Shreffler believes, what Webern 'valued most in twelve-tone composition'

**Example 1** Op.30 Variations, the opening double bass tetrachord compared with the opening of Op.25 no.1

26 Shreffler, 'Vocal origins', p. 335.

Example 2 Op.30, bs 0–20

was 'a kind of eternally present meaning that he found also in nature',[27] we are presumably dealing not only with the constant presence of closely interrelated subsets (like Op.30's first and third tetrachords, for example: see Example 2, bs 0-1 and 3) but also with the kind of 'pantheistic piety'[28] evident in Webern's conviction that 'God's presence in nature ... is revealed

[27] Ibid., p. 323.
[28] Ibid., p. 320.

most immediately and purely on the mountain peaks'.[29] Just as 'the technique was never an end in itself', so Webern's identification of the technique 'as a metaphor for the ineffable in nature and heaven'[30] reinforces the relevance of that metaphor to all his later works. It may be impossible to translate the enigmatic references to topographical and botanical phenomena on the outline of Op.28 into concrete musical equivalents, but the analytical task is rather to explore, in all its ambiguity, a spiritual progression between a natural state and a musical context, a belief in 'the divine within' and a technique that depends on 'continual metamorphosis'. In Webern's music, as in Jone's verse, there is not so much a narration of a spiritual odyssey as a discourse whose rhetoric seeks to persuade listeners to adopt – instinctively – the beliefs and attitudes represented as their own, even if the chosen, post-tonal language is not ideally suited to such a task, and the task is therefore liable to failure.

The ways in which music can be persuasive have been addressed with particular pertinence by Daniel Harrison in his analysis of the fugue from Bach's Toccata S915. Harrison's assumption that 'the composition is a persuasive discourse with a self-defined topic, and not a collection of ornaments, graces, and techniques having a purely aesthetic meaning',[31] may be controversial and even problematic in its concern with pursuing literal parallels between rhetorical and musical procedures. Yet Harrison's desire to promote an analysis 'written with conviction in terms of a rhetoric that emphasizes substance over style', and which is meant 'not so much to be about structure as about the effects of structure',[32] leads to a focus on the particular qualities of that intensely contrapuntal process that is fugue. Harrison argues that 'fugue achieves artistic success . . . because its various thematic treatments, harmonic modulations, contrapuntal devices, and so forth interest, convince, and perhaps even amaze, persuading the listener that it has not only displayed but also earned its unity'.[33] The Bach-admiring Webern's obsession with canonic counterpoint may be interpreted

29 Ibid., p. 328.

30 Ibid., p. 335.

31 Daniel Harrison, 'Rhetoric and fugue: an analytical application', *Music Theory Spectrum* 12/1 (Spring 1990), p. 7.

32 Ibid., p. 41.

33 Ibid., pp. 40–1.

similarly, and we might therefore propose that Op.30 evolves as it does because Webern is attempting to explore associations between technical procedures and abiding beliefs in ways that could persuade listeners that unity has been 'displayed but also earned'; and even that the 'ungraspable' can be grasped.[34] Just as Webern's pantheistic and organicist/evolutionary meditations cannot be detached from the music as he conceived it, so – once we are aware of them – they cannot be separated from the music as we perceive it. It is not that the music somehow metamorphoses into concepts; rather, that its 'purely musical' metamorphoses shadow, ambiguously, concepts that lie behind the composer's most cherished convictions. It is in the interaction of musical language and conceptual language that tension and ambiguity arise.

Webern's Variations, Op.30, is dominated by contrapuntal combinations which demonstrate different degrees of interaction at the levels of set structure and motivic process. But the implication, if we adopt Harrison's perspective, is that these processes themselves, as they might be represented in tabulated summaries of formal relationships, are insufficiently persuasive as metaphors for the divine in nature and within man: there must also be a persuasive 'tone', a spirit that seems to reach out beyond earthly reality.

Webern's emphasis on contrapuntal combination itself promotes the idea of discourse as dialogue. Parallel yet distinct voices pursue related motives in ways which point up the purely musical nature of the process. At the same time, however, purely musical coherence is challenged by Webern's rejection of linear continuity as practised by the tonal masters, and the advancing of fragmentation, a special mobility in musical space which seems to draw attention to the non-gravitational character of the musical fabric. In tonal composition, sudden shifts of register are not by definition structurally disruptive, as long as the actual or implied harmony conforms to accepted procedures, and even in Wagner the dialogue of relatively vulnerable and relatively assertive 'voices' is not dependent on an equivalence between the vulnerability of a character and a lack of purely textural continuity. In post-tonal music, by contrast, it is the concept of line as a smooth, registrally focused phenomenon that may appear conceptually

[34] Shreffler argues that 'to grasp the ungraspable' was one of Webern's 'longest-held goals in music' (Schreffler, 'Vocal origins', p. 336).

dissonant, and contrast may be more a matter of register than motive. The discussion of Op.30 that follows is an attempt to pursue this topic in greater depth, and ultimately to focus on the interaction between texture and 'tone'.

## IV

The opening of Op.30 has the uncompromising transparency of Webern at his most personal: short statements for double basses and trombone (bs 0–3) frame a brief duet for oboe and solo viola (see Example 2). The contrasts of colour are striking, but the similarities of contour – one interval rising or falling, followed by two falling or rising – indicate that essential Webernian continuity, the consequence of his concern to derive twelve-note sets from (in this case) a single tetrachord.

**Figure 1** Generation of the Op.30 row

| | | | | | | | | | | | | |
|---|---|---|---|---|---|---|---|---|---|---|---|---|
| | | | | | [0 | 3 | 4 | 7] | | | | |
| $P_0$: | A♮ | B♭ | D♭ | C♮ | B♮ | D♮ | E♭ | G♭ | F♮ | E♮ | G♮ | A♭ |
| | [0 | 1 | 4] | 3 | | [0 | 1 | 4] | 3 | | | |
| | | | | 1 | 0 | 3 | 4 | | 1 | 0 | 3 | 4 |
| | | 1 | | | | | 2 | | | | 3 | |

The set for Op.30 has versions of the unordered collection [0,1,3,4] as its first and third tetrachords. The central tetrachord, the very different but also symmetrical collection [0,3,4,7], can be generated from [0,1,3,4], as several commentators have shown (see Figure 1). Webern's immediate concern, in bs 0–3 of Op.30, seems to be to make explicit the ultimate, essential dependence of tetrachord 2 on tetrachord 1, by way of the common trichord [0,1,4]. In b. 2, tetrachord 2 of $P_0$ is superimposed on tetrachord 1 of $RI_0$, with the common dyad B/D highlighted. What is particularly striking about this initial strategy is that an aurally explicit identity – the B/D dyad – is countered, on analytical reflection, by the divergent texture. There is a switch from monody to duet which, once the conventions of twelve-note composition are appreciated, signals in the clearest possible way that 'duet' involves two different set forms rather than different segments of a single set form.

According to Webern, 'everything that occurs in the piece is based on the two ideas given in the first and second bars',[35] and Kathryn Bailey has shown that these ideas are matters of rhythm as well as of pitch and interval.[36] Bars 0–2 might appear preliminary, given that such simple alternation between 'monody' and 'duet' is not one of the principal ideas of the work, yet the balance of similarity and difference in b. 2 is the key to the basic strategy of the Variations as a whole, in the sense that separate linear events are vertically co-ordinated in ways that acknowledge degrees of interdependence. 'Harmony' is the result of sharing, and the type of sharing demonstrated in b. 2 will be reinforced at the end of the work as different set forms converge on the same pitches in the same registers.

Most commentators on Webern seem persuaded that such techniques justify the composer's claims for unity and synthesis, embodying, perhaps, a degree of self-knowledge that prevents his music from disintegrating into unconnected fragments. For example, Christopher Hasty, in his close reading of the first twenty bars of Op.30, proposes a three-phrase segmentation (0–6, 7–12, 13–20) which progresses from juxtaposition and rupture to synthesis.

> Phrase 2 does nothing to clarify or continue the structure of phrase 1. The juxtaposition of phrase 2 to the relatively closed phrase 1 is a rupture in the form. Phrase 3 in many ways heals this rupture and at the same time joins the three units into a continuous line, inverting the initial gesture of opening . . . into a gesture of repose.[37]

Hasty is sensitive to the continuing ambiguities – 'In spite of the remarkable consolidation effected by phrase 3, the immediate sense of closure at the end of phrase 3 is considerably weaker than that produced by the last unit of phrase 1' (b. 6)[38] – but he remains true to his perception that 'phrase

35 Webern, *Path*, p. 62.
36 Bailey, *Twelve-Note Music*, pp. 224–36.
37 Christopher F. Hasty, 'Composition and context in the twelve-note music of Anton Webern', *Music Analysis* 7/3 (October 1988), p. 305.
38 Ibid., p. 307.

3 functions to close the first variation as a whole', and 'it does this by reconciling or synthesizing previous musical developments'.[39]

My object is not to presume that Hasty's contention is incorrect, but rather to consider the circumstances, relevant to Op.30 as a whole, in which Webern is able to persuade some close readers of the work that reconciliation and synthesis are in fact achieved, while other readers may resist that conclusion, preferring to hear a more evenly balanced dialogue between the reconciling impulse and a persistent susceptibility to the properties of 'juxtaposition and rupture'. Even if Op.30 can be characterised as Webern's attempt to recover the 'success' of Bach's fugal models (not only displaying but also earning its unity, in Harrison's terms), it may also relate to the more immediate model of the Wagnerian dialogue, whose inherent tension between continuity and discontinuity seems reflected in Webern's work as a tension between his (optimistic) faith in certain Goethean concepts and the nature of his musical language. As a post-tonal post-Wagnerian, Webern transferred the continuity into his twelve-note substructure, the discontinuity into his motivic surface, and the vulnerability into what we hear as lyric material under constant threat from more assertive, more dramatic statements, which prevent it from achieving stability and closure. This tension between substructure and surface can also be reflected in the distinction between smaller and larger-scale structures – the kind of thing to which Paul Griffiths referred in his comment, concerning the second movement of the Concerto, Op.24, that 'the play of two- and three-note groups . . . can divert attention from the patterning of units of two and three bars. There is thus a subtle relation between small and large structures, the former being necessary to, but also compromising, perception of the latter.'[40]

Any listener who senses that, in Webern, 'small' structures are truly more *real* than larger ones may be particularly persuaded by the argument that in Op.30 Webern is not so much satisfying his aspiration to a unity that reflects the power of God in Nature, and his most cherished spiritual commitment to celebrating 'the divine within'; rather, he is struggling to realise, on the

39 Ibid., p. 304. For a different interpretation of the 'theme's' periodic structure, see Bailey, *Twelve-Note Music*, p. 228.

40 Paul Griffiths, s.v. 'Webern', *The New Grove Dictionary of Music and Musicians*, ed. Stanley Sadie (London: Macmillan, 1980), vol.20, p. 276 (col.1).

musical surface, a simulacrum of that powerful, evident unity provided by his twelve-note substructure, as if in constant homage to the last line of Jone's 'Wie bin ich froh': 'und bin auf Erde'. To be mortal is indeed to be vulnerable to the failure of divinity to make any significant impression on humanity, and technically this implies an acute awareness of the 'limits on how much music can be successfully held together', in Hasty's perceptive phrase.[41]

It would be dangerous to suggest that every Webern work is exactly the same when the interaction of structure and meaning is considered. On the one hand, the String Quartet, Op.28, in its progress between the two types of formal ambiguity embodied in its outer movements, may well be felt to counter the vulnerable aspect of its first movement's emphasis on lyric variation with the drama of the finale's fugue, whose powerfully integrative climax (bs 42—3) leads to a stretto that seems recollected in tranquillity, the tension between fugue and scherzo unambiguously resolved. On the other hand, Op.30 may be deemed a more 'Wagnerian' work, even as much a reaction against Bach, Beethoven and Brahms as a celebration of them, a work in which fundamental instabilities are less convincingly dispelled.

## V

Returning to the music of Op.30 in the light of these considerations, I believe that the first twenty bars (see Example 2) can be described as the theme for the variations which follow on the grounds that they present a dialogue between the work's contrasted expressive states – lyric vulnerability and more assertive, dramatic affirmation – in its most elementary form. It should nevertheless be clear that the real 'theme' of the work is the principle of metamorphosis itself, characterised in terms of various types of dialogue: between the [0,1, 3, 4] and [0,3,4,7] tetrachords (with their salient rhythms) and the two principal tempos (*Lebhaft* and *Ruhig*), in conjunction with various inflections of the vulnerable and assertive 'states'.

Following Webern's own description of the first twenty bars as a period,[42] we can identify varieties of dialogue within the antecedent and consequent respectively, as well as a 'higher order' exchange between the

41 Hasty, 'Composition and context', p. 305.
42 Webern, *Path*, p. 62.

two parts of the period as a whole. The antecedent (bs 0–9) presents three monodies and three duets in alternation, and the musical image of vulnerability is graphically conveyed in monody 1, the exposed double bass statement. No less graphic is the lack of a simplistic monody= vulnerable / duet=assertive opposition, at least where 'vulnerable' is interpreted simply to mean relatively evanescent in expression. Monody is vulnerable to extinction, partly through its lack of formal richness (a single tetrachord at a time) and partly because the evanescent mood can be assumed no less effectively by duet textures, most obviously in the solo violin/harp+double bass statement at the end of the antecedent (bs 7–9).

In the consequent of the thematic period (bs 10–20) the dialogue is between duet as close, canonic imitation (with one of the two voices usually shared between two instruments) and duet as motivic statement (sometimes doubled) with chordal punctuation – a verticalised tetrachord. As far as the consequent being in dialogue with the antecedent is concerned, it is clear that the consequent greatly intensifies the solo/tutti contrast present in the antecedent, while the louder dynamics and use of ***sf*** (***f***) also suggest a more decisive, assertive tone, before the shading down at the end. There is therefore a basic expressive contrast between the two components of the thematic period which overreaches the various internal contrasts within each of the main sections, and Webern's characteristic twelve-note strategy – set forms with significant invariant pitch-class membership of the various salient subsets (tetrachords) is deployed to serve the dialogic characterisation of the actual material.

Kathryn Bailey has described Variation I (bs 21–55) as a nine-segment arch form which presents 'a consistent alternation of the two generating [rhythmic] motives: odd-numbered sections deal with a, even-numbered sections with b'.[43] The dialogic function of these alternations is promoted by Webern's avoidance of precisely complementary alternations of dynamics and tempo: while the *Ruhig* segments are always ***pp***, and the *Lebhaft* segments ***f***, the statements of rhythmic motive a (and ar) may be associated with either expressive type. The treatment of motive b is therefore more stable than the treatment of motive a.

Webern's own description of Variation I as 'the first subject' unfolded

43 Bailey, *Twelve-Note Music*, p. 229.

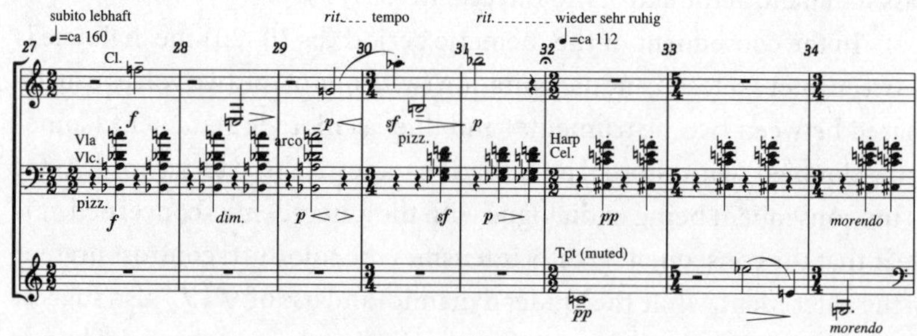

**Example 3** Op.30, bs 21–39 (reduction)

'in full'[44] means, in practice, a fuller exploration of the tensions presented in the theme itself, in the context of greater textural continuity. *Sehr ruhig* now becomes the principal alternative to *Lebhaft*, and the progress of the variation as a whole can be interpreted in terms of the *Ruhig* tone resisting the assault of the *Lebhaft* tone, although the end result is motivic dissolution

44 Webern, *Path*, p. 62.

rather than harmonic resolution. The first six bars of Variation I offer the prospect of a melody with chordal accompaniment whose antecedent (bs 21–3) and consequent (bs 24–6) share two pitch classes, and one actual pitch, the B♭. This relationship, which also functions as *dux*/*comes* of the submerged canonic texture, rather overrides the absolute contrast of the rhythmic motives stressed by Bailey, and from my own perspective consolidates the expression of vulnerable evanescence adumbrated in the theme itself. The first gesture in the direction of the alternative expressive topic comes at the start of the *subito lebhaft* (segment 3) at b. 27. Yet assertiveness shades down within that segment, and vulnerability is then reinforced in segment 4 from b. 32 (Example 3), where the muted trumpet is allocated a form of tetrachord 2 [0,3,4,7], which will have an important role in the work's final stages.

Another aspect of formal ambiguity in Variation I is that, since segment 4 (bs 32–4) follows a pause mark, it might be thought to begin a new stage of the variation. It may indeed do so, but the fact remains that the moment of maximum contrast and discontinuity comes between bs 34 and 35 – between segments 4 and 5. From segment 5 on, the contest between the two expressive topics is fully engaged, at first in terms of the loud, widely spaced *Lebhaft* melody from b. 35, then in the still more fragmented brass and woodwind texture from b. 43, a crucial variant in that the accompanying string chords begin to share the more assertive quality of the other material, as well as opposing fragmentation with simple repetition. Segment 7 (bs 43–7) provides the crisis of the variation. Then the last two segments (bs 48–55: Example 4), far from offering themselves as the simple, retrograde complements of the first two segments, as a literal arch form might suggest, continue the liquidation of the tetrachordal motive begun in earnest between bs 43 and 47. A particularly disruptive form of assertiveness has not eliminated the vulnerable, *Ruhig* topic altogether, but that topic is now less clearly defined than it was in the variation's first two segments. While it is true that the underpinning set structure acts as a kind of guarantee of essential continuity and coherence, this is countered rather than composed out by the persistent, even intensifying conflicts on the musical surface.

Variation II (bs 56–73) and Variation III (bs 74–109) are less intense, befitting their parallel formal functions as transition and secondary theme. Bailey's terminology does not conceal an element of double function in Variation II: 'the entire variation proceeds in layers of four-note

Example 4 Op.30, bs 48–55 (reduction)

chords', yet it is also 'a rhythmic canon in two voices'.[45] Significantly, however, and despite the presence of fairly strong dynamic contrasts, the variation inflects a single tempo rather than continuing the dialogue of tempos established in the theme and Variation I. The effect is therefore essentially assertive, the absence of linear motives at the level of the tetrachord making the linear processes of the canon a purely formal backdrop for an exercise in shifting, sharply sculpted densities.

For the purposes of this essay it would be strategically convenient to be able to assign Variation III entirely to the 'vulnerable' topic. The contrast between it and the assertive Variation II is indeed extreme, though perhaps more in texture – the shift from chord to line – than in temperament. Contrasts of tempo return, but this remains the most carefree, perhaps the most 'secular' music in the piece, evoking the floating maple leaves and other emblems of the organic natural world so important to Webern and Jone. Even the statements which are the most potentially aggressive, like the trombone/viola duet (bs 105–6), are mitigated, in this case by muting the trombone. In effect, therefore, the role of Variation III, as of Variation V later on, is to set off the more complex processes and characteristics of Variations IV and VI, directly linked as these are with the 'fully developed' version of the theme in Variation I.

Kathryn Bailey has discussed the extent to which Variation IV can be shown to comprise nine segments paralleling those of Variation I.[46] Understandably, she writes in terms of complexity and overlapping, even though the similarities of formal outline remain significant. Undoubtedly, the

45 Bailey, *Twelve-Note Music*, pp. 229–30.
46 Ibid., p. 231.

greater continuity and technical richness of Variation IV (it is the first section of Op.30 to deploy four chains of sets simultaneously) brings with it a refinement of the 'asymmetric dualism' embodied in the confrontation and interaction between the topics of vulnerability and assertiveness. From this perspective, Variation IV can be divided into two principal parts. In the first part, from the last beat of b. 109 to the first beat of b. 126, the dynamic level is predominantly low, and the high degree of melodic continuity, with longer note values and, on occasion, narrower intervals, suggests that the purer form of vulnerability is yielding to a more positive, confident tone, a sense of lyric aspiration in keeping with the achievement of the fully realised, four-chain, contrapuntal fabric, representing Webern's self-knowledge as a serial composer (Example 5). There is a significant moment of transition when this

Example 5 Op. 30, bs 109–21 (set chains)

Example 6 Op. 30, bs 125–34

mood is sustained as the basic tempo increases (bs 122–4). Then, from b. 125, the music embodies a crisis: assertiveness and aggressiveness are to the fore, yet a feeling of aspiration is not abandoned. As at b. 45 in Variation I, there is some indication of the two opposed emotional states coming together – a possibility of synthesis which, however, is belied by the relatively fragmented texture (Example 6). In Variation IV, as in Variation I, this crisis provokes a degree of liquidation (bs 132–4), but the thread of linear continuity is not wholly lost. In addition, the final C/B in the cello (b. 133) foreshadows the still more confident use of that interval (an octave higher) at the end of the whole work.

Variation IV may retain some elements of a pointillist approach to orchestration, but it is nevertheless consistently linear in texture, the polyphony unfolding note by note, however difficult it may be to hear the actual linear relations. The brief, transitional Variation V, like the Theme and like Variation II, rediscovers the dialogue between line and chord which is then further explored in Variation VI. Bailey has skilfully unravelled the rhythmic intricacies of this final section, noting the employment of the *Ausfall* technique, later so crucial to Op.31.[47] Webern's use of this technique in Op.30 can be interpreted as the result of his wish to progress beyond the polyphonic consistency of Variation IV, and to reinforce the large-scale formal function of Variation VI as a coda which is also a second development, a structure which achieves closure through drawing the most decisive conclusions from the composition's basic materials.

Variation VI interprets those materials asymmetrically, in that the four set-chains employed are of two types. Chains 1 and 2 present closely related sequences of seven prime forms each. Chains 3 and 4 are sequences of nine set forms, arranged palindromically around the central, fifth form: one chain of P versions, the other of R (Figure 2). Just as this choice of materials deconstructs the fully achieved consistency of Variation IV, with its four R-form chains, each of seven members, so Variation VI fragments the polyphonic consistency of Variation IV into a sequence of nine segments, in which chordal constructs constrain the canonic processes that alternate with them.

At the start of Variation VI (Example 7) Webern initiates a complex exploration of the dialogue between difference and similarity which invites interpretation in terms of a strategy for distancing the composer from the

47 Ibid., pp. 234—6.

more obviously logical properties of his basic material. That material is, after all, not a single set but a matrix comprising the forty-eight forms of the set, an entity embracing many kinds of relationship. Three of these can be observed in connection with the four tetrachords deployed in the first four bars of the Variation (146-9), as analysed in Figure 3: (a) the ordered dyadic content shared by $P_9$ and $R_2$; (b) the single dyadic exchanges, with pitches mirrored, of $P_7$ and $P_{10}$; (c) the shared spanning dyad of $P_{10}$ and $R_2$, creating the effect, for the tetrachords, of a $t_3$(inv) relation.

**Figure 2** Variation VI: the four set-chains (see Example 7)

| | | | | | | | | | |
|---|---|---|---|---|---|---|---|---|---|
| 1 | $P_7$ : | $P_0$ : | $P_5$ : | $P_{10}$ : | $P_3$ : | $P_8$ : | $P_1$ | | |
| 2 | $P_{10}$ : | $P_3$ : | $P_8$ : | $P_1$ : | $P_6$ : | $P_{11}$ : | $P_4$ | | |
| 3 | $P_9$ : | $P_2$ : | $P_7$ : | $P_0$ : | $P_5$ : | $P_0$ : | $P_7$ : | $P_2$ : | $P_9$ |
| 4 | $R_2$ : | $R_9$ : | $R_4$ : | $R_{11}$ : | $R_6$ : | $R_{11}$ : | $R_4$ : | $R_9$ : | $R_2$ |

There is a seven-note overlap between adjacent sets in Chains 1 and 2, and for the first five entries of Chains 3 and 4; e.g. P0 begins on the sixth pitch (A) of P7. Webern has to use different overlapping relationships for the second halves of Chains 3 and 4.

**Figure 3** Tetrachords in bs 146–9

(a) Chain 3 : $P_9$ : F♯ G♮ B♭ A♮
Chain 4 : $R_2$ : B♭ A♮ F♯ G♮

(b) Chain 1 : $P_7$ : E♮ F♮ A♭ G♮
Chain 2 : $P_{10}$ : G♮ A♭ B♮ B♭

(c) Chain 2 : $P_{10}$ : G♮ A♭ B♮ B♭
Chain 4 : $R_2$ : B♭ A♮ F♯ G♮

**Figure 4** A hypothetical alternative to Figure 3

$P_7$ : E♮ F♮ A♭ G♮
$R_0$ : A♭ G♮ E♮ F♮

$P_9$ : F♯ G♮ B♭ A♮
$P_0$ : A♮ B♭ D♭ C♮

If Webern had chosen $R_0$ rather than $P_{10}$, or $P_0$ rather than $R_2$, a more stable and explicit initial symmetry would have been created (Figure 4). As it is, he counters the actual asymmetry by drawing attention to invariant elements – most notably the fact that three of the four Gs in bs 146–9 are the same G.[48] Webern is, in a sense, demonstrating his freedom from the more literally complementary balancing and self-reflective properties of the matrix: he acknowledges them in order to question them. The most strongly connective, integrating strand (horn G/A♭; cello A♭/G) is embedded in a context of different degrees of parallelism. The organicism here has nothing to do with 'a morphology of diminution',[49] which might ultimately derive from a single, movement-spanning source – an *Ursatz*. The *Urphänomen* is rather the range of possibilities present in the set group, and while the group as an entity may be regarded as an organic structure, the process of using that structure, of developing a discourse by way of various choices and selections, creates a situation in which organicism itself is called into question.

In the early stages of Variation VI (bs 146–57) the discourse avoids direct dialogue between vulnerability and assertiveness; despite the textural diversity, the tone of lyric aspiration is sustained, moving towards the more assertive quality focused around the trumpet statement in bs 154–7. As in previous variations, the strongest sense of dramatic confrontation comes in the later stages, when the more forceful initiative stemming from the tuba statement (b. 163) and focusing into the highly invariant *Lebhaft* segment (bs 165–6) is countered by the relative rhythmic stability and sustained lyric poise of the *Wieder sehr ruhig* (bs 167–73). To end, if that were serially possible, at b. 173 would surely leave the listener with a sense of the relative serenity which essentially vulnerable but spiritually aware humanity could attain – an ending akin to that of Op.28. But Webern may be seeking a different image, closer to the positive evocation of love as perfection in the final stages of Op.29. The last two segments of Op.30 (bs 174–80) are complementary to each other – the first lyric, the second dramatic – in a way designed to counter the tendencies to motivic liquidation between bs

48 This technique of registral retention is important throughout Variation VI, as a more exhaustive narrative would show. Of particular significance to the topical focus are the anticipation and echo of the trumpet's G♯ (bs 156–7), the sharings of A, C, F and G♯ (bs 165–6) and the sustained transfers of B and D (bs 167–72).

49 See Thomas Clifton, 'An application of Goethe's concept of *Steigerung* to the morphology of diminution', *Journal of Music Theory* 14/2 (Winter 1970), pp. 165–89.

Example 7 Op. 30, variation 6 (set chains)

166 and 173. Indeed, the last two bars seem determined to persuade the listener that closure and resolution have been earned, that unity has been rediscovered and reinforced. Yet the formal and textural diversity of Variation VI as a whole may still leave us in some doubt as to whether closure is as complete and confident as, in isolation, it may appear to be. The last two bars have the effect of restoring a balance rather than of creating a resolution, and the role of the short pause bar (178) is to enhance the persistent difference between the work's principal emotional poles and to

Example 7 (*cont.*)

prevent the first from being finally and decisively absorbed into the second. In bs 176–7 both line and chord employ versions of tetrachord 2 [0,3,6,7]. In the countering statement of the last two bars, using the alternative tetrachord, the pitch classes of b. 177's chord all appear again, but recontextualised: the organic and the polarised co-exist. Lyric vulnerability yields, gracefully, to the assertive, and even if the fundamental instabilities are not convincingly dispelled, a persuasive equilibrium is finally achieved. That sense of equilibrium may even have something to do with the relation between the very beginning of Op.30 and the very end. The final statement (bs 179–80) offers an assertive transformation of the 'vulnerable' version of tetrachord 1 (bs 0–1), while the final versions of tetrachord 2 (bs 175–7) are altogether more stable and reflective than the volatile presentations in b. 2. The end is quite unlike the beginning, except that the basic shapes remain the same. The 'obsessive foreground motives' are not 'superimposed on continuous middleground transformation',[50] as in Strauss's *Metamorphosen*, but wrest coherence from a fragmented surface, offering correspondences suggestive of the model which, Webern declared, 'I would like to find within myself'. In the end, the work's 'plurality of relations' fines down to a dialogue between Webern and his inner sense of 'that which expresses itself "up there"'.[51] We may not be persuaded to accept Webern's beliefs as our own, but the power of those beliefs remains remarkable.

The fact that Op.30 ends with an assertion, like a Webernian translation of 'Es muß sein', indicates, in association with the composer's Goethean predispositions, that what 'must be' is not just the pursuit of self-knowledge, which in itself might merely reinforce a romantic agony, but the belief that fulfilment and achievement are practicable propositions. By definition, post-tonal music lacks that relatively stable topical vocabulary available to analysts of baroque, classical and romantic music. To this extent, Webern's Variations must remain unstable and ambiguous in its meanings, even when we know from letters, lectures and other materials that the composer was a man of particular beliefs who made certain associations between musical and extra-musical elements. Above all, Webern was not a man for whom 'experience' was the negative counterpole of 'innocence'; rather, in the spirit of Goethe, it implied the possibility of positive self-knowledge. Op.30 was surely intended as a persuasive discourse celebrating the presence of the divine within man and nature: there is a dialogue between this celebratory rhetoric and the tensions that are its counterpole, but Webern had no reason in principle to leave the dialectic unresolved. It was the nature of his musical language that made the unambiguous achievement of a new synthesis so difficult.

50 See p. 265 above.
51 See p. 264 above.

## VI

In a lecture in 1971, Karlheinz Stockhausen described various early Webern works (Opp.7, 9, 10) as 'so very short, we can call them moments'. He went on to relate this concept of 'extremely condensed music' to his own concern to create larger structures.

> [T]he great difficulty in moment-forming is the hair-raising problem of creating unity, because moment-forming is primarily about individuality. It has to be the degree of immediacy, or presence, that unites these individual moments: the fact that everything has presence to the same degree, because as soon as certain events are more present than others, then immediately we have a hierarchy . . . and that means direction and development of a sequential kind. And it is not at all easy to compose moments with equal degrees of presence.[52]

Elsewhere Stockhausen pointed to what, in Webern, 'was almost an atomization of the thematic concept: single ascending or descending intervals really were meant to replace an entire *theme* of classical music', as a concept contemporary composers might start with 'in order to go in a new direction'.[53] But the picture of Webern that emerges is of a composer torn between impulses to atomise and to integrate. Webern might have declared, like Stockhausen, 'ultimately I want to integrate everything' and 'create some kind of harmony and balance'[54] – but a balance that was not as divorced from thematicism, or from elements of hierarchy, as Stockhausen imagined.

The sequence of events in Op.30, and especially the distinct segments of Variation VI, can be held to state the problem: to represent the tension between an impulse to integrate, creating hierarchic imbalance, and the impulse to achieve a stable equilibrium. The fact that motivic connections are still fundamental to the structure of Variation VI – perhaps most explicitly in the three trumpet versions of the [0,3,4,7] tetrachord (bs 154, 165, 175) – provides the kind of evolutionary invariance that the wholehearted

[52] Karlheinz Stockhausen, *Karlheinz Stockhausen on Music. Lectures and Interviews*, compiled by Robin Maconie (London and New York: Marion Boyars, 1989), pp. 60–61.

[53] Jonathan Cott, ed., *Stockhausen. Conversations with the Composer* (London: Robson, 1974), p. 225.

[54] Ibid., pp. 79 and 44.

radicalisation of *Momentform* aimed to reject. All-embracing synthesis is precisely what Webern himself appears to describe in a letter to Willi Reich, written five months after Op.30's première in 1943:

> It did me a lot of good to be able to hear my piece. Because it was very important for me to check personally what it proves – and I believe I was right; namely, that when that kind of unity is the basis, even the most fragmented sounds must have a completely coherent effect, and leave hardly anything to be desired as far as 'comprehensibility' is concerned.[55]

Is it possible, after all, that Webern was guilty of wishful thinking? That even if he did not, like Strauss in Timothy Jackson's formulation, turn Goethe's 'view of metamorphosis' inside out, his techniques as a composer could not match his expressive intentions as, ultimately, a religious artist?

Webern was wholly justified in claiming, to Reich, that 'even the most fragmented sounds' in Op.30 have 'a completely coherent effect'. There is indeed a basic background unity. Yet this unity is not so much projected on to the musical surface as challenged by an essential diversity which is coherent, well-balanced, in a different way. The motivic metamorphosis that drives Webern's twelve-note discourse preserves the oppositions of lyric and dramatic topics in a way that comes naturally to the post-tonal composer, and leaves his status as an heir to the organic tonal tradition a matter for continuous, constructive debate.

Hearing Webern's music, as we must, comparatively, there is likely to be a sense of textural fragility partially offset by the logical strength of motivic consistency. Webern's own image of free floating (with reference to Op.29), of a 'looseness' that, in effect, counters the unified coherence of the serial substructure, is apt.[56] Even though all compositions, in all styles, can be discussed in terms of the ways in which they present degrees of similarity and difference, Webern offers a special transparency, in conjunction with an intense concern for uniformity. This gives voice to a special kind of instability, the precarious equilibrium of canons that are constantly breaking apart and reforming themselves in new ways. In this music, the present confronts the past as it seeks to continue it, in a dialogue that makes the

55 Webern, *Path*, p. 37.
56 Webern, *Letters*, p. 37.

central topic of 'comprehensibility' deeply ambiguous. Webern's discourse is as much about the cultural value of logic, complexity, the avoidance of simplicity, as it is about oneness with nature and aspirations to apprehend the presence of the divine within the human. Op.30 is a special work because we can sense more clearly than elsewhere in Webern the elements of a spiritual conflict between vulnerability (seeking serenity) and assertiveness (a tendency to violence) that outlines a profound dramatic tragedy. That is not to say that Webern was not, like Goethe, 'essentially optimistic', but it is to suggest that the 'greater seriousness' which the tragic perspective creates for pastoral, as 'the pantheistic sense of God in Nature',[57] confirms Webern's place in the great tradition stemming from Beethoven. Op.30 may fail to achieve that precise equivalence to a Goethean philosophical pronouncement which I have chosen to align with it, but the richness and power with which the Goethean structural principle acknowledged by Webern himself is projected is reason enough to celebrate a score whose meaning remains as compelling as it is verbally elusive.

57 Hatten, *Meaning*, p. 92.

# 9 A Webern bibliography

NEIL BOYNTON

The aim of the bibliography is to present a comprehensive list of publications pertaining to Anton Webern, comprising a list of all primary sources and a list of secondary sources from 1976 to 1994. Printed music is not listed except for the few publications that have appeared during the last twenty years or so. The list of primary sources divides into the following sections: catalogues, music, lectures, writings, letters, other. The list of secondary sources divides into two sections: bibliographies and list of sources.

Zoltan Roman's bibliography in Hans and Rosaleen Moldenhauer's *Anton von Webern: a Chronicle of his Life and Work* (London: Gollancz, 1978) is the most comprehensive of all previous Webern bibliographies (comprising some 430 entries), except for his own *Anton von Webern: an Annotated Bibliography* (comprising 859 entries). As the former is more widely available than the latter, which had a print run of only about 800, I consider it to be the standard and have taken the last date of this bibliography – the end of 1975 (with the exception of a couple of later entries) – as the starting date for my own list of secondary sources. Some earlier publications not listed in Roman's *Chronicle* bibliography are also included. Doctoral theses and dissertations are listed, Masters' are not. In general book and record reviews, and conference reports, have not been included. Almost all of the items listed in the present bibliography are held in the Paul Sacher Stiftung in Basel.

References to works without opus numbers have been supplied with Moldenhauer numbers, following the numbering adopted in the German edition of their biography, *Anton von Webern. Chronik seines Lebens und Werkes*, trans. Ken W. Bartlett (Zürich: Atlantis, 1980), and by Felix Meyer and Sabine Hänggi-Stampfli in *Anton Webern. Musikmanuskripte*, 2nd edn, Inventare der Paul Sacher Stiftung 4 (Winterthur: Amadeus, 1994). (The numbering in *Chronik* differs from that in *Chronicle.*)

I should like to thank Zoltan Roman (University of Calgary), Felix Meyer and Christina Dreier (Paul Sacher Stiftung), Franz Födermayr (Universität Wien), Sigrid von Moisy (Bayerische Staatsbibliothek, Munich), Harry Joelson (Stadtbibliothek, Winterthur), Leslie Morris (Houghton Library, Cambridge MA), Christopher Walton (Zentralbibliothek, Zürich), Jon Newsom (Library of Congress, Washington DC), John Guido (Washington State University), Hans Bynagle and Juanita Johnston (Whitworth College Library, Spokane WA), J. Rigbie Turner (Pierpont Morgan Library, New York), Don L. Roberts (Northwestern University, Evanston IL), Andreas Meyer and Inge Kovács (Humboldt Universität, Berlin), Regina Busch (Vienna), Reinhard Kapp (Hochschule für Musik und darstellende Kunst, Vienna), the staff of the Musiksammlung at the Österreichische Nationalbibliothek (Vienna), the staff of the Musiksammlung at the Stadt- und Landesbibliothek (Vienna) and the staff of the Salle de Musique at the Bibliothèque Nationale (Paris) for their help during the preparation of this bibliography. I am grateful to the Leverhulme Trust for financial assistance.

## Abbreviations

| | |
|---|---|
| *23 WMZ* | *23. Eine Wiener Musikzeitschrift* (1932–7); repr. with an introduction by Willi Reich (Vienna: Kerry, 1971) |
| *AfMw* | *Archiv für Musikwissenschaft* |
| *AW 1883 1983* | *Anton Webern 1883 1983. Eine Festschrift zum hundertsten Geburtstag*, ed. Ernst Hilmar (Vienna: UE, 1983) |
| *AW I, AW II* | *Anton Webern I* and *Anton Webern II*, ed. Heinz-Klaus Metzger and Rainer Riehn, Musik-Konzepte Sonderband (Munich: Edition Text+Kritik, 1983, 1984) |
| *Cento anni* | *Webern. Cento anni. La scelta trasgressiva. Festival Internazionale di Musica Contemporanea Venezia 1983* (programme), ed. Luigi Ferrari (Venice: La Biennale di Venezie, 1983) |
| *Chronicle* | Hans and Rosaleen Moldenhauer, *Anton von Webern: a Chronicle of his Life and Work* (London: Gollancz, 1978) |

| | |
|---|---|
| *Chronik* | Hans and Rosaleen Moldenhauer, *Anton von Webern. Chronik seines Lebens und Werkes*, trans. Ken W. Bartlett (Zürich: Atlantis, 1980) |
| *Comporre arcano* | *Comporre arcano. Webern e Varèse poli della musica moderna*, ed. Antonino Fiorenza (Palermo: Sellerio, 1985) |
| *ISGM* | *Internationale Schönberg-Gesellschaft. Mitteilungen* |
| *ITO* | *In Theory Only* |
| *JASI* | *Journal of the Arnold Schoenberg Institute* |
| *JMT* | *Journal of Music Theory* |
| *MitPSS* | *Mitteilungen der Paul Sacher Stiftung* |
| *MQ* | *The Musical Quarterly* |
| *MT* | *The Musical Times* |
| *MTS* | *Music Theory Spectrum* |
| *MusA* | *Music Analysis* |
| *NRMI* | *Nuova Rivista Musicale Italiana* |
| *NZM* | *Neue Zeitschrift für Musik* |
| *ÖMz* | *Österreichische Musikzeitschrift* |
| *Opus AW* | *Opus Anton Webern*, ed. Dieter Rexroth (Berlin: Quadriga, 1983) |
| *PNM* | *Perspectives of New Music* |
| *Die Reihe* | *Die Reihe* 2, 2nd edn (Vienna: UE, 1955); trans. Leo Black and Eric Smith (Bryn Mawr: Presser, 1959; copyright assigned to UE, 1975) |
| *SMz* | *Schweizerische Musikzeitung* |
| UE | Universal Edition |
| *Weg und Gestalt* | *Anton Webern. Weg und Gestalt. In Selbstzeugnissen und Worten der Freunde*, ed. Willi Reich, Sammlung Horizont (Zürich: Verlag der Arche, 1961) |
| *ZfM* | *Zeitschrift für Musik* |

## Primary sources

Unpublished primary sources are not listed. Publications in which primary sources are reproduced to illustrate an argument are given in the list of secondary sources.

### *Catalogues*

Published catalogues of private and public collections open to scholars are listed here; some exhibition catalogues are also listed.

The principal part of the Sacher Stiftung's Sammlung Anton Webern came from Moldenhauer's Webern Archive (Spokane WA). A summary of the holdings of the Sacher Stiftung's Sammlung Anton Webern is given in the Stiftung's own publication, *Paul Sacher Stiftung* (information brochure), 1st edn (1986), pp. 21–2; later acquisitions are noted in *Paul Sacher Stiftung*, 2nd edn (1989), pp. 28–9; *MitPSS* no.1 (January 1988), 4, 12; no.2 (January 1989), 13–14; no.4 (January 1991), 12; no.5 (January 1992), 9; no.8 (March 1995). Felix Meyer has produced a catalogue of Webern's music manuscripts in the Sacher Stiftung (see below). A rough guide to the contents of Moldenhauer's Webern Archive, including items other than music manuscripts, is given in Hans Moldenhauer, 'A Webern archive in America', in *Anton Webern: Perspectives*, compiled by Hans Moldenhauer, ed. Demar Irvine (Seattle and London: University of Washington Press, 1966; repr. New York: Da Capo Press, 1978), pp. 117–66.

The former Moldenhauer Archives were not only sold to the Paul Sacher Stiftung, but were also sold or given to the Library of Congress (Washington DC), Northwestern University (Evanston IL), Harvard University (Cambridge MA), the Washington State University (Pullman WA), Whitworth College (Spokane WA), the Stadt- und Landesbibliothek in Vienna, the Bayerische Staatsbibliothek in Munich and the Zentralbibliothek in Zürich, as reported in 'Moldenhauer archives', *International Webern Society Newsletter* no.21 (Fall 1987), 10–11. Of these it appears that in addition to the Sacher Stiftung only the Library of Congress and the Stadt- und Landesbibliothek in Vienna hold autograph material pertaining to Webern from the Moldenhauer archives. A catalogue of the archives, *The Rosaleen Moldenhauer Memorial: 'Music History from Primary Sources'. A Guide to the Moldenhauer Archives*, is currently being prepared by Jon Newsom for publication by the Library of Congress; the projected date of publication is 1995. Besides a comprehensive inventory, the book will include a series of historical essays on important items in the archives. Lauriejean Reinhardt will contribute essays on Webern's Two Songs Op.19, the fourth of *Fünf geistliche Lieder* Op.15 ('Mein Weg geht jetzt vorüber') and Webern's autograph copy of Hildegard Jone's poems. Felix Meyer will contribute an essay on Webern's 1920 arrangement of his Six Pieces Op.6 for chamber ensemble. (Some of the items from the Moldenhauer archive that are now in Munich are listed in *Sources for 20th-Century Music History: Alban Berg and the Second Viennese School; Musicians in American Exile; Bavarica* (catalogue of the joint exhibition of the Houghton Library (Harvard University) and the Bayerische Staatsbibliothek), ed. Helmut Hell, Sigrid von Moisy and Barbara Wolff, Bayerische Staatsbibliothek, Ausstellungskataloge 45 (Munich and Cambridge MA: Bavaria-Harvard Committee for 20th-Century Music History, 1988). This catalogue does not list any primary sources pertaining to Webern.)

Entries from the National Union Catalog are arranged according to place.

A brief summary of some of the catalogue entries is included. The wording of the original has not always been retained; the entries of some German catalogues have been translated into English.

**Austin TX**

*The National Union Catalog Pre-1956 Imprints*, DCLII, p. 415. The University of Texas holds a photocopy of the holograph of *Kinderstück* (M.267), originally in the Moldenhauer archive

**Basel**

*Anton Webern. Musikmanuskripte*, ed. Felix Meyer in collaboration with Sabine Hänggi-Stampfli, 2nd edn, Inventare der Paul Sacher Stiftung 4 (Winterthur: Amadeus, 1994; 1st edn 1988)

**Cambridge MA**

*Music Manuscripts at Harvard: a Catalogue of Music Manuscripts from the 14th to the 20th Centuries in the Houghton Library and the Eda Kuhn Loeb Music Library*, ed. Barbara Mahrenholz Wolff (Cambridge MA: Harvard University Library, 1992), p. 168 (no.358, 'Aufblick' (voice and piano), text by Richard Dehmel, autograph manuscript, fair copy, two leaves (two pages); this manuscript is at variance with the autograph M.14 and the published version, no.2 of Eight Early Songs (New York: Fischer, 1965)

**Cologne–Geneva**

*Musikhandschriften der Bodmeriana. Katalog*, ed. Tilman Seebass,

Bibliotheca Bodmeriana, Kataloge 6 (Cologne–Geneva: Fondation Martin Bodmer, 1986), pp. 83–4 (sketches of two songs for voice and piano: p. 1, 'Aufblick' (M.14), text by Richard Dehmel; p. 2, 'Du träumst so süß im Sommerwind' (M.21)), plate 16 (facsimile of p. 2)

**London**

*Handlist of Music Manuscripts Acquired 1908–67*, ed. Pamela Willetts (London: The British Library, 1970), pp. 57–8 (nos.52256–7, letters to Edward Clark, composer and conductor of the BBC, from musicians, including Webern (no.52257))

*The Catalogue of Printed Music in the British Library to 1980*, LX, p. 72 (*Variationen für Klavier* Op.27. The copy used by Peter Stadlen for the first performance, with annotations in the composer's hand. With a letter from Stadlen inserted)

Arthur Searle, *Music Manuscripts* (London: The British Library, 1987), pp. 67–8 (facsimile of part of a page of autograph score from the fourth of Six Pieces Op.6 (Zweig MS 128, p. 15))

**Los Angeles**

*Arnold Schoenberg Institute Archives: Preliminary Catalog*, ed. Kathryn P. Glennan, Jerry L. McBride and R. Wayne Shoaf, 3 vols. (Los Angeles: Arnold Schoenberg Institute, 1986). I: *Scores*, pp. 671–8 ('Archival scores', includes printed scores, the reprod. of a manuscript, a manuscript in the hand of a copyist and a manuscript in the hand of Schoenberg, some with dedications to Schoenberg from Webern); III: *Recordings, Text Manuscripts, Photographs*, p. 51 ('Text manuscripts', letter to Schoenberg of 6 September 1912)

**New York**

*The Mary Flagler Cary Music Collection* (New York: Pierpont Morgan Library, 1970), p. 99 (fourteen letters from 1912–29, to various correspondents, including Hermann Scherchen and Alexander von Zemlinsky)

J. Rigbie Turner, 'Nineteenth-century autograph music manuscripts in the Pierpont Morgan Library: a check list' (in two parts), *19th Century Music* 4/1, 2 (1980), 49–69, 157–83 (182–3). Reprinted with minor revisions as *Nineteenth-Century Autograph Music Manuscripts in the*

*Pierpont Morgan Library: a Check List* (New York: Pierpont Morgan Library, 1982)

**Paris**

*Bibliothèque Nationale. Lettres autographes conservés au Département de la Musique. Catalogue sommaire*, ed. Antoine Bloch-Michel (Paris: Bibliothèque Nationale, 1984), p. 307 (telegram to Paul Dukas, 1908)

**Spokane WA**

*The National Union Catalog Pre-1956 Imprints* DCLII, p. 415. The Gonzaga University holds a photocopy of the holograph of *Kinderstück* (M.267), originally in the Moldenhauer archive

**Vienna**

*Sechs Ausstellungen, 22. Mai – 20. Juni 1966. Die Handschriften der Meister. Berühmte Werke der Tonkunst in Autograph. Gesellschaft der Musikfreunde in Wien*, ed. Franz Grasberger (Vienna: Gesellschaft der Musikfreunde, 1966), pp. 247–50 (Vitrine 8,1: Passacaglia Op. 1, score; 8,2: *Zwei Lieder nach Gedichten von Rainer Maria Rilke Op.* 8, piano score; 8,3: *Drei Volkstexte* Op. 17, score; 8,4: photograph of Webern; 9,1: *Das Augenlicht* Op. 26, score; 9,2: *II. Kantate* Op. 31, piano score; 9,3: letter to Ernst Krenek (6 March 1934); 9,4: *Schatzwalzer aus dem Zigeunerbaron, für Salonorchester eingerichtet* (M.249)), 255 (facsimile of a letter to Ernst Krenek (6 March 1934))

*Schönberg–Webern–Berg. Bilder–Partituren–Dokumente*, ed. Werner Hofmann, Museum des 20. Jahrhunderts 36 (Vienna: Rosenbaum, 1969). Catalogue of the exhibition at the Museum des 20. Jahrhunderts (Vienna) from 17 May to 20 July 1969. The same exhibition was also shown in the Hague at the Haags Gemeentemuseum from 28 February to 28 April 1969, and a catalogue in Dutch was prepared on this occasion: *Schönberg/Webern/Berg. Portretten–partituren–documenten.*

*Alban Berg Studien* (Vienna: UE, 1980–), ed. Franz Grasberger and Rudolf Stephan. I[/1]: *Katalog der Musikhandschriften und Studien Alban Bergs im Fonds Alban Berg und der weiteren handschriftlichen Quellen im Besitz der Österreichische Nationalbibliothek*, prepared by Rosemary Hilmar (1980), p. 94 (no. 297: 'Entwürfe, Musikbeispiele, fremde Aufsätze', including Anton Webern, 'Der neue Stil Arnold

Schönbergs'. This essay was not written by Webern but by Erwin Stein and was published as 'Arnold Schönbergs neuer Stil' in *Merkur* 12/1 (1921), 3–8. See Rosemary Hilmar, 'Das Sprachchor. Eine Erläuterung zu einem falsch identifizierten Aufsatz von Anton Webern' (Secondary sources)); p. 97 (no.312: 'Typoskript (fragment)'. At the end of the typescript Helene Berg noted: 'Dieser Aufsatz scheint von Anton v. Webern zu sein'. The typescript is not by Webern, but is presumed to come from notes taken by an unknown person from Berg's lectures at the Urania (Vienna) in 1932. The typescript is reproduced in Rudolf Stephan, 'Ein frühes Dokument zur Entstehung der Zwölftonkomposition', in *Festschrift Arno Forchert zum 60. Geburtstag am 29. Dezember 1985*, ed. Gerhard Allroggen and Detlef Altenburg (Kassel: Bärenreiter, 1986), pp. 296–302); pp. 128–9 ('Fremde Werke in Originalhandschriften. Anton Webern', nos.423–5). I/2: *Katalog der Schriftstücke von der Hand Alban Bergs, der fremdschriftlichen und gedruckten Dokumente zur Lebensgeschichte und zu seinem Werk*, prepared by Rosemary Hilmar (1985), pp. 101–2 (no.787: 'Kunstpreis der Stadt Wien', including a letter from Webern addressed to the 'Direktion der Städtischen Sammlungen' (3 May 1930))

*Zum 100. Geburtstag Anton Webern. Musiksammlung der Österreichischen Nationalbibliothek, Institut für Österreichische Musikdokumentation. Konzertabend mit Vorträgen und Ausstellung, Montag, den 20. Juni 1983*, ed. Günter Brosche, catalogue prepared by Rosemary Hilmar (Vienna: Österreichische Nationalbibliothek, 1983)

*Alban Berg: 1885–1935. Ausstellung der Österreichischen Nationalbibliothek. Prunksaal. 23. Mai bis 20. Oktober 1985* (catalogue), ed. Rosemary Hilmar and Günter Brosche (Vienna: UE, 1985), cat. nos. 84, 128, 167, 171, 173, 179, 204, 282, 363, 416, 467

*Katalog der Sammlung Anton Dermota. Musikhandschriften und Musikerbriefe*, ed. Thomas Leibnitz and Agnes Ziffer, Publikationen des Instituts für Österreichische Musikdokumentation 12 (Tutzing: Schneider, 1988), pp. 180–1 (no.586: sketches for chorale preludes; no.587: leaf with musical quotation in Webern's hand with signed dedication; no.588: letter to Gottfried Kassowitz, with envelope)

Hilmar, Rosemary. 'Anton von Webern. Op.3. Fünf Lieder aus "Der siebente Ring" von Stefan George. Nr. 1: "Dies ist ein Lied…"', in *Beiträge zur musikalischen Quellenkunde. Katalog der Sammlung Hans P. Wertitsch in der Musiksammlung der Österreichischen Nationalbibliothek*, ed. Günter Brosche, Publikationen des Instituts für Österreichische Musikdokumen-tation 15 (Tutzing: Schneider, 1989), pp. 473–85. A description of the source is given on p. 473, and is followed by an essay on the significance of George for Webern.

*Die Nachlässe in der Wiener Stadt- und Landesbibliothek. Ein Verzeichnis*, compiled by Gerhard Renner (Vienna: Wiener Stadt- und Landesbibliothek, 1993), pp. 123 ('Moldenhauer, Hans. Teil der Sammlung Moldenhauer', including an autograph copy of 'Die Einsame', no. 2 of Four Songs Op. 13); ('Polnauer, Josef. Teilnachlaß', includes copies of letters from Webern to Polnauer); 187–8 ('Universal-Edition. Teil des Verlagsarchivs', includes correspondence between Webern and UE); 195 ('Webern, Anton von. Teilnachlaß', approximately fifteen items including printed music with corrections in Webern's hand, printers' proofs of works by Arnold Schoenberg with corrections in Webern's hand and studies in counterpoint by Webern's pupil Ludwig Zenk (with some entries in Webern's hand))

**Washington DC**

*The National Union Catalog Pre-1956 Imprints* DCLII, pp. 413–18. The Library of Congress holds a holograph score of the String Quartet Op. 28 ('Gift of Mrs. [Elisabeth Sprague] Coolidge, May 24, 1938'), p. 417. In addition it holds the following copies of holographs originally in the Moldenhauer archive. Photocopies: cello sonata (M.202), *Drei Stücke für Streichquartett* (Op. 9 no. 1, M.179, Op. 9 no. 6); orchestra pieces (1913) (M.187, 183, 189, 188); four Stefan George songs (M.144, 143, 145, 146); *Hochsommernacht* (M.65); *Kinderstück* (M.267); rondo (M.115); *Satz für Klavier* (M.112); *Sonatensatz (Rondo) für Klavier* (M.114); two songs after poems by Ferdinand Avenarius (M.4, 8); *Vorfrühling II* (M.6). Microfilms: three poems (M.3, 12, 11); five songs (M.83, 130, 131, 119, 132); *Im Sommerwind* (M.63); concerto (M.347); *Langsamer Satz* (M.78); five songs (M.83, 119, 130, 131, 132); string quartet (M.79);

*Siegfrieds Schwert* (M.16; not an original composition, but an arrangement of a song by Martin Plüddemann: see Martin Hoyer, 'Neues zu Anton Weberns frühen Liedern' (Secondary sources)); songs (M.7, 14, 20, 15, 61, 17, 19, 59, 60, 62, 18, 64).

*Music*

The list of music comprises works that are not listed by the Moldenhauers in *Chronicle* as published works. These are in large part works that have been published since 1976. The list divides into the following subsections: works with opus numbers, works without opus numbers and arrangements of works by other composers.

Works with opus numbers

*Entflieht auf leichten Kähnen* (Op.2), arranged for chorus, violin, viola, cello, harmonium and piano (1914), UE 14878 (Vienna: UE, [copyright 1977])

*Sechs Stücke für großes Orchester op.6. Faksimile-Ausgabe der autographen Partitur und des von Webern korrigierten Handexemplars des Erstdruckes*, ed. Franz Patzer (Vienna: Stadt- und Landesbibliothek, 1983). The accompanying booklet includes an introduction and analysis by Claudio Abbado (in Italian), translated into German by Ernst Hilmar, pp. 7–11; Ernst Hilmar, 'Dokumente zur Entstehungs- und Aufführungs-geschichte der Orchesterstücke op.6', pp. 12–14; and a brief commentary, also by Ernst Hilmar, 'Zum Manuskript und zu Weberns "Handexemplar" des Erstdruckes', p. 15

*Sechs Stücke* (Op.6), arranged for flute, oboe, clarinet, percussion, two violins, viola, cello, double bass, harmonium and piano (1920), UE 14778 (Vienna: UE, [copyright 1977])

*Variationen für Klavier Op.27* [...] *Webern's ideas on the work's interpretation set out for the first time by Peter Stadlen with the aid of the facsimile of his working copy containing Webern's instructions for the world première*, UE 16845 (Vienna: UE, 1979)

*Variationen für Orchester Op.30. Für 2 Klaviere gesetzt von Leopold Spinner*, UE 18199 (Vienna: UE, [copyright 1985])

Works without opus numbers

Quintet for Strings & Piano (1907) (M.118), ed. Jacques-Louis Monod, revised edn 1974, score (Hillsdale NY: Boelke-Bomart [?1974]). First published as Quintet for String Quartet and Piano (Hillsdale NY: Bomart Music, [1953])

*Satz* for piano (M.112). A manuscript copy in the hand of Friedrich Wildgans from a lost autograph score is reproduced in facsimile with critical commentary in Gareth Cox, *Anton Weberns Studienzeit. Seine Entwicklung im Lichte der Sätze und Fragmente für Klavier*, Europäische Hochschulschriften. Reihe XXXVI Musikwissenschaft 77 (Frankfurt a.M.: Lang, 1992), pp. 163–83. First published as *Satz für Klavier (c.1906) from the Composer's Autograph Manuscript in the Moldenhauer Archive* (New York: Fischer, [1970]). Cox suggests the work was composed c.1905 (pp. 126–9), a revision which has since been adopted by Meyer in *Anton Webern. Musikmanuskripte* (see Primary sources, Catalogues, Basel)

Arrangements of Works by Other Composers

Strauss, Johann. *Schatzwalzer* for orchestra, from *Zigeunerbaron* Op.418, arranged for string quartet, harmonium and piano (1921, M.249), UE 17101 (Vienna: UE, [copyright 1977])

### *Lectures*

*Der Weg zur Neuen Musik*, ed. Willi Reich (Vienna: UE, 1960). Published in English as *The Path to the New Music*, trans. Leo Black (Bryn Mawr: Presser, 1963); in Italian (with the letters to Jone and Humplik), trans. G. Taverna, as *Verso la nuova musica e lettere a H. Jone e J. Humplik* (Milan: Feltrinelli, 1963), and later as *Il cammino verso la nuova musica* (Milan: SE, 1990); in Russian as *Lekcii o muzyke. Piśma* (*Lectures on Music. Letters*), ed. M[ichaila] S[emenoviča] Druskina and A.G. Śnitke, trans. V.G. Śnitke (Moscow: Muzyka, 1975); in French as *Chemin vers la nouvelle musique*, trans. Anne Servant, Didier Alluard and Cyril Huvé (Paris: Lattès, 1980); in Catalan as *El camí cap a la nova música*, trans. Josep Casanovas, Música d'avui 2 (Barcelona: Bosch, 1982); in Hungarian as *Előadások, írások, levelek* (*Lectures, Writings, Letters*), ed. [?and trans.] András Wilheim

(Budapest: Zenemukiadó, 1983); in Portuguese as *O Caminho para a música nova*, trans. Carlos Kater, Coleção ensaios 7 (São Paulo: Novas metas, 1984); in Rumanian as *Calea spre muzica nouă*, trans. Mircea Bejinariu (Bucharest: Editura muzicală, 1988). Extracts from the lectures were published by Willi Reich as 'Weberns Vorträge', *23 WMZ* no. 14 (end of February 1934), 17–22. Reich also published a résumé of the 1932 lectures, 'Grenzgebiete des neuen Tons', *Die Musik* 25/2 (November 1932), 120–3 ('Webern-Abende in einem Wiener Bürgerhaus', pp. 121–2, 'Der Weg zur Komposition in 12 Tönen', pp. 122–3; the latter is reproduced in 'Brahmsschänder', *23 WMZ* no. 10 (15 May 1933), 1–5); extracts from these articles by Reich are reproduced in *Weg und Gestalt*, pp. 36–43. An extract from the lecture given on 20 February 1933 is reproduced in 'Was ist Musik?', *Melos* 25/10 (October 1958), 305–8. Ploderer's notes from the lecture given on 14 March 1933 are reproduced in 'Der Weg zur Neuen Musik', *Musik und Gesellschaft* 15 (1965), 624–7. Extracts from the lectures on 26 February 1932, 20 February 1933 and 10 April 1933 are reproduced in 'Dokumente', in *Opus AW*, pp. 79, 76 and 80. Extracts from the lectures on 4, 12 and 26 February 1932 and 3 April 1933 are published in English in 'Towards a New Music', *The Score* 28 (January 1961), 29–37. Leo Black's English translation of the lecture given on 15 January 1932 appears in 'Anton Webern: The Path to Twelve-Note Composition (1932)', in *Writings of German Composers*, ed. Jost Hermand and James Steakley (New York: Continuum, 1984), pp. 225–9. Extracts from the lectures and from the letters to Willi Reich in the 'Nachwort' of *Der Weg* have been translated into Japanese by Toyoji Takeuchi in *Anton Webern* (Tokyo: Hosei University Press, 1974).

### *Writings*

The sources are listed chronologically by date of publication within this section.

'Einleitung', in Heinrich Isaac, *'Choralis Constantinus'. Zweiter Teil. Graduale in mehrstimmiger Bearbeitung (a capella)*, ed. Anton von Webern, Denkmäler der Tonkunst in Österreich 32 (Vienna,

1905–6), pp. [vii]–xii. Extracts from the 'Einleitung' are reproduced in 'Choralis Constantinus', *Die Reihe*, 30–2 (Eng. trans., 23–5); and in *Weg und Gestalt*, p. 17

'Schönbergs Musik', in *Arnold Schönberg*, [?ed. Karl Linke] (Munich: Piper, 1912; repr. Wels: Welsermuhl, 1980), pp. 22–48. This essay is also published as 'Über Arnold Schönberg', *Rheinische Musik- und Theater-Zeitung* (17 and 24 February 1912), [?pp.], with an additional 'Nachwort' not included in 'Schönbergs Musik'. The 'Nachwort' is reproduced in Willi Reich, 'Ein verschollener Webern-Text', *Melos* 36/1 (January 1969), 9. An extract from p. 22 of 'Schönbergs Musik' appears in *Die Reihe*, 17 (Eng. trans., 10).

'Der Lehrer', in *Arnold Schönberg*, [?ed. Karl Linke] (Munich: Piper, 1912; repr. Wels: Welsermuhl, 1980), pp. 85–7. This essay is reproduced in 'Über Arnold Schönberg', *Rheinische Musik- und Theater-Zeitung* (17 and 24 February 1912), [?pp.]; in *Weg und Gestalt*, pp. 24–6; in *Die Reihe*, 16–17 (Eng. trans., 9); in Friedrich Wildgans, *Anton Webern*, trans. Edith Temple Roberts and Humphrey Searle (London: Calder and Boyars, 1966), pp. 160–2; and, in a different translation, in *Composers on Music: an Anthology of Composers' Writings*, ed. Sam Morgenstern (London: Faber, 1956), pp. 455–6. The first part of this essay is published as 'Der Schönbergschüler [1912]', *23 WMZ* no. 14 (end of February 1934), 4–5

'Analyse der Passacaglia op. 1', *Allgemeine Musikzeitung* 49/21–2 (1922), 465, 467; reproduced in Rudolf Stephan, 'Weberns Werke auf deutschen Tonkünstlerfesten. Mit zwei wenig beachteten Texten Weberns', *ÖMz* 27/3 (1972), 121–7 (123–4)

For Schoenberg's 50th birthday, *Musikblätter des Anbruch* 6 (Sonderheft: Arnold Schönberg zum fünfzigsten Geburtstage) (August–September 1924), 272. Reproduced in *Weg und Gestalt*, p. 28; and *Die Reihe*, 17 (Eng. trans., 10)

For Adolf Loos's 60th birthday, in *Adolf Loos zum 60. Geburtstag am 10. Dezember 1930* (Vienna: Lányi, 1930), p. 67

'An die Redaktion der *Muziek* in Amsterdam', *De Muziek* 5/1 (October 1930), 22. Reproduced in Willi Reich, 'Anton Webern über Alban Berg', *NZM* 124/4 (April 1963), 143

'Sechs Orchesterstücke [op. 6]', *Zeitschrift für Musik* 100/6 (June 1933),

566–7. Reproduced in Rudolf Stephan, 'Weberns Werke auf deutschen Tonkünstlerfesten. Mit zwei wenig beachteten Texten Weberns', *ÖMz* 27/3 (1972), 121–7 (126)

'Aus Schönbergs Schriften', in *Arnold Schönberg zum 60. Geburtstag. 13. September 1934* (Vienna: UE, 1934), 11–14. Reproduced without preface in *Musikblätter des Anbruch* 16 (September 1934), 138–40. Preface reproduced in *Weg und Gestalt*, p. 57; and *Die Reihe*, 17 (Eng. trans., 10)

'Gustav Mahler', in *Weg und Gestalt*, pp. 15–17. This article is composed of diary entries on Mahler (January 1902 and 4 February 1905).

'Über Arnold Schönberg als Dirigent [Mai 1914]', in Rudolf Stephan, 'Ein unbekannter Aufsatz Weberns über Schönberg', *ÖMz* 27/3 (March 1972), 127–30

Four early poems (1902), in Eng. trans. of Friedrich Wildgans, *Anton Webern*, pp. 163–5 ('Sonnenaufgang', 'Waldweg', 'An den Preglhof', 'Frauen-Schönheit'). The German original is given next to the English translation. Reproduced in *Chronicle*, pp. 65–6 (*Chronik*, pp. 55–6)

'Dokumente', in *Opus AW*, pp. 67–85, 121–8 (p. 76: diary entry from November 1904)

'Tot. Sei quadri per la scena', ed. Joachim Noller, trans. Nada Carli Alliney, in *Com'era dolce il profumo del tiglio. La musica a Vienna nell'età di Freud*, ed. Carlo di Incontrera ([?Monfalcone]: Teatro Communale di Monfalcone, 1988), pp. 381–95

### *Letters*

The sources are listed chronologically by date of publication within this section.

'Aus unveröffentlichten Briefen', *Der Turm* 1/12 (1945/46), 390–1

'Aus dem Briefwechsel', *Die Reihe*, 20–8 (Eng. trans., 13–21). These letters are reproduced in chronological order in 'Briefe der Freundschaft (1911–1945)', in *Die Stimme der Komponisten. Aufsätze, Reden, Briefe 1907–58*, ed. Heinrich Lindlar, Kontrapunkte. Schriften zur deutschen Musik der Gegenwart 2 (Rodenkirchen: Tonger, 1958), pp. 126–33

'Letters of Webern and Schoenberg (to Roberto Gerhard)', *The Score* 24 (November 1958), 36–41

*Briefe an Hildegard Jone und Josef Humplik*, ed. Josef Polnauer (Vienna: UE, 1959). Published in Italian in *Verso la nuova musica e lettere a H. Jone e J. Humplik* (see above, Lectures); in English as *Letters to Hildegard Jone and Josef Humplik*, trans. Cornelius Cardew (Bryn Mawr: Presser, in assoc. with UE (Vienna), 1967); in French as *Journal à une amie. Lettres à Hildegard Jone et Joseph Humplik*, ed. and trans. Élisabeth Bouillon (Paris: Lattès, 1979). Extracts from Webern's letters to Jone and Humplik are reproduced in 'Briefe an zwei Freunde', *Melos* 26/12 (December 1959), 377–9; *Weg und Gestalt*, pp. 14, 50, 58–67 (*passim*); and 'Dokumente', in *Opus AW*, pp. 67–85, 121–8 (*passim*).

Letters to Willi Reich are reproduced in *Der Weg*, pp. 63–72 (*Path*, pp. 58–67; see Lectures); *Weg und Gestalt*, pp. 50–1 ('Dank', 4 March 1934), 58–67 ('Aus Briefen der letzten Zeit'), 75 (facsimile of letter of 26 February 1943); 'Briefe aus Weberns letzten Jahren', ed. Willi Reich, *ÖMz* 20 (August 1965), 407–11. Extracts from most of the letters in *Der Weg* are also in *Weg und Gestalt*; extracts from a few are in *ÖMz* 20 (1965). Both *Weg und Gestalt* and the article in *ÖMz* contain material not included in *Der Weg*.

'Briefe an Alban Berg', in *Weg und Gestalt*, pp. 19–22 ('Mahlers "Lied von der Erde"': 30 October, 8 November and 23 November 1911; 'Ein Weihnachtsbrief an Alban Berg': 21 December 1911)

'Previously unpublished composers' letters as written to Claire R. Reis', *Musical America* 83/1 (January 1963), 16

'Zwei Briefe an Hanns Eisler', in *Sinn und Form. Sonderheft Hanns Eisler* (Berlin: Rütten & Loening, 1964), pp. 108–9 (26 February 1925, 19 April 1929). The letter of 19 April is reproduced in 'Ein Brief Anton Weberns an Hanns Eisler', *Musik und Gesellschaft* 8 (1958), 338–40; and in *Tagebuch* 10 (?1957)

'Brief an Frau Schreker', in *Programmheft des Staatstheaters Kassel 1964/65* no. 1, p. 8

'Arnold Schönberg, Anton Webern, Alban Berg, Unbekannte Briefe an Erwin Schulhoff', ed. Ivan Vojtěch, *Miscellanea Musicologica* (Prague) 18 (1965), 31–83 (38–40)

Facsimile of letter to Ernst Krenek (6 March 1934) in *Sechs Ausstellungen, 22. Mai – 20. Juni 1966. Die Handschriften der Meister. Berühmte Werke der Tonkunst in Autograph. Gesellschaft der Musikfreunde in*

*Wien*, ed. Franz Grasberger (Vienna: Gesellschaft der Musikfreunde, 1966), pp. 249 (catalogue description), 255 (facsimile)

'Berg und Webern schreiben an Hermann Scherchen', ed. Willi Reich, *Melos* 33/7–8 (July–August 1966), 225–8

Hans Moldenhauer, 'Paul Amadeus Pisk and the Viennese triumvirate', in *Paul A. Pisk: Essays in his Honor*, ed. John Glowacki (Austin: University of Texas Press, 1966), pp. 208–16 (p. 215, letter from Webern to Pisk (7 May 1934); p. 216, facsimile)

Letter to Darius Milhaud (1923), in *XII festival Gulbenkian de musica. Exposição Darius Milhaud, Salão Nobre de Teatro nacional de S. Carlos de 28 de maio a 8 de junho de 1968*, ed. François Lesure (Lisbon: Neogravura, 1968), no. 52 (text reproduced at end of catalogue; pages not numbered)

*Die Streichquartette der Wiener Schule. Schoenberg, Berg, Webern. Eine Dokumentation*, ed. Ursula von Rauchhaupt (Munich: Ellermann, [1971]), *passim*. Published in English as *Schoenberg, Berg, Webern: the String Quartets. A Documentary Study*, trans. Eugene Hartzell (Hamburg: Deutsche Grammophon Gesellschaft, 1971)

'Unveröffentlichte Briefe von Alban Berg und Anton Webern an Daniel Ruyneman', ed. Paul Op de Coul, *Tijdschrift voor Muziekwetenschap* (Utrecht) 20/3 (1972), 201–20

'Zur Webern-Epistolographie', ed. Rudolf Flotzinger, *ÖMz* 27/12 (December 1972), 663–4

'Briefe von Anton von Webern und Alban Berg an Adolf Loos', ed. Franz Glück, *ÖMz* 30/3 (March 1975), 110–13

Letter to Erwin Stein written sometime between 8 and 31 May 1939, concerning the String Quartet Op. 28, in Friedhelm Döhl, *Weberns Beitrag zur Stilwende der Neuen Musik. Studien über Voraussetzungen, Technik und Ästhetik der 'Komposition mit 12 nur aufeinander bezogenen Tönen'*, Berliner musikwissenschaftliche Arbeiten 12 (Munich: Katzbichler, 1976), pp. 443–7. (Originally doctoral thesis, University of Göttingen, 1966). Also in Döhl, 'Zum Formbegriff Weberns. Weberns Analyse des Streichquartetts op. 28 nebst einigen Bemerkungen zu Weberns Analyse eigener Werke', *ÖMz* 27/3 (March 1972), 131–48; Rauchhaupt, *Die Streichquartette der Wiener Schule*, pp. 137–41 (Eng. trans., pp. 132–6); *Chronik*, pp.

669–72 (*Chronicle*, trans. Zoltan Roman, pp. 751–6). Note that this is not the only published letter in which Webern gives a detailed description of Op.28. See also the letter to Rudolf Kolisch (19 April 1938), reproduced in Rauchhaupt, *Die Streichquartette der Wiener Schule*, pp. 131–5 (Eng. trans., pp. 127–9). Kolisch published extracts from this letter in the programme notes for the first performance at the Tenth Berkshire Festival of Chamber Music in South Mountain MA, 22 September 1938.

'Webern an Hartmann. Bisher unveröffentlichte Briefe und Postkarten', ed. Hans Moldenhauer, in *Karl Amadeus Hartmann und die Musica Viva. Essays. Bisher unveröffentlichte Briefe an Hartmann. Katalog* (of the exhibition from 19 June to 29 August 1980), ed. Renata Wagner, Margot Attenkofer and Helmut Hell, Bayerische Staatsbibliothek. Ausstellungs-Kataloge 21 (Munich: Piper; Mainz: Schott, 1980), pp. 81–91

'Webern schreibt Briefe', in *AW 1883 1983*, pp. 59–91. Extracts from letters to Ernst Diez, Arnold Schönberg, Alban Berg, Emil Hertzka, Guido Adler, Hans Heinsheimer, Josef Polnauer, Hildegard Jone and Josef Humplik, members of the Freie Typographia, Hanns Eisler, the editor of *Muziek*, Hermann Scherchen, Rudolf Kolisch, Erwin Stein, Willi Reich, Alfred Schlee and Webern's daughters Maria and Christine. Some of these letters have appeared elsewhere: extracts from several letters to various addressees are reproduced in 'Aus dem Briefwechsel', *Die Reihe*, 20–8; the extracts from the letters of 6 August 1928, 8 September 1930, 18 July 1936, 4 December 1943 and 29 April 1944 to Jone and Humplik are in Polnauer, *Briefe*; the letter of 19 April 1929 to Eisler is in 'Zwei Briefe an Hanns Eisler', in *Sinn und Form. Sonderheft Hanns Eisler*; the letter of 12 April 1938 to Scherchen is in 'Berg und Webern schreiben an Hermann Scherchen'; the letter of 19 June 1938 to Kolisch is in Rauchhaupt, *Die Streichquartette der Wiener Schule*, pp. 131–5; extracts from letters of 27 July 1939, 9 December 1939, 30 October 1940, 28 February 1942 and 10 January 1943 to Reich are in 'Briefe aus Weberns letzten Jahren', ed. Reich; and extracts from letters of 3 March and 23 August 1941 to Reich are in *Weg und Gestalt*, pp. 61, 63 (where the date of the letter of 23 August is incorrectly given as 21 August); extracts from some of these letters to Reich are also in *Der Weg*, pp. 63–72; some of the extracts from letters to Schoenberg and Berg are in 'Dokumente' (see below).

'Dokumente', in *Opus AW*, pp. 67–85, 121–8. This article presents extracts from various primary sources, including Webern's letters to Schoenberg, Berg, Hildegard Jone, Josef Humplik and Eduard Steuermann. Some of these letters have appeared elsewhere: the extracts from letters of 6 August 1928, 27 September 1930, 20 February 1934 and 25 January 1939 to Jone and Humplik are in Polnauer, *Briefe*; the entire letter to Steuermann is reproduced in 'Aus dem Briefwechsel Webern–Steuermann' (see below); some of the extracts from letters to Schoenberg and Berg are in 'Webern schreibt Briefe'; an extract from the letter of 23 November 1911 to Berg is in 'Briefe an Alban Berg'.

'Anton Webern. Vier Briefe an Alban Berg', in *Opus AW*, pp. 86–92 (12 July 1912, 14 July 1920, 29 July 1920, 8 October 1925). Extracts from some of these letters are in 'Webern schreibt Briefe', pp. 65–6, 72, 76.

Peter Sulzer, *Zehn Komponisten um Werner Reinhart*, 3 vols. (Winterthur: Atlantis, 1979–83). I and II: *Ein Ausschnitt aus dem Wirkungskreis des Musikkollegiums Winterthur 1920–50* (1979, 1980). I, pp. 95–220 ('Schönberg–Webern–Berg–Krenek)'; Abb.36 (p. 201), facsimile of Webern's entry in the guest book of the 'Rychenberg' (February 1940); Abb.37, facsimile of letter from Webern to Reinhart (8 February 1943). III: *Briefwechsel* (1983), pp. 117–50 ('Anton Webern'), twenty-one letters from Webern to Reinhart (28 November 1922 – 11 November 1944)

'Briefe an Theodor W. Adorno', ed. Rolf Tiedemann, in *AW I*, pp. 6–22

'Aus dem Briefwechsel Webern–Steuermann', ed. Regina Busch, in *AW I*, pp. 23–51. An extract from the letter of 6 December 1936 is reproduced in 'Dokumente', p. 126.

'Aus dem Briefwechsel Webern–Krenek', ed. Claudia Maurer Zenck, in *AW II*, pp. 151–61

'Briefe Weberns an Johann Humpelstetter', ed. Rainer Riehn, in *AW II*, pp. 354–64

*Zemlinsky Briefwechsel mit Schönberg, Webern, Berg und Schreker*, ed. Horst Weber, Bd I of Briefwechsel der Wiener Schule, Thomas Ertelt, gen.

ed., Staatlichen Instituts für Musikforschung Preußischer Kulturbesitz Berlin (Darmstadt: Wissenschaftliche Buchgesellschaft, 1995). Contains sixteen letters from Webern to Zemlinsky, from 14 June 1912 to 22 October 1924, on pp. 281–302. Most of these letters are held by the Pierpont Morgan Library.

*Other*

'Der UE-Lektor. Aus Gutachten Weberns für die UE', *Die Reihe*, 29 (Eng. trans., 22)

Extracts from Reich's notes made between September 1936 and February 1938 during his study of the theory of form as Webern's private pupil, in *Der Weg*, pp. 62–3 (*Path*, pp. 57–8). Reproduced in 'Aphorismen beim Unterricht', in *Gespräche mit Komponisten*, ed. Reich (Zürich: Manesse, 1965), pp. 219–21

Johann Humpelstetter, 'Anton Webern als nachschaffender Künstler, als Chorleiter und Dirigent', in *AW I*, pp. 52–73. This article is based on Humpelstetter's notes taken during rehearsals of the Singverein der Sozialdemokratische Kunststelle directed by Webern

**Secondary sources**

*Bibliographies*

The bibliographies are listed chronologically.

DELIÈGE, Célestin. 'Bibliographie [de la musique atonale et sérielle]', *Revue Belge de Musicologie* 13 (1959), 132–48

MCKENZIE, Wallace C. 'The music of Anton Webern' (unpublished dissertation, North Texas State College, 1960), pp. 478–94

KOLNEDER, Walter. *Anton Webern. Einführung in Werk und Stil*, Kontrapunkte: Schriften zur deutschen Musik der Gegenwart 5 (Rodenkirchen: Tonger, 1961), pp. 184–92. Published in English as *Anton Webern: an Introduction to his Works*, trans. Humphrey Searle (London: Faber, 1968), pp. 206–23

BASART, Ann Phillips. *Serial Music: a Classified Bibliography* (Berkeley and Los Angeles: University of California Press, 1963)

AUSTIN, William. *Music in the 20th Century: from Debussy through Stravinsky* (New York: Norton, 1966), pp. 644–7

DÖHL, Friedhelm. *Weberns Beitrag zur Stilwende der Neuen Musik* (see Letters, Erwin Stein), pp. 448–57

IRVINE, Demar. 'Selected bibliography', in *Anton Webern: Perspectives* (see Catalogues), pp. 167–81

REDLICH, Hans Ferdinand. 'Anton (von) Webern', in *Die Musik in Geschichte und Gegenwart*, ed. Friedrich Blume, 17 vols. (Kassel: Bärenreiter, 1949–86), XIV (1968), cols. 347–9

FINK, Michael. 'Anton Webern: supplement to a basic bibliography', *Current Musicology* 16 (1973), 103–10

KRAUS, Egon. 'Bibliographie. Anton Webern', *Musik und Bildung* 5/6 (June 1973), 330–3

KRELLMANN, Hanspeter. *Anton Webern in Selbstzeugnissen und Bilddokumenten*, Rowohlts Monographien 229 (Reinbek bei Hamburg: Rowohlt, 1975), pp. 148–52

ROMAN, Zoltan. 'Selected bibliography', in *Chronicle*, pp. 757–73; *Chronik*, pp. 673–88

——— *Anton von Webern: an Annotated Bibliography*, Detroit Studies in Music Bibliography 48 (Detroit: Information Coordinators Inc., 1983)

ZUBER, Barbara. 'Auswahlbibliographie', in *AW II*, pp. 417–27

WENK, Arthur. *Analyses of Nineteenth- and Twentieth-Century Music: 1940–1985*, MLA Index and Bibliography Series 25 (Boston: Music Library Association Inc., 1987)

ROMAN, Zoltan. 'Supplement to Webern bibliography', *Newsletter of the International Webern Society* no. 21 (Fall 1987), 11–17 (supplement to Roman's 1983 bibliography)

DIAMOND, Harold J. *Music Analyses: an Annotated Guide to the Literature* (New York: Schirmer, 1991), pp. 620–34 (nos. 4507–34)

### *List of sources*

ABEL, Angelika. 'Adornos Kritik der Zwölftontechnik Weberns. Die Grenzen einer "Logik des Zerfalls"', *AfMw* 38/3 (1981), 143–78

——— *Die Zwölftontechnik Weberns und Goethes Methodik der Farbenlehre. Zur Kompositionstheorie und Ästhetik der neuen Wiener Schule*, Beihefte zum Archiv für Musikwissenschaft 19 (Wiesbaden: Steiner, 1982). Originally doctoral dissertation (Marburg/Philipps-Universität, 1980)

———'Musik als Sprache. Über Webern und Goethe', *NZM* 144/12 (1983), 10–13

ACKERE, Jules E., and Johan Bruxelles B. COOSAERT. 'Arnold Schönberg, Alban Berg, Anton Webern. De moderne Weense school', *Tijdschrift voor Kunst en Cultur* 164 (1978), 145–80

ADAM, Max. *Anton von Webern und Emanuel Swedenborg. Ein Beitrag zum Bühnenstück* Tot [*von*] *A. v. Webern* (Blauen: Otto Franz Erb-Stiftung, 1986)

ADAMY, Bernhard. 'Schopenhauer und einige Komponisten. Rezeptionsansätze bei Humperdinck, Schönberg, Berg und Webern', *Schopenhauer Jahrbuch* 61 (1980), 70–89

ADORNO, Theodor Wiesengrund. 'Meister und Jünger', *23 WMZ* no. 14 (end of February 1934), 8–9

———*Gesammelte Schriften*, ed. Rolf Tiedemann and others, 20 vols. (Frankfurt a.M.: Suhrkamp, 1970–86). XII: *Philosophie der Neuen Musik*, ed. Tiedemann (1975; 2nd edn 1990). First published by Mohr (Tübingen, 1949); trans. Anne G. Mitchell and Wesley V. Blomster as *Philosophy of Modern Music* (London: Sheed and Ward, 1973; repr. New York: Continuum, 1984)

———'Das Altern der Neuen Musik', in *GS* XIV (*Dissonanzen. Einleitung in die Musiksoziologie*, ed. Tiedemann, 1973), pp. 143–67. Published in English as 'Modern music is growing old', *The Score* 18 (1956), 18–29

———'Anton Webern: Lieder op. 3 und op. 12', in *GS* XV (*Komposition für den Film* (with Hanns Eisler); *Der getreue Korrepetitor*, ed. Tiedemann, 1976), pp. 251–76. First published in *Der getreue Korrepetitor. Lehrschriften zur musikalischen Praxis* (Frankfurt a.M.: Fischer, 1963), pp. 101–26

———'Anton Webern: Sechs Bagatellen für Streichquartett op. 9', in *GS* XV, pp. 277–301. First published in *Der getreue Korrepetitor*, pp. 127–51

———'Anton Webern: Vier Stücke für Geige und Klavier op. 7', in *GS* XV, pp. 302–12. First published in *Der getreue Korrepetitor*, pp. 152–61

———'Anton von Webern', in *GS* XVI (*Musikalische Schriften I–III: Klangfiguren (I), Quasi una fantasia (II), Musikalische Schriften (III)*, ed. Tiedemann, 1978; 2nd edn, 1990), pp. 110–25. First published as

'Webern als Komponist', *Merkur* 13/3 (March 1959), 201–14; repr. in *Klangfiguren* (Berlin: Suhrkamp, 1959), pp. 157–81, and *Nervenpunkte der Neuen Musik (Ausgewählt aus «Klangfiguren»)*, Rowohlts deutsche Enzyklopädie 333 (Reinbek bei Hamburg: Rowohlt Taschenbuch Verlag, 1969), pp. 54–66; Italian trans. by Augusto Carli in *Cento anni*, pp. 67–76

——— 'Vers une musique informelle', in *GS* XVI, pp. 493–540. First published as 'Vers une musique informelle. Nach einer Kranichsteiner Vorlesung', *Darmstädter Beiträge zur Neuen Musik* 4 (1961), 73–102. Repr. in *Quasi una Fantasia* (Frankfurt a.M.: Suhrkamp, 1963), pp. 365–437; English trans. by Rodney Livingstone in *Quasi una Fantasia* (London: Verso, 1992), pp. 269–322

——— 'Form in der neuen Musik', in *GS* XVI, pp. 607–27. First published in *Darmstädter Beiträge zur Neuen Musik* 10 (1966), 9–21. Repr. in *Neue Rundschau* 77/1 (1966), 19–34

——— 'Anton von Webern', in *GS* XVII (*Musikalische Schriften IV: Moments musicaux, Impromptus*, ed. Tiedemann, 1982), pp. 204–9. First published in *SMz* 72 (1932), 679–83; repr. in *Auftakt* 16/9–10 (1936), 159–63, and *Impromptus* (Frankfurt a.M.: Suhrkamp, 1968), pp. 45–50

——— 'Anton Webern. Zur Aufführung der Fünf Orchesterstücke, op. 10, in Zürich', in *GS* XVIII (*Musikalische Schriften V*, ed. Tiedemann and Klaus Schultz, 1984), pp. 513–16. First published in *Musikblätter des Anbruch* 8/6 (1926), 280–2; repr. in *AW I*, pp. 269–71

——— 'Anton von Webern', in *GS* XVIII, pp. 517–18. First published in *Vossische Zeitung*, 3 December 1933, p. 30

——— 'Über einige Arbeiten von Anton Webern', in *GS* XVIII, pp. 673–9. First published in *AW I*, pp. 272–89

——— Review of Walter Kolneder, *Anton Webern. Einführung in Werk und Stil* (Rodenkirchen: Tonger, 1961), in *GS* XIX (*Musikalische Schriften V*, ed. Tiedemann and Klaus Schultz 1984), pp. 420–4. First published in *Neue Deutsche Hefte* 96 (November–December 1963), 163–7

——— 'Drei Dirigenten', in *GS* XIX, pp. 453–9. First published in *Musikblätter des Anbruch* 8/7 (1926), 315–39. An extract from this article ('Beschwörung: Anton Webern', in *GS* XIX, pp. 457–9) is reproduced in *AW I*, pp. 74–5

———'Berg und Webern', in *GS* XX/2 (*Vermischte Schriften II*, ed. Tiedemann, Gretel Adorno, Susan Buck-Morss and Klaus Schultz, 1986), pp. 782–92. Previously published as 'Berg und Webern (1930)', *ÖMz* 39/6 (June 1984), 290–5. Published in English as 'Berg and Webern: Schoenberg's heirs', in *GS* XVIII, pp. 446–55 (English translation first published in *Modern Music* 8/2 (1931), 29–38)

———'Berg Gedenkkonzert im Londoner Rundfunk', in *GS* XX/2, pp. 802–3

ALBRECHT, Otto E. 'Autographs of Viennese composers in the USA', in *Beiträge zur Musikdokumentation. Franz Grasberger zum 60. Geburtstag*, ed. Günter Brosche (Tutzing: Schneider, 1975), pp. 17–25

ALEGANT, Brian. 'A model for the pitch structure of Webern's Op.23 no.1, "Das dunkle Herz"', *MTS* 13/2 (1991), 127–46

ALLENDE–BLIN, Juan. 'Die Letzten. Anton Webern und seine Schüler [Herschkowitz and Focke]', *Musiktexte* nos. 28/29 (March 1989), 109

ANDRASCHKE, Peter. 'Webern und Rosegger', in *Opus AW*, pp. 108–12

ANGERER, Manfred. 'Die Opera 1 bis 31', in *AW 1883 1983*, pp. 185–204

———'Betrachtungen zur Webern-Literatur. Oder Warum seine Musik noch nicht auf der Straßen gepfiffen wird', *ÖMz* 38/11 (November 1983), 606–14

———'Das Umkreisen der Sonne. Zu Anton Weberns Trakl-Lied op.14/I', *Melos* 49/4 (1987), 94–117

———'Anton Webern und die Tradition', in *Musik in Österreich. Eine Chronik in Daten, Dokumenten, Essays und Bilden*, ed. Gottfried Kraus (Vienna: Brandstätter, 1989), pp. 346–9

ANTESBERGER, Günther. 'Die Passacaglia in der Wiener Schule. Analytische Studien zu einem barocken Formtypus in Werken von Arnold Schönberg, Alban Berg und Anton Webern', in *Festschrift für Franz Koschier. Beiträge zur Volkskunde, Naturkunde und Kulturgeschichte* (Klagenfurt: Verlag des Landesmuseums für Kärnten, 1974), pp. 121–38

ARAGONA, Livio. 'Il Lied di Abelone e il sopracciglio di Senecio. I Lieder di Webern tra figura e struttura', *Rivista Italiana di Musicologia* 23 (1988), 279–310

ARGOSH, Richard Steven. 'Nine short pieces: brevity in the music of Beethoven, Webern, and Kurtag' (unpublished dissertation, Princeton University, 1991)

BABBITT, Milton. *Words about Music*, ed. Stephen Dembski and Joseph N. Straus (Wisconsin: University of Wisconsin Press, 1987). Some of the material in these lectures first appeared in 'Some aspects of twelve-tone composition', *The Score and I. M. A. Magazine* 12 (1955), 53–61; 'Twelve-tone invariants as compositional determinants', *MQ* 46 (1960), 246–59; 'Set structure as a compositional determinant', *JMT* 5 (1961), 72–94; and 'Since Schoenberg', *PNM* 12/1–2 (1973–4), 3–28

BACH, Hans Elmar. 'Anton v. Webern. "Der Tag ist vergangen", 1915' and 'Anton v. Webern. Variationen op.27, I. Satz, Takt 1–18, 1936', in *Aufbruch der Jungen Musik. Von Webern bis Stockhausen*, ed. Hugo Wolfram Schmidt and Aloys Weber, Die Garbe Musikkunde Teil 4, 6th edn (Cologne: Gerig, 1979), pp. 211–18, 219–23

BAILEY, Kathryn. *The Twelve-note Music of Anton Webern: Old Forms in a New Language* (Cambridge: Cambridge University Press, 1991). Earlier versions of parts of this book have appeared as 'Formal and rhythmic procedures in Webern's Opus 30', *Canadian Association of University Schools of Music Journal* 2/1 (1972), 34–52; 'Webern's symmetrical row formations with particular reference to Opus 30', *Cahiers canadiens de musique* 5 (1972), 159–66; 'The evolution of variation form in the music of Webern', *Current Musicology* 16 (1973), 55–70; 'A note on Webern's graces', *Studies in Music from the University of Western Ontario* 6 (1981), 1–6; 'Webern's Opus 21: creativity in tradition', *Journal of Musicology* 2/2 (Spring 1983), 184–95; 'Willi Reich's Webern', *Tempo* no.165 (June 1988), 18–22; 'Canon and beyond: Webern's Op.31 Cantata', *MusA* 7/3 (1988), 313–48

——— 'Rhythm and metre in Webern's late works', *Journal of the Royal Musical Association* 120/2 (1995), 251–80

——— 'Coming of age', *MT* 136/1832 (October 1995), 644–9

——— 'Symmetry as nemesis: Webern and the first movement of the Concerto, Opus 24', *JMT* 40/2 (1996: forthcoming)

BAKER, James M. 'Coherence in Webern's Six Pieces for Orchestra, Op.6', *MTS* 4 (1982), 1–27

BARKIN, Elaine. 'About tunes and tetrachords', *ITO* 3/1 (1977–8), 29–30 (in response to Robert Gauldin, 'Pitch structure in the second movement of Webern's Concerto, Op.24')

BARUCH, Gerth-Wolfgang. 'Anton von Webern', *Melos* 20 (December 1953), 337–42

BEACH, David W. 'Segmental invariance and the twelve-tone system', *JMT* 20/2 (Fall 1976), 157–84

——— 'Pitch structure and the analytic process in atonal music', *MTS* 1 (1979), 7–22

BECKER, Peter. 'Ausdruck und Konstruktion bei Webern. Aspekte für den Musikunterricht in der Sekundarstufe II', *Musik und Bildung* 10/3 (1978), 174–9

——— '"Freilich ist es wieder Lyrik geworden." Auf der Suche nach dem Exemplarischen bei Webern', *Musik und Bildung* 15/12 (1983), 4–10

BEECHEY, Gwilym. 'Anton Webern 1883–1945', *Musical Opinion* 107/1272, 1274 (October, December 1983), 13–17, 26; 69–73

BEHNKE, Elizabeth A. 'The hermeneutics of silence: Webern's "Eingang" and the works of Jean Tardieu' (unpublished dissertation, Ohio University, 1978)

BENJAMIN, William E. 'Ideas of order in motivic music', *MTS* 1 (1979), 23–34

BERRY, Wallace. *Structural Functions in Music* (Englewood Cliffs NJ: Prentice-Hall, 1976), pp. 397–408 (discusses Op.11 no.3 and Op.5 no.4)

BERTINI, Gary. 'Anton Webern und die musikalische Praxis', in *Opus AW*, pp. 61–4

BLASL, Franz. Review of *Chronik*, *Musikerziehung* 34 (April 1981), 182

BLUMRÖDER, Christoph von. 'Webern und die serielle Musik', *Musikforschung* 38/4 (1985), 300–3

BOEHMER, Konrad. 'Webern. Klang – Natur. Varèse', in *AW I*, pp. 211–24

BOISSOU, Hélène. 'La forme chez Webern' (unpublished dissertation, University of Aix-Marseille I, 1979)

BON, Claude. 'Webern chorégraphe ou la notion d'espace dans la musique d'Anton Webern', *La Recherche en danse* 2 (1983), 75–8

BORRIES, Christian von. 'Webern op.6. Eine außergewöhnliche Erfahrung', in *Opus AW*, pp. 54–60

BOSCH, Horst. 'Ein Webern-Film für das Fernsehen', *ÖMz* 38/11 (November 1983), 634–5

BOULEZ, Pierre. 'Note to tonight's concert: Webern's work analyzed', *New York Herald Tribune*, 28 December 1952, §4, p. 4

——— 'Hommage à Webern', *Domaine musical* 1 (1954), 123–5

——— 'La conjonction Stravinsky/Webern', in *Points de repère*, ed. Jean-Jacques Nattiez, 2nd edn ([?Paris]: Bourgois, 1985), pp. 369–75 (372–5). Published in English as 'The Stravinsky–Webern conjunction', in *Orientations: Collected Writings*, trans. Martin Cooper (London: Faber, 1986), pp. 364–9 (367–9). From the sleeve note for a recording directed by Boulez (Véga C30 A 120)

——— *Jalons (pour une décennie). Dix ans d'enseignement au Collège de France (1978–1988)*, ed. Jean-Jacques Nattiez ([?Paris]: Bourgois, 1989)

——— 'Anton Webern. "Une oeuvre clé du XXe siècle"' (Boulez interviewed by Patrick Szersnovicz), *Le monde de la musique* 157 (July–August 1992), 42–7

BOYNTON, Neil. 'The combination of variations and adagio-form in the late instrumental works of Anton Webern' (unpublished thesis, University of Cambridge, 1993)

——— 'Formal combination in Webern's Variations Op. 30', *MusA* 14/2–3 (July–Oct. 1995), 193–220

BRADSHAW, Susan. 'The piano music of Schoenberg, Webern and Berg', *Composer* 68 (Winter 1979–80), 21–3

BRAUNEISS, Leopold. 'Zu einigen neu aufgefundenen Webern-Autographen', *ÖMz* 43/6 (June 1988), 307–14

BRELET, Gisèle. 'L'esthétique du discontinu dans la musique nouvelle', *Revue d'esthétique* 21 (1968), 253–77

BRESGEN, Cesar. 'In memoriam Anton Webern. Zum 20. Todestag', *Musikerziehung* 19 (1965), 55–60

——— 'Bemerkungen zu "Anton Webern ist tot" (*Musikerziehung*, Maiheft 1972, S. 223)', *Musikerziehung* 26 (1972), 25

——— *Mittersill 1945. Ein Weg zu Anton Webern* (Vienna: Österreichischer Bundesverlag, 1983). Reprint, 'Erinnerungen an Anton Webern', in *Zum 100. Geburtstag Anton Webern* (see Catalogues, Vienna), pp. 15–20

——— 'Anton Webern (1883–1945) aus heutiger Sicht', *Österreichische Autorenzeitung* 35/4 (December 1983), 18–19

BREUER, János. 'Anton von Webern dirigiert Kodály. Zur Wiener Erstaufführung des Psalmus Hungaricus', *Studia musicologica Akademiae scientarum Hungaricae* 25 (1983), 111–29

BRINDLE, Reginald Smith. *The New Music: the Avant-Garde since 1945* (London: Oxford University Press, 1975)

BRINKMANN, Reinhold. 'Ein Webern-Manuskript in Berlin', in *Festschrift Rudolf Elvers zum 60. Geburtstag*, ed. Ernst Herttrich and Hans Schneider (Tutzing: Schneider, 1985), pp. 63–71

——— 'Anton Webern. Eine Situationsbeschreibung', in *Vom Einfall zum Kunstwerk. Der Kompositionsprozess in der Musik des 20. Jahrhunderts*, ed. Hermann Danuser and Günter Katzenberger, Publikationen der Hochschule für Musik und Theater Hannover 4 (Laaber: Laaber Verlag, 1993), [?pp.]

BRISTIGER, Michal. 'Webern e Bach, Varèse e Hoene Wronski. Radici romantiche del pensiero musicale di due musicisti moderni', in *Comporre arcano*, pp. 42–51

BRÖMSE, Peter. 'Graphische Strukturveranschaulichung der Zwölftontechnik', in *Der Einfluß der technischen Mittler auf die Musikerziehung unserer Zeit*, ed. Egon Kraus (Mainz: Schott, 1968), pp. 278–82

BROOKS, Richard James. 'Structural functions of musical gesture as heard in selected instrumental compositions of the twentieth-century: a graphic analytic method' (unpublished dissertation, New York University, 1981). Includes a discussion of the Quartet Op.22

BROWNE, Earle. 'Toute police d'assurance est impensable', *Preuves* 16 (1966), 39–42

BUDDE, Elmar. 'Formen der Einfachheit in der Musik. Einige Aspekte kompositorisch-ästhetischer Wertung', in *Zur "Neuen Einfachheit" in der Musik*, ed. Otto Kolleritsch, Studien zur Wertungsforschung 14 (Vienna and Graz: UE for the Institut für Wertungsforschung an der Hochschule für Musik und darstellende Kunst in Graz, 1981), pp. 25–37

——— 'Musik als Sprache und Material. Anmerkungen zu Weberns Konzeption einer musikalischen Sprache', in *Die Wiener Schule in der Musikgeschichte des 20. Jahrhunderts. Bericht über den 2. Kongreß der*

*Internationalen Schönberg-Gesellschaft*, ed. Rudolf Stephan and Sigrid Wiesmann (Vienna: Lafite, 1986), pp. 161–6

——— 'Webern und Bach', in *Alte Musik als ästhetische Gegenwart. Bach, Händel, Schütz. Bericht über den internationalen musikwissenschaftlichen Kongress Stuttgart 1985*, ed. Dietrich Berke and Dorothee Hanemann, 2 vols. (Kassel: Bärenreiter, 1987), I, pp. 198–203

——— 'Anton Webern: Op.5/IV – Versuch einer Analyse', in *Die Wiener Schule*, ed. Rudolf Stephan, Wege der Forschung 643 (Darmstadt: Wissenschaftliche Buchgesellschaft, 1989), pp. 322–33. First published in *Erich Döflein. Festschrift zum 70. Geburtstag*, ed. Lars Ulrich Abraham (Mainz: Schott, 1972), pp. 58–66

BUDWEG, Harald. 'Der (fast) ganze Webern sollte es sein. Notizen zum bisher größten Projekt der Jungen Deutschen Philharmonie', *NZM* 144/11 (1983), 29–30

BURDE, Wolfgang. 'Komponieren um 1910. Notizen zu den instrumentalen Miniaturen Anton von Weberns', in *Opus AW*, pp. 94–9

BURKHART, Charles. 'The symmetrical source of Webern's Opus 5, no.4', *Music Forum* 5 (1980), 317–34

BUSCH, Regina. Review of *Chronik*, *Musica* 35/2 (1981), 179–80

——— 'Über die Musik von Anton Webern', *ÖMz* 36/9 (September 1981), 470–82

——— 'Leopold Spinner', *ÖMz* 37/10 (October 1982), 545–53

——— 'Aus dem Briefwechsel Webern–Steuermann', in *AW I*, pp. 23–51

——— 'Über die horizontale und vertikale Darstellung musikalischer Gedanken und den musikalischen Raum', in *AW I*, pp. 225–50. Published in English as 'On the horizontal and vertical presentation of musical ideas: and on musical space', trans. Michael Graubart, *Tempo* no.154 (1985), 156 and 157 (1986), 2–10, 7–15, 21–6

——— 'Wie Berg die richtige Reihe fand', in *AW II*, pp. 365–87

——— 'Verzeichnis der von Webern dirigierten und einstudierten Werke', in *AW II*, pp. 398–416

——— 'Taktgruppen in Weberns Konzert op.24', *Musica* 40/6 (1986), 532–7

——— *Leopold Spinner*, Musik der Zeit. Dokumentationen und Studien 6 (Bonn: Boosey and Hawkes, 1987). A shortened version of the

'Einleitung' (pp. 11–32) was published in English as 'The identity of Leopold Spinner', *Tempo* no. 165 (June 1988), 24–36

——— 'A recent Webern discovery', *Tempo* no. 165 (June 1988), 58

——— Letter to the editor, *Tempo* no. 166 (September 1988), 67–9

——— 'Thematisch oder athematisch?', *ISGM* nos. 3–4 (December 1989), 5–9

——— 'Else Cross', *ISGM* nos. 3–4, 11–12

——— 'Oktaven in Weberns Bagatellen', *Dissonanz* 27 (February 1991), 10–12. Published in English as 'Octaves in Webern's Bagatelles', trans. Inge Goodwin, *Tempo* no. 178 (September 1991), 12–15

CAGE, John. 'Defense of Satie', in *John Cage*, ed. Richard Kostelanetz (New York: RK Editions, 1970), pp. 77–84

CAPPELLI, Ida. 'Webern rückt in die erste Reihe auf', *Melos* 29 (1962), 377–83

CARAPEZZA, Paolo Emilio. 'Macrocosmo–micrologo', in *Comporre arcano*, pp. 20–33

CARNER, Mosco. 'Webern and the avant-garde', *Listener*, 9 August 1962, 225

CARTER, Beverly Holder. 'Goethe's color theory as a model for artistic analysis: an examination of selected works by Paul Klee and Anton Webern' (unpublished dissertation, Ohio University, 1991)

CASEY, Ethel. 'Webern: architect of silence', *Music Journal* 19/6 (1961), 52, 89

CASTIGLIONI, Niccolò. 'Entstehung und Krise des tonalen Systems', *Melos* 27 (1960), 369–72

CERHA, Gertraud. 'Zu den Arbeiten aus dem Nachlaß Weberns', in *AW 1883 1983*, pp. 205–22

——— 'Zum Verhältnis von Idee, Ideal, Ideologie und Wirklichkeit in der Welt Anton von Weberns', *ÖMz* 43/12 (December 1988), 650–8

CHADWICK, Nick. 'Webern, the BBC and the Berg Violin Concerto. The Berg Violin Concerto in London: Webern's correspondence with the BBC 1935–6', in *Sundry Sorts of Music Books: Essays on The British Library Collections*, ed. Chris Banks, Arthur Searle and Malcolm Turner (London: The British Library, 1993), pp. 330–45

CHAMFRAY, Claude. '*Variations pour piano* (op. 27) de Webern; *Quatuor à cordes*, de P. Wissmer; *Deux pièces pour piano*, de Lajtha (Schola

Cantorum)', *La revue musicale* 19/180 (1938), 386–7 (concert review)

CHOLOPOW, Juri. 'Über Webern's Begriffssystem der Formenlehre', *MitPSS* no.5 (January 1992), 27–30

CHOLOPOW, Valentina. 'Chromatische Prinzipien in Anton Weberns Vokalzyklus *Sechs Lieder nach Gedichten von Georg Trakl*, op.14', *Beiträge zur Musikwissenschaft* 17 (1975), 155–69

CHOLOPOW, Valentina and Juri. *Anton Webern. Leben und Werk*, trans. Christoph Hellmundt (Berlin: Henschelverlag, 1989). First published in Russian (Moscow: Sowjetski Kompositor, 1984); published in Italian as *Anton Webern*, Le Sfere 12 (Milan: Ricordi, 1990)

CHRISMAN, Richard. 'Anton Webern's Six Bagatelles for String Quartet, Op.9: the unfolding of intervallic successions', *JMT* 23/1 (Spring 1979), 81–122

CLIFTON, Thomas. 'Music as constituted object', in *In Search of Musical Method*, ed. F[idelis] J[oseph] Smith (London: Gordon and Breach, 1976), pp. 73–98. Repr. in *Music and Man* 2/1–2 (1976), 73–98. Discusses Op.9 no.1

——— *Music as Heard: a Study in Applied Phenomenology* (New Haven: Yale University Press, 1983). See esp. pp. 129–35, 231–5

CLÜVER, Claus. 'Klangfarbenmelodie in polychromatic poems. A. von Webern and A. de Campos', *Comparative Literature Studies* 18 (September 1981), 386–98

COLAZZO, Cosimo. 'Le metamorfosi del tempo. Per un webernismo critico. La concezione musicale di Anton Webern in rapporto al pensiero di J.W. Goethe', *NRMI* 28/1 (1994), 57–68

COLLISANI, Amalia. 'Spazio e tempo', in *Comporre arcano*, pp. 84–94

CONE, Edward T. 'Analysis today', *MQ* 46 (April 1960), 172–88

COOK, Nicholas. *A Guide to Musical Analysis* (London: 1987, Dent), pp. 294–312 ('Analyzing serial music', I–III)

COOSAERT, Johan Bruxelles B. See Ackere

COSTÈRE, Edmond. 'Pour une analyse structurale des variations opus 27 de Webern', *Canadian University Music Review* 7 (1986), 103–26

COVINGTON, Katherine Russell. 'A study of textural stratification in twentieth-century compositions' (unpublished dissertation, Indiana University, 1982)

COX, Gareth. 'Einige quellenkritische Bemerkungen zu Weberns *Satz für Klavier* (M. 112)', *MitPSS* no.4 (January 1991), 18–20

——— *Anton Weberns Studienzeit. Seine Entwicklung im Lichte der Sätze und Fragmente für Klavier*, Europäische Hochschulschriften, Reihe XXXVI Musikwissenschaft 77 (Frankfurt a.M.: Lang, 1992). Originally doctoral dissertation, 'Die Sätze für Soloklavier aus der Studienzeit Anton Weberns' (Albert-Ludwigs-Universität, Freiburg im Breisgau, 1991)

CRAFT, Robert. 'Anton Webern', *The Score* 13 (September 1955), 9–22. Includes the text of the booklet for Craft's recording of the complete works of Webern (Philips L09414–17; Columbia Records K4L–232)

——— 'A concert for Saint Mark', *The Score* 18 (December 1956), 35–51 (44–5)

——— 'A personal preface', *The Score* 20 (June 1957), 7–13 (12–13)

——— 'Boulez and Stockhausen', *The Score* 24 (November 1958), 54–62

CROSS, Else. 'Anton von Webern as I knew him', *Royal Academy of Music Magazine* 197 (Michaelmas 1969), 11–15. Published in German as 'Webern wie ich ihn kannte', *ÖMz* 41/11 (November 1986), 560–4

CROTTY, John E. 'A preliminary analysis of Webern's Opus 6 no.3', *ITO* 5/2 (1979–80), 23–32

DAGNES, Edward P. 'Symmetrical structures in Webern: an analytical overview of the Symphonie, movement II, variation 3', *ITO* 1/9–10 (1975–6), 33–[?54]

DAHLHAUS, Carl. 'Webern heute', *NZM* 133/5 (1972), 242

——— Review of *Chronik*, *German Studies. Section 3: Literature, Music, Fine Arts* 15 (1982), 77–8

——— 'Probleme des Rhythmus in der Neuen Musik', in *Schönberg und andere* (Mainz: Schott, 1978), pp. 97–110. Published in English as 'Problems of rhythm in the New Music', in *Schoenberg and the New Music*, trans. Derrick Puffett and Alfred Clayton (Cambridge: Cambridge University Press, 1987), pp. 45–61

——— 'Rhythmische Strukturen in Weberns Orchesterstücken opus 6', in *Schönberg und andere*, pp. 204–9. Previously published in *Beiträge der Österreichischen Gesellschaft für Musik 1972/73. Webern Kongress* (Kassel: Bärenreiter, 1973), pp. 73–80; published in English as 'Rhythmic structures in Webern's Orchestral Pieces, Op.6', in *Schoenberg and the New Music*, pp. 174–80

——— 'Analytische Instrumentation – Bachs sechsstimmiges Ricercar in der Orchestrierung Anton Weberns', in *Schönberg und andere*, pp. 210–17. Previously published in *Bach-Interpretationen. Walter Blankenburg zum 65. Geburtstag*, ed. Martin Geck (Göttingen: Vandenhoeck & Ruprecht, 1969), pp. 197–206; published in English as 'Analytical instrumentation: Bach's Six-Part Ricercar as orchestrated by Anton Webern', in *Schoenberg and the New Music*, pp. 181–91

DAHLHAUS, Carl, and Rudolf STEPHAN. 'Eine "dritte Epoche" der Musik? Kritische Bemerkungen zur elektronischen Musik', *Deutsche Universitätszeitung* 10/17 (1955), 14–17

DALLAPICCOLA, Luigi. 'In memoria di Anton Webern', *Emporium* 105 (1947), 18–20

DE VELDE, Henk. See Velde

DELAERE, Mark. *Funktionelle Atonalität. Analytische Strategien für die frei-atonale Musik der Wiener Schule*, Veröffentlichungen zur Musikforschung 14 (Wilhelmshaven: Noetzel, 1993)

DELIÈGE, Célestin. 'La *set theory* ou les enjeux du pléonasme', *Analyse musicale* 17 (October 1989), 64–79 (75–6)

DEPPERT, Heinrich. 'Über einige Voraussetzungen der musikalischen Analyse', *Zeitschrift für Musiktheorie* 4/2 (1973), 10–16

DIBELIUS, Ulrich. 'L'oeuvre désoeuvrée', *Musique en jeu* 6 (1972), 3–12

——— 'Gegenpositionen. Webern und Varèse oder Diamant und Kristall', *Philharmonische Blätter* (Berlin) 5 (1977), 10–12

DONAT, Misha. 'Second Viennese School?', *Tempo* no.99 (1972), 8–13

DOPHEIDE, Bernhard. 'Anmerkungen zu Anton Weberns Orchesterstück op.6/1', *Zeitschrift für Musikpädagogik* 7 (May 1982), 30–2

DREW, David. 'Twelve questions for Leopold Spinner', *Tempo* no.99 (1972), 14–17

DREYER, Lutz. 'Der tonale "Atonale". Zur Harmonik im Spätwerk Anton Weberns', *NZM* 147/1 (1986), 14–18

DREYER, Martin. 'Mainly Webern', *MT* 125 (February 1984), 101. Report on the Olivetti International Webern Cycle

DRUSKIN, Mihail. 'Zur Persönlichkeit Anton Weberns', *Beiträge zur Musikwissenschaft* 16/1 (1974), 31–44

DUJMIĆ, Dunja. 'Anton Webern ili trijumf strukture' ('Anton Webern or the Triumph of Structure'), *Zvuk*, [?]/1 (1980), 44–9

DÜMLING, Albrecht. '"Dies ist ein Lied für dich allein". Zu einigen Motiven von Weberns Textwahl', in *AW I*, pp. 251–61

DUNSBY, Jonathan, and Arnold WHITTALL. *Music Analysis in Theory and Practice* (London: Faber, 1988), pp. 186–200 ('Twelve-note composition')

DURNEY, Daniel. 'Aspects du problème de la forme dans la musique instrumentale au tournant du siècle. Mahler–Schönberg, Berg, Webern–Debussy, 1890–1910' (doctorat de troisième cycle, Université Paris IV, 1981)

EGGEBRECHT, Hans Heinrich. 'Punktuelle Musik', in *Bericht über das zweite Colloquium der Walcker-Stiftung, März 1972*, ed. Eggebrecht, Veröffentlichungen der Walcker-Stiftung 5 (Stuttgart: Musikwissenschaftliche Verlags-Gesellschaft, 1974), pp. 162–87

ELSTON, Arnold. 'Some rhythmic practices in contemporary music', *MQ* 42/3 (July 1956), 318–29 (325–9)

ERDMANN, Martin. 'Webern und Cage. Zur Genese der Cageschen Losigkeit', in *John Cage II*, ed. Heinz-Klaus Metzger and Rainer Riehn, Musik-Konzepte Sonderband (Munich: Edition Text+Kritik, 1990), pp. 237–59

ERICSON, Raymond. 'New Webern haul found in a dark attic', *New York Times*, 10 April 1966, §X, p. 11

ESCOT, Pozzi. 'Webern's Opus 25, No. 1: perception of large-scale patterns', *Theory and Practice* 4/1 (March 1979), 28–9

——— 'Towards a theoretical concept: non-linearity in Webern's Op. 11, no. 1', *Sonus* 3/1 (Fall 1982), 18–29

ESSL, Karlheinz. *Das Synthese-Denken bei Anton Webern. Studien zur Musikauffassung des späten Webern unter besonderer Berücksichtigung seiner eigenen Analysen zu op. 28 und 30*, Wiener Veröffentlichungen zur Musikwissenschaft 24 (Tutzing: Schneider, 1991). Originally doctoral dissertation (University of Vienna, 1989)

EVANS, Tamara S. 'Thomas Mann, Anton Webern, and the magic square', in *German Literature and Music. An Aesthetic Fusion: 1890–1989*, ed. Claus Reschke and Howard Pollack, Houston German Studies 8 (Munich: Fink, 1992), pp. 159–72

FEDERHOFER, Hellmut. 'Ein Hörprotokoll neuer Musik', in *Scritti in onore di Luigi Ronga* (Milan and Naples: Ricciardi, 1973), pp. 157–77

FLOROS, Constantin. 'Das Kammerkonzert von Alban Berg. Hommage à Schönberg und Webern', in *Alban Berg. Kammermusik II*, ed. Heinz-Klaus Metzger and Rainer Riehn, Musik-Konzepte 9 (Munich: Edition Text+Kritik, 1979), pp. 63–90

FONTANELLI, Simone. 'Chitarra e ricerca timbrica nelle opere di A. Webern', *Fronimo* 37 (October 1981), 53–5

FOREMAN, Lewis. 'Webern, the BBC and the Berg Violin Concerto', *Tempo* no. 178 (September 1991), 2–10

FORTE, Allen. 'A program for the analytic reading of score', *JMT* 10 (1966), 330–64

——— 'Aspects of rhythm in Webern's atonal music', *MTS* 2 (1980), 90–109

——— 'A major Webern revision and its implications for analysis', *PNM* 28/1 (1990), 224–55

——— 'An octatonic essay by Webern: No. 1 of the *Six Bagatelles for String Quartet*, Op. 9', *MTS* 16/2 (1994), 171–95

FRIED, Philip Aaron. 'Webern's Concerto, Opus 24: an analysis' (unpublished dissertation, University of Chicago, 1985)

FUCHS, Anton. *Auf ihren Spuren in Kärnten. Alban Berg, Gustav Mahler, Johannes Brahms, Hugo Wolf, Anton Webern* (Klagenfurt: Kärnter Druck- und Verlagsgesellschaft, 1988)

GARCÍA LABORDA, José M. 'Tradición y progreso en Anton Webern', *Ritmo* (1984), 17–21

GAULDIN, Robert. 'Pitch structure in the second movement of Webern's Concerto, Op. 24', *ITO* 2/10 (1976–7), 8–22

——— 'The magic squares of the third movement of Webern's concerto, Op. 24', *ITO* 2/11–12 (1976–7), 32–42

GEFORS, Hans. 'Stockhausen kontra Webern eller Vad kan lära av 50-talet?', *Nutida Musik* 19/4 (1975–6), 19–24

——— Review of *Chronicle*, *Dansk Musiktidsskrift* 54 (1979–80), 211–12

GENTILUCCI, Armando. *Oltre l'avanguardia. Un invito al molteplice*, Contrappunti 4 (Fiesole: Discanto Edizioni, 1979)

GERLACH, Reinhard. 'Die Funktion des Textes in Liedern Anton Weberns', in *Colloquium Music and Word Brno 1969*, ed. Rudolf Pečman, Colloquia on the history and theory of music at the International Music Festival in Brno 4 (Brno: IMF, 1973), pp. 263–85. A slightly more detailed version of Gerlach's conference paper is published as 'Anton Webern. "Ein Winterabend" Op.13, Nr. 4. Zum Verhältnis von Musik und Dichtung oder Wahrheit als Struktur', *AfMw* 30/1 (1973), 44–68

——— 'Mystik und Klangmagie in Anton von Weberns hybrider Tonalität', in *Die Wiener Schule*, ed. Rudolf Stephan, Wege der Forschung 643 (Darmstadt: Wissenschaftliche Buchsgesellschaft, 1989), pp. 334–69. First published in *AfMw* 33 (1976), 1–27

GOEBELS, Franzpeter. 'Bemerkungen und Materialien zum Studium neuer Klaviermusik', *SMz* 113/5, 6 (1973), 265–8, 329–40

GOŁĄB, Maciej. 'Technika struktur dodekachordalnych w 6 Bagatelach op.9 i w 3 małych utworach op.11 Antona Weberna' (The technique of dodecaphonic structures in the Six Bagatelles Op.9 and the Three Little Pieces Op.11 by Anton Webern), *Muzyka* 23/3 (1978), 67–84 (includes an abstract in English)

GRASBERGER, Franz and Rudolf STEPHAN (eds). *Alban Berg Studien* (Vienna: UE, 1980–), I[/1]: *Katalog der Musikhandschriften und Studien Alban Bergs im Fonds Alban Berg und der weiteren handschriftlichen Quellen im Besitz der Österreichische Nationalbibliothek*, prepared by Rosemary Hilmar (1980), pp. 109–10 ('Analysen und Studien zu und in anderen Werken. Anton Webern', nos.368–74). See Busch, 'Wie Berg die richtige Reihe fand', for a discussion of no.373, Webern's Trio Op.20

GREISSLE, Felix. 'Weberns Eigenzeit', in *AW II*, pp. 5–7

GRIFFITHS, Paul. 'A Webern winter: concerts and chronicles', *MT* 120 (March 1979), 211–14

——— 'Webern', in Oliver Neighbour, Paul Griffiths and George Perle, *The New Grove Second Viennese School* (London: Macmillan, 1983), pp. 89–134. First published in *The New Grove Dictionary of Music and Musicians*, ed. Stanley Sadie, 20 vols. (London: Macmillan, 1981), XX, pp. 270–82. Published in German as *Schönberg, Webern, Berg. Die Zweite Wiener Schule*, trans. Sebastian Loelgen (Stuttgart: Metzler, 1992)

——— 'Schoenberg, Berg and Webern', in *Heritage of Music*, ed. Michael Raeburn and Alan Kendall, 4 vols. (Oxford: Oxford University Press, 1989), IV: *Music in the Twentieth Century*, pp. 187–205

GRITSCH, Robert. 'Schönberg op.19 und Webern op.9. Ein Vergleich', *Der*

*Komponist. Information des Österreichischen Komponistenbunds* (May 1979), 9–14

GROSSE, Ulrich. 'Erster Satz des "Konzert für neun Instrumente" op.24 von Anton Webern', in *Analyse*, ed. E. Karkoschka and others, 2 vols. (Herrenberg: Döring, 1976). I, pp. 82–9 (text); II, tables 16–25

GRUHN, Wilfried. 'Anton von Webern (1883–1945). Fünf Stücke für Orchester op.10 (1911/1913)', in *Perspektiven neuer Musik. Material und didaktische Information*, ed. Dieter Zimmerschied (Mainz: Schott, 1974), pp. 13–40

HAGLUND, Rolf. Review of *Chronicle*, *Svensk Tidskrift für Musikforskning* 61/2 (1979), 67–9

HAIMO, Ethan. 'Secondary and disjunct order-position relationships in Webern's Op.20', *PNM* 24/2 (1985–6), 406–19

HAMILTON, Iain. 'Alban Berg and Anton Webern', in *European Music in the Twentieth Century*, ed. Howard Hartog (London: Routledge and Kegan Paul, 1957; repr. Westport CT: Greenwood Press, 1976), pp. 94–117

HAMM, Charles. 'Solo songs: Anton von Webern', *Notes* 23 (1966–7), 840–1

HANNA, John. See Ismer

HANSBERGER, Joachim. 'Anton Webern. Die vierte Bagatelle für Streichquartett als Gegenstand einer Übung im Musikhören', *Musica* 23 (1969), 236–40

HANSEN, Bernard. 'Dimensionen des Komponierens. Varèse und Webern', in *Edgard Varèse, die Befreiung des Klangs. Symposium Edgard Varèse Hamburg 1991*, ed. Helga de la Motte-Haber (Hofheim: Wolke, 1992), [?pp.]

HANSEN, Matthias. 'Zusammenhang im Dienste der Faßlichkeit. Anmerkungen zu einer Konstellation. Brahms–Schönberg–Webern', *Musik und Gesellschaft* 33/12 (December 1983), 700–4

HANSEN, Peter S. *Twentieth-Century Music* (Boston: Allyn and Bacon, 1978), pp. 192–219 ('Berg and Webern')

HANSON, Robert Frederic. 'Anton Webern's atonal style' (unpublished dissertation, Southampton University, 1976). Discusses Op.10

——— 'Webern's chromatic organisation', *MusA* 2/2 (1983), 135–49. Discusses Op.3 no.5 ('Kahl reckt der Baum'), Op.7 no.1 and Op.10 no.4

HARTMANN, Karl Amadeus. 'Lektionen bei Anton Webern. Briefe an meine Frau', in *Opus AW*, pp. 9–11. First published in *Kleine Schriften*, ed. Ernst Thomas (Mainz: Schott, 1965), pp. 26–32. Extracts from the letters are published in *Chronicle*, pp. 540–3 (*Chronik*, pp. 491–3), and in *Karl Amadeus Hartmann und die Musica Viva. Essays. Bisher unveröffentlichte Briefe an Hartmann. Katalog* (of the exhibition from 19 June to 29 August 1980), ed. Renata Wagner, Margot Attenkofer and Helmut Hell, Bayerische Staatsbibliothek. Ausstellungs-Kataloge 21 (Munich: Piper; Mainz: Schott, 1980), pp. 247–51

HARTWELL, Robin. 'Rhythmic procedures in the serial music of Anton Webern' (unpublished dissertation, University of Sussex, 1980)

——— 'Duration and mental arithmetic: the first movement of Webern's First Cantata', *PNM* 23/1 (1984–5), 348–59

HARVEY, Jonathan. 'Atonality', *MT* 122 (November 1980), 699–700

HASTY, Christopher. 'Rhythm in post-tonal music: preliminary questions of duration and motion', *JMT* 25/2 (1981), 183–216

——— 'Segmentation and process in post-tonal music', *MTS* 3 (1981), 54–73

——— 'Phrase formation in post-tonal music', *JMT* 28 (1984), 167–89

——— 'Composition and context in the twelve-note music of Anton Webern', *MusA* 7/3 (1988), 281–312

HAUGAN, Edwin Lyle. 'Anton von Webern's String Quartet in A minor (c.1907), M.121: a reconstruction' (unpublished dissertation, Louisiana State University and Agricultural and Mechanical College, 1989)

HAYES, Malcolm. *Anton Webern* (London: Phaidon, 1996)

HEIMANN, Walter. 'Autonomie und soziale Bildung. Musikgeschichte als Problem im Unterricht, dargestellt am Beispiel der Variationen op.27/I von Anton Webern. Unterrichtsbeispiel für Sekundarstufe II', *Musik und Bildung* 10/3 (1978), 165–73

HELLER, Friedrich C. Review of *Chronik*, *ÖMz* 37/10 (October 1982), 589, 592

HENZE, Hans Werner. 'Gefahren in der neuen Musik', *Texte und Zeichen* 1 (1955), 213–15. A shorter, revised version of this essay was published as 'Die Zeichen', in *Musik und Politik. Schriften und Gespräche*

*1955–1975*, ed. Jens Brockmeier (Munich: Deutscher Taschenbuch Verlag, 1976), pp. 26–8; published in English as 'Signs', in *Music and Politics: Collected Writings 1953–81*, trans. Peter Labanyi (London: Faber, 1982), pp. 205–6

HERSCHKOWITZ, Filipp. *O muzike*, ed. L. Hoffmann (Moscow: Sowjetski Kompositor, 1991)

HILMAR, Ernst. 'Versuch einer Bestandsaufnahme. Hans Moldenhauers "Webern-Archiv"', *ÖMz* 37/10 (October 1982), 574–5

——— (ed.). 'Aus einem Gespräch mit Weberns Tochter Maria Halbich-Webern', in *AW 1883 1983*, pp. 93–7

———See also *Sechs Stücke für großes Orchester op. 6* (Primary sources, Music)

HILMAR, Rosemary. 'Das Sprachrohr. Eine Erläuterung zu einem falsch identifizierten Aufsatz von Anton Webern', *SMz* 122 (1982), 326–32

———See also *Katalog der Sammlung Dermota* (Primary sources, Catalogues, Vienna)

H[ILMAR]-VOIT, Renate. 'Dokumente zu Anton Weberns Mahler-Pflege', *Nachrichten zur Mahler-Forschung* 13 (1984), 11–16

HOFFMANN, Peter. 'Post-Webernsche Musik? György Kurtágs Webern-Rezeption am Beispiel seines Streichquartetts op. 28', *Musiktheorie* 7/2 (1992), 129–48

HOLLAND, Dietmar. 'Musikwissenschaftliche Ideologiekritik. Zur Methode der Webern-Dissertation von Wolfgang Martin Stroh', *Die Musikforschung* 29 (1976), 187–90. (Stroh, *Anton Webern. Historische Legitimation als kompositorisches Problem*, Göppinger Akademische Beiträge 63 (Göppingen: Kümmerle, 1973))

HOPF, Helmuth. Review of *Chronik*, *Zeitschrift für Musikpädagogik* 6 (1981), 195

HORCICKA, Hans. 'Musikalischer Denkmalschutz', in *Beiträge zur Musikdokumentation. Franz Grasberger zum 60. Geburtstag*, pp. 107–13

HOYER, Martin. 'Neues zu Anton Weberns frühen Liedern', *MitPSS* no. 5 (January 1992), 31–5

HUFSCHMIDT, Wolfgang. 'Musik aus Zahlen. Prinzipien der musikalischen Formgestaltung in der seriellen Kompositionspraxis', in *Reflexionen über Musik heute*, ed. Wilfried Gruhn (Mainz: Schott, 1981), pp. 24–57

HUPFER, Konrad. 'Webern greift in die Reihenmechanik ein', *Melos* 34 (1967), 290–4

IJZERMAN, Job. 'Die Symmetrie in Weberns Orchesterstück op. 10 Nr. 1. Anmerkungen zur Analyse von Daniel A. Plante in *Musiktheorie* 4 (1989), S. 235–246', *Musiktheorie* 5/2 (1990), 165–7

ISAACSON, Eric John. 'Similarity of interval-class content between pitch-class sets: the IcVSIM relation and its application', (unpublished dissertation, Indiana University, 1992). Discusses Op. 5 nos. 2 and 4

ISMER, Ursula, and John HANNA. 'Studien zur Entwicklung der Variation vom 19. Jahrhundert bis zur spätbürgerlichen Musik' (unpublished dissertation, Martin-Luther-Universität, Halle-Wittenberg, 1976)

JANK, Werner. '"Wenn schon, dann bitte Genosse von Webern!" Zu den Beziehungen zwischen IGNM-Österreich und Arbeitermusikbewegung in der Ersten Republik', *ÖMz* 36/2 (February 1981), 73–82

——— 'Zur Arbeitermusikbewegung in der Ersten Republik', in *Arbeiterkultur in Österreich 1918–1945. Konferenz (Wien, 12. bis 14. Februar 1981)*, ed. Brigitte Galanda, Geschichte der Arbeiterbewegung. ITH-Tagungsberichte 16 (Vienna: Europaverlag, 1981), pp. 127–37

JAROCIŃSKI, Stefan. *Orfeusz na rozdrożu. Eseje o muzyce i muzykach XX wieku* (*Orpheus at the Crossroads: Essays on Music and Musicians of the 20th Century*), [?3rd] edn (Cracow: Polskie wydawnictwo muzyczne, 1983; [1st] edn, [?1958], pp. 105–16 ('Anton Webern (1958)')

——— 'Problem ekspresji i ekspresjonizmu w muzyce' (Expression and Expressionism in music), *Miesiecznik literacki* 12/2 (1977), 62–8

JELINEK, Hanns. *Anleitung zur Zwölftonkomposition nebst allerlei Paralipomena. Appendix zu "Zwölftonwerk" op. 15*, 2 vols., each accompanied by an appendix comprising analyses of twelve-note works (Vienna: UE, 1952–8; 2nd edn, 1967)

JENSEN, Eric Frederick. 'Webern and Giovanni Segantini's *Trittico della natura*', *MT* 130 (January 1989), 11–15

JETTER, Elisabeth. 'Ordnungsprinzipien im ersten Satz von Anton Weberns Symphonie op. 21', *Musik und Bildung* 10/3 (1978), 151–8

JOHNSON, Peter. 'Studies in atonality: non-thematic structural processes in the early atonal music of Schoenberg and Webern' (unpublished dissertation, University of Oxford, 1978)

——— 'Symmetrical sets in Webern's Op.10, no.4', *PNM* 17/1 (1978–9), 219–29

KABBASH, Paul Andrew. 'Form and rhythm in Webern's atonal works' (unpublished dissertation, Yale University, 1983)

——— 'Aggregate-derived symmetry in Webern's early works', *JMT* 28/2 (Fall 1984), 225–50

KARKOSCHKA, Erhard. 'Der mißverstandene Webern', *Melos* 29 (1962), 13–15

——— 'Kommentar zur Analyse von S. Silver', in *Analyse* I, pp. 41–5. See Silver, 'Erster Satz aus "Drei Kleine Stücke" op.11 von Anton Webern'

——— 'Nochmal: Weberns Orchesterstück op.10 Nr.1. Anmerkungen zur Analyse von Daniel A. Plante in *Musiktheorie* 4 (1989), S. 235–46', *Musiktheorie* 5/2 (1990), 161–4

KATER, Carlos. 'Sinfonia op.21, de A. Webern. Análise gráfica do movimento II', in *Anton Webern, O Caminho para a música nova*, trans. Carlos Kater, Coleção ensaios 7 (São Paulo: Novas metas, 1984), pp. 183–205

KATZ, Erich. 'Vokalmusik im Schaffen der Gegenwart', *Musikblätter des Anbruch* 10 (1928), 399–408 (403–4)

KAUFMANN, Harald. 'Figur in Weberns erster Bagatelle', in *AW II*, pp. 337–41

KERR, Elisabeth. 'The variations of Webern's Symphony Op.21: some observations on rhythmic organization and the use of numerology', *ITO* 8/2 (1984–5), 5–14

KHOLOPOVA. See Cholopow

KINZLER, Hartmuth. 'Webern kam aus Wien nach Darmstadt ohne sein Gewand [...] Bemerkungen zu Opus 27/I', in *Geisteswissenschaften öffentlich. Studium generale am Fachbereich Erziehungs- und Kulturwissenschaften 1987/88*, ed. Reinhold Mokrosch, Schriftenreihe des Fachbereichs 3, 10 (Osnabrück: Selbstverlag der Universität Osnabrück, 1988), pp. 139–73

KLEIN, Heribert. 'Anton von Webern. Passacaglia op.1', *NZM* 147/2 (1986), 30–2

KLEIN, Rudolf. 'Neue Musik in Österreich', *Musica* 16 (1962), 107–15

——— Review of Anton Webern, *Variationen für Klavier Op.27* [...]

*Webern's ideas on the work's interpretation set out for the first time by Peter Stadlen* [...] (see Primary sources, Music), *ÖMz* 37/11 (November 1982), 658

KLEMM, Eberhardt. 'Das Augenlicht. Analytische Betrachtung zu einer der späten Kantaten Weberns', *Musik und Gesellschaft* 33 (1983), 696–9

KOEGLER, Horst. 'Choregraphen adaptieren moderne Musik', *Melos* 28 (1961), 104–8 ('Anton Webern. Orchesterstücke op.10 und op.6', pp. 105–6)

KÖHLER, Rafael. 'Der Kristall als ästhetische Idee. Ein Beitrag zur Rezeptions- und Ideengeschichte der Zweiten Wiener Schule', *AfMw* 42/4 (1985), 241–62

KOHOUTEK, Ctirad. *Tehnika kompozicii v muzyke XX veka* (*Compositional Technique in 20th-Century Music*), trans. from the Czech (Moscow: Muzyka, 1976). (Details of original not known)

KOLISCH, Rudolf. 'Webern – Opus 5 and Opus 7', in *Rudolf Kolisch. Zur Theorie der Aufführung*, ed. Heinz Klaus Metzger and Rainer Riehn, Musik-Konzepte 29–30 (Munich: Edition Text+Kritik, 1983), pp. 120–1

KOLMAN, Peter. 'Anton Webern. Tvorca novej hudby', *Slovenska hudba* 7/10 (1963), 301–4

KOLNEDER, Walter. *Anton Webern: an Introduction to his Works*, trans. Humphrey Searle (Berkeley: University of California Press, 1968; repr. Westport CT: Greenwood Press, 1982)

KONOLD, Wulf. *Weltliche Kantaten im 20. Jahrhundert. Beiträge zu einer Theorie der funktionalen Musik* (Wolfenbüttel: Moseler, 1975), pp. 120–3 ('Anton Webern. Erste Kantate op.29'). Originally doctoral dissertation (Christian-Albrechts-Universität, Kiel, 1974)

KORTSEN, Bjarne. 'Anton Webern i brev og foredrag', *Dansk musiktidskrift* 36/2 (1961), 47–8, 51–2

KOVÁCS, Sándor. 'Ordnungen mit Tonhöhen', *Magyar Zene* 25/4 (1984), 377–83

KOVAROVICS, Ludwig. 'Die Wiener Schule (Schönberg–Berg–Webern)', *Der Komponist. Information des Österreichischen Komponistenbunds* (November 1978), 3–10

KRAEMER, Uwe (ed.). *Komponisten über Komponisten. Ein Quellen-*

*Lesebuch*, 3rd edn, Taschenbücher zur Musikwissenschaft 16 (Wilhelmshaven: Heinrichshofen, 1983), pp. 210–16. Includes contributions from Krenek, Adorno, Fortner, Stravinsky, Erhard Karkoschka, Jürg Baur, and Philipp Jarnach

KRAMER, Jonathan D. *The Time of Music: New Meanings, New Temporalities, New Listening Strategies* (New York: Schirmer, 1988), pp. 183–200 ('Analytic interlude: Webern's Opus 29')

KRAMME, Joel I. 'Introducing the chorus to atonal music: a study of Anton Webern's *Entflieht auf leichten Kähnen*, Opus 2', *Choral Journal* 15/8 (April 1975), 8–13

KRASNER, Louis, and Don C. SEIBERT. 'Some memories of Anton Webern, the Berg Concerto, and Vienna in the 1930s', *Fanfare* 11 (1987), 335–47. Extracts from this article are published in French as 'Souvenirs. Anton Webern, le concerto de violon de Berg et la Vienne des années 30', trans. Jacques Lasserre, *Dissonanz* 27 (1991), 4–9

KRAUS, Gottfried. 'Weberns Nachlaß in die USA', *ÖMz* 16/11 (November 1961), 558

KRELLMANN, Hanspeter. 'Was Anton Webern uns heute bedeutet', in *Opus AW*, pp. 172–5

KRENEK, Ernst. 'Der ganze Webern in drei Stunden', *Melos* 24 (1957), 304–5

——— 'Anton Weberns Skizzenbücher', *Musica* 24 (1970), 121–3

——— 'Einsiedler-Kongreß', *ÖMz* 38/11 (November 1983), 605

——— 'Freiheit und Verantwortung', in *AW II*, pp. 3–4; first published in *23 WMZ* no. 14 (end of February 1934), 10–11; repr. in *Zur Sprache gebracht. Essays über Musik* (Munich: Langen and Müller, 1958), pp. 156–7; and *Weg und Gestalt*, pp. 34–6

——— 'Zu Anton Weberns 100. Geburtstag', in *AW II*, pp. 26–50

——— 'Anton Webern', in *Komponisten des 20. Jahrhunderts in der Paul Sacher Stiftung*, ed. Hans Jörg Jans, Felix Meyer and Ingrid Westen (Basel: Paul Sacher Stiftung, 1986), pp. 127–9

KREYSZIG, Walter Kurt. 'Das Bach-Motiv als Grundlage für Symmetriebildungen in Anton Weberns Quartett für Geige, Klarinette, Tenorsaxophon und Klavier', *Musiktheorie* 4/3 (1989), 247–68

KRONES, Hartmut. 'Die Komponisten der Wiener Schule und die Wiener Philharmoniker', in *Klang und Komponist. 150 Jahre Wiener Philharmoniker. Ein Symposium der Wiener Philharmoniker, Kongressbericht*, ed. Otto Biba and Wolfgang Schuster (Tutzing: Schneider, 1992), pp. 201–[?]

KRONICK, Melanie S. 'Musical invention and poetry in the late vocal works of Anton Webern' (unpublished dissertation, Lousiana State University and Agricultural and Mechanical College, 1992)

KUDRJASOV, Jurij. 'Hudozestvennoe mirovozzrenie Antona Veberna' (The artistic and philosophical outlook of Anton Webern) (unpublished dissertation, Leningradskij gos. institut teatra, muzyki i kinematografii, [?1975])

KÜHN, Hellmut. 'Versuch über Weberns Geschichtsbegriff', in *Zwischen Tradition und Fortschritt. Über das musikalische Geschichtsbewusstsein. Neue Versuche*, ed. Rudolf Stephan, Veröffentlichungen des Instituts für neue Musik und Musikerziehung 13 (Mainz: Schott, 1973), pp. 96–111

——— 'Gleich und Gleich?', in *Opus AW*, pp. 13–17

KUHNLE, Kristian. 'Anton Webern. Anmerkungen zum 100. Geburtstag am 3. Dezember', *Musica Sacra* 103 (1983), 464–8

LAUGWITZ, Burkhard. 'Das Konzert war eine Demonstration. Louis Krasner und die Uraufführung von Bergs Violinkonzert', *NZM* 152/10 (October 1991), 4–10

LECLÈRE, François. *Premières pierres* (Paris: de Maule, 1987), pp. 161–5 ('Anton Webern. Réseaux et symétries dans la "Symphonie opus 21"')

LEGRAND, Joseph. Review of *Chronicle*, *Études classiques* 48/2 (April 1980), 180–1

LEIBOWITZ, René. *Schoenberg and his School*, trans. Dika Newlin (New York: Philosophical Library, 1949; repr. Da Capo, 1970)

——— 'Webern und Mahler. Ein unveröffentlichter Text', *Musiktexte* no. 1 (October 1983), 42–3

LELEU, Jean-Louis. 'L'organisation du temps musical dans les cinq pièces op. 10 d'Anton Webern', *L'Éducation Musicale* 40 (1983), 7–14

——— 'Le problème de la forme musicale dans les compositions dodécaphoniques d'Anton Webern' (doctorat (nouveau doctorat), Université Paris IV, 1987)

——— 'Webern et Mondrian. Notes sur la conjonction', *Inharmoniques* 5 (1989), 118–32

LESPINARD, Bernadette. 'Webern et l'art poétique. A propos du Lied "Wie bin ich froh" opus 25 no 1, sur un poème de H. Jone', *Analyse musicale* 3 (1986), 51–5

LESTER, Joel. *Analytic Approaches to Twentieth-Century Music* (New York: Norton, 1989)

LEWIN, David. 'An example of serial technique in early Webern', *Theory and Practice* 7/1 (August 1982), 40–3

——— 'Transformational technique in atonal and other music theories', *PNM* 21/1–2 (1982–3), 312–71. Discusses Op.5 no.2

——— *Generalised Musical Intervals and Transformations* (New Haven: Yale University Press, 1987)

——— 'A metrical problem in Webern's Op.27', *MusA* 12/3 (1993), 343–54. Re-examines metrical issues in the second movement of the Piano Variations that Lewin had initially discussed in 'A metrical problem in Webern's Op.27', *JMT* 6/1 (1962), 124–32

——— 'Set theory, derivation, and transformational structures in analyzing Webern's Opus 10, Number 4', in *Musical Form and Transformation: 4 Analytic Essays* (New Haven: Yale University Press, 1993), pp. 68–96

LIGETI, György. 'Aspekte der Webernschen Kompositionstechnik', in *AW II*, pp. 51–104

LIMMERT, Erich. 'Hannover. Webern-Ballet wie auf Taubenfüßen', *Melos* 29 (1962), 198–9

LINDLAR, Heinrich. 'Anton Webern. Zur 75. Wiederkehr seines Geburtstages am 3. Dezember', *Musica* 12 (1958), 761–2

LUDVOVA, Jitka. 'Schonbergovi zaci v Cechach' (Schoenberg's pupils in Czechoslovakia), *Hudebni Veda* 20/4 (1983), 322–42

LYNN, Donna Levern. '12-tone symmetry: Webern's thematic sketches for the Sinfonie, Op.21, second movement', *MT* 131 (December 1990), 644–6

——— 'Genesis, process and reception of Anton Webern's twelve-tone music: a study of the sketches for Opp.17–19, 21, and 22/2 (1924–1930)' (unpublished dissertation, Duke University, 1992)

MACHLIS, Joseph. *Introduction to Contemporary Music*, 2nd edn (London: Dent, 1980), pp. 269–82 ('Anton Webern 1883–1945')

MACK, Dana. 'Schoenberg and the battles of modern music', *New Criterion* 6/6 (February 1988), 17–26. Includes Eng. trans. of extracts from Webern's letter of 2 September 1922 to Egon Wellesz, pp. 22–3

MACKAY, John William. 'The analysis of phrase structure and tonal centering in early twentieth-century tonalities' (unpublished dissertation, University of California at San Diego, 1983). Includes an analysis of the second and third movements of both Op.24 and Op.27

MACONIE, Robin. 'Towards a psychology of musical aesthetics', *Soundings* 8 (1979–80), 37–54 (esp. pp. 52–4)

MAEGAARD, Jan. 'Weberns Zwölftonreihen', in *Analytica*, ed. Anders Lönn and Erik Kjellberg (Stockholm: Almqvist and Wiskell, 1985), pp. 249–67

——— 'Die Komponisten der Wiener Schule und ihre Textdichter sowie das Komponisten-Dichter-Verhältnis heute', in *Zum Verhältnis von zeitgenössischer Musik und zeitgenössischer Dichtung*, ed. Otto Kolleritsch, Studien zur Wertungsforschung 20 (Vienna and Graz: UE for the Institut für Wertungsforschung an der Hochschule für Musik und darstellende Kunst in Graz, 1988), pp. 168–83

MAREN, Roger. 'The music of Anton Webern: prisms in twelve tones', *Reporter* 41 (1957), 38–41

MARKIEWICZ, Leon. 'Z zagadnien analizy utworow dodekafonicznych' (On analysing dodecaphonic compositions), in *Studia musicologica, aesthetica, theoretica, historica* (Lissa Festschrift), ed. Elżbieta Dzięebowska (Cracow: Wyd. Muz., 1979), pp. 295–305

MARRA, James Richard. 'Interrelations between pitch and rhythmic structures in Webern's Opus 11 no.1', *ITO* 7/2 (1983–4), 3–33

——— 'Webern's 1904 Lieder: a study in late tonal practice', *Indiana Theory Review* 8/2 (1987), 3–44

MARVIN, Elizabeth West. 'The structural role of complementation in Webern's *Orchestra Pieces* (1913)', *MTS* 5 (Spring 1983), 76–88

MASEDA, Eduardo Pérez. See Pérez

MATTER, Henri-Louis. *Anton Webern – essai* (Lausanne: L'âge d'homme, 1981)

MAURER ZENCK, Claudia. 'Bruch und Summe. Die Beziehung zwischen Krenek und Webern', in *Ernst Krenek*, ed. Otto Kolleritsch, Studien zur Wertungsforschung 15 (Vienna and Graz: UE for the Institut für Wertungsforschung an der Hochschule für Musik und darstellende Kunst in Graz, 1982), pp. 174–88

——— 'Der Sinn von Weberns Variationen', in *AW II*, pp. 342–53. An earlier version of this article appears in Claudia Maurer Zenck, *Ernst Krenek – ein Komponist im Exil* (Vienna: Lafite, 1980), pp. 147–54

MAUSER, Siegfried. 'Webern und die musikalische Tradition', in *Opus AW*, pp. 100–2

MEAD, Andrew. 'Webern, tradition, and "composing with twelve tones"', *MTS* 15/2 (1993), 173–204

MELLERS, Wilfrid. *Caliban Reborn: Renewal in Twentieth-Century Music* (London: Harper and Row, 1967), pp. 52–60

MESNAGE, Marcel and André RIOTTE. 'Les variations pour piano opus 27 d'Anton Webern', *Analyse Musicale* 14 (1989), 41–67

METHLAGL, Walter. 'Woge und Kristall. Georg Trakl, Hildegard Jone, Anton von Webern', *Das Fenster* 42 (1987), 4130–3

METKEN, Günter. 'L'élévation en musique. Anton Webern et Segantini', *Revue de l'art* 96 (1992), 82–4

METZ, Günther. 'Das Webern-Zitat in Hindemiths Pittsburgh Symphony', *AfMw* 42/3 (1985), 200–12

METZGER, Heinz-Klaus. 'Über Anton Weberns Streichquartett 1905', in *AW I*, pp. 76–111. Published in Italian as 'Il «Quartetto per archi» del 1905 di Webern', in *Comporre arcano*, pp. 64–83

——— 'Addendum in motu contrario. Zum Schicksal des Webernschen Espressivo in der revolutionären Phase der seriellen Bewegung', in *AW I*, pp. 207–10. Addendum to Martin Zenck, 'Weberns Wiener Espressivo', pp. 179–206

——— 'Zur möglichen Zukunft Weberns', in *AW I*, pp. 306–15. Published in Italian as 'Per il possibile futuro di Webern', trans. Augusto Carli, in *Cento anni*, pp. 77–84

MEYER, Felix. 'Im Zeichen der Reduktion. Quellenkritische und analytische Bemerkungen zu Anton Weberns Rilke-Liedern op. 8', in *Quellenstudien I. Gustav Mahler–Igor Strawinsky–Anton Webern–Frank Martin*, ed. Hans Oesch, Publications of the Paul Sacher Stiftung 2 (Winterthur: Amadeus Verlag, 1991), pp. 53–100

——— '"O sanftes Glühn der Berge". Ein verworfenes "Stück mit Gesang" von Anton Webern', in *Quellenstudien II. Zwölf Komponisten des 20. Jahrhunderts*, ed. Felix Meyer, Publications of the Paul Sacher Stiftung 3 (Winterthur: Amadeus, 1993), pp. 11–38

MEYER, Felix, and Anne SHREFFLER. 'Webern's revisions: some analytical implications', *MusA* 12/3 (1993), 355–79

MILA, Massimo. Review of *Chronicle*, *NRMI* 13 (1979), 444–7

MILNER, Anthony. 'The vocal element in melody', *MT* 97 (March 1956), 128–31

MOLDENHAUER, Hans. 'Excelsior! Die Genese des Webern-Archivs', in *Komponisten des 20. Jahrhunderts in der Paul Sacher Stiftung*, ed. Hans Jörg Jans, Felix Meyer and Ingrid Westen (Basel: Paul Sacher Stiftung, 1986), pp. 130–47

MOOSER, R.-Aloys. *Visage de la musique contemporaine, 1957–1961* (Paris: Juillard, 1962). See esp. pp. 28–9 (*Drei Volkstexte* Op.17), 204–26 (Six Pieces Op.6)

MORTON, Lawrence. Review of *Chronicle*, *JASI* 3/2 (October 1979), 189–93

MOSER, Roland. 'Flaschenpost', *Dissonanz* 28 (1991), 23–4. On Louis Krasner and Don C. Seibert, 'Souvenirs' (see Krasner and Seibert)

MOTTE-HABER, Helga de la. 'Musikkritik und Reklame', *NZM* 133/5 (1972), 242–3

MURRAY, Edward Michael. 'New approaches to the analysis of Webern' (unpublished dissertation, Yale University, 1979)

NEUWIRTH, Gösta. 'Rotas – Sator. Für Ernst Krenek zum 23. August 1980', *ÖMz* 35/9 (September 1980), 461–72

——— 'Die Suche nach der endgültigen Unwirklichkeit', in *AW I*, pp. 262–8

——— 'Weberns Rede', in *AW II*, pp. 112–36. Pages 112–17 of this article were first published as 'Weberns Rede. Wahn & Witz, mit beschränkter Haftung', *ÖMz* 38/11 (November 1983), 614–19; passages from this article also appear in the previous item ('Die Suche [...]')

NEWLIN, Dika. Review of the Quintet for Strings and Piano, M.118 (New York: Bomart, 1953), *Notes* 10 (1953), 674–5

———Review of *Chronicle*, *Notes* 36/1 (September 1979), 97–8

NICOLODI, Fiamma. 'Luigi Dallapiccola e la Scuola di Vienna. Considerazioni e note in margine a una scelta', *NRMI* 17/3–4 (1983), 493–528

NOLAN, Catherine. 'New issues in the analysis of Webern's 12-tone music', *Canadian University Music Review* 9/1 (1988), 83–103

——— 'Hierarchic linear structures in Webern's twelve-tone music' (unpublished dissertation, Yale University, 1989)

NOLLER, Joachim. 'Das dodekaphone Volkslied. Studien zu Weberns op. 17, 18 und 19', in *AW II*, pp. 137–50

——— 'Faßlichkeit. Eine kulturhistorische Studie zur Ästhetik Weberns', *AfMw* 43/3 (1986), 169–80

——— 'Webern e il teatro', trans. Nada Carli Alliney, in *Com'era dolce il profumo del tiglio. La musica a Vienna nell'età di Freud*, ed. Carlo di Incontrera ([?Monfalcone]: Teatro Communale di Monfalcone, 1988), pp. 363–79

——— 'Bedeutungsstrukturen. Zu Anton Weberns "alpinen" Programmen', *NZM* 151/9 (September 1990), 12–18

——— 'Weberns Innerlichkeit und das Theater', *ÖMz* 47/9 (September 1992), 502–13

OBERKOGLER, Wolfgang. *Das Streichquartettschaffen in Wien von 1910 bis 1925*, Wiener Veröffentlichungen zur Musikwissenschaft 22 (Tutzing: Schneider, 1982)

OEHLSCHLÄGEL, Reinhard. 'Wider Tod und Krieg. Anton Webern heute', *Musiktexte* no. 1 (October 1983), 44–6

——— 'Anton Webern heute', in *Opus AW*, pp. 162–6

OESCH, Hans. 'Weberns erste Bagatelle', in *Das musikalische Kunstwerk. Geschichte, Ästhetik, Theorie. Festschrift Carl Dahlhaus zum 60. Geburtstag* (Laaber: Laaber Verlag, 1988), pp. 695–712

——— 'Weberns Plan einer Gesamtausgabe', in *Neue Musik und Tradition. Festschrift Rudolf Stephan zum 65. Geburtstag*, ed. Josef Kuckertz, Helga de la Motte-Haber, Christian Martin Schmidt and Wilhelm Seidel (Laaber: Laaber Verlag, 1990), pp. 501–9

——— 'Webern und das SATOR-Palindrom', in *Quellenstudien I. Gustav Mahle–Igor Strawinsky–Anton Webern–Frank Martin*, ed. Hans Oesch, Publications of the Paul Sacher Stiftung 2 (Winterthur: Amadeus, 1991), pp. 101–56

OKABE, Shin'ichiro. 'Stylistic changes in Webern: an analysis of different versions of Opera 5 and 6', *Ongakugaku* (*Journal of the Musicological Society of Japan*) 33/1 (July 1987), 35–61. In Japanese; a summary in English is given on p. 35

——— 'Manuscript studies of Webern's vocal compositions from the late 1910s and the early 1920s', *Polyphone. Biannual Series of Music Criticism* 6 (1990), 230–44. In Japanese

O'LEARY, Jane Strong. 'Aspects of structure in Webern's Quartet, Op.22' (unpublished dissertation, Princeton University, 1978)

OLSON, Christine. 'Tonal remnants in early Webern: the first movement of the Orchestral Pieces (1913)', *ITO* 5/2 (1979–80), 34–46

PALOMERO, Félix. 'Webern y el expressionismo vienes', *Ritmo* [?55] (1984), 9–15

PARK, Jae-Sung. 'A study of pitch-class structure in Anton Webern's fourteen early atonal songs (1908–1909)' (unpublished dissertation, State University of New York at Buffalo, 1989)

PARSONS, Michael. 'Webern's late works', *Listener*, 25 August 1966, p. 286

PARTSCH, Erich Wolfgang. 'Ergänzungen zur Verbreitungsgeschichte von Weberns *Sechsorchesterstücken op. 6*', in *40.000 Musikerbriefe auf Knopfdruck. Methoden der Verschlagwortung anhand des UE-Briefwechsels. Untersuchungen — Detailergebnisse*, ed. Ernst Hilmar, Schriftenreihe zur Musik 2 (Tutzing: Schneider, 1989), pp. 55–62

PASQUET, Yves-Marie. 'Dans les hauts pâturages weberniens', *Analyse musicale* 18 (January 1990), 61–7

PASS, Walter. 'Weberns Presse-Echo in den Jahren 1907 bis 1945', in *AW 1883 1983*, pp. 99–150

——— 'Zum Wiener Webern-Fest 1983', *ÖMz* 38/11 (November 1983), 636

——— 'Webern-Kongress Wien 1983', *ÖMz* 39/2 (February 1984), 98–9

PATZER, Franz. 'Zu Anton v. Weberns 100. Geburtstag', in booklet accompanying *Sechs Stücke für großes Orchester op. 6. Faksimile-Ausgabe der autographen Partitur und des von Webern korrigierten Handexemplars des Erstdruckes*, ed. Franz Patzer (Vienna: Stadt- und Landesbiblio-thek, 1983), p. 5

PAULI, Hansjörg. 'Aus Gesprächen über Webern' (with Gottfried Michael Koenig, Rudolf Kolisch, Walter Levin, Peter Stadlen, Willi Reich and Josef Hueber), in *AW II*, pp. 238–93

PÉREZ MASEDA, Eduardo. 'Anton Webern', *Ritmo* [?55] (1984), 7–8

PERLE, George. *Serial Composition and Atonality: an Introduction to the Music of Schoenberg, Berg, and Webern*, 4th edn (Berkeley: University of California Press, 1977; 5th edn, 1981; 6th edn, 1991)

PERLOFF, Nancy. 'Klee and Webern: speculation on modernist theories of composition', *MQ* 69/2 (Spring 1983), 180–208

PERRY, Jeffrey. 'A study of Anton Webern's Six Bagatelles for String Quartet, op.9' (unpublished dissertation, Princeton University, 1990)

PETAZZI, Paolo. 'Introduzione a Webern', in *Cento anni*, pp. 23–66

PHIPPS, Graham H. 'Tonality in Webern's Cantata 1', *MusA* 3/2 (1984), 125–58

——— 'Harmonic thought in Webern's sketches', *MitPSS* no. 4 (January 1991), 31–3

——— 'Harmony as a determinant of structure in Webern's Variations for Orchestra', in *Music Theory and the Exploration of the Past*, ed. Christopher Hatch and David W. Bernstein (Chicago: University of Chicago Press, 1993), pp. 473–504

PISK, Paul A. 'Seattle. Auch von Webern gibt es noch Uraufführungen', *Melos* 29 (1962), 252–3

PLANTE, Daniel. A. 'Weberns Orchesterstück op.10 Nr. 1', *Musiktheorie* 4/3 (1989), 235–46

POLANSKY, Larry, and James Tenney. 'Temporal Gestalt perception in music', *JMT* 24/2 (1980), 205–41. Discusses the second movement of Op.24

POPELJAS, Lidija. 'Svoeobrazie imitacionno-kanoničeskoj tehniki v pozdnij sočinenijah A. Veberna' (The originality of the imitative-canonic technique in the late works of Anton Webern), in *Teoretičeskie problemy polifonii* (*Theoretical Problems of Polyphony*), ed. Lidija Popeljas, Sbornik trud. Gosudarstvennyj muzykal'noj-pedagogiceskij institut imeni Gnesinyh 52 (Moscow: Gos. Muz-Ped. Inst. Gnesinyh, 1980), [?pp.]

PORFIR'EVA, Anna. 'Ėstetika avstro-nemeckoj poėzii načala XX veka i kamernoe vokal'noe tvorčestvo Veberna' (The aesthetics of Austrian and German poetry of the twentieth century and the chamber vocal art of Webern), in *Žanrogo-stilističeskie tendencii klassičeskoj i sovremennoj muzyki* (*Genre and Stylistic Trends in Classic and Contemporary Music*), ed. Anna Porfir'eva (Leningrad: Leningradskij Inst. teatra, muzyki i kinomatografii, 1980), [?pp.]

POUSSEUR, Henri. 'Textes sur l'expression', in *La musique et ses problèmes contemporains 1953–63*, ed. Jean-Louis Barrault, André Frank and Simone Benmussa, Cahiers de la Compagnie Madeleine Renaud — Jean-Louis Barrault (Paris: Julliard, 1963), pp. 169–202 (IV. 'Webern et le silence', pp. 190–202)

——— 'Webern und wir', in *AW 1883 1983*, pp. 17–27

——— 'Eine Aktualität, die sich nicht umgehen läßt', in *Opus AW*, pp. 48–53

PRIEBERG, Fred. Musik und Macht (Frankfurt a.M.: Fischer Taschenbuch Verlag, 1991), 'Die krummen Rücken', pp. 255–77. Concerning Webern and the Third Reich: his application to the Reichskulturkammer for financial support.

PUFFETT, Derrick. 'A notational peculiarity in early Webern and its implications', *Tempo* 196 (August 1996), forthcoming.

RAHN, John. 'Analysis one: Webern's *Symphonie* op. 21: Thema', in *Basic Atonal Theory* (New York: Longman, 1980), pp. 4–18

RAIDT, Jürgen. '"Instrumentale Analyse" – "analytische Instrumentation". Weberns Instrumentation des Ricercars à 6 von J. S. Bach in der Sekundarstufe II', *Musik und Bildung* 24/1 (1992), 52–7

RAISS, Hans-Peter. 'Anton Webern. Symphonie Op. 21, 2. Satz (1928)', in *Neue Musik seit 1945*, ed. Hans Vogt, 3rd edn (Stuttgart: Reclam, 1982; 1st edn, 1972), pp. 209–28

RATHERT, Wolfgang. 'Musikgeschichtliche Nomothetik. Zum Formdenken Weberns', *Musiktheorie* 6/3 (1991), 199–220

REICH, Willi. 'Grenzgebiete des neuen Tons', *Die Musik* 25 (1932–3), 120–3

——— 'Zur Geschichte der Zwölftonmusik', in *Festschrift Alfred Orel zum 70. Geburtstag*, ed. Hellmut Federhofer (Vienna: Rohrer, 1960), pp. 151–7

——— 'Das Gesamtwerk Anton Weberns auf Schallplatten', *SMz* 100 (1960), 320–[?]

——— 'Weberns fem orkesterstycken opus 10', *Nutida Musik* 21/4 (1977–8), 37–8

———See also 'Schönbergs Musik' (1912) (Primary sources, Writings)

REIMERS, Gerd. *Beethovens flyttlass och andra essaer kring musiker och deras boninger i Osterrike* (*Beethoven's Furniture Wagons and other Essays on Musicians and their Lodgings in Austria*) (Stockholm: Reimers, 1977). Includes maps

REINHARDT, Lauriejean. 'Webern's literary encounter with Hildegard Jone', *MitPSS* no. 5 (January 1992), 36–40

——— 'From poet's voice to composer's muse: text and music in Webern's Jone settings' (unpublished dissertation, University of North Carolina at Chapel Hill, 1994)

——— '"Ich und Du und Alle": Hildegard Jone, Ferdinand Ebner, and Anton Webern's *Drei Gesänge* Op.23', *Proceedings of the XV Congress of the International Musicological Society: Free Papers* (Madrid), forthcoming

RESTAGNO, E. 'Da Venezia – Webern alla Biennale', *NRMI* 18/1 (1984), 92–6

——— 'Da Palermo – Convegno di studi e concerti dedicati a Webern e Varèse', *NRMI* 18/1 (1984), 96–8

RICHTER, Arnd. 'Anton von Webern. Kinderstück (1924)', *Üben und Musizieren* 2 (March 1985), 170–4

RIEHN, Rainer. 'Chronologisches Werkverzeichnis', in *AW II*, pp. 388–97

RIETHMÜLLER, Albrecht. 'Hermetik, Schock, Faßlichkeit. Zum Verhältnis von Musikwerk und Publikum in der ersten Hälfte des 20. Jahrhunderts', *AfMw* 37/1 (1980), 32–60

RINGGER, Rolf Urs. 'Zur Wort-Ton-Beziehung beim frühen Anton Webern', *SMz* 103 (1963), 330–5

——— 'Sprachmusikalische Chiffern in Anton Weberns Klavierlieder', *SMz* 106 (1966), 14–19

——— 'Reihenelemente in Anton Weberns Klavierliedern', *SMz* 107 (1967), 144–9

RIOTTE, André. See Mesnage

ROCHE, Maurice. 'Des précurseurs ...', *Esprit*, n.s.1 (January 1960), 39–51

RODE, Susanne. 'Zur Rezeption von Kraus' Offenbach-Vorlesungen', *Kraus-Hefte* 49 (1989), 5–11

——— '"Schweigt auch die Welt, aus Farben ist sie immer ..." Ganz kleine Sachen zu Anton Webern und Hildegard Jone', *MitPSS* no.3 (January 1990), 29–31

——— 'Gedanken über Kunst. Anton Webern, Karl Kraus, Hildegard Jone', *Das Fenster* 47 (Spring 1990), 4592–7

——— 'Anton Webern und Karl Kraus – Aspekte einer ungewöhlnlichen Kraus-Rezeption', *ÖMz* 46/6 (June 1991), 313–24

——— 'Wagner und die Folgen. Zur Nietzsche-Wagner-Rezeption bei Alban Berg und Anton von Webern', in *Der Fall Wagner. Ursprünge und Folgen von Nietzsches Wagner-Kritik*, ed. Thomas Steiert, Thurnauer Schriften zum Musiktheater 11 (Laaber: Laaber Verlag, 1991), pp. 265–91

ROGNONI, Luigi. *La scuola musicale di Vienna* (Turin: Eunaudi, 1966). Published in English as *The Second Vienna School: Expressionism and Dodecaphony*, trans. Robert W. Mann (London: Calder, 1977)

——— 'Meditazione su Anton Webern', *Quadrivium* 14 (*Testimonianze, studi e ricerche in onore di Guido M. Gatti (1892–1973)*) (1973), 405–11

——— 'Webern e Varèse. Ragion dialettica di un cammino parallelo', in *Comporre arcano*, pp. 13–19

ROMAN, Zoltan. 'Prelude and finale: musical *Jugendstil* in selected songs by Mahler and Webern', in *Focus on Vienna 1900*, ed. Erika Nielsen (Munich: Fink, 1982), pp. 113–24

——— 'From congruence to antithesis: poetic and musical *Jugendstil* in Webern's songs', *Miscellanea Musicologica* (Adelaide) 13 (1984), 191–202

ROSCHITZ, Karlheinz. 'Webern-Fest in Wien', *ÖMz* 39/2 (February 1984), 104–5

ROSTAND, Claude. 'Paris begeistert sich für Webern und Schönberg', *Melos* 22 (1955), 150–1

RUMMENHÖLLER, Peter. 'Versuch über den Eindruck von Weberns Musik', in *Opus AW*, pp. 167–71

RUSS, Michael. 'Temporal and pitch structure in Webern's Orchestral Piece Op. 10, no. 2', *MusA* 7/3 (1988), 247–79

SAARY, Margareta. *Verfremdung von Zitaten als Basis früher musikalischer Kreativität. Hugo Wolfs Stilmittel in einem Frühwerk Anton Weberns* ('Aufblick', M. 14), Mitteilungen der Österreichischen Akademie der Wissenschaften: Kommission für Musikforschung 38 (Vienna: Verlag der Österreichischen Akademie der Wissenschaften, 1986). (*Sonderabdruck* from the *Anzeiger der phil.-hist. Klasse der Österreichischen Akademie der Wissenschaften* 122 (1985), So[nderabdruck] 8, pp. 155–80)

SALZMAN, Eric. 'The miniaturist and the swashbuckler: Webern and Varèse', *Keynote* 7/10 (1983), 6–10

SAMSON, Jim. *Music in Transition: a Study of Tonal Expansion and Atonality, 1900–1920* (London: Dent, 1977)

SCHAEFFER, Pierre. 'Avant et après', *Preuves* 15/178 (1965), 29–34 (31–2)

SCHAFFER, Sarah. 'Analytical issues in the segmentation of atonal music: an investigation based on selected pre-serial works of Schoenberg, Berg, and Webern' (unpublished dissertation, Indiana University, 1992)

SCHÄFFER, Boguslaw. 'C'est au public à se hausser au niveau de l'oeuvre ...', *Preuves* 16/183 (1966), 51–3

SCHMIDT, Christian Martin. *Brennpunkte der Neuen Musik. Historisch-Systematisches zu wesentlichen Aspekten* (Cologne: Gerig, 1977), pp. 33–68 ('Der Komponist als Theoretiker – Karlheinz Stockhausen'). Discusses Stockhausen's essay on Webern's String Quartet Op.28 (see Stockhausen, 'Struktur und Erlebniszeit')

SCHNEBEL, Dieter. 'Die Variationen für Klavier op.27' (1952), in *AW II*, pp. 162–217. Part I of this article was first published in Schnebel, *Denkbare Musik. Schriften 1952–1972*, ed. Hans Rudolf Zeller (Cologne: DuMont Schauberg, 1972), pp. 156–70

SCHNEIDER, Frank. 'Variationen über Opus Webern', *Musik und Gesellschaft* 33/12 (December 1983), 690–5

SCHNEIDER, Norbert J. '"Ausdruck" bei Anton von Webern', in *Opus AW*, pp. 113–19

SCHOLLUM, Robert. *Das österreichische Lied des 20. Jahrhunderts*, Publikationen des Instituts für Österreichische Musikdokumentation 3 (Tutzing: Schneider, 1977), pp. 83–98 ('Anton Webern'). An earlier version of this article was pub. as 'Stilistische Elemente der frühen Webern-Lieder', in *Beiträge der Österreichischen Gesellschaft für Musik 1972/73. Webern Kongress*, pp. 127–34

——— 'Wolf–Webern–von Einem. Anmerkungen zu Deklamatorik, musikalischer Gestik, Szenik', in *Wort–Ton–Verhältnis. Beiträge zur Geschichte im europäischen Raum*, ed. Elisabeth Haselauer (Vienna: Böhlau, 1981), pp. 109–25

——— 'Was um und nach Schönberg geschah', *Sborník prací filozofické fakulty Brněnské univerzity. Rada hudebnevedná* nos. 19–20 (1984), 155–63 (161)

SCHÖNY, Heinz. 'Musikgeschichte und Genealogie (91). Anton von Webern', *Genealogie* 19/2 (February 1989), 433–9

SCHUBERT, Giselher. 'Die Einsamkeit auf hohen Bergen. Aus der Webern-Rezeption der 20er Jahre', in *Opus AW*, pp. 156–61

——— 'Zur Rezeption der Musik Anton von Weberns', in *Die Wiener Schule heute. 9 Beiträge*, ed. Carl Dahlhaus, Veröffentlichungen des Instituts für Neue Musik und Musikerziehung Darmstadt 24 (Mainz: Schott, 1983), pp. 63–86

SCHULTZ, Donna Gartman. 'Set theory and its application to compositions by five twentieth-century composers' (unpublished dissertation, Michigan State University, 1979)

SCHULZ, Reinhard. *Über das Verhältnis von Konstruktion und Ausdruck in den Werken Anton Weberns*, Studien zur Musik 1 (Munich: Fink, 1982)

SCHWEIZER, Klaus. 'Anton Webern. Sechs Stücke für Orchester op. 6', *NZM* 145/10 (1984), 25–8

——— 'Neue Musik aus dem Fundus. Anton Weberns Orchesterstücke als Erstaufführung bei der Basler IGNM', *Basler Zeitung*, 1 December 1987, p. 37

——— 'Schürfarbeit im Nachlaß Weberns. Basler workshop mit Opus 10', *NZM* 149/2 (1988), 40–1

——— 'Der Webern-Nachlaß in Basel', *Basler Zeitung*, 3 March 1984, p. 35

SCHWENDINGER, Herbert. 'Anton Webern ist tot', *Musikerziehung* 25/5 (1972), 223–5

SEARLE, Humphrey. 'Webern the evolutionist', *Sunday Telegraph*, 16 April 1961, p. 11. Reproduced in Searle's 'Translator's preface' to Eng. trans. of Friedrich Wildgans, *Anton Webern*, pp. 8–12

——— 'Webern and his musical legacy', *Composer* 38 (1970–1), 1–3

SEIBERT, Don C. See Krasner

SEMENOVA, Tat'jana. 'Esteticeskie osnovy ekspressionisma v muzyke' (Aesthetic fundamentals of Expressionism in music) (unpublished dissertation, Moskovskij gosudarstvennyj universitet, 1979)

SHREFFLER, Anne C. 'Webern's Trakl settings' (unpublished dissertation, Harvard University, 1989)

——— 'Webern and Trakl: evolution of a style', in *Atti del XIV congresso della Società internazionale di musicologia. Trasmissione e recezione delle forme di cultura musicale* (Bologna, 1987), III: *Free Papers*, ed. Angelo Pompilio, Donatella Restani, Lorenzo Bianconi and F. Alberto Gallo (Turin: Edizione di Torino, 1990), pp. 369–80

——— 'A new Trakl fragment by Webern: some notes on "Klage"', *MitPSS* no.4 (January 1991), 21–6

——— 'Webern, Trakl, and the decline of the West: Webern's setting of "Abendland III"', in *German Literature and Music. An Aesthetic Fusion: 1890–1989*, ed. Claus Reschke and Howard Pollack, Houston German Studies 8 (Munich: Fink, 1992), pp. 145–57

——— *Webern and the Lyric Impulse: Songs and Fragments on Poems of Georg Trakl* (Oxford: Clarendon Press, 1994)

——— '"Mein Weg geht jetzt vorüber": the vocal origins of Webern's twelve-tone composition', *Journal of the American Musicological Society* 47/2 (1994), 275–339

——— See also Meyer

SICHARDT, Martina. 'Zur Uraufführung von Volksliedbearbeitungen Schönbergs für gemischten Chor durch Anton Webern', *ISGM* nos.3–4 (December 1989), 2–4

SIEVERS, Gerd. 'Anton von Webern zum Gedenken', *Musica* 8 (1954), 20

SILVER, Sheila. 'Erster Satz aus "Drei kleine Stücke für Violoncello und Klavier" op.11 von Anton Webern', in *Analyse* I, pp. 38–45 (text); II, tables 3–5. Followed by Erhard Karkoschka, 'Kommentar zur Analyse von S. Silver', I, pp. 41–5

SIMMS, Bryan. 'The Society for Private Musical Performances', *JASI* 3 (1979), 125–49

SLONIMSKY, Nicolas (ed.). *Lexicon of Musical Invective: Critical Assaults on Composers since Beethoven's Time* (New York: Coleman-Ross, 1953), pp. 249–51 ('Webern')

SMIRNOV, Dmitri. 'Geometr zvukovikh kristalov' (Geometer of sound crystals), *Sovetskaia muzika* 3, 4 (1990), 74–81, 84–93. Concerns Smirnov's lessons with Herschkowitz

——— 'A visitor from an unknown planet: music in the eyes of Filipp Herschkowitz', trans. Rosamund Bartlett, *Tempo* no.173 (June 1990), 34–8

SMITH, Charles Justice, III. 'Patterns and strategies: four perspectives of musical characterization' (unpublished dissertation, University of Michigan, 1980). Includes an 'analytical sketch' of Op.10 no.4

——— 'Comment' (on Edward Dagnes, 'Symmetrical structures in Webern'), *ITO* 1/9–10 (1975–6), 53–4

SMITH, Joan Allen. *Schoenberg and his Circle: a Viennese Portrait* (New York: Schirmer, 1986)

SNARRENBERG, Robert. 'Hearings of Webern's "Bewegt"', *PNM* 24/2 (1985–86), 386–404

SNOW, Rosemary Allsman. 'Cadence or cadential feeling in the instrumental works of Anton von Webern' (unpublished dissertation, Case Western Reserve University, 1977)

SOMFAI, László. '"... Csak utólag vettem észre". Anton Webern elemzése op.28-as Vonósnégyesének adagio-formájáról', *Magyar Zene* 25/4 (1984), 367–76

SOUSTER, Tim. 'The second Viennese school: Pierre Boulez talks to Tim Souster', *MT* 110 (1969), 473–6

SPINNER, Leopold. *A Short Introduction to the Technique of Twelve-tone Composition* (London: Boosey and Hawkes, 1960)

——— 'The abolition of thematicism: and the structural meaning of the method of twelve-tone composition', *Tempo* no. 146 (September 1983), 2–9. Published in German as 'Über die strukturelle Bedeutung der Methode der Zwölftonkomposition und einen "Abbau des Thematischen"', trans. Michael Kopfermann in Regina Busch, *Leopold Spinner*, Musik der Zeit. Dokumentationen und Studien 6 (Bonn: Boosey and Hawkes, 1987), pp. 192–201

——— 'Zwei Scherzo-Analysen', in Busch, *Leopold Spinner*, pp. 180–91 ('Anton Webern, 2. Satz aus dem Streichquartett op.28', 187–91)

——— 'Anton Weberns Kantate Nr.2, Opus 31. Die Formprinzipien der kanonischen Darstellung (Analyse des vierten Satzes)', in *Die Wiener Schule*, ed. Rudolf Stephan, Wege der Forschung 643 (Darmstadt: Wissenschaftliche Buchgesellschaft, 1989), pp. 313–21. First published in *SMz* 101 (1961), 303–8

STADLEN, Peter. 'Webern symposium', *The Score* 25 (June 1959), 65–8

——— 'The Webern legend', *MT* 101 (1960), 695–7. Published in German as 'Die Webern-Legende', *Musica* 15 (1961), 66–8

——— 'Das pointillistische Mißverständnis', *ÖMz* 27/3 (March 1972), 152–61

——— 'Das pointillistische Mißverständnis', in *Beiträge der Österreichischen Gesellschaft für Musik 1972/73. Webern Kongress* (Kassel: Bärenreiter, 1973), pp. 173–84 (not the same as previous item)

STAEMPFLI, Edward. 'Das Streichtrio Opus 45 von Arnold Schönberg', *Melos* 27 (1970), 35–9 (38–9)

STAHMER, Klaus Hinrich. *Jugendstil in der Musik* (Darmstadt: Roether, 1976)

——— 'Analytische Orchestration. Bach-Transkriptionen von Schönberg, Webern und Berg', in *57. Bachfest der Neuen Bachgesellschaft in Würzburg 22. bis 27. Mai 1982. Bach und die Barockkunst*, ed. Christian Kabitz (Kassel: Neue Bachgesellschaft, 1982), pp. 151–4

STAŃSKA, Elżbieta. 'Dodekafonia A. Weberna', in *Zeszyty naukowe państwowej wyższej szkoły muzycznej w Katowicach* (*Scholarly Literature from the State Higher School of Music in Katowice*), ed. Barbara Lankowska-Guzy, Zeszyty naukowe 24 (Katowice: Państwowa Wyższa Szkoła Muzyczna, 1978), pp. 32–79

STARR, Daniel. 'Derivation and polyphony', *PNM* 23/1 (1984), 180–257 (202–7, 'Analytical vignette. Webern Op.27')

STEGEN, Gudrun. *Studien zum Strukturdenken in der Neuen Musik*, Kölner Beiträge zur Musikforschung 117 (Regensburg: Bosse, 1981), pp. 31–108 ('Der Strukturbegriff in der Neuen Musik, dargestellt an Werken von Webern, Boulez und Stockhausen. [Teil] A, Webern')

STEIN, Erwin. 'Schoenberg and the German line', *Modern Music* 3/4 (May–June 1926), 22–7

——— 'Webern's Trio op.20', *Neue Musikzeitung* (1928), 517–[?]

STEINER, Ena. 'Mödling revisited', *JASI* 1/2 (February 1977), 75–86

——— Review of *Chronicle*, *Music Review* 40/3 (August 1979), 222–6

STEMPEL, Larry. 'Varèse's "awkwardness" and the symmetry in the "frame of twelve tones": an analytic approach', *MQ* 65/2 (April 1979), 148–66 (esp. 151–5)

STEPHAN, Rudolf. *Neue Musik* (Göttingen: Vandenhoeck und Ruprecht, 1958; 2nd edn, 1973)

——— 'Zu Anton Weberns Orchesterwerken', *Philharmonische Blätter* (Berlin) 4 (1976–7), 9–13

——— 'Überlegungen zur Taktgruppenanalyse. Zur Interpretation der 7. Symphonie von Gustav Mahler', in *Logos Musicae. Festschrift für Albert Palm*, ed. Rüdiger Görner (Wiesbaden: Steiner, 1982), pp. 202–10. Includes presentation of Webern's own metric analysis from an autograph fair copy of his Concerto Op.24

———'Über Anton Webern', in *Zum 100. Geburtstag Anton Webern* (see Catalogues, Vienna), pp. 6–14. Reproduced in *Opus AW*, pp. 39–46

———Review of Anton Webern, *Sechs Stücke für großes Orchester op. 6 (erste Fassung). Faksimile Ausgabe* [...] (see Primary sources, Music), *ÖMz* 39/6 (June 1984), 346

———*Vom musikalischen Denken. Gesammelte Vorträge*, ed. Rainer Damm and Andreas Taub (Mainz: Schott, 1985)

———'Schönberg und der Klassizismus', in *Die Wiener Schule*, ed. Rudolf Stephan, pp. 157–73

———See also Dahlhaus, Grasberger

STEUERMANN, Edward. 'On Anton Webern and his music', in *The Not Quite Innocent Bystander: Writings of Edward Steuermann*, ed. Clara Steuermann, David Porter and Gunther Schuller, trans. Richard Cantwell and Charles Messner (Lincoln and London: University of Nebraska Press, 1989), pp. 53–5

———'The possibilities and impossibilities of serial composition: an unscientific inquiry', in *The Not Quite Innocent Bystander*, pp. 56–62

STEVENSSON, Kjell-Inge. 'En kammarsymfonis öde. Något om Weberns arrangemang av Schönbergs Kammarsymfoni opus 9', *Nutida Musik* 25/4 (1981–2), 47–9

STIEBLER, Ernstalbrecht (interviewer and ed.). '1968er Erinnerungen (Reaktionen). Stellungnahmen von Komponisten anläßlich des 25. Todestages Weberns am 15. September 1970', in *AW II*, pp. 105–11. Contributions from Ligeti, Schnebel, Giuseppe G. Englert, Stockhausen, Rainer Riehn, Kurt Schwertsik, Hans-Joachim Hespos, Nicolaus A. Huber, Lachenmann, Gottfried Michael Koenig and Kagel

STOCKHAUSEN, Karlheinz. 'Weberns Konzert für neun Instrumente', in *Texte*, 6 vols. (Cologne: vols. I–III, DuMont Schauberg, 1963–71; vols. IV–VI, DuMont, 1978–89). I: *Zur elektronischen und instrumentalen Musik. Aufsätze 1952–1962 zur Theorie des Komponierens*, ed. Dieter Schnebel (1963; repr. 1988), pp. 24–31. First published in *Melos* 20 (1953), 343–8

———'Arbeitsbericht 1952/53. Orientierung', in *Texte* I, pp. 32–8 (36)

———'Zur Situation des Metiers', in *Texte* I, pp. 45–62 (46)

———'Gruppenkomposition. Klavierstück I (Anleitung zum Hören)', in *Texte* I, pp. 63–74 (73–4)

——— 'Von Webern zu Debussy. Bemerkungen zur statistischen Form', in *Texte* I, pp. 75–85

——— 'Struktur und Erlebniszeit', in *Texte* I, pp. 86–98. First published in *Die Reihe*, 69–79 (Eng. trans., 64–74)

——— 'Zum 15. September 1955 (Über Anton Webern)', in *Texte* II (*Zu eigenen Werken, zur Kunst Anderer, Aktuelles. Aufsätze 1952–1962 zur musikalischen Praxis*, ed. Dieter Schnebel, 1964; repr. 1975, 1988), pp. 140–3. First published in *Die Reihe*, 42–4 (Eng. trans., 37–9)

——— 'Die aktuelle Bedeutung Weberns', in *Texte* III (*Texte zur Musik 1963–1970. Einführungen und Projekte, Kurse, Sendungen, Standpunkte, Nebennoten*, ed. Dieter Schnebel, 1971), pp. 351–2

——— 'Webern-Seminar. "Da hatten die Leute kaum aufgehorcht, und schon war alles wieder vorbei"', in *Karlheinz Stockhausen. Im Musikwissenschaftlichen Seminar der Universität Freiburg i. Br., 3. bis 5. Juni 1985*, ed. Hans Heinrich Eggebrecht, Veröffentlichungen der Walcker-Stiftung 11 (Murrhardt: Musikwissenschaftliche Verlags-Gesellschaft, 1986), pp. 9–45

STRAUS, Joseph N. 'Recompositions by Schoenberg, Stravinsky, and Webern', *MQ* 72/3 (1986), 301–28

——— *Remaking the Past: Musical Modernism and the Influence of the Tonal Tradition* (Cambridge, MA: Harvard University Press, 1990)

STROH, Wolfgang Martin. *Webern: Symphonie Op. 21*, Meisterwerke der Musik 11 (Munich: Fink, 1975)

——— 'Wie hat Webern Geschichte gemacht?', in *AW II*, pp. 294–303

STUCKENSCHMIDT, Hans Heinz. 'Anton Webern', *Philharmonische Blätter* (Berlin) [?no. 4] (1978–9), 2–5

STUPPNER, Hubert. 'Anankastische Aspekte im Werk Anton Weberns', in *AW I*, pp. 112–18

SWAROWSKY, Hans. *Wahrung der Gestalt. Schriften über Werk und Wiedergabe, Stil und Interpretation in der Musik*, ed. Manfred Huss (Vienna: UE, 1979). 'Anton von Webern' (pp. 235–40) trans. into Italian by Barbara Barbini, in *Cento anni*, pp. 85–9

SZMOLYAN, Walter. 'Schönbergs Wiener Skandalkonzert', *ÖMz* 31/6 (June 1976), 293–304

——— 'Die Wiener Stadtbibliothek erwarb Musikautographen aus der Moldenhauer-Sammlung', *ÖMz* 36/3 (March 1981), 160

———'Wiederbeginn 1945 mit Anton Webern und Rückblick in die dreißiger Jahre', *ÖMz* 37/11 (November 1982), 623–30

TENNEY, James. See Polansky

TESTA, Susan Eileen. '"Atonalita" and "dodecafonia" in Italy to 1935' (unpublished dissertation, Columbia University, 1982)

THEINER, Lieselotte, and Lucia VOGEL (eds.). *Die Österreichische Nachfolge der Wiener Schule. Musiksammlung der Österreichischen Nationalbibliothek, Institut für Österreichische Musikdokumentation. Sonderausstellung 2.–21. Mai 1974* (Vienna: Musiksammlung der Österreichischen Nationalbibliothek, 1974). Catalogue with bibliographies and discographies

THOMAS, Jennifer. 'The use of color [timbre] in three chamber works of the twentieth century', *Indiana Theory Review* 4/3 (Spring 1981), 24–40. Discusses the Op.22 Quartet

TODD, Larry. 'The genesis of Webern's Opus 32', *MQ* 66/4 (October 1980), 581–91

TRABER, Jürgen Habakuk. 'Zum Verhalten von bürgerlichen Komponisten im ersten Weltkrieg', *Zeitschrift für Kunst und Gesellschaft* 1 (February 1976), 40–7

TREMBATH, Shirley Elizabeth. 'Text and texture in the solo vocal works, Opp.14–25, of Anton Webern' (unpublished dissertation, University of Texas at Austin, 1985)

———'Text and texture in the "Lieder" of Anton Webern', *Miscellanea Musicologica* (Adelaide) 16 (1989), 135–58

TÜRCKE, Berthold. 'Gurrelieder and Orchestral Pieces, Op.16, for two pianos: a rediscovery of reductions by Schoenberg/Webern and Erwin Stein', *JASI* 7/2 (November 1983), 239–54

———'Ein Stehenbleiben, das in die Weite geht. Der Gestus der Zeit in Weberns Spätwerk', in *AW II*, pp. 8–25

UNDERWOOD, James. 'Time and activity in Webern's Opus 10: a composer's viewpoint', *Indiana Theory Review* 3/2 (Winter 1980), 31–8

VANDER WEG, John Dean. 'Symmetrical pitch- and equivalence-class set structure in Anton Webern's Opus 5' (unpublished dissertation, University of Michigan, 1983)

VARGA, Ovidiu. *Quo vadis musica?*, 3 vols. (Bucureşti: Editura muzicalǎ, 1980–3), III: *Cei trei vienezi* [Arnold Schoenberg, Anton

Webern, Alban Berg] *şi nostalgia lui Orfeu. Triplă monografie polemică* (1983)

VELDE, Henk de. '"Es stürzt aus Höhen Frische..." Anmerkungen zur dodekaphonen Poetik Anton Weberns', in *AW I*, pp. 167–78

VELTEN, Klaus. 'Über das Verhältnis von Ausdruck und Form im Werk Gustav Mahlers und Anton Weberns', *Musik und Bildung* 10 (1978), 159–64

VIVIER, Odile. 'Varèse e Webern', in *Comporre arcano*, pp. 34–41

VLAD, Roman. 'Anton von Webern e la composizione atematica', *Rassegna musicale* 25 (1955), 98–102

——— 'Le avanguardie musicali e la SIMC [Societé Internationale de Musique Contemporaine]', *Chigiana* 35, n.s. 15 (*Atti del Convegno di Studi. Avanguardie musicali e spettacolari italiene nell'Europa degli anni Venti. Programmi di sala della XXXV settimana musicale, Siena, 29–31 agosto 1978*) (pub. 1982), 9–23. Includes a reprint of the programme note for Webern's Op. 20 from the first ISCM festival (Siena, September 1928), pp. 15–16

——— 'Forme geometriche e forme organiche in Webern', in *Comporre arcano*, pp. 95–113

VON BORRIES, Christian. See Borries

WALACIŃSKI, Adam. 'Poetyka muzyczna Weberna', in *Poetyka muzyczna. Autorefleksje kompozytorów. Warsztatowe, teoretyczne i estetyczne*, ed. Ewa Mizerska-Golonek and Leszek Polony (Cracow: Akademia Muzyczna, 1983), pp. 159–72

WALLNER, Friedrich. 'Anton Webern und die Philosophie', *ÖMz* 38/11 (November 1983), 620–9

WASON, Robert. 'Webern's *Variations for Piano*, Op. 27: musical structure and the performance score', *Intégral* 1 (1987), 57–103

——— 'Remnants of tonality in Webern's Op. 3/2', *MitPSS* no. 4 (January 1991), 27–30

WATKINS, Glenn. *Soundings: Music in the Twentieth Century* (New York: Schirmer, 1988), pp. 38–44 ('Webern: Opus 1 to Opus 2'), 383–91 ('Webern's path to the New Music')

WEBER, Markus. 'Der Schaffensprozess im VI. Satz aus Anton Weberns *Zweiter Kantate* op. 31. Versuch einer Rekonstruktion', *Schweizer Jahrbuch für Musikwissenschaft* n.s. nos. 13–14 (1993–4), 99–155

WELLESZ, Egon. 'Reminiscences of Mahler', *The Score* 28 (January 1961), 52–7 (54)

WHITTALL, Arnold. 'After Webern, Wagner: reflections on the past and future of Pierre Boulez', *Music Review* 28 (1967), 135–8

———*Music since the First World War* (London: Dent, 1977)

———Review of *Chronicle*, *Music and Letters* 61/1 (January 1980), 92–5

———'Webern and atonality: the path from the old aesthetic', *MT* 124 (December 1983), 733–7

———'Webern and multiple meaning', *MusA* 6/3 (1987), 333–53

———See also Dunsby

WIESMANN, Sigrid. 'Weltanschauungsmusik? Anton Webern und Ferdinand Ebner', *ÖMz* 38/11 (November 1983), 630–4

WILDBERGER, Jacques. 'Webern gestern und heute', *Melos* 27 (1960), 126

WILHEIM, András. 'Modszer és mű – Elemző megjegyzések Webern *Das Augenlicht* című kompozíciójához', *Magyar Zene* 25/4 (1984), 384–8

WILLAM, Wolfgang. *Anton Weberns II. Kantate op.31. Studien zu Konstruktion und Ausdruck*, Beiträge zur Musikforschung 8 (Munich and Salzburg: Katzbichler, 1980). Originally doctoral dissertation (University of Heidelberg, 1977)

WILLIAMS, Edgar Warren, Jr. 'On mod 12 complementary interval sets', *ITO* 7/2 (1983–4), 34–43. Discusses Op.11 no.3 and Op.13 no.1 ('Wiese im Park')

WINTLE, Christopher. 'An early version of derivation: Webern's Op.11/3', *PNM* 13/2 (1974–5), 166–77

———'Analysis and performance: Webern's Concerto Op.24/ii', *MusA* 1/1 (1982), 73–99. Reproduced in *Die Wiener Schule*, ed. Rudolf Stephan, pp. 370–404

WITZENMANN, Wolfgang. 'Naturphilosophie und musikalisches Denken. Zu Anton Weberns Auseinandersetzung mit Goethes *Farbenlehre*', *Neue Zürcher Zeitung*, 24–5 March 1984, p. 66

WOCKER, Karl Heinz. 'London. Viel von Webern', *Musica* 24 (1970), 562–4

WOOLDRIDGE, David. 'Some performance problems in contemporary music', *Tempo* no.79 (Winter 1966–7), 9–14

WÜBBOLT, Georg. 'Weberns Goethe-Rezeption. Ein Beitrag zum Thema Natur und Kunst', in *Opus AW*, pp. 103–7

YANG, Tsung-Hsien. 'Webern's Symphony: beyond palindromes and canons' (unpublished dissertation, Brandeis University, 1987)

ZABIEGA, Tadeusz. 'La musique universelle d'Anton Webern', *Revue musicale de Suisse Romande* 33/1 (1980), 8–18

——— 'Anton Webern et l'idée de la nature', *Revue musicale de Suisse Romande* 34/2 (1981), 73–80

——— 'La pensée musicale d'Anton von Webern et la philosophie de la nature de Goethe' (doctorat d'état, Université Paris IV, 1987)

ZACCARO, Gianfranco. 'Smagrimenti musicale', *Ponte* 44/4–5 (1988), 218–24

ZACHER, Gerd. 'Zu Anton Weberns Bachverständnis. Die Instrumentation des Ricercars', in *AW I*, pp. 290–305

ZAPPA, Frank. 'My favourite records [1967]', in Dominique Chevalier, *Viva! Zappa*, trans. Matthew Screech (London: Omnibus, 1986), p. 108

ZAUNSCHIRM, F. 'Cesar Bresgen. "Requiem für Anton Webern"', *Musica* 37/6 (1983), 525–8

ZENCK, Claudia Maurer. See Maurer

ZENCK, Martin. *Kunst als Begriffslose Erkenntnis. Zum Kunstbegriff der ästhetischen Theorie Theodor W. Adornos*, Theorie und Geschichte der Literatur und der schönen Künste 29 (Munich: Fink, 1977), pp. 211–44 ('Indifferenz von Konstruktion und Ausdruck in Weberns Trakllied "Gesang einer gefangenen Amsel"')

——— 'Weberns Wiener Espressivo. Seine Voraussetzungen im späten Mittelalter und bei Beethoven', in *AW I*, pp. 179–206

——— 'Die theoretische und kompositorische Auseinandersetzung Henri Pousseurs mit Anton Webern', in *AW II*, pp. 218–37

——— 'Tradition as authority and provocation: Anton Webern's confrontation with Johann Sebastian Bach', in *Bach Studies*, ed. Don O. Franklin (Cambridge: Cambridge University Press, 1989), pp. 297–322

ZILLIG, Winfried. 'Zur Geschichte der neuen Musik. Von der Dodekaphonie zur Elektronik', *Musica* 14 (1960), 777–80 (778–9)

ZUBER, Barbara. 'Erforschung eines *Bildes*. Der VI. Satz aus Anton Weberns Kantate op. 31', in *AW I*, pp. 119–66

——— 'Reihe, Gesetz, Urpflanze, Nomos. Anton Weberns musikalisch-philosophisch-botanische Streifzüge', in *AW II*, pp. 304–36

ZULIAN, Claudio. 'Les trois moments de la composition déductive. Schönberg, Webern et Xenakis' (doctorat (nouveau doctorat), Université Paris VIII, 1990)

# Index